MW00779297

HISTORY AND ITS OBJECTS

Praise for *History and Its Objects*

"In its clarity, *History and Its Objects* is a pure pleasure to read. Peter N. Miller tells his story with great erudition and in a personal tone, elegantly composing it from numerous historical examples."—Matthias Bruhn, Humboldt University Berlin

"Peter N. Miller offers an original approach to the history of things, bringing what he calls a 'submerged history' of things to the surface."—Peter Burke, Emmanuel College, Cambridge

"In this remarkable book, Peter N. Miller unearths an unsuspected genealogy for material culture studies and cultural history. We owe Miller a debt of gratitude for laying bare this deep history and revealing that in our present celebration of material culture, we are joining a long conversation."—Pamela H. Smith, Columbia University

"Weaving together literary and scholarly insights, *History and Its Objects* will prove indispensable reading for historians and cultural historians, as well as anthropologists and archeologists worldwide."—Nathan Schlanger, École nationale des chartes, Paris

HISTORY
AND ITS OBJECTS

ANTIQUARIANISM
AND MATERIAL
CULTURE SINCE 1500

PETER N. MILLER

CORNELL UNIVERSITY PRESS
Ithaca and London

Published with support from the Book Subvention Fund of
Bard Graduate Center

First published 2017 by Cornell University Press

Printed in the United States of America

Library of Congress Cataloging-in-Publication Data

Names: Miller, Peter N., author.
Title: History and its objects : antiquarianism and material
    culture since 1500 / Peter N. Miller.
Description: Ithaca ; London : Cornell University Press,
    2017. | Includes bibliographical references and index.
Identifiers: LCCN 2016045224 (print) | LCCN 2016049373
    (ebook) | ISBN 9780801453700 (cloth : alk. paper) |
    ISBN 9781501708237 (epub/mobi) |
    ISBN 9781501708244 (pdf)
Subjects: LCSH: Antiquities—Study and teaching. |
    Material culture—History. | Europe—Historiography.
Classification: LCC GN406 .M555 2017 (print) |
    LCC GN406 (ebook) | DDC 930.1071—dc23
LC record available at https://lccn.loc.gov/2016045224

For Livia and Samuel, again
Quick now, here, now, always—

❦ Contents

CONTENTS

✺ ILLUSTRATIONS

✎ HISTORY AND ITS OBJECTS

Now, the question "To what question did So-and-So intend this proposition for an answer?" is an historical question, and therefore cannot be settled except by historical methods.

—R. G. Collingwood, *An Autobiography*

 INTRODUCTION

Why Historiography Matters

The question to which this book is an answer is:
what is the history of thinking about how to study the past through things?
The skeptic might ask another question: Is it important to know the history
of what we do? Do medical doctors, for example, need to know the history
of medicine in order to properly diagnose and treat their patients? Do com-
puter scientists need to know the history of computing for their programs to
work? Do astronomers need to know the history of astronomy in order to be
better astronomers? We know that painters, architects, and composers have
by tradition been schooled in the past of their practice. Some philosophers
are, but not all. Robert Pippin has recently argued that between those who
deny any role for history in tackling philosophical problems, and those who
treat the history of philosophy as a closed canon of past problems, there is
a middle course: engaging with the history as a way of "doing philosophy."
For philosophers, there is the weight of the great ancestors pressing down,
like atmospheric pressure: invisible, but of undeniable impact.[1]

What, then, of historians? Are they more like physicians or painters?
I would argue that they are much closer to the philosophers. Both groups
are, so to speak, born into existing research paradigms, inheriting questions
and historiographies, sometimes insensibly, but usually with at least some
notion of how the questions of the past have shaped their field. The partial
awareness creates its own challenge because sometimes it is not the visible

but the submerged, or forgotten, parts of the history that matter. We see the trees, but it is not the forest that we miss so much as the roots.

That is very much the case, I would argue, with the history of the study of objects as historical evidence. The subject has hardly attracted much attention. But with the great swelling of interest in material culture in the past twenty-odd years, we can no longer proceed as if this approach to the past

FIGURE 1   Friedrich Nietzsche's death mask, Nietzsche-Archiv, Weimar. Herzogin Anna Amalia Bibliothek (www.klassik-stiftung.de)

has no history. We need now to map out the submerged history that bears and orients the visible practice. There is more depth to the use of objects as evidence than we might think, and a more sophisticated inventory of approaches and arguments on which to draw than we might imagine. We need to know the history of our questions in order to make sure that we are asking them in the best possible way, that is, in the formulation likely to elicit the most valuable answers. The history of disciplines as the history of questions, rather than answers, is not only better history, it is also history we can use.

Friedrich Nietzsche was a young professor of classics at the University of Basel when in the summer semester of 1871 he offered a lecture course on the history and meaning of classical philology. In the very first lecture he declared that "in Antiquity philology was in no way a science, but only a general passion for every kind of knowledge." What was this omnivorous passion? Turning to the question of ancient remains, he explained that the "next sign of the revival of antiquity is the sentimentality of ruins, especially Rome's, and in excavations this longing [*Sehnsucht*] was satisfied."[2]

I remember reading these words on a train going from Bern to Berlin. I had come from Rome, where I had stood before Hermanus Posthumus' astonishing reflection on the psychodynamics of the Renaissance encounter

FIGURE 2   Hermanus Posthumus, *Landscape with Roman Ruins* (1536). Collection of the Princes of Lichtenstein, Vaduz.

with Roman antiquities. Those small figures darting about the field of ruins drawing and measuring were engaged in an unequal battle with time. Small chance triumphs were wagered against unrecoverable loss. What might it have felt like to be those people?

In an instant a whole piece of the emotional landscape of scholarship suddenly became clear. The painting prepared me for Nietzsche. Posthumus had painted that longing. I also perceived how radical Nietzsche's challenge was. Scholars were in the habit of not allowing feelings like yearning to enter into their work. Nietzsche was unmasking the passion that expressed itself through outward denial of its existence. A year later, Nietzsche delivered a series of lectures on the subject of education for the Basel public that began to expose the extent of his critique of contemporary scholarly approaches.[3] This deepened and widened in the two *Untimely Meditations* on history (1874) and philology (1875, unfinished). By 1878, he had decided to devote himself fully to the way he thought the past should be put to work, but the product of his labor, *Human, All Too Human*, had no place in a philology department. In 1879 Nietzsche resigned his post.

Nietzsche's revelation of the 1870s was that the academic study of the past—the glory of the German university system—systematically obscured a basic truth: It is not normal to study history. Oh, yes, he would say, past-ness has always weighed on living people, but the professionalized, dispassionate treatment of facts, as if while wearing white coats and using instruments to hold them at arms' length, was something entirely novel. Where once the past was bound into a person's lived experience, it was now kept apart from it.

In "On the Advantage and Disadvantage of History for Life," which he later re-titled "We Historians," Nietzsche expressed his discomfort with the regime of facts. For the "painstaking micrologists" with their technical mastery had "reduced" historical phenomena to an intellectual experience, and in the process killed them off. Their motto, he mused, was *Fiat veritas pereat vita*—let there be truth and let life perish. On the other hand, those able to find in the past an easy interlocutor for present purposes could only do so at the cost of precision and detail (Darwin's lumping rather than splitting). Another group of past-lovers—Nietzsche called them "antiquarians"—rooted themselves in time and place through studying things. In the first instance, these were the objects the antiquary grew up with as a child: "The possession of ancestral furniture changes its meaning in such a soul; for the soul is rather possessed by the furniture." The domestic scale was, for the child, monumental. And so it was that in "the small and limited, the decayed . . . the preserving and revering soul of the antiquarian" made his home and "nest."

Later, as his scope expanded, "His city's history becomes for him his own biography. He understands its wall, its towered gate, its council ordinances and its popular festivals as an illustrated diary of his youth, and finds himself in all of these things—his strength, his energy, his joy, judgment, his folly and rudeness."

Antiquarians were already in bad odor when Nietzsche was writing this. But he grasped the intimate connection between their commitment to research and the kind of imagination he prized. His admiration is registered in that string of biographical markers. The antiquarian's ability to feel himself a part of the past was the product of long hours of research, not an alternative to it. And there was a human element to this that was admirable: "Empathy and a feeling for the future, a nose for almost obliterated traces, an instinctive capacity for reading accurately a past still concealed beneath many later layers, a quick understanding of palimpsests, indeed polypsests—these are his gifts and virtues." Perhaps a more beautiful description of the virtues of antiquaries has never been written.[4] Elsewhere, Nietzsche praises their commitment to truth.[5]

But Nietzsche also feared the allure, the seduction, of knowing many things. That same antiquarian habitus, turned on itself and disconnected from reverence for life led to "the wretched drama of a blind mania for collecting, a restless compiling together of everything that ever existed." He saw this as a peril in an educational system that venerated the accumulation of facts. "Are these still men, we ask ourselves, or perhaps only machines for thinking, writing, and speaking?" The lack of connection between the subject studied and the subject doing the studying—this seemed to Nietzsche the great mark of systemic failure:

> One of them, let us say, is busy with Democritus; but the question always comes to my lips: why Democritus? Why not Heraclitus or Philo or Bacon? Or Descartes? And so on. And then: Why a philosopher anyway? Why not a poet or orator? And why a Greek at all? Why not an Englishman or a Turk?. . . So it does not matter what they study, as long as they—who could never themselves make history—keep history nicely "objective."[6]

Historismus was a culture of facts but also a culture of the status quo because no one had questioned the commitment to "objectivity." Hence Nietzsche's head-shaking judgment that historical education led to "a kind of congenital grayness."[7]

Nietzsche's essay "We Philologists" went a step further. Not in the argument—classical philology's problems were the same as history's. But as the years passed Nietzsche's sense of personal betrayal kept intensifying. "The philologist," he writes, "must first be a man. Only then will he be creative as a philologist." The love of facts had displaced education from its real purpose: making individuals.[8] Nietzsche lamented the soul-killing technical achievements of the contemporary historical and philological sciences with a different vision of research in mind. He saw scholarship not as the triumph of the technicians but as a way of nourishing the person. He signaled this hoped-for connection between erudition and sensibility with the word *Sehnsucht*.

Nietzsche was deeply attached to the poetry of Friedrich Hölderlin, and *Sehnsucht* was a central theme in his work, linked to the impossible yearning to return home. In his poem "Mnemosyne," Hölderlin pictures humans as forced to carry our memories, like pack animals, even as we yearn always to be released from our burden, to live as unbounded ("Und immer / Ins Ungebundene gehet eine Sehnsucht"). For Hölderlin, we manage to stay on the narrow path by looking neither forward nor back. Instead, we focus on the material world around us.

> . . . . on the ground
> Sunshine we see and the dry dust
> And, a native sight, the shadows of forests, and on roof-tops
> There blossoms smoke, near ancient crests
> Of the turrets, peaceable; for good indeed
> [. . .] are the signs of the day.[9]

It is as though Nietzsche took over Hölderlin's material "solution" for the soul's yearning for reconstruction—the poem's *nostos*, after all, is about the recapturing of past time—and applied it to the scholar's yearning to reconstruct the past. Hence the therapeutic role assigned to archaeology. In his essay on history, Nietzsche identified the yearning and the therapy with the objects of antiquarian study: "Small, humble, fragile, old-fashioned things are endowed with dignity and sanctity" by "his antiquarian spirit." We are halfway between Hölderlin and a later admirer of both Hölderlin and Nietzsche, Rainer Maria Rilke. In his *Duino Elegies* (1923) Rilke affirmed: "Perhaps we are *here*, in order to say: house, bridge, fountain, gate, pitcher, fruit-tree, window—at most: column, tower."[10]

Sehnsucht as watchword means acknowledging the human in the scholarly. Later in the lecture course on classical philology, as Nietzsche put the last strokes to his portrait of the philologist, *Sehnsucht* returns to mark the individual's desire both to incorporate antiquity into a fully modern life and to imagine himself back into an earlier world.[11]

Sigmund Freud and Marcel Proust, Nietzsche's successors as psychologists of European culture (as he imagined his calling), both affirmed the emotional meaning of antiquities. In *Civilization and Its Discontents* (1938), Freud imagined the human mind as an archaeological site—he, too specifically refers to Rome—with layers upon layers of memories, all intact and all simultaneously present. Proust, in the first volume of *Remembrance of Things Past* (1915), likened the voracious and boundless curiosity of the lover for the beloved to that of the antiquary for "the deciphering of texts, the weighing of evidence, and the interpretation of old monuments."

That for Nietzsche, Freud, and Proust the threads of memory and passion twine around things may not surprise us. That they all refer to antiquities may. Now is the time to go back and rethink the relationship between *antiquarianism*, the term we habitually use to describe the historical scholarship that put things at the center, and *history*, understood somewhat awkwardly as both what happened in the past and the study of that past. The received view, whose monuments we might take to be the critique of "Erudition" in Diderot and D'Alembert's *Encyclopédie* (1750) and George Eliot's treatment of Edward Casaubon in *Middlemarch* (1871), sees the antiquarian as a myopic pedant and antiquarianism as an obsession with details of the deep past at the expense of the living present. Marc Bloch, our patron saint of history, makes just this point in his famous *Historian's Craft* (1943). He recounts that on his way back to France from the 6th International Congress of Historical Sciences held in Oslo in 1928, he and his traveling partner Henri Pirenne stopped off in Stockholm. Pirenne insisted they go off to see the town. "If I were an antiquarian," he said, "I would have eyes only for old stuff, but I am a historian. Therefore, I love life."[12]

Michael Shanks, a classical archaeologist who has looked to the antiquaries' practice as a model for working with objects, wants us instead to think of antiquarianism as the study of the past-in-the-present. And thus Pirenne and, to the extent that he was endorsing the view, Bloch have it backwards. The reason has to do with the subject of antiquarian research: things. Simply put, when we hold an artifact in our hands or walk a historical landscape, we have an immediate bodily experience of the past that affects us in a way that reading words cannot.

On March 28, 1859, Henry David Thoreau paddled along the Concord River thinking about the collection of arrowheads he planned to publish. He found them everywhere and found them enormously evocative. "Each one yields me a thought," he wrote. But the harvest they yielded was directly related to the nature of the objects and not some generalized sentimentality. With these man-made artifacts, Thoreau continued, "I come nearer to the maker of it than if I found his bones. His bones would not prove any wit that wielded them, such as this work of his bones does. It is humanity inscribed on the face of the earth." These arrowheads were precise records of people. "At every step I see it, and I can easily supply the 'Tahatawan' or 'Mantatuket' that might have been written if he had had a clerk." They were, he concluded, "not fossil bones, but, as it were, fossil thoughts, forever reminding me of the mind that shaped them."[13]

With this, Thoreau knowingly took his place in a New World restaging of Posthumus' Roman reflection. "Time," Thoreau acknowledged, "will soon destroy the works of famous painters and sculptors." But these arrowheads, because they were so numerous and yet so culture-specific, "will balk his"— Time's—"efforts" and reward the patient seeker after the past.[14]

This encounter of thought and feeling, of a hard-headed hope, is what Thoreau's younger contemporary, Nietzsche, was pointing us toward with his one word: *Sehnsucht.* That electric moment connecting object with imagination can open as many doors in us as we possess—hence the inherent relationship between the study of things and the older German aspiration to *Bildung,* or the American liberal arts education.

Thucydides used *archaeology* to refer to the oldest legends, not only to physical remains from time out of mind. We cannot be sure of the line of transmission, but a generation later we find Plato putting the same word in the mouth of the sophist Hippias, who explained that it referred to "the genealogy of heroes and men, and in stories of the foundation of cities in olden times and, to put it briefly, in all sorts of antiquarian lore."[15]

Plato was especially attentive to the question of how to learn from these things. In a discussion about naming and necessity, Socrates pushed the philosopher Cratylus to acknowledge the disjunction between names and the things they named. Cratylus had wanted to insist on a kind of natural identity between the two, something we might think of as a sort of romantic philology—or plain old mysticism. Socrates worked hard to pry the names apart from the things. In so doing, however, he also made an argument for ways of knowing: "How real existence is to be studied or discovered is, I suspect, beyond you and me. But we may admit so much, that the knowledge of things is not to be derived from names. No, they must be studied and investigated in themselves."[16]

The Greeks were late-born compared to the Egyptians and the Mesopotamians. For two thousand years these peoples, with their pyramids, foundation deposits, and stamped bricks, had been thinking about the ways "things" and "the past" were connected. But where their attention was focused on the stakes we humans have in the desperate game of memory, Socrates shifted the conversation. Things are no longer *aide-mémoires*, or tokens of longing; they are now containers of information. We can learn from the things themselves. This exchange does not figure in the charge sheet Nietzsche drew up against Socrates in *The Birth of Tragedy*, from that same decade as his reflections on history, but it could have.[17]

It is Marcus Terentius Varro, an ancient Roman contemporary of Cicero and lover of Roman cultural heritage, who brought together Thucydides and Plato, archaeology, and "learning from things." The Greek *archaiologia* became the Latin *antiquitates*. It referred to subjects such as religion, law, government, and calendars sorted under four headings: people, places, things, and times. We only know of Varro's work from the long passages copied out by Augustine in his *City of God* in order to mock the pagan rituals he took so seriously.

From the Renaissance on, people who called themselves antiquarians (*antiquarii*) investigated the physical remains of antiquity and used them, alongside textual evidence, to understand it. As they did, they remade Varro's fourfold classification system into private, public, sacred, and military antiquities. William Stenhouse, a historian of classical scholarship, has noted that the work of antiquarians fell along a spectrum from gathering the remains of the past to researching its customs and institutions. Historians employed chronological ordering, while antiquaries organized their narratives around structures or systems—law, religion, sports, warfare, dining, and so on. Not for nothing did Arnaldo Momigliano, the historian of the ancient world whose work on antiquarianism kickstarted the renewal of interest that has marked the past decades, call sociology a form of "armed antiquarianism" and later in life seek answers from anthropology.

The practice of antiquaries began with collecting. From the fifteenth to the eighteenth centuries, lists, catalogue entries, and short essays filled thicker and thicker folio volumes recording erudition's slow reconquest of the past. After amassing objects, they described them carefully and then compared them with other objects and with texts. Reconstruction—that was the aim of antiquarian scholarship. Francis Bacon in *The Advancement of Learning* (1605) had developed the metaphor of a shipwreck for the fall of the ancient world, with spars and flotsam standing for the fragments of antiquity that had survived into the present. The antiquaries tried to put it all back together again.

The shipwreck of antiquity was, of course, too vast for any one of them to put it back together on his own. Hence they made recourse by default to collaboration. Scholars developed their interpretations in conversation with each other. When they weren't physically proximate, they wrote letters. By the second half of the seventeenth century, the exchange of letters and manuscripts evolved into the first learned journals. The Republic of Antiquaries flourished within the ecosystem that was Europe's Republic of Letters.

Collecting, describing, comparing—all are deeply empirical practices. It is not surprising, then, that antiquarians corresponded with artisans and scientists in order to obtain the best instruments and latest experimental data; that they worked closely with merchants who could acquire novelties on their distant commercial circuits; and that they maintained good relations with farmers so as to hear of finds newly emerged from under the plow. Nor were human practices beyond the scope of their curiosity. Nicolas-Claude Fabri de Peiresc (1580–1637), the Provençal antiquary whom Momigliano called "that archetype of all antiquarians," documented state funeral rituals in France, collected information on the negotiating techniques of sub-Saharan African traders, and investigated the music of the Eastern Christians as performed in the Church of the Holy Sepulchre.[18]

Momigliano argued that the antiquaries of Renaissance and early modern Europe, though maligned by later generations, had invented research. He might also have said that they stood at the beginning of the history of what we call "interdisciplinarity." While the historians of the ancient world essentially rewrote the surviving written sources, the antiquaries dug—in the ground, in archives, in collections—added what they found to the record of the past, and then tried to follow the resulting questions wherever they led. It was only toward the end of the eighteenth century that this research vocation and its related evidence-handling technologies were eventually taken over by historians. But once in possession of these tools, the historians no longer needed the antiquaries, whose untimely backward-looking led to their rapid fall in an age obsessed by the "Moderns." Meanwhile, the birth of archaeology as a discipline created another object-studying center of gravity.[19] The antiquary fell between these chairs. By 1963 Momigliano could argue that the antiquary had himself become a problem worth studying, "a figure, so near to my profession, so transparently sincere in his vocation, so understandable in his enthusiasms, and yet so deeply mysterious in his ultimate aims."[20]

The history of antiquarianism, in all its forms, is a very big story. It is a story that Momigliano lamented had not yet been told when he published his field-making "Ancient History and the Antiquarian" in 1950, and that is only now beginning to come into focus.[21] In this book, I am not trying to write that history of antiquarianism itself. Rather, I am attempting an outline history of how people have thought about studying objects as evidence. Solving for this x will, indeed, lead us to travel for a time along the same route that a history of antiquarianism might take, but our points of departure and arrival lie elsewhere.

More than twenty years ago, Francis Haskell published *History and Its Images*. It provided the historical content for the theoretical turn in art history that emphasized the documents and archives of the discipline itself: self-examination in the form of scholarship. It, too, contained parts of what a history of antiquarianism would have to encompass. *History and Its Objects* may serve a similar historiographical function for the current wave of material culture studies; at the very least it will illustrate the long and rich history of thinking about objects as evidence. It, too, has parts of what a full-scale history of antiquarianism would need to include. But rather than pursuing comprehensiveness, as did Haskell, I wanted to document some of the questions we have been posing to objects over time, and how those questions have changed.

Haskell had recourse to cultural history as the rubric under which the study of images fell. Momigliano was the first to call attention to the connection between antiquarianism and cultural history. This seemed to me one of his promising asides. But they meet in a vast and murky terrain, and he himself chose not to venture upon it. When I started thinking about the questions that became this book, I thought that terrain could be crossed on the high road: from Peiresc to Voltaire to Burckhardt and on to the present. But I soon learned that a straight road is not always a true road. There were so many things that could be called cultural history and so many side routes that promised much but wound up as dead ends. While trying to pick my path across the swamp I read very carefully in the oeuvre of Hans Schleier, Germany's leading expert on nineteenth-century cultural history. Schleier made me realize that there could only be a "baggy" history of cultural history, because its contents were so various. To make any sense of the legacy of the antiquary, I had to narrow the focus.[22]

This turned out to be more straightforward than I first thought. A history of thinking about how objects have worked as historical evidence ended up offering a direct route from antiquarianism to material culture. It explained the origins of the part of cultural history that worked with things. The other parts of cultural history, the ones that dealt with the "creative spirit" or "the high points of the human spirit," are not relevant to me here. Even Jacob Burckhardt, who was an art historian, did not really belong to the discussion about objects.

Haskell's and Momigliano's antiquarians were sometimes also philologists. Both texts and artifacts emerged from the same time and place and could be studied together comparatively. Philology, however, early on—by the seventeenth century—developed a defined set of practices and a scholarly literature, while antiquarianism didn't. Like some luxuriant tropical vine, its tendrils extended from ancient Rome to Greece and the Orient as well as northern Europe and Africa. But self-conscious discussions of method were few. Philology talked a lot about itself. I therefore expected the nineteenth-century German debate between "thing philology" and "word philology" (*Sach- und Wort-Philologie*) to yield up an authentically nineteenth-century language of material culture that we could draw upon today. But in this I was disappointed. The debate was less a debate than the headline suggests, and the ground of agreement was much greater. However, those who now maintain that the "word philologists" followed the later Kant (or, better, Hamann and Herder) in seeing language as offering privileged access to the soul of a people are in effect identifying the "thing philologists," by contrast, as anti-romantic. We cannot simply think ourselves into the past because we think in words. We need things to help us.

This attempt to think through a cultural history of objects and their study led me to the present-day "material turn." But then I proceeded to find "material turns" at, well, every turn. There was the material turn in Rome in the 1430s and 1440s, when Poggio Bracciolini, Cyriac of Ancona, Flavio Biondo, and Leon Battista Alberti were making the revival of antiquity something real. Then there was the material turn in Rome in the 1560s and 1570s driven by Pirro Ligorio, Onufrio Panvinio, and Pedro Chacón. In the 1630s, along the Rome–Aix-en-Provence–Paris axis of the Peiresc correspondence, there was yet another burst of material intelligence. In Göttingen, in the 1760s, the material turn of Gatterer, Schlözer, and Heyne produced the new auxiliary sciences of history, *Statistik*, and archaeology. Then again in the 1830s and 1840s the scholarship in the German regional historical associations led to an expansion of the material corpus beyond the bounds of *antiquitates*, and cultural history was born. In the 1880s there was the decisive material turn driven by Karl Lamprecht, who worked on books, manuscripts, art, and economic life. It was decisive because it inspired the principals of the next material turn, in Hamburg and Strasbourg, Warburg and Bloch, who produced the *Mnemosyne Atlas* and the *Annales d'histoire économique et sociale*. If all of these could legitimately be viewed as material turns and none of them figure in our standard histories of history, then two things follow. First, there was a more or less continuous engagement of history and historians with objects and the questions objects ask of us. And, second, we need a new history of history. This book is a step on that path: it is a history of all these material turns.[23]

Fritz Stern began *Einstein's German World* by recounting Raymond Aron's melancholic counterfactual, "This could have been Germany's century." That the twentieth could have been is due to the fact that the nineteenth actually was. In the history of historical scholarship, of academic institutions, of learned publications, the German discourse of the nineteenth century had the kind of global dominance we now associate with universities in the United States.[24] Yes, we can find some of these arguments running in parallel in other places, such as France or England—and I have tried to point them out where possible.[25] Lionel Gossman, for instance, explicitly argued that earlier eighteenth-century French medieval scholars such as La Curne de Sainte-Palaye "anticipated" the Göttingen historians in their thinking about research, sources, and evidence.[26] But I would argue that only in Germany was there a sustained, century-long, intergenerational conversation at the highest level of conceptual self-consciousness about how to think about an object historically. Maybe another way to say "conceptual self-consciousness" is "unremitting tendency to self-examination and self-theorization." If this doesn't make for readable texts, it does make for a rich discursive field that stretches from the textbooks of the university professors to the journal articles by local historians to the multi-volume syntheses of provincial polymaths to the administrative memoranda of museum directors. All of these look back to the Renaissance for sources even as they point toward the issues of our own time and our own "material turn." If we want our work on the past to yield resources for living in our present, not just the pleasures of reconstruction, then this wide German debate will provide us with the most nourishment.

In the German century that actually was, museums began to emerge as knowledge institutions on a par with the university. In fact, it is precisely the people who turned to material evidence for history who were the proponents of museum-making. The first professor to lecture on archaeology began by working on a collection of ancient gems. The local historians who articulated the shape of a German cultural history based on things were also the first to propose regional museum collections. The most interesting of the mid-nineteenth-century multi-volume cultural histories was written by a provincial polymath who began his career as a porcelain curator, then became a librarian, built a personal collection of thousands of objects that he then used as the basis of his written history, and fantasized about recomposing his history as a museum exhibition. None of this, by the way, happened in Berlin. If the "nation" was a driving force on the periphery, where this was translated into institutionalized scholarly activity, the "state" was nowhere to be seen. Finally, the first cultural historical museum—in a small Bavarian town—was founded to produce a history of the German nation from things. It would not be going too far to say that the museum and material culture were born twins.

So, too, were material culture and medieval studies. For if the first objects studied historically were of venerated Roman and then Greek antiquity, by the seventeenth century antiquaries were turning their attention to period between antiquity and themselves. Giants of erudition of such standing that, like Brazilian footballers, they are known by only one name, viz. Peiresc, Mabillon, and Leibniz, changed the way a thousand years of European history were studied. Their work on medieval material evidence was then incorporated into the curriculum at Göttingen and made the subject of cultural historical investigation, first by amateurs and then by professional historians. The Middle Ages became a museum "discipline" at the same places where the idea of the nation defined a museum's collecting policy, such as the Germanisches Nationalmuseum. And from the 1870s, economic history in Germany focused intensively on the Middle Ages (Karl Lamprecht, Theodor von Inama-Sternegg). The next generation, which included Pirenne, Huizinga and later, Bloch, followed Lamprecht in treating medieval economic history as a form of cultural history.

We are called *Homo sapiens*. Once upon a time there were other species in the genus *Homo*. In East Africa there was *Homo rudolfensis*, in East Asia *Homo erectus*, in Europe *Homo neanderthalensis*, in Indonesia *Homo floresiensis* and in Siberia *Homo denisova*. But of all these different species, only one survived, so that it became possible to equate human beings with *Homo sapiens* and to forget that *sapiens* was just one species of human being.[27] Similarly, we have come to think that history is identical to the university-based discipline of history just because the other kind of historical scholarship—the object-studying antiquarianism—disappeared. Just as we're told that *Homo sapiens* may have hunted Neanderthals to extinction, university-based history in some quarters made the old antiquarianism its first target. In both cases, the species that disappeared was absorbed into the successor's gene pool.

Imagine the effect on our sense of human-ness were we to discover that the other species of humans had survived into our present. Imagine if we were to find that antiquarianism had survived into the present, and not in some marginal location, weakened form or genetic marker, but as a force to be reckoned with.

If histories of history have not found a way to include antiquarianism, the absence of histories of antiquarianism, lamented already by Arnaldo Momigliano in 1950, has not helped.[28] Momigliano was a historian of the ancient world and its later study. To the extent that this second focus put him in position to provide such an account, he argued that in the eighteenth century antiquaries and historians had selectively interbred—to the advantage of the historians. For this reason, the genome of the university-based historian—to stay with the analogy—has a high proportion of antiquarian DNA. And then, Momigliano argued, in the nineteenth century the still-surviving antiquaries continued to evolve, branching into the distinct species of archaeologist, anthropologist, art historian, and, later, sociologist. By the turn of the twentieth century, history was not the only modern human science that contained a high proportion of antiquarian DNA: they all did.[29] Having found their way into the university as distinct disciplines, some of them continued to evolve beyond the genus of past-loving creatures altogether. But the ones the university-based scholars left for dead also kept evolving. They became museum curators, conservators, local folklorists, artists inspired by the past to create new visions, writers of historical fiction, re-enactors, and the large and late-born clan of public historians.

What does it mean for our story that university-based history is not the only kind of past-loving? While distinct species often compete for resources, sometimes the recognition of distinctiveness allows for collaboration instead. It might even yield an agenda for action. Take the relationship between curators and historians, for example, or between writers of historical fiction and historians. Each can bring something different and important to the understanding of the past. Over the course of the twentieth century, university history departments have gotten better at broadening the category of what counts as history. Think of the contributions of social history, women's history, history from below, history of everyday life, history of science, and environmental history, among others. But we haven't gotten any better at broadening the category of who counts as a historian. Why shouldn't a serious documentary filmmaker like Frederick Wiseman or a deeply evidence-based conceptual artist like Mark Dion be part of ongoing dialogue with university-based historians? The interest in "experiential learning" on the part of historians of science and archaeologists has shown how much university-based scholars can learn from past-loving artisans.

If curators are one of the other species of past-lovers, so are artists. The little figures clambering about the Roman ruins in the great painting by Hermanus Posthumus were drawing and sketching in order to draw and sketch better. The engagement of contemporary conceptual artists with material evidence and even the methodologies of producing it (for instance, archaeology) might lead us to encourage more interspecies communication, so to speak. Programs that link together the inquiries of artists and scholars could take advantage of their different but related kinds of material knowledge. We see this beginning to happen in some places.[30]

Objects conservation, which emerged from the practices of antiquaries—Peiresc, for instance, gave instruction about how to conserve the skin of a crocodile which had fallen into the sea en route from Alexandria to Marseille, and the antiquary John Milner launched a debate about the gothic in England which was continued by Ruskin half a century later—requires a scientist's knowledge of materials, a practitioner's knowledge of techniques, and a historian's knowledge of context. No wonder that conservation is now finding its way back into university curricula that are themselves trying to integrate textual and material knowledge.[31]

Unlike textual knowledge, materials often exceed the capacities of any one person or approach. Institutions with collections and institutions with learned practices could find more justification for the collaborations that are otherwise often difficult to organize. University museums are the likeliest to do this first; projects underway at Göttingen and Glasgow suggest that this great convergence—or should we say re-convergence?—is possible. Antiquarians like Peiresc were creatures of the *Kunst- und Wunderkammer*, and this same way of organizing knowledge was still animating the amateur historical associations of the nineteenth century all across Europe.

The university-based past-loving species may indeed face declining enrollments and thus grimmer prospects in future years. This much we may grant the prophets of doom. But if we look outside the university to the broader genus of the past-lovers, we see no diminution of the past's popularity. Historical fiction sells and sells and sells; Hilary Mantel has turned a sixteenth-century administrator into a star of stage and screen. At the most recent Venice Biennale, archaeology was one of the most powerful of the artistic languages on display. The most popular museums in the world are all historical: the British Museum, the Louvre, the Metropolitan Museum of Art, and the Palace Museum in Beijing. And Venice, like Colonial Williamsburg, exists for us as an example of the past in the present that attracts more and more worshipers each year.

Scholarly practices developed by the antiquaries still drive the activities of many of the past-lovers. (It's in the DNA.) Collecting is registered in the ever greater importance of material culture and object-based learning, both inside and outside the university. Without description and the close-looking it memorializes, there would be no curatorial activity. Comparing may actually be fundamental to a globalized world fascinated by the encounter—sometimes shaken, sometimes stirred—between different genera of sources, questions, or bodies of knowledge. Reconstruction, whether of lost structures, such as the *Schloss* in Berlin, or of past practices, for example, by American Civil War re-enactors, looms large in an ever fragmenting world. Because of that fragmentation and because of the explosion of at-our-fingertips knowledge, collaboration appeals to past-lovers more than before. Facebook, Twitter, and Instagram are nothing if not amped-up republics of letters. The digital revolution empowers each of these methods. But it also pushes us in the direction of the antiquaries' *style* of presentation: non-linear, focusing on the fragment, curatorial in approach, and aspiring always to the database. In all of this what has dropped out is the "piety," or reverence, that Nietzsche identified in the antiquaries' posture of reconstruction. Those who now reach into the antiquaries' toolkit, whether or not they know that's what it is, are doing so not out of any sentimentality but because it contains the tools they want.

The founding of the Germanisches Nationalmuseum in 1852 as a platform for object-based historical research launched a full-throttle, decades-long debate in Germany about how historical subjects could be addressed in a museum setting where they could speak to scholars and to the general public. Perhaps the details of that debate, and its broader nineteenth-century context, could contribute to our own discussions about the future of museums in a twenty-first-century research environment.[32]

In the nineteenth century, the university-based gatekeepers of academic knowledge rejected this move as imperiling their carefully drawn boundaries, as did the museum-based connoisseurs who, in parallel, feared for their oases consecrated to higher things and better sorts of people. Aby Warburg's complaints about "border guards" in his 1912 lecture on the movement of Greek astrological imagery eastward to India and back to Renaissance Ferrara, not to mention the marginality of his own "Library for Cultural Sciences" in Hamburg, highlight the price of trespassing disciplinary or other conventions.[33] A century later, many of these issues are still live. Universities struggle with the tension between discipline-based departments and centers or institutes organized around themes or practices. Power still remains with the departments. Only on the fringes, where local context serves as a counterweight, can something as innovative as Stanford's Institute of Design (known as the "d.school") thrive. Its collaborative, experimental, problem-driven approach and its crossing the university and business worlds seems tailor-made to the new world Nietzsche advocated in his two "untimely meditations." Yet Stanford's d.school abandons the deep commitment to research characteristic of the antiquaries and does not even try much to speak to humanities departments, suggesting that the perfect Nietzschean hybrid remains to be found—or created.[34]

Momigliano identified the 1870s as one of the great turning points in the history of studying the ancient world. He singled out the publications of

E. B. Tylor, Johann Jakob Bachofen, Lewis Henry Morgan, and Numa Denis Fustel de Coulanges.[35] We might want to add Nietzsche to that list. From our perspective, we can see that Nietzsche in the 1870s was groping toward an answer to the question of how to think about the meaningfulness of the past in an age of "deep history" (our term, not his). Along with Bachofen, who was also working in Basel at the time, Nietzsche was realizing that the advent of prehistory had to change how we thought about the past. Rousseau, in his *Discourse on Inequality* (1755), invoked the latest anthropological research to argue that previous thinking about the state of nature did not get far enough back in time and thus presented as natural what was just conventional (most pertinently the origin of property). Nietzsche and Bachofen now did the very same thing to Rousseau, saying that he didn't go back far enough to the foundation of things like morality and family. For Nietzsche, the breakthrough came in the work whose completion was responsible for "We Philologists" remaining incomplete.

In *Human, All Too Human* (1878) Nietzsche shows us what the discovery of prehistory could mean. He proclaimed that compared to the vastness of the past, philosophers and historians had generalized from "a very restricted stretch of time." He wished his readers "to imagine a human being eighty thousand years old." Everything important about human development "occurred during primeval times, long before those four thousand years with which we are more or less acquainted." Nietzsche called what could be done with this deep past not history but "historical philosophy." We might think of this as something akin to the philosophical histories of the Enlightenment, but with a still greater emphasis on the broad philosophical strokes and a commensurately diminished attention to historicity.[36]

One of the examples of this new approach is, precisely, the earliest attention to things. With hominids viewing mighty, invisible actors—let us call them gods—as causal agents, objects were worshipped for the indwelling divinity who needed to be propitiated: "the corporeal element provides the handle with which one can grasp the spiritual," as Nietzsche put it.[37] Thus a tool or a bauble or a garment or a place—anything that could play a causal role in the world—gained meaning by association with the invisible power causing all things. We might call this the "birth of aura": like the Big Bang, thousands of years later it is still shaping the horizon of our experience. Having come to the conclusion that the really big issues could not be treated philologically and that, by contrast, the issues philologists could treat were superficial, Nietzsche felt that there was only one course of action left to him: to abandon his essentially historical perspective for a philosophical one. Half a century later, this same idea, mediated by the philosopher and sociologist

Max Scheler, appears in Alfred Weber's *Cultural History as Cultural Sociology* (1935). Weber, the brother of the more famous Max and a professor at Heidelberg, argued that humans' self-awareness was a function of recognizing in the self the same kind of object-ness that they perceived all around them. Related to this was the unprecedented practice of tool-making, something that happened very early on. As with Nietzsche, accommodating prehistory meant generalizing, in this case toward sociology.[38]

But what is the conclusion that historians might draw from the same realization about how long our history really is? Daniel Lord Smail's *On Deep History and the Brain* (2007) and *Deep History: The Architecture of Past and Present* (2011, with Andrew Shryock) have suggested some answers to this question, but have not yet changed the way historians do business. If historians are only capable of working on the last four thousand of the seventy or eighty thousand years of *Homo sapiens*, then, effectively, all our work is antiquarian in the specific sense of being research-driven but basically de-contextualized, looking at a piece of the whole only. In the Hayden Planetarium in New York, the length of the universe in time corresponds to the length of a ramp visitors descend from the Big Bang "theater." Measured against this, the length of the history of *Homo sapiens* is the breadth of a single human hair (the ramp is four hundred feet long). And almost all the history historians do focuses on the last part of that hair's breadth. Compared to the forty-odd centuries of recorded history and the hundred centuries since the Neolithic Revolution, even the world wars of the twentieth century might be just a kind of "histoire événementielle," to use Braudel's slight. On the other hand, perhaps this discovery offers an opportunity to appreciate anew what antiquarianism does well—something Nietzsche was pointing to in his meditation on history. And, of course, the more students of the past reach for a way to access the deeper past with questions about humans and not just nature's history, the greater a role there will be for material culture among university-based students of the past.[39]

This book did not set out to be even a partial history of antiquarianism. It began life as a kind of dark binary star orbiting *Peiresc's Mediterranean World*. Where that project approached a single life as a vast cosmos, this one treats a vast theme in the form of an outline sketch. If that one adopted the style of antiquarianism to unmoor a set of received assumptions about antiquarianism, this one deploys one narrative in order to replace another one. For if Peiresc provided me with a way into the history of using—and thinking with—material evidence, I also realized that I needed an understanding of the longer, broader impact of antiquarianism to assess the shorter, sharper impact of Peiresc's antiquarian practices. In that book, I suggested that taking antiquarianism more seriously would open up the possibility of a Copernican revolution in the history of historical research, in which the object-centered, research-oriented approach of the past-lovers would appear as typical, and the grand historical narrative of the sort we associate with the century from Gibbon to Burckhardt as the exception. This book provides that counter-history.

Having completed this two-sided project, I can now see that thinking about things is also the key to perceiving the ongoing relationships between the different species that constitute the genus of the past-lovers. Antiquaries and object-lovers like Peiresc have turned out to be more instructive than they seemed. But even more, the longing trapped in things helps connect the professional students of the past, of whatever species, with *Homo sapiens* writ large. All of us experience the power of the past in things, whether cleaning out the closets of deceased parents or cradling our grown children's mementos or experiencing the shock of connection to an impersonal past through the magic of the haptic. History with objects obliterates so many of the false walls that partition off our experience of living that it is hard not to feel, with Nietzsche, that getting this relationship right will help us, finally, make history work for life.

❧ CHAPTER 1

History and Things in the Twentieth Century

From my childhood trips to the Hayden Planetarium at the American Museum of Natural History I remember two things: the giant, metal, ant-shaped Zeiss Mark IV projector in the planetarium and the Northwest Coast canoe crewed by wooden Indians perpetually paddling out the 77th Street entrance. The one impressed as space-age wizardry, the other with a primitiveness that belied its artifice. One was a piece of technical rationality put in the service of the imagination, the other a piece of re-imagining—where did that crew come from, anyway?—that was somehow supposed to inspire rigorous scientific investigation.

No one has written more knowingly nor more lovingly about the canoe as an object than Bronisław Malinowski (1884–1942). Marooned on Papua New Guinea during the First World War while doing fieldwork, the product of his prolonged residency was one of the most perfect books of the twentieth century—and an astonishing engagement with material culture. The chapter Malinowski devoted to the canoe in *Argonauts of the Western Pacific* (1922) surveys its meanings from 360 degrees, and in so doing models all the questions anyone might have about any kind of artifact. Acknowledging that a canoe "is an item of material culture," and therefore can be described, photographed, and collected, "the ethnographic reality of the canoe," he writes, "would not be brought much nearer to a student at home, even by placing a perfect specimen right before him." For even though it was material, the canoe's meaning

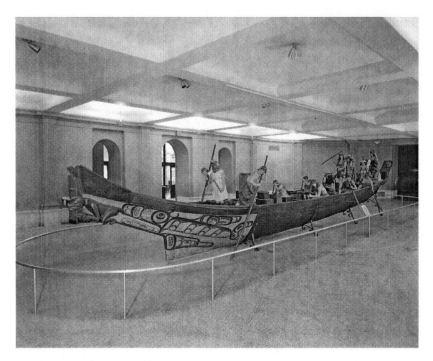

FIGURE 3   The native canoe at the 77th Street entrance of the American Museum of Natural History. Image #328834, American Museum of Natural History Library.

was derived from its role in society and in the individual imagination. Nevertheless, as Nietzsche himself might have believed, Malinowski explained that "it is in this emotional attitude of the natives towards their canoes" that researchers would find the "deepest" reality, the "innermost self."

That same year, Rilke completed the *Duino Elegies*. The ten poems represent—among other things, certainly—the working out of a metaphysics of objects. Read this way, they may be the culmination of a series of reflections that began in Rilke's earlier work on Rodin. Rilke encountered Auguste Rodin in 1902 and soon after became his secretary. He looked very carefully at Rodin's work and saw not concepts or ideas but hands. "Hands," he wrote, "are a complicated organism, a delta in which much life from distant sources flows together and is poured into the great stream of action." For him, hands are real, and what they make is real. In fact, what they make is history. "Hands have a history of their own, they have, indeed, their own culture."[1]

Rilke's "culture of the hand" is a way of defining human activity: training the hand, the works of the hand, the world made by many hands. But then Rilke tried to imagine what a historical practice would look like that took this world as its subject. "If my subject were personalities," Rilke began, "I could begin where you have just left off on entering this room; breaking in upon your conversation, I would, without effort, share your thoughts."[2] This is the ideal of history as it actually was, Ranke's famous *wie es eigentlich gewesen ist.* It is the *Historismus* upon which was founded the university-based discipline of history. But it is not the history Rilke wants to write or might want us to write. "When I attempt to visualize my task," he continues, "it becomes clear to me that it is not people about whom I have to speak, but things."[3]

Rilke probes deeply. "How does it come about at all that things are related to us? What is their history?" Rilke's answer meets the depth of his challenge. He offers up a conjectural history of the creative soul that would seem to follow Nietzsche's turn to "historical philosophy" in *Human, All Too Human.* Things, he writes, were made very early, with difficulty, after the pattern of natural things already existing. "The earliest images were possibly nothing but practical applications of this experience, attempts to form out of the visible human and animal world something immortal and permanent, belonging to an order immediately above that world: a thing."[4]

By 1907, then, Rilke had developed an ontology that linked humans and things. Building on this, he sketched out a model of what a historical study fit for this approach might look like. He also hinted at a possible metaphysics, too, in which things explained not only the place of humans in this world, but also our relationship to things eternal. This project may owe something to Nietzsche's vision of artifacts in *Human, All Too Human* as residually auratic because of their original investiture with divine potency. Rilke zeroed in on that divine residue and gave it voice in the *Duino Elegies*, begun in 1912 and then completed, on the other side of the cataclysm, in 1923. The first six elegies are devoted to the various obstacles to connecting the material and the transcendent aspects of existence, while the final four make it the centerpiece of Rilke's quest for healing.

From a generalized affirmation of the world, warts and all, Rilke began, in the seventh elegy, the process of connecting in the realm of ruins with the antiquarian's work of reconstruction: "Where once an enduring house was, now a phantom structure crosses our path, completely belonging to the realm of concepts."[5] The things themselves were gone, but they had been reconstructed and preserved as mental realities. Temples that once existed, he writes, were no longer known: "It is we who secretly save up these extravagances of the heart. Where one of them still survives, a Thing that was formerly prayed to, worshipped, knelt before—just as it is, it passes into the invisible world."

This is indeed the fate of all material things. But, Rilke argues, the recovery and reconceptualization of these monuments within us, through

FIGURE 4   Duino Castle and Cliff.

imagination, is an even greater triumph. "Many no longer perceive it, yet miss the chance to build it *inside* themselves now, with pillars and statues: greater!" Objects and monuments even in their decayed, ruinous state functioned still as internalized placeholders of materiality. "This once *stood* among mankind, in the midst of Fate the annihilator, in the midst of Not-Knowing-Whither, it stood as if enduring."[6] Those who had no ability to take the ruin inside he calls the "disinherited ones, to whom neither the past belongs, nor yet what has nearly arrived." Moving from inner to outer, from psychology to archaeology, Rilke recapitulates the history of antiquarianism as metaphysical assertion. To the angels, Rilke speaks the monuments of Western culture: "Pillars, pylons, the Sphinx, the striving thrust of the cathedral."[7] And yet, Rilke is also instructing the instructor, as poet to the historian, that reconstructing the past is an act of imagination, not just archival skills, and that this act is itself encoded in the encounter with the thing as the paradigmatic "source."

But then, in the ninth elegy, Rilke takes the interest in reconstructing the past in a direction it hadn't gone to before, or at least not as archaeology. For he argues that things give us not so much the grand monuments of the past but the monumentality of the ordinary. In other words, the same ontology connects the study of the material past to the study of daily life—a connection that the *Annales* School and the Yidisher Visnshaftlekher Institut (YIVO) made that same decade, though in different languages. "Why then have to be human?" he asks. "Because truly being here is so much," is his answer. Trying to "hold it firmly in our simple hands" was the goal, but what could ever be taken into the realm beyond, of the angels? The answer, he writes, was not something "unsayable" or transcendent for us humans, like a sphinx or pillar or cathedral. All this would be obvious to the angels. Instead, evoking a Nietzschean descent from the mountaintop, Rilke's envoy brings "some word he has gained, some pure word, the yellow and blue gentian," referring to a common flowering, alpine plant. Unlike Aby Warburg, then, who worried about how he would get from the "heights of Sils-Maria to the lowlands of the scholar's study," Rilke trusted in that connection. Flowers, simple in their own way, could yet be staked against the eternal. And this, in turn, led Rilke into an extraordinary sequence of lines in which it is material culture that is pledged in the game of meaningfulness. "Perhaps we are *here*," he writes, "in order to say: house, bridge, fountain, gate, pitcher, fruit-tree, window—at most: column, tower."[8]

Rilke's choices are not random. These are not merely common objects, they each define a point on the map of human existence and taken together map the significant contours of life itself. The "house" stands for family and human society; the "bridge" for what connects people and stories; the "fountain" is the life-giving power of nature; the "gate" marks thresholds and regulates crossings; the "pitcher" is the man-made instrument for bringing sustenance from nature to bodies; the "fruit-tree" is both product of the elements and nourishment for people; the "window" how we, and through which we, see the world. The "at most" suggests that the typical art-historical objects only occupy one end, the obvious end, of a much richer spectrum.

It is of this daily realm that Rilke sings: "Praise this world to the angel." He insists that we focus on the here and the now and that things mediate this encounter. In some of his most arresting mix of registers and images he writes:

> . . . So show him [the angel]
> something simple which, formed over generations,
> lives as our own, near our hand and within our gaze.
> Tell him of Things. He will stand astonished; as *you* stood
> by the rope-maker in Rome or the potter along the Nile.[9]

Rilke's metaphysics of objects was laid out by 1923. It remains a unique perspective on why things matter. And, as far as I know, it has played no role in subsequent discussions of material culture.

In that same year, at the sanatorium in Kreuzlingen, Aby Warburg delivered his now-famous lecture on the Hopi snake dance. Warburg had traveled in the American Southwest in 1897 and delivered a few lectures upon his return to Germany at ethnological museums in Hamburg and Berlin. He had even thought of gaining his *Habilitation* with a dissertation on the Hopi.[10] But the material had otherwise remained in the drawer until, as part of an effort to demonstrate a wellness sufficient to warrant his discharge from care, Warburg pulled it all together for a bravura presentation. And still the lecture remained unpublished. After his death, and the Kulturwissenschaftliche Bibliothek Warburg's flight to London, a small summary was published in English. But the full text did not reappear until the end of the twentieth century, first in German and then in English.[11]

The reader of "Images from the Region of the Pueblo Indians of North America" encounters not just photographs and drawings of objects, both sacred and profane, but also a discussion that turns around space and things. At the center, of course, is the snake—a particular kind of object—and the snake's home and the human performance of the snake. We are half a world away, and more, from Malinowski's canoe, but the laser-like penetration through layers of the material, all the way to the innermost immaterialities, is the same. Warburg not only photographed things like the native kachina dolls, he had himself photographed wearing the god-doll. Warburg's library, which he described as a "Problem-Bibliothek"—we might call it a "problem-focused collection"—functioned as a magnet for historians and anthropologists of religion. His own work crossed borders between disciplines, materials, and institutions in pursuit of its intellectual quarry. Warburg, was, for instance, interested in clothing, hairstyles, jewelry, pots, wall-coverings, furniture, and the like, all without regard for the object's status or aesthetics. For the purpose of understanding

> the decoration of a marriage chest could be just as relevant as the fresco cycles of a palace, a temporary structure erected for a pageant as revealing as a cathedral; popular broadsheets, ballads, customs, rituals, amulets, games, anything and everything that formed part of the life of a community also deserved to be considered by *Kulturwissenschaft* as a cue to the mental life of a civilization. Of course antiquarians had always been interested in such evidence, but they were after the quaint and picturesque curiosity.[12]

When Warburg talked about antiquarians, he knew whereof he spoke. His legendary work in the Florentine archives inspired his fellow "archive rat," the economic historian Alfred Doren, to dedicate to him his history of the

Florentine woollens industry. Warburg could bemusedly describe himself as a kind of antiquary in the same way as he referred to himself as a "truffle hunter." In his lecture on Francesco Sassetti's injunction to his children, he referred to the effect of research on the researcher as the "reawakened past of his home ground"—almost quoting Nietzsche's description of the positive effects of antiquarian research on the antiquarian.[13] If Warburg never inspired others to work on material culture or on the history of antiquarianism it is because he himself did not recognize these terms in his practice of *Kulturwissenschaft*, or "cultural science," devoting no set piece to explicating his own key term.

But a younger follower did. In a lecture delivered at the Warburg Library a year after Warburg's death, Edgar Wind clarified the method behind his border-crossing logic. "Instead of positing *in abstracto* that inter-relationships exist," Wind wrote, "search for them where they may be grasped historically—in individual objects." Wind explained that in practice it meant "studying this concrete object, as conditioned by the nature of the techniques used to make it."[14]

This keyword, "Kulturwissenschaft," remains without a history, lost along with the German world whence it came. It had been coined in the middle of the nineteenth century, originally to explain the material workings of society (see chapter 7).[15] It soon became the pivot in a debate about the kind of knowledge produced in the humanities with the intent of securing these in the face of the increasing dominance—and swagger—of the natural sciences. The most far-ranging of these interventions was Heinrich Rickert's *Kulturwissenschaft und Naturwissenschaft* (1898; revised and reprinted in 1910, 1915, 1921, and 1926). He argued that historical knowledge, unlike natural scientific knowledge, had as its *telos* the individual, whether person or event. What gave historical knowledge its legitimacy, however, was the historian's ability to abstract, or generalize, without sacrificing the specificity of past reality. Hence for him the "Kulturwissenschaften" were always the "historische Kulturwissenschaften." We are here only one step away from Weber with his historical sociology and "ideal types." In fact, sociology immediately replaced the neologistic *Kulturwissenschaft* as the way of talking about multidisciplinary analysis in the early twentieth century.[16]

In the years that followed Warburg's death in 1929, his closest collaborators, Ernst Cassirer and especially Erwin Panofsky and Fritz Saxl, led the institution toward a more intensive engagement with the meanings of images—Panofsky's famous *Iconology*. They paid less attention to the material support on which the images were found and to the anthropological and religious contexts in which those images were developed and deployed. Had

Warburg lived longer, that might not have been the case. In any event, with his death the Warburg Institute, as it was known after moving to London in 1933, became identified with an intellectualized cultural history.[17]

Rilke's approach to the object, via Rodin and the encounter at Duino, led to metaphysics. Around the same time, Giorgio de Chirico came to the same conclusion, but through a different vector: Nietzsche. "After having read the works of Friedrich Nietzsche," he wrote, "I became aware that there is a host of strange, unknown, solitary things which can be translated into painting." There was, in fact, a "language that the things of this world sometimes speak."

From *Thus Spake Zarathustra* De Chirico came to understand his own experience of "the whole enigma of sudden revelation," the way "the sight of something—a building, a street, a garden, a square" could become a moment of the uncanny, connecting the visible realm with the invisible. "To see everything, even man, in its quality of thing. This is the Nietzschean method," he wrote. For example, when Nietzsche wrote of the pleasure in reading a book or listening to a piece of music, what he was saying was that "the one is no longer a book, nor the other a piece of music; each is a thing from which one gets a sensation." Nietzsche opened up for De Chirico "the psychological language of things"; painting this became the program of his "metaphysical" paintings in a parallel to Rilke's metaphysical poems. The scope he assigned to his paintings was vast—"things generally considered insignificant . . . certain phenomena of feeling, of the character of a given people, even to arrive at the point where one can picture the creative geniuses of the past as things . . . things we examine from all sides." Like Nietzsche, for whom the discovery of "prehistory" opened up a new vision of the natural, so too for De Chirico acquiring a "sense of prehistory" or of "Hellenic prehistory" enabled him to reimagine the artist as the mythmaker he once was.[18]

De Chirico painted the feeling in architecture, Virginia Woolf wrote about architecture as if it had feelings. Her description of the ruination of a house by time, told from the perspective of the house, is a marvel of material imagination that remains unsurpassed to this day (*To the Lighthouse*, "Part II: Time Passes," 1927). But all through the 1920s and 1930s there was a comprehensive artistic conversation about materiality. To give three examples: the conflict between words and things—or between matter and the idea—as incarnated in the Golden Calf was on center stage in Arnold Schönberg's opera *Moses und Aron* (1930–1932). Through the 1930s Francis Ponge began to develop a form of poetry devoted to the concrete. Ponge himself explained that he wanted to write "a kind of *De Rerum Natura*." At the heart of this

FIGURE 5 Giorgio De Chirico, *Les Jeux du Savant* (The Scholar's Playthings), 1917. Bridgeman, De Chirico. © 2016 Artists Rights Society (ARS), New York/SIAE, Rome.

project was an extraordinary effort to convey the detail of material reality in immaterial words.[19] Italo Calvino actually called him "the Lucretius of our time, reconstructing the physical nature of the world by means of the impalpable, powder-fine dust of words."[20] Finally, at the exact same time, on the other side of the ocean, William Carlos Williams turned to concreteness to communicate a socialist's aesthetic. But, for him, "no ideas but in things" was part of a paring down and focus—his iconic "The Red Wheelbarrow" has only sixteen words—whereas Ponge's Lucretian ekphrases could be stunningly baroque.[21]

But moving from art back toward scholarship, while Ponge and Williams tried to make poetry of everyday things, Walter Benjamin, in his contemporary exploration of Second Empire Paris, was using the study of everyday material culture to explode the limits of history as practiced. At the heart of the work are the arcades, but Benjamin's roving eye takes in cast iron, gas lamps, mirrors, clothing of all sorts, furniture, sewers—in short, the full range of the built and occupied city. He went one step further, however, leaving the work itself as a collection of notes in which the materiality of the historical operation is left on view for his readers. The *Arcades Project* as we have it is a kind of Beaubourg of scholarship in which the wiring and plumbing are on view and the discussion of wiring and plumbing hidden within.[22]

Benjamin spent the summers of 1934, 1936, and 1938 visiting Bertolt Brecht on the Danish island of Funen. Their discussions were memorialized in Brecht's own "Arcades Project," the *Messingkauf Dialogues*, an extended, unfinished series of fragmentary theatrical discussions of the nature of theater and representation. One of the characters, "the Philosopher," who could well have been inspired by Benjamin, expresses his uneasiness with the world of illusion on stage by comparing his relation to the stage with that of a man who "deals in scrap metal, and goes to see a brass band wanting to buy not a trumpet or any other instrument, but simply brass." The trumpeter's trumpet is made of brass, but the trumpeter does not see his instrument as pure material. "But that is," the Philosopher concludes, "exactly how I am approaching you in my search for incidents between people." Materiality for Brecht's Philosopher was a means of clarifying history.[23]

While Benjamin in the 1930s recovered the lost Paris of the nineteenth century by reading in the archive, his slightly younger contemporary, Emanuel Ringelblum, directed a research project in the early 1940s devoted to making the archive: collecting spent streetcar tickets, programs from children's theater, and maps of doorbells as well as ethnographies of everyday life. Only a little historiographical digging is needed to connect its director to the

YIVO, the Yiddish Scientific Institute in Vilnius, whose program was based on collecting objects from the Jews of Eastern Europe that documented their quotidian existence, and to the *Annales d'histoire économique et sociale*, edited by Marc Bloch and Lucien Febvre, one of whose contributors was Ringelblum's teacher in Warsaw, Marceli Handelsman. That Ringelblum and his team were operating clandestinely under the excruciatingly harsh conditions of the Warsaw Ghetto should not obscure the intellectual audacity of the "Oyneg Shabes" self-archiving project.

The war years saw two parallel milestones in material history, neither executed by self-identifying historians. J.R.R. Tolkien in Oxford used his skills as a Norse philologist to reconstruct a material past and then reverse-engineer the languages and poetry of Middle Earth. As scholarship, this method had been the standard practice of philologists since the Renaissance and had led to fascinating convergences—and conflicts—between philologists and historians. Tolkien turned the toolkit to fantasy and created Middle Earth's scripts, literature, laws, cults, weapons, foods, and entertainments—though even here, he was preceded by learned early modern fantasists such as Pirro Ligorio, Giovanni Battista Piranesi, and Louis-Sébastien Mercier.

Archaeologists and anthropologists had been working with artifacts from their disciplines' origins in the nineteenth century. But that didn't necessarily translate into theorizing the encounter with the object. At the same time that Tolkien was inventing Middle Earth in Oxford, the anthropologist André Leroi-Gourhan was doing fieldwork in eastern Siberia and among the Ainu of northern Japan. The first fruits of his labors were published in 1943 as *L'homme et la matière*. He drew a range of objects of daily life and showed them in motion. He called the study of objects in use "technology." For any future fetishization of the material artifact, Leroi-Gourhan's book of 1943 awaits as an already-made antidote.[24]

In the same year of Malinowski's "canoe" and Rilke's "potter on the Nile," Henri Pirenne opened the Fifth International Congress of Historical Sciences in Brussels with a lecture titled "On the Comparative Method in History." Inspired by Pirenne, Bloch and Febvre began the project that culminated in 1929 with publication of the *Annales d'histoire économique et sociale*. As the first journal to make material history its focus, the *Annales* became a standard around which rallied a new kind of history. The scholarship it published aimed to move decisively toward material and away from "ideas," which at the time was associated with flaccid German *Geistesgeschichte*.

But it was not until after the Second World War and the publication of Fernand Braudel's *The Mediterranean and the Mediterranean World in the Age of Phillip II* (1949) that the appeal of material history began to spread more widely in academic circles. Even while this only became clear in retrospect, Braudel was already thinking very self-consciously about material culture. In two notes published in *Annales* in 1961 he sought to define "vie matérielle" so that it could be grasped and studied. We might now see this as forethinking toward *The Structure of Everyday Life* (1981).[25] That book, with its discussion of food, clothing, tools, furniture, metals, and the like was for a long time *the* classic presentation of material culture on the scale of the world.

At the same moment that Braudel finally published his *Mediterranean*, but on the other side of the ocean, Sigfried Giedion published *Mechanization Takes Command* (1948). A student of Heinrich Wölfflin—and thus a "grandchild" of Jacob Burckhardt—Giedion had written a play about work, a book about iron, and then, as a refugee in the United States, a book about cities. But *Mechanization Takes Command*, which began as a course he taught at Yale, is about the nature of industrial making and, at the same time, about how to think about history. It is almost a reflection on material history as a symbolic form, in counterpoint with the thinking of his fellow refugee and Yale colleague Ernst Cassirer, who also arrived there in 1941. Nor can we, his current readers, miss the connection between his interest in movement and that of Aby Warburg: Giedion is Warburg disenchanted. Above all, like Braudel on the other side of the globe, Giedion was trying to find a way to grasp, and then to represent, the underlying shaping reality beneath the welter of events. Like Braudel he was always attendant to the particularity of material. But unlike Braudel, and more like Benjamin, he eschewed grand narrative for the telling fragment. "History writing," he concluded, "is ever tied to the fragment."[26]

Giedion returned to Europe after the war, but his book remained. Though its prewar European style of cross-disciplinary conceptual meditation was unassimilable, the topics he studied—the American invention of the assembly line, the Yale lock—made it seem familiar and eased its way onto university reading lists. But it was still some time before "material culture studies" developed as an academic subject in the United States. The key figures here are James Deetz and Thomas Schlereth. Where Giedion talked about "anonymous history," Deetz referred to "commonplace activities." As an archaeologist working on historical periods, Deetz was able to move back and forth between texts and things. This practice, much closer to classical (Greek, Roman, Egyptian, and Near Eastern) than to prehistoric archaeology, links to the antiquarian heritage. So, too, his embrace of the "small things" as opposed to the monumental (in their time antiquaries were often mocked for their attraction to *Kleinkunst*, or the *kleingeschichtlich*), and the small people as opposed to the mighty. But even of the mighty he notes that while we may know of their thoughts, because they wrote them down, we may not know what they ate for breakfast on any given day.[27]

But it is Schlereth, who was trained as an intellectual historian of the nineteenth-century United States, whom Kenneth J. Ames identified as the person most closely associated with material culture studies in America and the one most responsible for its advancement. He was the first person, so far as I can tell, who asked the basic historiographical questions:

> When did a serious scholarly interest in material culture studies begin in this country and how was it nurtured by individuals, institutions, and events? How and why did this intellectual activity grow in terms of research, publications, teaching and pubic outreach? What was the historical relationship between formal material culture scholarship and a wider public interest in the extant artifacts of the American past?[28]

His attempt to answer these questions, in however narrow a compass, is exemplary and still, I think, unique. He noted how much interest there was in material culture dating back to the Centennial Exhibition (1876), the Columbian Exposition (1893), and the "Colonial Revival" of the 1920s, but also that all this happened outside of academia because of historians' total lack of interest in things. Institutional foundings dated to Winterthur–University of Delaware's 1952 MA program, followed by much more activity along these lines in the late 1960s. The bicentennial celebrations in 1976 provided a more recent impulse, perhaps a decisive one as it occurred subsequent to the creation of the academic programs that could finally credentialize and reward interest in these materials. That so much more institutionalization happened in the United States—compare the frequency of "material culture" with "culture matérielle" in France and "Sachkultur" in Germany, Austria, and Switzerland, and the difference is staggering—reflects the ongoing appeal of a fanfare for the common man. It is the slow awakening of interest on the part of academics, whether in departments of history or art history, that is the "material turn" so much spoken of so these days. Outside of the university the culture had already turned.[29] Speaking autobiographically, Schlereth explained his attention to things as a function of his happening to have received a postdoctoral fellowship to a museum, and his historiographical sensitivity as a result of his early training as an intellectual historian.[30]

This chronology of intensifying engagement may be even clearer if we look to the arts. In 1979 an exhibition of stuff belonging to ordinary people opened in Cologne. "La Musée sentimental de Cologne," as it was called, stands at the beginning of a whole series of such displays.[31] Some are completely earnest in their attempt to conjure up the lives of those who did not leave written testimony, such as the Lower East Side Tenement Museum. The summer of 2015 saw an exhibition at the Münchner Stadtmuseum of unabashedly idiosyncratic collecting by residents of the city over the course of its complicated twentieth-century history (including sneakers, record sleeves, and beer tankards).[32] The Boijmans van Beuningen Museum in Rotterdam is taking this idea to its completion. It is planning a public art depot in which the collections of ordinary people will be stored alongside the museum's in a purpose-built Collection Building.[33] Other displays of the ordinary can be deeply ironic, none more so than those of the Museum of Jurassic Technology in Los Angeles (though the Museum of Unheard Of Things in Berlin comes close). It seems that the very term *sentimental museum* to describe this scope was coined by the Catalan sculptor Frederic Marès for the collection of nondescript iron implements, keys, and pipes he donated to the city of Barcelona in 1946.[34]

Another urban visionary of the material is the Parisian artist and print-maker Érik Desmazières. He saw Paris with an eye educated by Walter Benjamin. His early series "Passages de Paris" directly acknowledges Benjamin's *Passagenwerk*. Desmazières' works in aquatint turn the living city into a graded grey pile of things to be studied. These prints call to mind nothing so much as Charles Méryon's oeuvre of a century earlier—and so lead us into a three-way conversation with Benjamin and Baudelaire. Desmazières' series on the print shop of his collaborator René Taze is a powerful celebration of the first industrial age. The piled-high depiction of the shop in the Passage Vero-Déodat (now gone) of his friend the collector Robert Capia gives us the modern store as an early modern *Kunst- und Wunderkammer*—itself the subject of earlier works by Desmazières. Objects, like those cluttering Capia's shop, are repositories of memory but also seem on the verge of themselves breaking into story. (I am always half-expecting the manikin slumped down against a display case to clamber to its feet and start jabbering like a revived C3PO.)

A generation ago David Macaulay began illustrating the material world. The titles of his books often refer to a single structure—*Castle, Cathedral, Mosque, Ship*—but if you read the books instead of just looking at the astonishing pictures you quickly see that what Macaulay is really doing is reconstructing worlds. Leafing through *City* (1974), for example, we find him a student of its markets, baths, government and sacred buildings, and private homes. *Mill* (1983), devoted to a New England town, shows Macaulay placing the building in the context of technology, geology, hydrology, sociology, and economics. You can't read these books and not come away with a respect bordering on awe for what amazing things humans have made out of pretty basic material.

FIGURE 6   Érik Desmazières, *Le Magasin de Robert Capia*, 2008. Érik Desmazières. © Studio Sébert, Paris. Courtesy of the artist and Fitch-Febvrel Gallery.

Reconstructing worlds from fragments is crucial in the books of the late W. G. Sebald. Contributing to the uncanniness of his novels, hovering as they do between the autobiographical and the fantastic, is the role of the concrete. Part of this, to be sure, is communicated by the plain and unadorned language. But part derives from the use of photography and, more generally, close attention to the details of artifacts. There's also an ethics here as well. As a German—perhaps especially as a German—who emigrated when he came of age, objects may have seemed to him more resistant to manipulation.[35] That Austerlitz, Sebald's most defined character, is a historian of the built environment who uses his research as a way back into his own suppressed memories suggests that if objects are bound up with our own life stories, then doing research on those objects can be a form of doing work on the self.

Something very like that was imagined by Orhan Pamuk. So great was Pamuk's sense of the power of objects that he decided to write a novel as a museum catalogue, with essays and entries serving as the text, to be called *The Museum of Innocence*. Even after abandoning this idea to write a more conventional book in which those utterly banal objects were props and not, so to speak, main characters, he still so strongly believed in the volubility of the things he had collected that he created a museum for them in Istanbul.

This kind of reflexiveness about materiality, often explicitly in the language of archaeology, is very current right now.[36] We can take the 2015 Venice Biennale as our sample. Tsibi Geva's "Archaeology of the Present" for the Israeli pavilion presented objects of daily life in recreated storage vaults typical of older Israeli homes. Jimmie Durham's "Venice: Objects, Work and Tourism" used objects to get past national histories and back to individual stories. His assemblage of bricks, entitled "In the Brickworks of Vicenza Many Histories Have Come Together," bears the mark of an individual, whose life he then recounts. But the mark is a fictive footprint—in Latin a *vestigium*—itself an absence pointing to a lost material reality. Grisha Bruskin cast, damaged, buried, and then excavated a series of Soviet-era figures which he restaged as "An Archaeologist's Collection." This was his way of using objects to talk about the past. It was also a commentary on archaeology.[37] Arseny Zhilyaev's "Cradle of Humankind" moved to the next stage in the life of an object, its musealization, in this case in a future museum built by a "Russian Cosmic Federation" based in outer space. His gesture at defamiliarization may have been more extreme even than Bruskin's, but his quarry was the same: understanding the Soviet experience. Zhilyaev's foray into the future followed his investigations of the contemporary museum through imagined but also curated exhibitions.[38] Zhilyaev's projects were presented alongside Mark Dion's "Wonder Workshop," in which he does not so much reconstruct the museum's origin in the early modern *Kunst- und Wunderkammer* as unveil the material techniques that took living things and made them into museum things. Dion's accompanying "Pursuit of William Hamilton" and "Bay of Naples Research" amount to an artist's history of how historical research was done with and on artifacts.[39] Traveling from Mark Dion in Venice to an exhibition of Joseph Cornell in London made Cornell's microcosmic engagement with the history and model of the *Wunderkammer* seem like a first step toward Dion's macro-scale installations. Cornell's "Elements of Natural History" from 1936 restages different kinds of knowledge as different kinds of media: powders in beakers in a cabinet with illustrations and photographs of buildings and names of scientists. And the various themes of later collages ("Celestial Theater," "Life of Ludwig of Bavaria") and explorations ("Museum without Walls," "Center of a Labyrinth") seem to speak to very contemporary interests.[40] Cornell was himself inspired by Juan Gris, whose still lifes stand near the beginning of the century's—and this chapter's—reflection on things.

It may, perhaps, be no coincidence that so much very good thinking about objects as a way back into the past has been done by artists. After all, painters, sculptors, even poets are, first and foremost, masters of the tangible. At the same time, professors of history, literature, and even art were, for most of the twentieth century, much less aware and less committed to the object as a document. Indeed, the story that will unfold in subsequent chapters could even be construed as suggesting that as the university-based scholars of the past pulled away from the object, those driven by imaginative access to the past took it up with greater and greater intensity.

That is a large claim, and it would be intriguing to try and substantiate it. Paul Veyne has observed that it very often happens "that history of history does not unfold among historians, but among novelists, travelers, or sociologists." My own interest here in the imagined access to the past is more programmatic. Paul Feyerabend concluded his thrilling examination of scientific research, *Against Method*, with a call for attention to the arts as a way of thinking. It bears repeating, if only because it explains my approach in these last pages more eloquently than I could.

> The arts, as I see them today, are not a domain separated from abstract thought, but complementary to it and needed to fully realize its potential. Examining this function of the arts and trying to establish a mode of research that unites their power with that of science and religion seems to be a fascinating enterprise. . . .[41]

When the classical archaeologist Michael Shanks teamed up with the English theater director and artist Mike Pearson to turn a modern ruin in the Welsh forest into a theatrical exploration of recent pasts (*Tri Bywyd*) he was doing no more nor less than a Feyerabendian "re-staging of evidence."[42]

Only two decades later, I would venture that this sort of re-staging is no longer shocking. The enormous success of books for a general audience in which material culture is the storytelling medium is proof. The huge impact of Neil MacGregor's *History of the World in 100 Objects*, followed by the history of America through 101 objects, of New York through 100 objects, of religion in 5½ objects, and of Jane Austen and the Brontë sisters through their things is a giant straw in the wind.[43] There is even a novel about a love story turned bad, presented as the post-divorce auction catalogue of a couple's possessions.[44] Mix intergenerational family history with political history and we have the potent brew that made Edmund de Waal's *The Hare with the Amber Eyes* (2010) an international bestseller. It's precisely the way in which things function as "memory palaces" independent of human intentionality that seems now so interesting to so many different kinds of inquirers. For the scholar, it's an opportunity to interrogate past society; for the biographer, to explore a subject from a different angle; for the artist, another way into world-making; and for some design thinkers a way of unleashing creativity to solve real-world problems.

Even "high" intellectual culture has been domesticated by approaching it through material culture. In the late 1990s, Peter Stallybrass, who helped focus our attention on the "material text," wrote an article entitled "Marx's Overcoat." He wove out of the story of Marx's repeated pawnings of his coat not only a family saga but an intensely personal meditation on Marx's own scholarship on commodities and materialism.[45] In short: Marx needed the British Library's collection to write *Kapital*. But according to the library's regulations, readers had to wear coats. Thus, when he was so poor that he needed to pawn his coat, he could not go to the library. If no coat, then no *Kapital*. Could there be a better example of the close relationship between material and intellectual history?

As for Marx, he would seem like an inevitable character in my story. "Marx and Material Culture" is such an obvious subject. Yet, to my astonishment I have found no book and no article with that title (accurate as of December 31, 2016). And on reflection, I can understand why. As a philosopher of history Marx may have believed that the quest for the material drove history, but he himself was not interested in the particular stories that particular pieces of material culture could help tell. Unlike Stallybrass, for instance, he would not have bothered with the story of one man's coat. The Revolution in France, yes; the English working class, yes, but one little life? No! In fact, he theorizes this rejection in the ninth and tenth of his *Theses on Feuerbach* (1845). And even the one time he pays close attention to the way in which things and people mutually interact, he can only characterize the phenomenon as "fantastic" and coins a term designed to emphasize the mystical nature of causation via a material entity: *fetish*. To be fair, as we have seen, Nietzsche and Rilke themselves both acknowledged that there was a complex metaphysics at work in the way things stood in for the realm of divinity. But from the time the Portuguese coined the term *feitiço* to describe the wonder-working idols they encountered in West Africa, the connotation of *fetish* was always and wholly negative: magical, primitive, obscuring, fundamentally false. Just to make the point, today we talk about the "agency" of objects. Between the fetish and the agent yawns an interpretive space that Marx could not cross.[46]

Nor did the century of Communist polities produce a distinctive scholarship on material culture. In 1919, right after the Revolution, while Malinowski was thinking about his canoes, the Soviet Union made to seize the term for itself. An Academy of Material Culture was formed in St. Petersburg to replace the tsarist-era Archaeological Commission. The academicians dropped "archaeology" for "material culture" in the new institute's name in order to evoke "historical materialism"—a resonant ideological term, but one that had never been given scientific content. Lenin, however, did not think the echo was clear enough and with his own hand added the word *history* to the institution's name just to make sure that no one missed the reference, turning it into the Academy of History of Material Culture.[47] But was there any argument behind the term? Or was it an empty gesture? V. I. Ravdonikas's "For a Marxist History of Material Culture" (1930) has all the right words in the right order but turns out to be a political screed denouncing pre-Soviet archaeology and archaeologists—and thus proving the hollowness of the previous decade's move.[48] Our conclusion must therefore be negative: Even the one place where Marxism-Leninism was the dominant culture did not make a contribution to thinking about how to study history through material sources.

A historian of scholarship reading today's literature on material culture—and reading its footnotes even more carefully—would find few references to the twentieth-century history I have been just been surveying, however breathlessly. The point of it has been to make clear that we are not talking here about a marginal phenomenon but about a consciousness of the active role of the material that pervades some of the most significant cultural creation of the twentieth century.[49] Aside from Schlereth, those working on the past through things seem not to have wondered much about the history of thinking with objects, nor about the history of the study of objects. If this chapter has shown anything, it is that we are not the first to think with and about things.

At this stage we might wonder instead why university-based scholars of the past have been so slow to take up this story. This is complicated and perhaps better left for a different kind of discussion, but some large part of the answer has to refer to the history of academic training as well as the shape of the enterprise. At least since Cicero made the clear and distinct identification between the "liberal arts" which were the domain of free men and the "mechanical arts" which were performed by slaves, the culture of the hand would always be found inferior to that of the head. The modern university system did not change this hierarchy, and even within art history, one field whose main body of evidence was strikingly material, scholars focused on the tower and column and not the pitcher or fruit-tree, to borrow Rilke's categories. Moreover, disciplines and departments tend to separate out inquiries for more precise control of content, and some kinds of inquiries have disappeared over the decades and centuries into the widening crevasses between those fields of knowledge. And maybe, too, the very personal nature of the relationship forged between memory and the material world simply could not be accommodated by scholars still resisting the turn inwards Nietzsche called for in the twinned "We Historians" and "We Philologists."

All of this is to say that when academics started using the term *material culture* in the last decades of the twentieth century, they were joining a conversation that had been going on for a long time without being noticed. Not having noticed, they felt little need to reconstruct its prior history. But we, having noticed, can ask: Where did it come from?

✿ CHAPTER 2

Karl Lamprecht and the "Material Turn" c. 1885

Before Bloch and Warburg, who talked about material culture? The answer to the question about how both Bloch and Warburg happened to be so open to material culture is surprisingly simple: they were both admirers of Karl Lamprecht, arguably the most important historian for the twentieth century and one of the least known, at least to non-specialists.

Lamprecht was Warburg's teacher at Bonn around 1880. During those same years he was patron to the young Belgian economic historian Henri Pirenne. After moving to Leipzig he attracted the attention of Johan Huizinga, who devoted his inaugural lecture to Lamprecht. Bloch came as a visiting student to the Institute for Cultural and Universal History that Lamprecht founded at Leipzig in 1911. Lamprecht's interest in social scientific laws made him a key figure in the histories of knowledge written by Ernst Cassirer and Karl Weintraub, and his role in trying—and mostly failing—to reshape German historical practice for his two most recent biographers, Roger Chickering and Luise Schorn-Schütte.[1] But if we bore into his oeuvre we find that his notion of cultural history is in fact deeply related to his thinking about material culture. It is here that his contribution is singular, here that his connection to those we have been studying is most obvious—and it is precisely here that his contribution has been most ignored.

Lamprecht began as a student at Bonn in the 1870s where he reviewed and attacked the most important contemporary historiographical theorist,

FIGURE 7   Karl Lamprecht. The Miriam and Ira D. Wallach Division of Art, Prints, and Photographs: Print Collection, The New York Public Library.

Johann Gustav Droysen (1808–1884), for ignoring material conditions.[2] He then moved to Leipzig in the summer of 1877 to study economic history with Wilhelm Roscher (1817–1894). Roscher had himself studied with K. O. Müller at Göttingen between 1835 and 1840, and then moved to Berlin to attend the seminars of August Boeckh, the leading philologist of the age, and Leopold von Ranke, the leading historian of the age. It was to

Ranke that Roscher dedicated his first book, on Thucydides. He set for himself the task of bringing to economics the kind of historical approach that Friederich Carl von Savigny had brought to law. His *Outline of Lectures on Political Economy in the Historical Method* (1843) was published the year before he took up a chair at Leipzig devoted to economics and *Statistik*, a kind of political science developed in the late eighteenth century (see chapter 4). His *System of National Economy* in five volumes began to be published in 1854 and his *Views of National Economy from a Historical Standpoint* in 1861. Roscher's masterpiece, the *History of National Economy in Germany* was published in 1874, just before Lamprecht's arrival in Leipzig. In all these works, Roscher tried to show that economic thinking could not be studied independently of the broader currents of thought in a given time and place. He brought a self-conscious historical methodology to bear on the problem of treating ideas about the material world as historical, and not philosophical, objects.[3]

By 1880, Lamprecht was back in Bonn, subsidized by the industrialist and political liberal Gustav von Mevissen (1815–1899) to study the economic and cultural history of the Rhineland.[4] In a memorandum of 1880, prepared for Mevissen before he had even begun his research, Lamprecht explained that the organismic perspective on history he favored was revealed in material culture—he used the term *reale Cultur*, which had been used by philologists for over a century to refer to the realm of the signified. "Accordingly," he concluded, "the focus of a consistent historical development lies in the area of 'real' culture, wherein are counted the history of classes, of law, and of economy."[5] Lamprecht saw material culture shaping intellectual culture, not separate from it or subservient to it.

Lamprecht's research and vigor helped establish the Rhenish Historical Society (1881), whose secretary he became.[6] Like the historical associations founded in a wave in the first half of the century, this society brought together academics, archivists, and lay supporters to organize, catalogue, and publish documentary sources for local history. Lamprecht worked closely with the director of the Trier museum, Felix Hettner, who helped coedit the Mevissen-supported *Westdeutsche Zeitschrift für Geschichte und Kunst*.[7] Lamprecht used the journal to publish Gustav von Schmoller (1838–1917) and other young members of the historical school of national economy, such as Theodor von Inama-Sternegg and August von Miaskowski. Lamprecht also provided a platform to Pirenne. Lamprecht explained to a teacher, Ernst Bernheim, in 1881 that his goal was to raise local history to the level of universal history.[8] It was only through looking locally and deeply that he thought one could grasp the bigger questions. As he wrote to Schmoller late in 1881 connecting local with material history, it was "here," in the *real* culture of the Rhineland, that "the universal first clearly and immanently" appeared.[9]

Lamprecht habilitated at Bonn with a study of the medieval chronicler Dietrich Engelhaus. The subject is unimportant, but the field to which it contributed is: "History and Historical *Hilfswissenschaften* with specific consideration of Rhenish Provincial History and Medieval Cultural History."[10] This highlights the way Lamprecht's work ties together the material forms of historical work: auxiliary sciences, regional history, and cultural history.

Lamprecht looked to draw together his academic interests and his work on behalf of Mevissen's association. His plan was to write a history of the medieval Rhineland that would reconstruct the material bases of life. Local culture was to provide the sources.[11] Achieving this was the task he set for his *German Economic Life in the Middle Ages*, a closely argued and statistically underpinned (and overflowing) study of economic life in the Mosel region in the High Middle Ages, published in three large volumes in 1885 and 1886.[12] One can see the influence of his teacher Roscher throughout.

This is a great work of historical scholarship. But it is not surprising that it is among the least-known great works of historical scholarship. The primary reason for this is that it makes no concessions to the reader. It begins, without introduction of any sort, in the Merovingian Rhineland with questions about law and politics, before turning directly to agriculture and land use. The first volume examines the nature of the economy over time, looking closely at the manorial system, political administration, free and bound labor, and social classes. The second volume is a supporting statistical compilation that ranges deeply into questions of property, production, consumption, and prices. The third volume prints the archival sources on which the entire labor is based. The whole bristles with argument but, like a balled-up hedgehog, is almost designed to make access difficult. Why Lamprecht, who thought much about the history of historiography, devoted so little attention to helping readers follow his own argument is hard to know. Based on his later patterns and performances, the likeliest answer is that he was impatient, in a hurry, and overly sure of himself. What need could there be to make plain what, he no doubt thought, was obvious (and brilliant) for all to see?

Only at the head of the statistical section in volume 2 do we find anything like an introduction. In it, Lamprecht focused on the key term in the book's subtitle: "material culture" (as in "Investigations into the Development of the Material Culture of the Countryside on the Basis of Sources Principally from the Mosel Lands"). Lamprecht explained that "the concept of material culture as a unifying total manifestation will be definitive" for the historian who hoped to tell a story neither from the sole perspective of law nor from that of economics. Lamprecht described this as "the basis of this work."[13] In *German Economic Life*, "material" or "real" culture offered a concrete context for integrating across disciplines (law and economy, for example). Lamprecht was convinced that the many-sidedness of culture was grasped much more authentically through a material synthesis than through an ideal one. The book, he writes,

> will investigate the legal and economic aspects of the development of all of the countryside's material culture, an investigation based on the conviction that in the total development of culture, one may indeed supplement a specific, ideal circle of faith, of art, and of science with the sphere of specific, real or material culture, that is, of economy and of law, and that it must be possible to subject the development of each particular circle, as well as their reciprocal relationships, to distinct investigations.[14]

In a letter of 1884, written while finishing the big book, Lamprecht argued that a treatment of the material conditions of life naturally lent itself to a regional framing.[15] Lamprecht's local focus enabled him to unite divergent registers of historical sources in their concreteness without falling back on an (ultimately) Hegelian mythology of unity.

Offering his judgment to the Royal Saxon Commission on History in 1900, Lamprecht maintained that regional history, which he now termed "Landesgeschichte," was intrinsically more easily adapted to the study of material culture than was politics because it was more attuned "to the development of local conditions."[16] Lamprecht's turn to the regional needs to be seen alongside his advocacy of cultural over and against the hegemony of political history as the chief framework for studying the past.[17] In an 1898 speech, Lamprecht explained that "cultural history, that is, social and economic history, literature, art history, etc., when looked at more closely, was characterized by such a mass of important material that it was hardly possible, to the extent that one was looking at its material branches, to solve the task other than by a locally delimited approach, that is, by working through the material at the level of provincial history."[18] By the time Lamprecht came to Leipzig in 1891, his work on the region converged with that of a new colleague, Friedrich Ratzel, the founder of modern geographical studies.[19] We will return in a moment to the posterity of Lamprecht's *Landesgeschichte*.

The second context of convergence—material culture—followed from the first. Lamprecht used the platform provided by the dedication to Mevissen of *German Economic Life* to argue explicitly that after legal and constitutional history, and after economic history, the time had now come to focus on "material culture in its totality as a goal of historical research in so far as this research specifically turns toward real things in contrast to research into the ideal developmental factors of faith, science, and art."[20]

This re-centering on material culture was, Lamprecht concluded, "a goal that is easy to state, but difficult to achieve." It was no small matter to master "the individual sides of sub-disciplines oriented toward real culture in a multidimensional manner." There was simply a lot to know. This kind of comprehensiveness was especially necessary when studying provincial culture. Because it represented the slowly moving register of time, its students had to excavate the sources before they could hazard a guess at the outline of a story. To do even this they had to utilize the most sophisticated of modern historical approaches: "Practically, because given the slow but uninterrupted development of rural culture in particular, a large number of questions of the present cannot be resolved without a genuine and comprehensive understanding of a far-distant past; scientifically, because the more recent developments in historical studies have not yet achieved a comprehensive and well-founded view of the history of rural culture in particular."[21] We have here laid out the program of Marc Bloch's *Les caractères originaux de l'histoire rurale française* (1931). And yet, like some earlier methodological pioneers, such as Johann Christoph Gatterer (1727–1799), Lamprecht put his emphasis on the writing of history rather than its researching, since only the former—"the artistic task of the history writer"—could "by means of empathy awaken the life of historical organisms and endow it with an ongoing presence."[22]

Material culture was the outcome of the interchange of economic, legal, and social conditions. As a result, its study helped uncover their varied impacts. But Lamprecht also argued that "every achievement of ideal culture in terms of faith and knowledge, poetry and art, places its stamp on the material forces."[23] Therefore, he continued, the task of the historian working within the framework of material culture was to use it as a tool for connecting bodies of evidence in order to make visible an otherwise invisible large-scale historical process. "It was thus our task in the history of material culture," he wrote, "to investigate particular developmental sequences based on specific grounds."[24] What material culture did not mean was that the "ideas" were to be thrown out. On the contrary, it was their integration that was the goal.[25] While passages such as this have led inquirers to focus on Lamprecht as a theorist of cultural history, they have overlooked the fact that it is the *material* trace that Lamprecht offers as the substrate on which all these other large processes have worked.

Material culture was itself connected to economy, law, and society. This was where Lamprecht had begun, as a student, with Roscher. Looking back on his own work from the vantage point of the mid-1890s, Lamprecht argued that "all of these studies would be as if suspended in air if I did not draw on their complement, the development of material culture, as I expressed it back then and for a long time thereafter in accordance with Roscher's procedure." His *German Economic Life* reflected this method.[26] Periodization by "spiritual" culture exactly matched that by "material" culture.[27] This reflected a physical reality, that material goods underlay cultural ones and that spiritual creations followed from the satisfaction of material needs. "Every question" about the origin of culture was actually asking, "What favored the development of the material foundations of culture?"[28]

That the "ideal" creations of the mind were connected to those of the hand was something he saw in the work of Jacob Burckhardt. Burckhardt helps us understand the third convergence at work in Lamprecht: cultural history. With the help of Burckhardt, Lamprecht turned in the 1880s toward art historical projects as necessary for capturing the fullest extent of the human experience. "In the meantime," he wrote, "I had read Burckhardt's *History of the Italian Renaissance. . . .* And there it seemed to me that no discipline was more important for further study in the specific area of intellectual development than art history, because it alone offers the monuments of the past that immediately give a complete view of the whole."[29] Thinking in terms of Burckhardt-like notions of cultural history led Lamprecht to explain that the "ideal culture," of literature and art, develops "only on the basis of the unfolding of the real culture, and can therefore be explained only on the condition that this real culture has been understood."[30]

In the lecture course on German economic history that he first delivered in winter semester 1882 and then repeated three times by the winter of 1889, Lamprecht described cultural history in these terms. To the "real" belonged the development of law, economics, and the social; to the "ideal" religion, art, and science.[31] Thus, we should see his *German Economic Life* as in parallel with two other simultaneous projects: his work on the Carolingian-era Ada Gospels in the Trier Stadtbibliothek (1880) and on decorated incipits in medieval German manuscripts (*Initial-Ornamentik des VIII. bis XIII. Jahrhunderts*, 1882). In these, Lamprecht sought to show how art could function as a source for cultural history. Indeed, he began the latter by proclaiming that "no other branch of the spiritual culture of our people" provides a better illustration of the development of spiritual culture than did art.[32]

The book projects were well received. This led him to work more and more in the history of art and literature, which he saw as rooted in religion, morals, and law. He believed that their foundations "were shared in common."[33] Thinking with Burckhardt in the late 1870s and early 1880s had led

Lamprecht to believe that material and intellectual history had to be united and that the study of art objects was the best way to accomplish this task. He then described the "goal" of his medieval studies as tracing "the interactions between the real and ideal lines of development."[34]

Lamprecht saw himself as doing something entirely novel. He did not wish to ground himself on any historical precedent, nor place himself in any one line of descent. Thus, his lecture course of the 1880s, *Fundamentals of German Cultural Development in the Middle Ages*, surveyed prior understandings of cultural history but with a focus on philosophy of history. He offered no survey of the literature and no special understanding of, nor empathy for, the work done by others on material sources.[35] The brief historical survey that introduced Lamprecht's *Introduction to Historical Thinking* (1912) demonstrated a familiarity with those predecessors who had worked on things, the early modern antiquaries, even to the point of noting that *antiquities* as a term extended to the Middle Ages. Yet Lamprecht also seemed to absorb the critical view of antiquaries as blinkered collectors and collators: "Industrious work in publishing sources occurred at the same time. In this area, once antiquity and up to the middle of the seventeenth century had been fairly well exhausted, there also appeared collections of medieval source authors, which today have been completed with the publication of critical modern editions, in particular the *Monumenta Germaniae Historica*, which eke out a silent existence in our libraries, their dust disturbed by no one."[36] He even sounded like the Nietzsche of the 1870s in likening modern, professional history to old-time antiquarianism. So much of the energy devoted to specialized research led to "nothing other than to a dead mass of well-prepared antiquarian material."[37] In his "Old and New Directions in Historical Studies" (1896) he complained about the "specialization in micrological precision."[38] Then there was the amateurish cultural history of things—"the archaeology of bric-à-brac," he called it, perhaps referring to work from the 1840s and 1850s (see chapter 7)—with which he wanted nothing to do. This was a history without theory and without the aspiration to be a science of human nature.[39] In all this, Lamprecht directly followed in the footsteps of his teacher, Roscher, who had described the "historical artisan"—as opposed to the "artist"—in just this demeaning, servile way.[40] Nietzsche might have derived the negative elements in his portrait of the antiquary in the second of the *Untimely Meditations* from Roscher as well—he checked Roscher's *Thucydides* out of the Basel library three times between 1869 and 1874.[41]

All this left the older Lamprecht at the edge of a new kind of historiography. In place of Ranke's political history based on a juridical foundation he now proposed "the morphological method of the economic and social sciences."[42] He believed that it offered the possibility of connecting the material with the ideal side of cultural history. *Morphology* was Goethe's term, which he used to help him track something that was changing due to both internal and external causes. In "Towards a General Comparative Theory" Goethe put the problem this way:

> An initial and a very general observation on the outer effect of what works from within and the inner effect of what works from without would therefore be as follows; the structure in its final form is, as it were, the inner nucleus molded in various ways by the characteristics of the outer element. It is precisely thus that the animal retains its viability in the outer world: it is shaped from without as well as from within.[43]

On the one hand, Lamprecht's approach to cultural history looked back to Goethe's morphology. On the other, he resorted to the most advanced of contemporary "theory," namely, social psychology. He followed Wilhelm Wundt's belief that different sets of conditions helped create different mental responses and that these held true across large numbers of people. The other immensely creative force in contemporary German history-writing, Johann Gustav Droysen, feared that the contemporary information overload would rupture the continuity of history and fragment the possibility of the particular kind of understanding that was history. In other words, Droysen could mark the beginning of the fundamentally defensive attitude of the humanities vis-à-vis the natural sciences, an attitude that persists to this day. Lamprecht disagreed.

At a time when Wilhelm Dilthey and Heinrich Rickert sought to uphold the autonomy and value of history, in particular, by anatomizing the *Geistes-* or *Kulturwissenschaften*—the human or cultural sciences—and differentiating them from the natural sciences, Lamprecht, like his teacher Roscher, argued for their convergence. He believed that history was "primarily a socio-psychological science."[44] He described social psychology as "nothing but the application of greater intensity of observation to historical material."[45] The scope of this material was vast, and documenting it all was the historian's task.[46] Rickert understood how Lamprecht could have felt that his scientizing vision was consistent with his own effort at upholding the autonomy of the history, but stressed that he was in no way arguing that its legitimacy depended upon being made into a natural science.[47]

At the far end of his career—but before the disgrace he brought on himself in 1915 by publicly endorsing the German ravaging of Belgium—Lamprecht observed that the biggest contribution of his twelve-volume *German History* was by including nontextual sources and in reaching across to new fields and distant bodies of learning. He summed up his contribution by transposing from psychology to history and so created a new kind of historical form. Rather than having students focus on a series of events, he aimed "above all to transmit the spirit, the culturally distinctive, the *mentalité*, of the nation in question."[48]

The scientific laws of the mind, he came to believe, provided him with the tool he needed to bring together the two different kinds of cultural history, Burckhardt's ideality and his own work on materiality. "The world of men," he wrote, "oscillates between the opposites of the natural and the spiritual in the same way as does the individual man. Thus, the science of history is faced with the same problems as the science of the individual man; it sees both a material and a spiritual side, and for it, too, arises the overarching question of the 'how' of these mutual connections."[49] In the previous generation, Auguste Comte had called for a "history without names," and Marx had identified the masses with history. Each had developed their own laws to explain the relationship between individual and mass. Lamprecht argued that what held these different measures together was not, however, "class" but mind. For Lamprecht, this new science of the mind made possible the conciliation of opposites, whether in the life of an individual or a group.[50]

What of Marx? Economic history–as–cultural history was what Lamprecht achieved in his work of the 1880s. Many associated this move with sympathy for Marx. But in fact, his attention to the individual within the group marked Lamprecht's distance-taking from Marx. Lamprecht saw Marx as having tried to create a new kind of history but failing because of a dogmatic commitment to monocausal explanation by class. "The real error in Marx's theory of history," Lamprecht wrote, "is that as a result of an error in the dialectical conclusion, which completely neglects the psychological factors of economic processes, conclusions are immediately drawn about spiritual manifestations and their consequences."[51] In fact, Lamprecht wrote elsewhere, without an understanding of psychic changes social and economic change did not add up to a theory: "We see that this is the doctrine of Karl Marx, the theory of the so-called, though most unhappily so-called, historical materialism."[52] Marx and Engels failed because they did not grasp—did not even try to grasp—the inner, individual, phenomena of socio-psychic progress. And yet, Lamprecht was clear that "it would, of course, be going too far simply to deny the real importance of their theory."[53]

Nevertheless, when readers lumped Lamprecht with Marx—not discouraged by Fritz Mehring's praise of Lamprecht's *German History* as a Marxian history—they could point to Lamprecht himself as a source.[54] For in stressing the importance of the material he sometimes struck an insistent, even exclusivist note: "The material is the foundation for spiritual cultural patrimony. Intellectual creations are a luxury elaborated after physical needs have been satisfied. All questions regarding the origins of culture are therefore resolved in the question, 'What fosters the development of the material foundations of culture?'" Lamprecht proceeded to quote Engels for support.[55] No surprise, then, that Lamprecht's critics could paint him a Marxist.

The debate about Lamprecht's cultural history, the *Lamprecht-Streit*, is how Lamprecht is mostly known today. It was, in fact, as much a debate about what history should constitute as it was a debate about whether Lamprecht was a good historian. Thus, Dietrich Schäfer in his 1888 Tübingen inaugural lecture attacked cultural history because it "turned attention away from politics and the state to the stuff of everyday customs and usages—the study of the unimportant [*Kleinleben*] in its most minute details—rather than the spiritual and moral character of the people." A year later, the Italian Renaissance historian Eberhard Gothein replied, denying that political history comprehended the full breadth of the human experience. Schäfer's was the more accepted view within the historical profession. Even a student of Lamprecht's from the later Leipzig years, Alfred Doren, described cultural history as akin to impressionist painting or free enterprise in economic life. It was, in other words, suggestive rather than scientific.[56]

Aside from its consequences for Lamprecht's career, the effect of the debate, amply narrated by Chickering and Schorn-Schütte, was to stigmatize cultural history in Germany. Those too conservative to be persuaded found their prejudices amply confirmed by revelations of Lamprecht's sloppiness. But even those who saw the innovativeness and opportunities in Lamprecht's approach became reluctant to be seen in the corner of someone whose methods were so suspect. Some of the most interesting German historical thinkers, such as Max Weber, Friedrich Meinecke, and Otto Hintze, were sympathetic to what Lamprecht was trying to do. But they felt unable to support him in public.[57] Outside Germany, Lamprecht's innovations seemed more appealing than his failings seemed disillusioning. Lamprecht was invited to America in 1905 to lecture at Columbia University and at the St. Louis World's Fair, where he appealed to the American vision of a "new" history. In France, he was invited to publish in Henri Berr's *Revue de Synthèse* as a representative of Berr's vision of the "new" history.

That Lamprecht's influence was great, despite his discredit in university circles, also reflected respect for his accomplishments as an innovative academic administrator. By 1909 Lamprecht had wrangled permission from the Prussian government to establish an institute in which his general ideas about cultural history could be transformed into curricula. If history was "the totality of historical life" ("Gesamtheit des geschichtlichen Lebens") and defining the "cultural age" ("Kulturzeitalter") was the goal, it had to be pursued through "work on the details" ("Arbeit am Detail") in a research seminar if the results were to have any value. Lamprecht imagined as subjects the new areas of "psycho-genetic" research, such as "the source materials of folklore, universal prehistory, via research into analogical thinking, [and] also child psychology."[58]

In 1911 the Institut für Kultur- und Universalgeschichte opened its doors to students and visitors. To scholars in the outside world, such as the young Marc Bloch and Johan Huizinga, and the already senior Henri Pirenne and Henri Berr, Lamprecht seemed to model a new kind of synthetic history, even if his manifest failings complicated their task of persuasion.[59] The institute's program of instruction was articulated across three levels. In the first tier, Lamprecht gave a lecture course introducing methodological principles. The rest of the curriculum included small classes on subjects such as socioeconomic history, legal history, and eighteenth- and nineteenth-century cultural history to prepare students for more advanced study. The second tier of courses was oriented around nations. In 1909 these included topics in French and Chinese cultural history and the history of social movements in the nineteenth century. In 1913, topics included English and Italian cultural history, heresy and millenarianism in the late Middle Ages, and Marx and historical materialism. The third tier of courses emphasized comparative method, such as the comparative ethical and expressive development of children in West European cultures, the ethnology of the Middle Ages, the development of the epic, and comparative history of German and Japanese art.[60]

The program was more Americanized than other seminars at Leipzig, with graduate instruction as well as an office designed to attend to the students' welfare. The instructors were mostly hangers-on, former students of Lamprecht who had not gotten employment elsewhere. Yet, students he attracted. His own seminar was so popular that he had to move to a new building, which he shared with the seminar on "Regional History and Settlement Studies"— his old interest in regional history must have made this seem a sweet connection—the seminar for East Asian studies, and the seminar for comparative history of religions. The library of his Institute grew to thirty thousand books, most on cultural history, as well as an archive of children's drawings. He bought the newest machinery for the reproduction and slide projection of photos. Lamprecht advised students, was a charismatic lecturer, and went to the pub after talks.[61] When Warburg was planning to establish his own institute in Hamburg, he turned to his old teacher for advice and experience.[62]

Lamprecht's language was obscure, and his *bona fides* as a scholar was undermined by his sloppiness. Both made him an easy target for a professoriate that in any event was too committed to the narrative of the state—and too celebratory of hierarchy—to be sympathetic to his truly innovative perspective. Nevertheless, there is no one else through whom run, like lines at a junction, the most significant historical practitioners of the twentieth century. If he had not been so discredited by the *Lamprecht-Streit* we might see him as the ancestor of cultural history in Germany. Of course, he was discredited and with him cultural history. Instead, it was sociology which, after Weber, functioned as the polydisciplinary integrative human science in the first half of the twentieth century. After the war, its role was taken over by social history; only toward the end of the twentieth century did cultural history strike new roots in Germany.

But back to Lamprecht. If he is the answer to the question of "Where did the *Annales*, and where did Warburg, come from?" then we must now ask a new question: Where did Karl Lamprecht come from?

Lamprecht presented himself as having no predecessors. We do know with whom he studied, and we know some of those whom he admired. If Lamprecht fills the role of grandfather to the formulators of "material culture studies"—and father to the pioneers who wrote history from material sources without giving their vision a name—and if we wish to continue pursuing a genealogical path, then it now seems that we will have to go back one more generation at least, to the *great*-grandfathers who taught Lamprecht.

One of them, Wilhelm Roscher, was professor of economic history at Leipzig, where Lamprecht was his student. Of Roscher's teachers, we know for certain of the impact on him of Karl Otfried Müller and Leopold von Ranke. If we were to keep following this genealogical approach, moving backward from what we know to what we know (that is, from Lamprecht, in this case, to the influence on him of those we can be sure to have influenced him), our next step would take us to Ranke—in order to understand better who Roscher was and what he might have given Lamprecht. At that point we would have arrived back to what would seem like an obvious and familiar beginning and would conclude that Ranke gave birth to both political and economic history. We would not, in short, need the remaining chapters of this book. Put another way, if we only followed the genealogical approach, we would not learn anything we did not already know.

But that's just it—what about what we don't know? The genealogist can never be surprised. Moreover, he or she starts from an assessment of the present and has no means of evaluating that assessment. (To be fair, Nietzsche and Foucault would deny the very possibility of standing outside of oneself in order to make that evaluation.) But if that initial assessment is wrong, then that error will affect every subsequent stage of the inquiry. Thus, in our example, a genealogical approach to the history of thinking about material evidence would move back from Bloch and Warburg to Lamprecht to Roscher and, finally, to Ranke. We would see no meaningful connection between the early modern use of objects as historical evidence and economic history, as indeed neither Henri Pirenne nor Marc Bloch did. A genealogical approach would be unable to discern the impact of a long-submerged terrain feature on the shaping of the present—which is a way of thinking about the continuing impact of early modern historical scholarship on modern historical scholarship—because it would never have had the chance to take the measure of that feature before its submergence. But what happens if we start from the past, from the the early modern antiquaries themselves? Where will a history of their practice take us? Might there be some way to combine approaches in an almost morphological way, studying development from the present backward to the past and from the past forward to the present?

Let us begin to find out.

CHAPTER 3

Things as Historical Evidence in the Late Renaissance and Early Enlightenment

There are many paintings of ruins. My favorite, ever since I first saw it twenty years ago, was executed by the Dutchman Herman Postma (Hermanus Posthumus) around 1536 (see fig. 2). It depicts a vast scene of ruined structures and sculptures. Dwarfed by the remains among which they find themselves, a small number of men can be seen drawing, measuring, and exploring. Some are clearly artists, engaged in copying for the sake of imitating. Others are clearly not. They are either adventurers or besotted lovers of old things.

The history of antiquarianism may have begun long before this painting; indeed, in some way it marks a kind of coming-of-age moment, but many of its lingering perplexities remain. Those who scoured the landscape for material traces of the Roman past (which they then proceeded to interrogate) were called antiquarians, from the *antiquarius* as lover of antiquities. The term also referred to copyists of ancient manuscripts, suggesting a view of books as artifacts with which scholars have only caught up fairly recently. This fascination with ancient physical remains acquired a self-consciousness in the fourteenth century with Petrarch. He collected ancient coins, imagined himself walking through ancient Rome, and wrote letters to ancient Romans. In the fifteenth century, Cyriac of Ancona began recording the Greek inscriptions he encountered during his travels as a merchant in the eastern Mediterranean. His drawings became sought-after sources on the ancient and Byzantine Greek world.

His contemporary, Poggio Bracciolini, like Petrarch before him, re-envisioned the ancient Roman cityscape from a walker's point of view while also collecting manuscripts of long-lost Roman works. A third contemporary, Flavio Biondo, not only wrote books that textually reassembled the imagined pieces of the ancient city but also extended the antiquarian's eye to the countryside and described and identified Roman places in the Italian provinces. A fourth, Leon Battista Alberti, organized, amid his writing and building, the first known underwater excavations. And all this happened in Rome in the 1430s and 1440s.[1]

The revival of antiquity was also the revival of the study of antiquity. And this study infused contemporary art, literature, manners, and what we might term *lifestyle*. The sixteenth century, to stay in Italy, saw an even deeper and broader engagement with antiquities, and the identification of a group of people devoted to the study of its material remains. Raphael, as the papal prefect of antiquities, wrote a letter in 1519 about the preservation of the Roman fabric. Northerners like Postma, in his painting of 1536, captured the sense of discovery and documentation that pervaded a whole group of people.[2]

Who were the antiquaries? They were doctors and lawyers, architects and professors, great merchants and clerics, collectors and small-scale dealers in old things. They were fascinated by antiquity, they read its surviving literature, and they approached its physical remains with seriousness. Some of their work produced buildings evoking classical structures or theories, some of their work took the form of images of buildings, and some of their work produced paper, whether books or notes or newsy letters. These labors documented coins and inscriptions, mapped the location of ancient towns and cities, and interpreted unknown words found in books on the basis of newly found artifacts. Previously unknown realms of ancient religion, law, calendars, warfare, clothing, food, and sport were the subject of discussion in learned circles and were eventually published for a reading public that was as vast outside of Italy as within it.[3] Through objects, Renaissance scholars gained access to parts of the past that were not discussed in texts or were discussed in texts that no longer survived. The intellectual avant-garde was devoted to reconstructing the past or, better, making a new present by way of reconstructing the past. *Antiquarianism* is the name given to this object-attentiveness, though it accompanied and never came at the expense of attention to complimentary texts.

At the end of the sixteenth century, even as the discussion of antiquities had become Europe-wide, the hub remained Rome, and within Rome the most sophisticated conversations were held in the circle of Cardinal Alessandro Farnese. For two or three decades, the scholars he supported were at the forefront of antiquarian scholarship. Pirro Ligorio, Onofrio Panvinio, Fulvio Orsini, Antonio Agustín, Alfonso and Pedro Chácon, and Antonio Bosio pushed forward the borders of the known, and they did it in one especially important way: by making the material culture of antiquity speak to the present. They represent a high point of Renaissance antiquarianism as well as the last moment of Italian dominance.[4] From 1600 onwards, even as the great Italian center pulsed on, leadership in the object-study of the ancient world began to move across the Alps. If we want to grasp this moment of profound change, the best person to investigate is Nicolas-Claude Fabri de Peiresc (1580–1637).

Peiresc

Peiresc may not have been a colossus, but from his perch in Provence he bestrode one of the highways traveled by antiquarianism on its way north. He was trained as a lawyer, studied everything that could then be studied from astronomy to zoology—with a heavy emphasis on antiquity—and lived as social a life as was possible for an ascetic, sickly, provincial intellectual. He wrote letters for several hours each day and at some point decided to channel his literary output into his correspondence. It was this combination of commitments to learning and to sociability that led him to prominence as the "prince" of the early seventeenth-century Republic of Letters, to borrow Marc Fumaroli's term (at the end of the same century, Pierre Bayle called him the "Procurator-General"). That his archive of seventy thousand unpublished papers has survived to the present day makes him a crucial figure for anyone wishing to understand the antiquarian culture of the early seventeenth century. Reading in this archive in the years around 1960, Arnaldo Momigliano concluded that Peiresc was "that archetype of all antiquaries."[5]

So, let us take a moment to acquaint ourselves with this example of antiquarianism in action around the year 1600. Educated by the Jesuits at Avignon, Peiresc traveled to Italy as an eighteen-year-old and spent two years visiting with and befriending as many scholars and erudites as possible, both young and old, moving between Naples and Venice. He returned to Provence to complete his legal training and then took a second Grand Tour to the Low Countries and England. By the time he returned home in 1607, he had met almost everyone who was anyone in the world of learning. From 1617 to 1623 he lived in Paris at the court of Louis XIII and acquired not only a whole other set of contacts but also a whole other context for understanding human action. In all these places, over all this time, he sought out and studied collections of

FIGURE 8 Portrait of Nicolas-Claude Fabri de Peiresc (1636) by Claude Mellan (1598–1688). OP-4635, Collection: European Art. The State Hermitage Museum, St. Petersburg, Photograph © The State Hermitage Museum. Photo by Svetlana Suetova and Konstantin Sinyavsky.

books, manuscripts, and objects. In 1623 he returned to Provence, where he stayed until his death in 1637. During these years he became deeply enmeshed in the study of the Mediterranean and the ancient Near East while continuing to develop his interest in astronomy and antiquities, facts that are preserved in his archive. Prospecting in it we encounter at every turn a vision of how objects functioned as historical evidence.

If we could have perched on his shoulder all those years watching him in action—or if we had spent almost as much time reading through the paper archiving of those actions—we might conclude that of all his talents it was his ability to make any kind of object the answer to some question that stands out. And this, in turn, was directly linked to his great curiosity. He seems to us to be fascinated by so many things. In this fascination we should see him responding to the object or document as if to a question, and as we all know, asking a good question is already half the way toward answering it. Peiresc's questions provide a red thread through the archive and, in their openness to possibility, suggest something of the intellectual freedom that must have helped make him such a cherished interlocutor.

Peiresc was attracted to big things, like volcanos, but also to very small things, like insects. He involved himself in conserving the skin of a Nile crocodile that had gone into the sea along with the rest of a ship's cargo. He personally instructed his correspondents how to make casts of objects, how to measure the content of ancient vases with millet seeds, how to use telescopes and sextants, and how to make "squeezes" of inscriptions. In other words, where even the most sophisticated collectors among his contemporaries, like Cassiano dal Pozzo, made their encyclopedic collections out of two dimensions, Peiresc believed that since knowledge came in three dimensions it had to be reproduced in three dimensions.

Like all antiquaries, Peiresc studied the remains of the ancient world. But he belonged also to a relatively recent phenomenon, the study of the postclassical world. In the Rome of the 1580s, the interest in early Christianity inspired by the Counter-Reformation had led the young Antonio Bosio into the Roman catacombs to begin the study of the "sacred," or Christian archaeology. The French jurists of the second half of the sixteenth century had already begun looking at the way Roman law had become the law in France. Peiresc, in a generation that included Théodore Godefroy and Antoine Duchesne, began to explore the sources that documented medieval France. These were more obviously numerous, but also more varied, than what survived from the ancient world. A brief survey of how Peiresc operated amidst these new sources will give us a good sense of the state of the art of thinking about objects as evidence. And since these same sources would serve as the basis for the expansion of medieval studies in the second half of the seventeenth century, the creation of an elaborate curriculum for teaching them in the eighteenth century, and then the establishment of a cultural history of the recent past in the nineteenth century, our larger story could be said to start right here.

Like those who followed him, Peiresc did not only read and copy out the words on the pages of a book or manuscript. He also viewed books and pages as objects, accounting for their support, script, container, setting, and even the location and physical form of their storage. For instance, he recalled a Marseille notary who said that he had colligated many titles and instructions of the affairs of the Abbey of St. Victor from "an old manuscript book in large paper," from an old roll "written in red ink" in one handwriting up through 1506, and from another that continued to the year 1591 all in a "large format quarto, three fingers thick, covered in wood and old leather."[6] A finding aid Peiresc composed for the royal archive, the "Tresor des Chartes," seemingly done in the field, moved from the location of documents to their physical form:

> In the first case in the corner, in the bundles "On Aurasia," three great charters, one a bull with lead [seal], the others without seal. In the bundles "Arles," two great parchments, two small parchments, a leaf of paper. The register of the Porcellet cases. In the bundle "Avignon" two small parchments, one all eaten away, the other of the vicomté of Nîmes, two grand, one with 4 wax seals and the other with one, and at the bottom of the box a parchment without seal, labelled 0.[7]

Books were also containers, also a form of physical storage. Peiresc paid attention to the material constitution of books from the inside. This codicological perspective is on display in a letter Peiresc sent to Hugo Grotius in 1629 describing the manuscript copy of the *Eclogues* of Constantine VII Porphyrogenitus that he had just obtained from Cyprus. Peiresc wanted to send the book to Grotius for assessment but would not bind it so that Grotius could see it in the state it was brought to him from the Levant, with the quires renumbered to allow Grotius himself to dismember and reorder them.[8]

Seals played a huge role in the cosmos of medieval document study because they were textual, visual, *and* material, all in one.[9] Peiresc was especially attentive to them. We find many elaborate verbal descriptions of seals in his dossiers devoted to medieval subjects.[10] The density of detail in these seal ekphrases is notable. He applied the same kind of verbal description to artifacts and naturalia that hitherto had been applied only to art objects and marvels. Looking at this practice, we might even think about description as a kind of antiquarian "technology."[11] But Peiresc did not only use words. He also documented these visual and material artifacts in images. He commissioned an artist to depict them in the most beautiful and detailed way—as beautiful as anything in Cassiano dal Pozzo's "paper museum." Interestingly, he did not treat his coins and gems—the more typical objects of antiquarian labor—as lovingly.

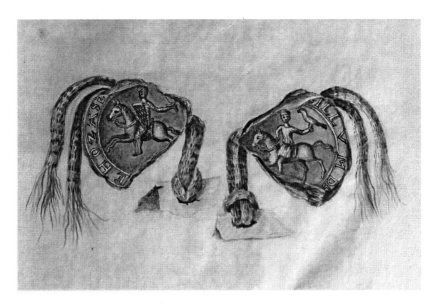

Figure 9a Drawing of seal. Bibliothèque Inguimbertine, Musées et Bibliothèques de Carpentras, MS. 1784 fols. 145r, 216r. Photo by author.

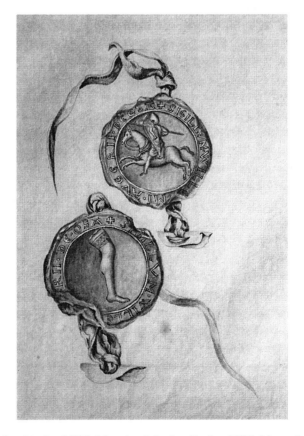

Figure 9b Drawing of seal. Bibliothèque Inguimbertine, Musées et Bibliothèques de Carpentras, MS. 1784 fols. 145r, 216r. Photo by author.

Moreover, the images on the seals spoke a language of their own, heraldry, which in turn inspired additional research. Peiresc's archive contains information on the coats of arms of great families and also on the presence of these emblems on various kinds of objects and structures. Much of his knowledge came from experience; he recorded it in "field reports." These were usually structured as a narrative; for instance, of a walk through a church during which Peiresc identifies the emblems in different parts of the building in more or less detail, sometimes adding rough depictions in his notes.[12] As Michel Pastoureau has shown in our own time, heraldry is an early modern iconographic science.[13]

Seals with emblems could be read as evidence for family history.[14] Genealogy is the immaterial science implied by these material traces, but in the hands of Peiresc the practice involved much more than tracing the lineage of a ruling family. It was a form of historical exploration.[15] It could also be heavily collaborative work, as it required the sifting of large quantities of archival information.[16]

Especially notable is that many of the most beautiful of Peiresc's images are of broken seals, reproduced in his archive in their state of unembellished and unrestored fragmentation with a precision that must have followed specific instructions from Peiresc himself. We could, I suppose, see this as an instance of the "cult of ruins," like that of Posthumus and Heemskerck in Rome, only writ small. But there is another way to approach these images that may bear more fruit.

Peiresc was fascinated by the late antique gems from Egypt with monstrous imagery and identified, from late antiquity onwards, with gnostic Christian sects. He devoted great energies to studying one type in particular, the "Abraxas" gem. It depicted a snake with a rooster's head holding a sword and shield bearing the Greek letters IAO. The workmanship was crude, and Peiresc not only acknowledged this to friends—its "si goffa maestria"—but went on to explain that what mattered was not whether something was pretty but whether it was interesting. He presented this approach as characteristic of his work more generally.[17]

The case of the interesting but un-aesthetic archaeological object pervades Peiresc's archive. He must have written so much about the "Abraxas" gem because doing so flew in the face of common practice. In the later eighteenth century this same insistence would create the demarcation line between ancient art history ("Archäologie der Kunst") and archaeology and, still later, in the nineteenth century, the split between art history and material culture. That antiquaries like Peiresc were catholic enough in their taste to work on such objects did not always redound to their credit as it helped fuel the stereotype of an antiquary as someone whose curiosity came at the expense of good taste.

We can also find here the beginnings of a distinction Alois Riegl later drew between those for whom monuments mattered because of their "age value" and those who focused on their "historical value." Because Peiresc was interested in the object as specifically historical evidence and because evidence is contextual, he wished to encounter the object altered as little as possible. Objects would necessarily bear the marks of time's eating teeth—but he could account for this natural decay. The work of an anonymous restorer, possessed of any number of *idées fixes*, could not be so easily accounted for. Peiresc trusted that his mastery of the antiquarian toolkit—and, to be sure, his own intuitions—could help him make sense of an object's biography. Requesting of the Portuguese converso jeweler Enrique Alvarés in Paris a sketch of some ancient vases, Peiresc asked that the jeweled settings be omitted "since they deter me more than they help, given that I am seeking there what the ancients made and not what moderns added."[18]

Peiresc was a keen student of papers and inks. He frequently relied upon his knowledge of paper to date manuscripts, especially those that came to him from the Levant. Paleography offered him the same firm footing in material evidence. On the bottom of a copied-out diploma of Louis V he wrote, "The writing is almost the same as under Charlemagne, with a form long and twisted."[19]

Paleography was to manuscripts what epigraphy was to stone. And so we find exactly the same kind of historical sensitivity in Peiresc's attention to inscriptions. His volume on French antiquities contains many funerary inscriptions. At one monastery he visited he transcribed one from 1294 along with its coats of arms.[20] He copied out the inscription on a five-hundred-year-old tomb in the old collegiate church at Poissy, tried to imitate the script, then transcribed, drew, and identified it.[21] And when he copied inscriptions, he made sure to preserve abbreviations and ligatures unexpanded, as he did at the shrine to St. Louis in the Sainte-Chapelle.[22]

Peiresc's ability to see the questions lurking within material forms helped open new possibilities for research. We could look at the work done by his collaborators Godefroy and Duchesne in this light. We could also look at the later practice of medieval studies to see how others took these efforts and made them more systematic.

Spon and Mabillon

Peiresc died in 1637. Pierre Gassendi sat in his house until 1639 writing the biography that he published in 1641, *The Life of the Great Man Nicolas-Claude Fabri de Peiresc, Senator of Aix*, which was reprinted several times in Holland and then translated into English in 1657, at the urging of Samuel Hartlib, as

The Mirrour of True Nobility and Gentility. It was through this book that many people encountered Peiresc, including Samuel Johnson, Laurence Sterne, and Benjamin Disraeli.

One of the few great scholars of the next generation to make the trip to Aix in order to immerse himself in the Peiresc papers was Jacob Spon (1647–1685), a physician from Lyon. (That he was himself a man of the South may not have been incidental to his positive disposition toward another provincial intellectual.)[23] He published incisively on the history of Lyon as well as on typical antiquarian topics such as vases and tripods. Most famously, he traveled to Greece in 1675 and then wrote about his experiences.[24]

Among contemporaries, Spon was especially sensitive to the landscape of artifacts. So, for example, he coined the term *Archaeographia* in 1685, which he defined as "knowledge of the monuments through which the Ancients transmitted their religion, history, politics and other arts and sciences, and tried to pass them down to posterity."[25] Though his very neologism refers to "writing," it is clear that Spon was trying to mark out a space where learning about the past could come from past things themselves.

This is especially clear if we turn to his slightly earlier *Response to the Criticism of Mr. Guillet* (1679), Spon's answer to the person who viewed printed books as "history itself" (*l'histoire mesme*) and inscriptions and medals as merely "monuments that serve history" (*monumens qui servent à l'histoire*).[26] In putting the difference between him and his antagonist in these terms, Spon helped articulate a major turning point in historical scholarship: the idea that things—objects, matter—constituted the building blocks of history; that words were not the only source of truth; that narrative was not identical with "history" but rather a rendering of it. Francis Bacon had classed antiquities among the "unperfect" histories, along with memorials. These were "history unfinished," while antiquities were "history defaced" or, more poetically, "some remnants of history which have casually escaped the shipwreck of time." The image of "planks of a shipwreck" (Bacon's "tanquam tabula naufragii") washing up on a distant shore beautifully conveys the de-contextualization of the past as it comes down to us—and precisely defines the challenge facing the historical researcher. The planks included "monuments, names, words, proverbs, traditions, private records and evidences, fragments of stories, passages of books that concern not story, and the like."[27] What Spon adds to Bacon is the clarification that "books are not more history than medals or inscriptions."[28]

Having turned books back into objects and thus into sources to be deciphered—not simply read off as innocently transparent vessels of content—Spon could set forth the science of monuments that his antagonist had mocked. *Archaeographia* had eight parts: numismatics, epigraphy, ancient architecture, iconography (including sculpture), glyptography, toreumatography (the study of reliefs), bibliography, and angeiography, "a vast and prickly" field that included weights, measures, vases, domestic and agricultural utensils, games, clothing, "and a thousand other things whose study does not easily fit among the existing sciences."[29] Spon gave names to some of these. "Deipnographia" was the study of dining customs, "dulographia" the study of slavery, and "taphographia" the study of funerary customs. All of these sub-inquiries added up to an *Archaeographia* that was cultural history done from objects. (Spon clearly felt the need for new terms, which is itself a fascinating window into his sense of the current state of historical practice.)

In formulating these categories Spon drew heavily on his fellow southerner, Peiresc.[30] Most telling is his use of Peiresc as the key figure when he needed a reply to his antagonist's doubt about the use of nontextual evidence: for Spon, Peiresc, "the most universal who ever there was in these matters," was the proof that an antiquarian could do better than a reader of books even for books themselves.[31] And then, a bit later, digressing to show "the merit of a real antiquary," Spon quoted verbatim Peiresc's memo summarizing a meeting with the Flemish artist and antiquary Wenceslas Coberg in 1606.[32] Spon reflected on Peiresc's study of artifacts when thinking about how material evidence could help illuminate the past. He and his colleagues were working out the rules of their trade as they practiced. Most of the time they did not offer self-consciously theoretical statements about what they were doing. For this we need to wait for Jean Mabillon's monumental *De re diplomatica* (1681).

Mabillon, a Benedictine monk whom his eighteenth-century emulators referred to simply as "the antiquary," helps us track the impact of Peiresc's treatment of medieval evidence on later scholars. Typically, histories of the textual-material practices associated with medieval historical scholarship begin with Mabillon and the Benedictines of the Congregation of Saint-Maur, and in particular with the reforms associated with the head of the order at midcentury, Dom d'Achery. While we cannot trace a direct link from Dom d'Achery and Mabillon back to Peiresc, we know of Peiresc's admiration for the Maurists as early as the 1620s; in a sense, Peiresc's practice and Mabillon's shared common intellectual ancestry. And Mabillon himself makes one direct reference to Peiresc.[33]

The subtitle of Mabillon's book announces that it will "explain and illustrate" anything relevant to the "antiquity, material, script and style" of ancient charters, including "the seals, monograms, subscriptions and chronological

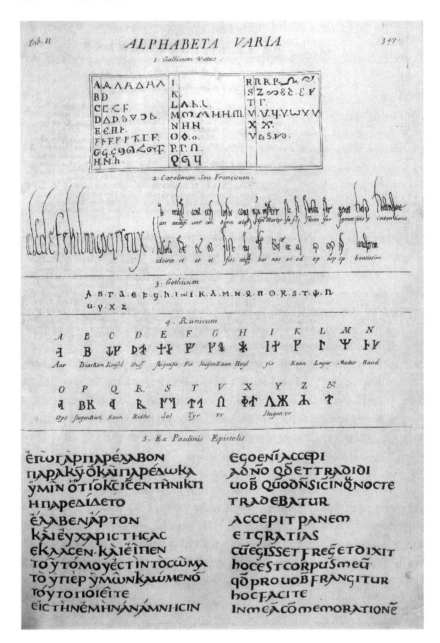

FIGURE 10 Mabillon, *De re diplomatica* (1681). Photo by author.

notes," from within the "antiquarian, historical and forensic discipline."[34] This mighty book is a primer on the material culture of the medieval public document, with treatments of ink, paper, parchment, seals, monograms, formulary, and vocabularies as tools for establishing authenticity and dating—all statements that are definitive for their time. Even the barest perusal of Mabillon's book is enough to establish its aim at definitiveness. The charts of letter forms in the book reflect both a wealth of learning and a desire to systematize technical tools for the heuristic benefit of others (fig. 3). This is what sets Mabillon's work apart from that of forerunners like Peiresc.

The first two of *De re diplomatica*'s six books focus on documents. Book 1 offers a history of the use of charters going back as early as Mabillon could verify their dating (the fifth century) and suggests an outline of their different uses. Book 2 examines the document's style, script, subscriptions, seals, and chronological markers. Being able to do this was essential in order to distinguish truth from falsehood. Mabillon represents both a continuity with the past—he generally used "antiquarius" as synonymous with "scribe"—and a break from it. "I am undertaking a new kind of antiquarian art," he writes, "in which the method, form and authority of ancient instruments are considered."[35] Scribes were masters of the material culture of writing. Mabillon's inquiry had the effect of taking that knowledge and organizing it such that scholars could use it in order to assess documents of scribal production.

Mabillon went on to note that while no one would doubt the utility of antiquarianism for ecclesiastical and civil history (Varro's "people" and "places" and Biondo's "sacred" and "public" antiquities), he wanted to insist also on its value for the history of individuals (Varro's "people," Biondo's "private antiquities"). But, above all, Mabillon wanted to emphasize the great value of his treatise "for the discipline of antiquarianism, history and law." Elsewhere he refers to "experts in antiquarian things," avoiding the abstract noun.[36]

Along with his command of the details, Mabillon brought a sense of scholarship as a calling. In his clerical context one can see the values that antiquaries like Peiresc attached to precision and accuracy as a secularization of the spiritual commitment to truth. The connection between Peiresc and Mabillon was admittedly tenuous: Mabillon did not make the pilgrimage to Aix to inspect Peiresc's archive, though Mabillon's successor Dom Bernard de Montfaucon did. It is only in Book 2 of *De re diplomatica*, deep into his discussion of seals, that Mabillon mentions Peiresc, and the reference is derived directly from Gassendi's printed *Life*. Reflecting on Peiresc's study of Merovingian and Carolingian seals as historical documents, Mabillon writes:

> Men expert in antiquities diligently and with much study inquired into these old seals, among them Peiresc, according to Gassendi [*Vita Peireski*, Book 2] "commending the ancient Seals which he saw, and taking away their impressed reliefs from the archives of St. Denis, St. Germain des Près, St. Maur and others, wherein were contained the true

effigies of Charlemagne, Ludovicus Pius, the Emperor Lothar, Pipin King of Aquitaine, Charles the Bald, Charles the Simple and other Kings of the second stock or family." These and other archives we have ourselves diligently searched through. . . .[37]

The first question that Mabillon asks is whether these kings were bearded; the second is what kind of crown they wore. Fifty years earlier, Peiresc and his friends had asked the same questions.[38] And Mabillon notes that the German polyhistor Hermann Conring supported his opinion that Constantine and his successors wore a gemmed diadem rather than a laurel by reference to a gem belonging to Peiresc.[39] Mabillon's breakthrough rested atop a half-century of antiquarian investigation of medieval source materials as documents of material and visual culture.

Leibniz and After

Mabillon established a Europe-wide field of diplomatics and thus, with it, a Europe-wide attention to the material culture of writing and its supports. Although there were those who disputed some of his conclusions or the way he interpreted particular pieces of evidence, no one denied his contention that there was legitimate information to be extracted from documents by following his method.[40] The Monastery of Saint-Germain-des-Prés was a center of historical learning in Europe because of Mabillon. Montfaucon, who followed him there, did for Greek paleography what Mabillon had done for Latin. He then took Mabillon's more instrumental interest in iconography and developed it into a free-standing field of study in his magnum opus, *L'Antiquité Expliquée* (1719, in 10 large vols.).[41] (Montfaucon also produced the first modern catalogue of the Peiresc manuscripts and incorporated many illustrations from them into his giant survey of ancient symbolism.)[42]

But Montfaucon, for all his significance, especially for Greek paleography, was not Mabillon's equal in shaping future practice. For that we must turn to Gottfried Wilhelm Leibniz (1646–1716), the German polymath whose historical writings remained mostly unfinished and unpublished, and whose insight and sheer brilliance as a historian may only now be visible. Günter Scheel noted that Leibniz was among the first to try to implement as a historian what Mabillon and the Maurists had developed as monkish operatives. He exploited the genealogical interests of the rulers for whom he worked to launch his own research projects. But he never finished what he began.[43]

But perhaps, rather than seeing this as a failure—the glass half-empty—we should recognize that the gap between the project as envisioned and as executed always constitutes a valuable intellectual marker. For when we come across examples of people who see the way to tackling certain new problems but do not yet possess the tools to tackle them we are in possession of a precise measurement of the state of the art. (We can probably all empathize with this gap between knowing in a flash how to do a project but needing years and years to carry it out.) "Success" and "failure" are much cruder and, in the end, less interesting ways of assessing the work of historical figures.

Leibniz, who was a great admirer of Mabillon and who learned from both the Maurists and their antagonists the Bollandists, broadened the vision of the historical by including the history of the earth and of nature and deepened the attention to material evidence with his commitment to the collecting of official sources. What Mabillon called "diplômes" he called *Urkunden*. Antiquarianism is the key for studying "Leibniz and history," but for all sorts of reasons—the general decline in the prestige of antiquarian research, the fact that Leibniz didn't publish his historical work, the vast scope of Leibniz's *oeuvre*, professional historians' ignorance of antiquarianism's history—this fact has only recently been grasped.[44]

In a sketch dating from around 1692, just after his return from visiting Italian scholars, archives, and sites, Leibniz proposed that history be shaped less by the order of time than by the nature of the sources drawn upon. These he enumerated as written, oral, and material. The latter he then divided into the remains of human bodies, mostly bones, and the products of human industry, such as tools, tombs, and buildings.[45] The discovery of prehistory was a long way off, but Leibniz in his brilliance had already mapped a new field.

In July 1692, in a note to himself laying out the plan of his future *History of Brunswick*, Leibniz talked about the need to amass "matériaux." These material objects included, among other things, "monuments," by which Leibniz meant old manuscripts, charters, seals, epitaphs, inscriptions, medals, panel paintings, and drawings. He would then choose "the best of these materials" ("matériaux") for his history.[46] Leibniz's formulation harkens back to Bacon's characterization of antiquarian sources in *The Advancement of Learning* ("out of monuments, names, words, proverbs, traditions, private records and evidences, fragments of stories, passages of books that concern not story") and looks ahead to the way Goethe described the section of sources he amassed in his *Farbenlehre* ("Materials for the History of Colour Theory").[47]

For Leibniz, history was a function of the intersection between a source—a manuscript, a coin, an inscription—and the researcher's ability to interpret and integrate it into a story or "plot" and then into some kind of text. Most famously, Leibniz described the relationship between sources and story in terms of that between the parts of the body and the whole, living form. "The bones support the whole, the nerves make the connection between them, the spirits give direction to the machinery of the humours, which is formed by the nourishing juice, and the flesh binds the whole together." In historical studies chronology is to be compared to the work of the bones, genealogy to the nerves, "the secret motives to the spirits, useful examples to the juice, and the detail of circumstances to the mass of flesh."[48] It was because of this recognition that without sources there could be no evidence, and without evidence there was no truthful account, that Leibniz defended the antiquarians. The details mattered.[49]

In his introduction to a volume of sources for writing the history of the House of Brunswick (1706), Leibniz explained that what he wanted to do was to offer a series of proof-texts. He explicitly opposed this to what he viewed as the style of history writing revived in the Renaissance, which was devoid of "document-supported narrative."[50] Eusebius was the alternative, showing how documents could be used. Documents aided the cause of truth because they allowed others to check one's work. Leibniz cited as predecessors the seventeenth-century French erudites Duchesne and Étienne Baluze and the clerics Jacques Sirmond, d'Achery, and Mabillon. Momigliano would make precisely the same argument 257 years later in the sixth of his Sather Lectures, on Eusebian historiography. Document-based history has a much longer history than is usually recognized.[51]

Leibniz's grasp of material evidence was comprehensive. It involved "the inspection of a quantity of monuments, which is to say, of old manuscripts, diplomas, seals, epitaphs, inscriptions, medals, paintings and drawings." But the striking thing is that he never managed to incorporate any of this extraordinary evidence-handling skill into a long-form narrative. The "History of the House of Brunswick" was never published. What of this history he did manage to write is a narrative of kings and marriages and battles, on the surface appearing not so different from the kind of humanist history-writing that Leibniz himself looked down upon. What he actually published were three volumes of preparatory materials toward that history containing the sources he had read, and prefaced with brief descriptions of those sources and, sometimes, how he got access to them (*Scriptores Rerum Brunsvicensium*, 1707–1710). As with Peiresc's *History of Provence*, whose conventional literary presentation belies the brilliantly variegated research materials that underpin it, Leibniz's work seems to underline a contemporary definition of what could be presented as "history." To see the evidentiary imagination in action one needs to look at the preparatory materials and not the finished edition—an indication of the power of conservative conventions of genre even for a creative thinker like Leibniz.[52]

Leibniz saw the history of the earth as the foundation of human history and so began his history of Brunswick with an account of the region's geological history. If we compare this with Braudel's historicizing of earth science the difference is sharp. Braudel emphasized the earth's unchanging aspect, while for Leibniz the *longue durée* was one of near-cataclysmic convulsion. "These traces," he wrote, "mark the great floods, the ruins of mountains, and even underground fires. The effect of violent fire is particularly evident in minerals, and in underground productions perfectly like those of furnaces or chemical laboratories . . . but water has no less caused changes and ravages. All appearances make it evident that a great part of this land was covered by water."[53]

He granted this vision its fullest presentation in the *Protogaea*, begun in Rome in 1691 and finished in the following two years (though not published in his lifetime). In it, Leibniz presented the natural world as a giant historical document. This vision is at the core of the chapter on marine fossils and also the one on the "changing of the land by water and the revolutions offered by its traces." And here, in a subject area to which few paid attention at the time, Leibniz wrote about the work of the Nile making its delta in Egypt and of the Rhone making its delta at Arles, citing Aristotle and Peiresc as his sources.[54]

Horst Bredekamp has taken Leibniz's "material" sensibility seriously, presenting him as someone who first collapsed the categories of optic and haptic and then sought a new way to transmit this kind of knowledge: the museum.[55] The best practice was, Leibniz wrote in 1679, "not only not to look at things superficially, but to consider them carefully piece by piece. . . . To this end it is extremely good to view many things and to look at them carefully, as [in] art, curiosity, and anatomy cabinets."[56] Later, in 1713, when framing a proposal for a scientific society, Leibniz divided up the three classes—physical, mathematical, and literary—based on their sources and tools. Literature was to be studied by reference to "all kinds of monuments, inscriptions, coins and other antiquities through documents from archives and registers and through manuscripts of all kinds of languages, including oriental languages." Leibniz concluded that the best way to present all three of these classes of materials was through "a cabinet and theater of Nature and Art."[57]

Surveying Leibniz's achievements, Henri Berr and Lucien Febvre emphasized early in the twentieth century his innovations in bringing materials into the inventory of sources. With him, they concluded, "the conception of the written text as the sole source of historical knowledge first appears as a relic of the past."[58] Leibniz's move created the need to evaluate the new kinds of evidence he was examining and constituted the origin of the auxiliary sciences.

Even where Leibniz seemed to value texts, he did so because he believed that at that moment the technical means of textual interpretation were simply more reliable than those available for material culture: "The complete rules of art and historical narrative can cover huge spans of time, while in stone and metal only painfully gathered together fragments are passed on, from which no ordered whole can be recovered."[59]

Leibniz's insistence on the importance of evidence and his reliance on the range of material evidence found an audience in Germany in the next generation, even though his chief historical works were either unpublished or published in truncated form. (Leibniz himself warned posterity about this: "He who knows me only from my published work does not know me.")[60]

Benjamin Hederich (1675–1748) was a schoolteacher who worked in Brandenburg and Saxony and published textbooks on various disciplines. His *Introduction to the Most Noble Historical Sciences* (1711) went through eight editions up through 1787. It contains an introduction to world history, to ancient writers, to prior schoolbooks on the subject, to the ancient gods (mythology), and to Roman antiquities. There are also detailed bibliographical treatments of geography, chronology, genealogy, and heraldry. The section on antiquities includes sub-categories devoted to physical monuments in the city, games, festivals, law, army, clothes, weights and measures, numismatics, titles, and much more. What makes this aggregation of sciences especially important is that it bridges the antiquarian orientation of the seventeenth century with the late eighteenth century's interest in academic auxiliary sciences (*Hilfswissenschaften*). In the preface to the sixth edition, published in 1742, Hederich notes only minor changes from the previous one: it contains, as before, "those sciences which for the most part make up the so-called 'galant studies', or the other part of 'Philology,' namely 'Real Philology' [*Philolgiam realem*]." This philology that dealt with *realia* he contrasted explicitly in the very next sentence with the content of a previous book of his, an *Introduction to the Most Noble Philological Sciences* (*Anleitung zu den vornehmsten Philologischen Wissenschaften*), which made up the first part of philology, namely "Philologiam verbalem," or "word philology."[61]

In Hederich we already have the divergence between words and things in the study of the past—what in the next century would be called *Wort-* and *Sachphilologie*. This divergence formed the backbone of a famous dispute between the two nineteenth-century philological schools of Gottfried

Hermann and August Boeckh (see below, chapter 5). Hederich coined the neologism *real philology* because he needed a term to refer to a kind of *historical* investigation of the material world. Its closest methodological analogue was philology—texts as a means for understanding something else, just as objects could be studied as a means for understanding something else—and so, it seems, Hederich reached for it and adapted it. The received view is that philology confronted materiality only in the nineteenth century. But Boeckh's *Sachphilologie* was just another way of making Hederich's point that objects could be studied the way texts were; Hederich was forced to make it precisely because Leibniz had paved the way for an integration of antiquities and other kinds of material sources into historical scholarship.

Hederich included these materials-based sources within the *Wissenschaften* of his title, affording them the same dignity as textual sources. But the equal standing wouldn't hold for long. In 1741 Anselm Desing gave these various materials-based sources a name of their own but also downgraded them. They were now *auxilia historica*, "aids to history."[62] No longer would genealogy or heraldry be considered a noble science alongside universal history, as in Hederich. This distinction between the subsidiary and the more noble sciences would endure, though Desing and his term have not.

In fact, like Hederich's book, Desing's account amounts to a collection of annotated bibliographies.[63] These allow for discussions of antiquarianism, genealogy, diplomatics, numismatics, paleography, history of learning, and *historia literaria*. It is through these last categories that Desing comes to the canonical "auxilium": the study of *Urkunden*. Linking the history of scholarly practice to a practical enumeration of those tools opens up the possibility of a new kind of self-consciousness about practice. This approach would facilitate the study of unfinished working materials rather than just printed books, opening into the world of the scholar's study rather than restricting scholarship to what was published—which was the rule for the great compilers of the previous generation, Daniel Morhof and Johann Fabricius. Desing did not take this step, but knowingly or not, he prepared for its coming.

Another way of making Desing's division into primary and secondary subjects came out of the study of legal history. In 1735 Johann David Köhler was called to a chair at Göttingen, where he taught modern European history and geography. In 1736 he published his *History of the German Empire*. It began with a short discussion of the necessary foundation in the sources—now called *Subsidia Historica*, not *Auxilia*, reinforcements perhaps less dismissive than aids.[64] There were domestic and foreign sources, each divided into primary and secondary. The primary domestic ones included contemporary narratives of various sorts as well as documents. These latter, in turn, consisted of "diplomata" (emanating from rulers), "acta publica" (concerning public events such as war and peace), and letters.[65] A discussion of the secondary literature and its varied kinds preceded that of foreign sources.[66]

If the Germans in the first half of the eighteenth century seemed to be developing Leibniz's initiative, the French returned to their hero Mabillon in 1750, when Charles-François Toustain and René-Prosper Tassin, two Benedictines of Saint-Maur, compiled the *Nouveau Traité de Diplomatique*. It is, to be sure, a work of piety, defending Mabillon against a half-century of criticism, but it also extends and deepens his project while incorporating a half-century of new discoveries.[67]

First and foremost, it is a defense of archives. "Archives supply everything," they write.[68] To their defense of Mabillon, reverently called "the Antiquary," they add a much broader notion of diplomatics:

> In addition to charters, diplomas, originals, juridical acts, one includes there state documents, annals, histories, books of laws, statutes, customs, privileges, legal titles, Princely or Republican claims, treaties of alliance and peace, transactions, genealogical books, fiefs, hundreds, tributes, impositions and revenues, registers of the kingdom containing names of provinces, cities, towns, villages etc.[69]

The authors define seven kinds of "sources": the material on which diplomata were written and the instruments and ink with which they were written, along with their letter forms, seals, styles, and formulae. What follows are long and fascinating discussions of inks, writing, and paper. (They even digress into an important discussion of oriental writing in which pride of place is given to the Samaritan Pentateuch.)[70]

It is clear from the two Benedictines' treatment of Mabillon that by the middle of the eighteenth century the practice of antiquaries had become institutionalized. In the discussion of different scripts, for example, they offered a full-blown articulation of the logic of comparison: "The antiquary is often reduced to comparing the characters of different centuries in order to determine the age and value of a monument. It is necessary therefore to place before his eyes these distinctive characters. The study of medals and inscriptions ceaselessly recalls the different shapes that letters have taken. Manuscripts need to be studied the same way, and diplomas cannot be overlooked."[71]

From their vantage point at the middle of the eighteenth century—and always looking backwards—the two Benedictines saw themselves as resting on centuries of work by antiquarians. The following passage, buried in a huge chapter that discusses changes in the shape of letters over time, is one of the most profound apologies for the practice of research ever written, let alone in Paris in the mid-eighteenth century—at the very same moment that the *Encyclopédie* was hammering a satirical nail into the antiquary's coffin. It is as close to a programmatic announcement as one gets in France of what, at the very same time in Germany, was about to burst into full flower, and with a different name, as an academic discipline:

> From such important motives we are justified, moreover, in going into the small details about each of the letters of the alphabet, images, and features, in order to discover the centuries in which they were in use. Each wheel, each spring, that is part of the marvels of art are trifles in themselves but contribute to produce prodigious effects. One will treat, if one wants to, of the minutiae of numerous observations which very few people know to appreciate to their just value, but it is the knowledge and precise application to these supposed minutiae which make the antiquary. . . . It will cost them some effort to become antiquaries; will it not cost them anything to become physicians or astronomers?[72]

The closest in spirit to this passage is what we find in the prefaces to the seven volumes of the Comte de Caylus's *Collection of Egyptian, Etruscan, Greek and Roman Antiquities* (1752–1763), especially to volumes Two and Five, where Caylus tries to communicate to readers the emotional experience of the scholar when he holds a piece of the past in his hands. "In the moment when his treasures arrive, he opens the cases that contain them with a sweet uncertainty, full of expectation. . . . The moment of the encounter is for him a living joy."[73]

But the age of the Benedictines, like that of antiquarian grandees like Caylus, was coming to an end. And though there remained the autumnal flourish of the Abbé Barthélemy's *Voyage of the Young Anacharsis* (1789), the tone would now be set in Germany. By the time the last volumes of the *Nouveau Traité* rolled off the presses in 1762 and 1765, Johann Christoph Gatterer at Göttingen had begun transforming the study of objects as historical evidence.

❧ CHAPTER 4

Material Evidence in the History Curriculum in Eighteenth-Century Göttingen

When Arnaldo Momigliano called the eighteenth century the "age of antiquaries" he was referring to an interest in antiquity and its physical remains that by then had spread from the stern erudites of Peiresc's cabinet to the softer salons of Paris and the wider readership of London's weekly magazines. The discoveries at Pompeii and Herculaneum were the Columbian encounter for Old World devotees. The Grand Tour brought more foreign tourists, many of them aristocratic louts looking for a lush life in the south at which they could also, especially if they were Protestant northerners, sniff disapprovingly. Among the tourists were architects and designers whose subsequent work was infused by antique encounters in the Mediterranean basin. If we think about the last half of the eighteenth century we can discern a "material turn" at least equal in profundity to our own. And if we think about Piranesi, Winckelmann, Caylus, Robert Adam, and Josiah Wedgwood, to name but a few, we can say that the most remarkable artistic geniuses of the time were fired up by their encounter with ancient materiality.

It is at just this time that the sophisticated discussions that grew out of the work of Mabillon and Leibniz were systematized. We find surveys of historical learning published by professors at a number of institutions. This was the moment when the first academic curriculum for material culture studies was created. It happened at the University of Göttingen, a new foundation (from 1734, formal opening in 1737) that was envisioned as the model of an enlightened university. With a professionalized training regimen for historians came the idea of required courses, and the auxiliary sciences of history were born. Up to then, as we have seen, there had been scattered efforts to systematize the study of particular bodies of evidence, such as documents, genealogy, numismatics, heraldry, epigraphy, chronology, and geography.[1]

Like all required courses, the "auxilia historica," too, were despised. Those who wanted to go on to become successful historians had to learn how to extract evidence from otherwise opaque, if not actually recalcitrant, materiality. But the tools themselves were to become transparent; once successfully incorporated and assimilated into the toolkit of the historian, they would be invisible to both writer and reader. They were certainly not deemed themselves worthy of study. And so, to this very day, no one has written the history of the development of this curriculum, though it lived on for a long time at Göttingen itself and was elsewhere sustained through a series of textbooks, each written by the professor teaching the course in the hope of supplementing his income. The books are not themselves great works of history. But they are great works for historians interested in the history of historical research. Written as they are for students, they offer self-conscious and explicit precepts about the why and the how of studying objects.[2]

The University of Göttingen during the last four decades of the eighteenth century was an extraordinary hothouse for humanities research. Johann Christoph Gatterer was creating the history curriculum; meanwhile, his rival historian, August Ludwig von Schlözer, was creating a blend of history, political science, and ethnography he called *Statistik*. In the neighboring faculty of philology, Christian Gottlob Heyne lectured on the history of the ancient world and almost singlehandedly created archaeology as a university-based discipline. All this while the Orientalist J. D. Michaelis was re-envisioning the Bible as the ancient history of the Near East. Their work, collectively, shaped the horizon of the future study of objects. We can even begin to trace out some of their legacy by reading the textbooks written by their students, who trained the next generation of thinking about material culture. We will follow this over the next two chapters, in this one, focusing on the *historische Hilfswissenschaften*, and in the next, on archaeology and philology.[3]

Gatterer

The *historische Hilfswissenschaften* came to Göttingen immediately after the university's founding. Johann David Köhler (1684–1755), who arrived there

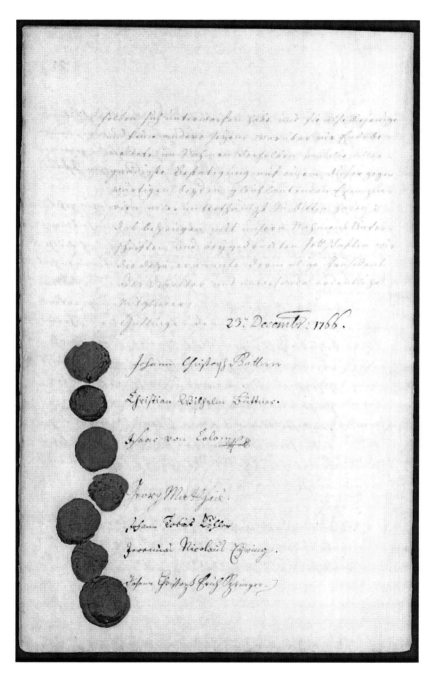

FIGURE 11B Historical Institute by-laws, last page. Gesetze des königl. Instituts der historischen Wissenschaften zu Göttingen. Göttingen University Archive, Kur 7540. Photo by author.

in 1739, worked on chronology and geography from a historical point of view but also heraldry, numismatics, and *Urkunden* (public documents).[4] But it was his successor, Johann Christoph Gatterer, who was the true father of source studies (*Urkundenlehre*).[5] Gatterer began teaching at Göttingen in 1759. 1764 is the date traditionally given for the foundation of the "Historical Institute," and 1766 for its recognition by the state—whether the Prussian or the Hanoverian state is not exactly clear—as "Academia historica."[6]

The institute began with eight members, two of whom were in the natural sciences. It published two journals, the *Allgemeine historische Bibliothek* (1767–1771) and the *Historisches Journal* (1772–1781). It organized the publication of translations, collections of sources, and editions of German historians of the Middle Ages. It possessed diplomatic, numismatic, and geographical study collections, held weekly meetings and lectures, and with its diplomas occupied a space somewhere between an academy and a university faculty.[7] Gatterer's plan was for a national network of such institutes, with Göttingen at the center.[8]

If Gatterer inherited the notion that certain kinds of mostly material artifacts, such as coins, inscriptions, charters, pictures, and family trees, could help establish the stable facts of names and dates upon which historians could build their accounts, his great achievement was to give the notion of the "auxilia historica" a curricular form. He taught a generation of students about these various objects and the way they worked. His flagship course was entitled, in the manner of the eighteenth century, "The Encyclopedia of Historical Study" ("Encyclopädie der Geschichtskunde"), later elaborated as "Historical Encyclopedia, that is, the principal chapters of Heraldry, Geography, Chronology, Numismatics, Genealogy, Diplomatics and general History."[9]

By Gatterer's own estimate, the second-largest number of historical books produced during the years 1769–1771, just behind German history, was in the *historische Hilfswissenschaften*.[10] Like his colleagues, Gatterer published textbooks devoted to all the individual subjects on which he lectured. These were repeatedly revised as he taught and re-taught the same subjects over the course of his career. As soon as he arrived at Göttingen he published one textbook on genealogy and heraldry (*Handbuch der neuesten Genealogie und Heraldik*, 1760) and another on universal history (part one, 1761; part two, 1765). The handbook on heraldry was systematized, revised, and published almost thirty years later as *Outline of Genealogy* (1788) and again three years later as *Practical Heraldry* (1791). The handbook on universal history went through seven editions by 1792 and also reappeared as *Outline of Universal History* (1765), *Introduction to Synchronistic Universal History* (1771), *A Brief*

Concept of World History (1785), *World History in its Fullest Scope* (1785), and finally as *An Essay on a General World History* (1792).[11]

Gatterer was aware that there were others who were turning to artifacts as sources for historical understanding. Students of the ancient world had for centuries examined remains and ruins. But for the *Altertumskundler* or *Altertumswissenschaftler*, the objects were studied as ancillary to texts. This would change with the birth of archaeology, but only very slowly and by way of art history.[12] Gatterer's *Hilfswissenschaften* were also auxiliary, but because they were material, or because their probative value lay in their materiality. In teaching students how to use them Gatterer was also teaching them about how objects could function as evidence.[13]

It was in the context of pedagogy that in 1771 Gatterer published "On Historical Education" ("Von der historischen Erziehung"), in which he suggested ways of making the teaching of genealogy, heraldry, and numismatics into a kind of game.[14] In this discussion, Gatterer revealed much about his understanding of doing history, or to use his verb, "historisieren." Using the example of heraldic materials, Gatterer's "historicizing" meant recounting the origin and changes in a coat of arms—the life-course of an artifact, one might say. So understood, the heraldist absorbed the ambition of the historian, and heraldry, in turn, was absorbed into the domain of the historian.[15]

"Historisieren" required a precise understanding of evidence and how to classify it. Gatterer here offered just such a classification scheme. The most relevant first-order sources included (1) coats of arms and patents of nobility, (2) seals, and (3) coins. Then there were the objects that did not emerge out of an explicitly heraldic context but that contained heraldic material, such as (1) monuments, including epitaphs, gravestones, paintings, church placards, and hatchments; (2) letters; (3) historical narratives; (4) tournament descriptions; (5) family materials, such as birth and ancestral documents, descriptions of formal rites and processions, and funerals; and (6) heraldry collections and books of coats of arms.[16]

Gatterer was trying to build a methodological structure out of the particular challenges posed by the various *Hilfswissenschaften*. His importance for us lies in this attempt to generalize about the historian's practice from the very minute details of reading these material sources. Turning coins or heraldic books or diplomas into evidence meant understanding how history was encoded into the material support and the material form of texts. The very creation of this curriculum at Göttingen moved questions of materiality and evidence to the center of historical pedagogy. We might understand this to be the import of his declaration that "the intelligent choice of events is the true touchstone of a historical genius."[17]

In 1767, as the introduction to the first volume of translations of the English "Universal History" series, Gatterer dedicated an entire essay to the subject "On Evidence in Historical Studies."[18] He began by emphasizing the link between the *Hilfswissenschaften* and the idea of "evidence," but he then turned from the critical examination of evidence to its literary presentation.[19] This is also important: The very person whose life work had the effect of forcing generations of history students to think about how the material constitution of evidence needed to be taken into consideration by the historian retained the older view that the historian was a writer.

Evidence was important because it helped in the task of effective historical writing, whose goal was to make the reader, who lived in the present, into something like a spectator of what had occurred in the past.[20] To serve the reader, though, the writer had first to be able to imagine himself into that time and place.[21] To write about Alexander's conquests, Catiline's betrayal or Spinoza's subversions, the historian had to be able to be "as-if present." Erudition, in short, had to work together with imagination. Only by first imagining herself into the past—and that is where command of the sources represented by the *Hilfswissenschaften* came in—could the historian help the reader imagine herself into the past being narrated.

The conclusion Gatterer drew from this was that *"the writer of history must hide himself from his readers as much as possible.* He must play all his roles as if he were speaking directly to the reader and, in the process, the writer of history must appear to be merely a bystander or observer, and occasionally no more than a provider of nomenclature for the reader."[22] Gatterer elsewhere distinguished between "Historiomathie," which taught how to study history and which seems coordinate with the evidentiary practices of the *Hilfswissenschaften*, and "Historische Kunst oder Geschichtswissenschaft (Ars historica oder Historiographia)," which was a set of premises about how to write a history book so that it would be readable.[23] Gatterer's biographer used these categories to assess his achievement. Whereas the goal of the "historical researcher" (*Geschichtsforscher*) was "the research of particular facts," that of the "history writer" (*Geschichtsschreiber*) was "the statement of how they cohere together."[24] He thought Gatterer more researcher than writer. Gatterer himself devoted some of his most important thinking to the historical writer. He brought "research" into the university training of the historian, whereas previously it had been associated with the identity of the antiquarian.[25]

Awareness of the reader, indeed the kind of reader Gatterer was addressing, speaks to the new horizon of readership that Mark Phillips sees emerging in the second half of the eighteenth century in England.[26] It was just then that

William Robertson consigned proof-texts to endnotes in his *History of the Reign of Charles V* (1769), an event Momigliano and then Grafton noted as material evidence for the effect on historical scholarship of having new readers who were not professionals and were not interested in checking on their authors' *bona fides* sentence by sentence. Johan Huizinga in 1929 offered a more general view of the change in historical writing attendant upon the democratization of the history-reading public in modern times.[27]

And yet, Gatterer did not propose going all the way in this direction. His imagination was still being held to account by his erudition; and his immediate audience remained scholars rather than urban elites. Hence his commitment to the *Hilfswissenschaften*. For, he believed, only through mastery of all the relevant sources could the historian in his guise as researcher understand the past sufficiently for the historian in his guise as writer to tell a story that could carry readers back into the past: "It goes without saying that *vivid descriptions of places and countries, of things and people,* are some of the preferred aids that create an ideal presence for the reader. . . . I only wish that one could draw these things precisely as they are in nature, paint them as vividly as circumstances allow."[28]

Gatterer seems to hesitate on the precipice of arguing for a more popular voice rather than a purely academic one. This is where his long familiarity with the old rhetorical side of history-writing came to the aid of his Enlightenment-era engagement with the new "social," reading public. Paradoxically, Gatterer, whose name is rightly attached to the professional training of historians, developed his scheme of evidence-based training in order "to find an entry into the heart of the reader"; that is, he developed the science of research behind the scenes so that he could deliver an enjoyable narrative to those not conducting the research themselves. This was another way of representing the ancient rhetorician's invocation to teach, delight, and move.[29] And yet, he writes that he was not trying "to make the historical writer into a poet nor to recommend a poetic prose as historical style." Gatterer may not have been trying to make historians into artists, but he was certainly arguing that historians would not be able to communicate effectively with their contemporary readers if they were cut off from contemporary ways of communicating.[30]

The real difference between the historian and the writer, Gatterer argued, was that while the writer had to create a whole that never was, the historian, using "evidence," could bring forth a past that once existed but survived in broken pieces only. And then, invoking the language used by Renaissance antiquaries like Cyriac of Ancona, Gatterer proclaimed that the trained historian "brings what is dead back to life and makes the past contemporary, and he offers his readers an imitation that may be weak, but that is nonetheless in a certain way a true imitation of the godhead." Even more than bringing the dead back to life, the historian was capable of abolishing time itself. In the kind of understanding he could achieve "there is nothing past, nothing future; all is present and nothing is abstract; everything is a unique, all-seeing insight."[31]

This essay was published only a year after the official recognition of the Historical Institute at Göttingen and could be construed as representing its mission statement. "Evidence," in short, secured the truth of the historian's argument—he offered the usual declaration about the importance of using original materials, whether texts, artifacts, or eyewitness accounts—but also the reader's passage to persuasion. Gatterer was telling his students that one had to be more than a good researcher to be a good historian; one had to be good at constructing an argument *and* presenting it to the reader.[32] The complexity of the historian's task was reflected in the small number of historians who had ever achieved this dual mastery of sources and of story. The number of those "who possess the necessary knowledge of diplomatics, of monument studies, the critical knowledge of people in general and of authors in particular is rather small," he wrote. Even scarcer, however, were readers who possessed enough knowledge not just to take the historian at his word but also to follow his proofs. "In a word, one sees that it is possible to take a historical example to the level of evidence, but that the number of history writers and readers that can ascend to this rarefied level of historical insight is rather small."[33] Gatterer was gesturing toward a feedback loop between historical writing and historical reading: changing the one always implied changing the other. He recognized that he was living through a transitional moment in the reading of history and that therefore the writing of history would have to change accordingly.

Summing up, Gatterer insisted, strikingly, that successfully deploying evidence in historical demonstration would have the effect of making the past "more seen than read." But even this did not mean sweeping the reader off her feet. It was the presentation of evidence to the mind that allowed the reader to participate, so to speak, in historical understanding, making the reader into a prime example of Enlightenment in action, daring to learn by daring to read (Gatterer explicitly connected the history book to the novel). Winning over the reader showed how much richer historical reality was than its fictional re-enactment.[34] This element, the "seeing" of the past, would return again in debates about cultural history in the 1840s and 1850s. Looking back from the 1920s, Huizinga wrote that the point of controlling the sources was to be able to pick out the piquant details and make a more engaging story: "The most modest historical research, that of the genealogist and the student of heraldry, that of the local dilettante, can be exalted and ennobled by this intellectual preoccupation."[35]

This challenge of writing history was one Momigilano placed at the heart of his classic essay, "Ancient History and the Antiquarian." For him, Gibbon's *Essai sur l'étude de la littérature* of 1761 marked the encounter between research and writing. In the small university town of Göttingen Gatterer was grappling with the same challenge. Evidence, in Gatterer's sense, transcended Mabillon's and even Leibniz's view of historical research. For it reached toward nonprofessional readers in a way that they had not envisioned, reflecting the new social realities of the era. Yet like Gibbon, Gatterer neither abandoned nor proposed that others abandon the connection to the sources that characterized the antiquary.

Statistik and Schlözer

Gatterer's ambition to bring together research and writing was part of his wider goal of synthesizing the diachronic and the synchronic, the micro- and the macro-scale—in short, of squaring the circle of historical understanding. "Universal history" was one arena in which he sought to perform this magic trick. The other was *Statistik*, the study of a state's power that included its constitution, demography, economy, and geography. It had developed in Germany in the previous generation. Gatterer advanced it but had also anchored it in a still deeper past. "Statistik," he wrote, "is the continuation and consequence of the science of Antiquities [*der Wissenschaft der Alterthümer*]."[36] The fifteenth-century Italian antiquarian Flavio Biondo had divided antiquities into public, private, sacred, and military.[37] Gatterer replaced "military" with "learned" but explicitly retained Biondo's old framework.[38] For Gatterer, antiquarianism provided the armature for *Statistik*.[39]

The link between antiquarianism and *Statistik* reflects the fact that the study of antiquities had been, of all the forms of early modern historical inquiry, the one in which material remains played the biggest role. In his "Ideal of a General World-Statistik," delivered as a lecture to the Historical Institute on October 2, 1773, Gatterer sought to differentiate history from *Statistik* by relating the former to the past and the latter to the present.[40] If Gatterer had struggled with the question of how historical research could be useful for historical narrative, his treatment of *Statistik* always gave priority to the material conditions of historical existence. These included physical and climatic evidence but also ideas—when they had an impact on the use of the material, as did forces such as religion.[41]

Gatterer illustrated his argument. He began with "People" and "Place." Places were divided by size, borders, and products and were to be evaluated in terms of centers and peripheries. Products of the land were then divided into those made by nature and those made by men. These latter divided into aesthetic (artistic) and material attainments ("Ways of living and types of inhabitants"). The material conditions included (1) hunting and fishing, (2) agriculture, (3) craft and manufacture, (4) trade, (5) religion and spirituality, (6) learning, and (7) nobility.[42] Gatterer's attention to the material conditions of life, to its very physical reality, extended directly to the human intervention in nature—the original definition of *culture*. Compared to *Historia literaria*, which looked only at book learning and "high culture," *Statistik* appears as much richer and more earthy. The late Renaissance genre of the "interest of states" like the books written by Giovanni Botero (1597) or Samuel von Pufendorf (1684), as well as travel literature, had previously introduced readers to these kinds of practical details.[43] The elaboration of *Statistik* belongs to the surge in sophisticated historical thinking about culture that we find at Göttingen in the second half of the eighteenth century.[44]

For the idea of *Statistik* as the ultimate science of material contextualization whether of past or present, we need to turn to Gatterer's contemporary and rival at Göttingen August Ludwig von Schlözer.[45] He had come to Göttingen to work with the great Orientalist Johann David Michaelis, who made him study Oriental languages and read Montesquieu's *Persian Letters*. Schlözer prepared himself for travel to the East by studying medicine, natural science, and history, the last as a student of Gatterer's. He was in Sweden from 1755 to 1758 and wanted very much to go on the Danish expedition to Arabia organized by Michaelis and led by Carsten Niebuhr, but he was excluded—and thus saved from almost certain death (of the ten who set out, only Niebuhr returned alive). Then Michaelis got Schlözer a job in St. Petersburg, where he lived between 1761 and 1767, with one year spent back at Göttingen.[46]

Upon his return from St. Petersburg, Schlözer published his "Lecture on Universal History" (1772). He argued that individual facts or events were to the historian what tesserae were for the mosaicist—they made sense only once they were ordered. "Putting things together is the work of the writer of history" ("die Zusammenstellung ist das Werk des Geschichtsschreibers") and the methods of that "putting together" defined the different kinds of history. Schlözer offered a new and precise vocabulary for the process of contextualization that Gatterer had put at the center of his work but had never fully explicated. Gatterer worked with the binary categories of universal and particular, while Schlözer worked outward from the type of evidence. He contrasted the contextualization of *realia* ("Realzusammenhang"), which he characterized as "synthetic," with the contextualization of the time-bound, which he called "Zeitzusammenhang" or "synchronistisch" (time-bound or synchronic). Things could be contextualized in varied ways: by time ("chronographisch"), by tool or process ("technographisch"), by location ("geographisch"), or by people ("ethnographisch").[47] What was time-bound—events—could only be contextualized in terms of unfolding over time.[48] In Schlözer's parceling out of the spectrum, *Statistik* dealt with *realia*, history with time-bound events.

Schlözer's pregnant idea was that *Statistik* was the great aggregator: "The physicist, the geographer, the nature expert (botanist, mineralogist, zoologist), the historian, the antiquarian, the economist, the public intellectual (*Publicist*), the religion teacher, and ten others, each limited to his own subject, will find material for descriptions in even the most minor state."[49] With all these specific perspectives, the danger was always of dissolving into a collection of micrologies, "the listing of anecdotes, minute details, monotonous and boring in themselves."[50] Just as every plant or insect interested the entomologist or botanist but was not important for anyone else, so too with details about the state.[51] Yet one never knew what fact might turn out to be important later.

Numbers, Schlözer answered, provided a means of assessing the significance of facts. He insisted on this: "Many a piece of information seems to be unimportant and is overlooked; its significance is hidden and is found only through combination. This is where the genius and erudition of the *Statistiker* shows itself: The more knowledge he possesses of things of all kinds, the more often he will find, sometimes surprisingly, that two events have a cause-and-effect relationship, a relationship that would never occur to the mere *homme de lettres*."[52] Schlözer's "combination" might echo Gatterer's ambition for universal history, but the word points toward Leibniz. Schlözer's attack on micrology and his effort to develop numbers as a measure of relevance suggest a new kind of answer to what I have elsewhere termed "the problem of detail."[53]

Again following Leibniz, Schlözer allowed that language was another body of information that could be read as evidence. This was important because "in the absence of written documents history can still be written by a systematic comparison of words." For this, Schlözer collected translations of the Lord's Prayer in as many languages as possible. The origins and homelands of all peoples, he argued, could be found out by a *historia etymologica*—another late Renaissance inquiry that looked different after Leibniz.[54] And yet, drawing the line at relevance, this defense of the possible

utility of what were often dismissed as "Kleinigkeiten"—little things, antiquarian curiosities, pedantry—was coupled with a dismissal of old-fashioned
polymathy. *Statistik*, no matter its attention to little details, was a rigorous
science and hence to be distinguished from antiquarianism: "Four emissar-
ies would be needed for an initial effort. Each would have to be a trained
expert in his own subject: the additions to nearly all of the sciences in recent
years no longer allow for pansophy, polyhistory, or *ex omnibus aliquid*; the
most brilliant mathematician, when considering matters of agriculture, is as
simple-minded as a child, and the reverse is equally true."[55] The "combinato-
rialness" of Enlightenment *Statistik* was different from that of Renaissance
polyhistory—to paint in broad strokes—because it was systematic rather
than idiosyncratic, convergent rather than digressive.

Schlözer insisted that contemporary importance—"relevance"—would
be determinate. The fact is that Schlözer was engaged with the contemporary world in ways that we would now call "social science" and that the
nineteenth century termed "political economy" or "national economy,"
even though he thought and worked historically.[56] This commitment to relevance would exclude, he thought, most knowledge of painting, history, or
antiquities—though he gave as an example of an exception to the latter the
amount of money tourists spent in Rome each year. The razor of relevance
would defend *Statistik* from the charge of pedantry or the lurking peril of
detail for detail's sake and was a clear leave-taking from the antiquarian heritage still owned by Gatterer.[57]

It is in the context of talking about the possibility of a historical
Statistik—that is, *Statistik* for the ancient world—that Schlözer cast the relationship between his work and that of the antiquaries in the clearest light.
Why, he asks, should there be *Statistik* for the present but not for the past? After
all, "History is *Statistik* in motion and *Statistik* is history at rest."[58] This is a
succinct way of capturing the difference between these forms as well as what
they have in common. They also make clear the relationship that Momigliano
articulated between history and antiquarianism. For a nineteenth-century
German, *Statistik* as history-made-stationary is another way of saying "antiquitates." Schlözer even says so himself: "We already have such old statistics from times long past; we just use names for them that not everyone
would expect: *antiquitates* persicae, graecae, romanae, germanicae. . . ."[59]
Schlözer was fully aware of the antiquarian foundation of the kind of structural investigation of the material world he presented in new terms and with
a new focus.

Like antiquarianism and history, *Statistik* and history were also part of
a binary system. Changes in thinking about history shaped thinking about

Statistik. Recent times had altered the definition of the field considerably: "History is no longer merely the biography of kings, a chronologically-exact recitation of the succession to the throne, wars and battles, a narration of revolutions and alliances." This change, Schlözer continued, began "half a century ago, when the British and French awakened us with better examples."[60] The development of philosophical history was one dimension of this change, the growth in readership another. Like Gatterer, Schlözer explicitly identified the new role of the public as an engine of change: "But even if I did know all those things that are, by themselves, indisputably useful, do I know—and this is what I really wanted to know in the first place—how the nation (*le peuple est TOUT*) was doing during that time?"[61] The French Revolution's creation of "the People" suggested to Schlözer the possibility of a wholly new shape to "history." Once focused on the social constitution of the nation, the whole panoply of that social entity's existence opened up as subject matter. Agriculture, trade, industry, and many other activities "are truly noteworthy matters of the state, and the history writer must register them by virtue of his office; so he must be a *Statistiker*."[62] The discovery of fire or bread-making was as important as any battle, "and thousands of other things that are disdained as *Kleinigkeiten* by straightforward political and folk history are drawn out of the dust, and known through use are honored."[63] *Statistik*, in Schlözer's hands, was not knowledge of an abstract whole, as it was for Gatterer; it was a vision of social life articulated through the material realities of daily life, for all people. If we understand this, we can understand Schlözer's conclusion in this same passage: "to put it differently: history is the whole, and *Statistik* is a part of that whole."[64] More broadly, where Gatterer's thinking about objects as evidence was limited to his thinking about the rules for evaluating and deploying that evidence in narrative, Schlözer was actually trying to imagine fields of historical inquiry shaped by their material content.

Gatterer's Heirs

While Gatterer was giving his lectures on the *Hilfswissenschaften* at Göttingen, Georg Andreas Will, a prominent historian of Nuremburg at the University of Altdorf prepared his own manuscript, *Introduction to Historical Learning and the Method for Teaching and Learning History* (c. 1766). His book included a discussion of "the current historical *Hilfswissenschaften*." Unlike Gatterer, his list included antiquities (*Alterthümer*) and identified its subject areas as "Religion, law and governance, domestic and military matters, trade, manners, speech and literature." He also included as predecessors the seventeenth- and eighteenth-century scholars who had written about antiquities, such as Gruter, Gronovius, Graevius, Montfaucon, and Muratori. But when including antiquities, he could not resist sneering that in practice *antiquitates* "took unimportant little things from ancient households, clothing, and plasterwork for investigation." Nevertheless, Will still looked to the study of classical antiquities as a model for studying modern things: "German antiquities should have a special worth to us, and it is to be wished that the quantity of short writings composed for their explanation should be gathered up into a *Treasury of Teutonic Antiquities*."[65] This wish would be fulfilled in the century to come (see chapter 6).

A generation later, Friedrich Maier, in his *Essay of an Encyclopedia of History, in all its parts naturally connected* (1796), introduced a significant new idea. He explained that the materials of history could be organized according to either space or time—and that their organization directly shaped the writing of history. "We directly perceive the occurrence of things, and thus the cause of events, as proximal, *in the form of space*; occurrences in space are represented by description, ergo the *describing historical sciences* [beschreibende Geschichts-Wissenschaften]; or *in the form of time*, occurrences in time are represented by narration, ergo the *narrating historical sciences* [erzählende Geschichts-Wissenschaften]."[66] Maier was trying to forge a connection between types of inquiries and types of representation; we might see this as a way of explaining why certain subjects lent themselves to diachronic exposition and others to the synchronic variety. Making description the touchstone reaches directly back to the antiquarian by way of Schlözer's *Statistik*.

This fascinating distinction between narrating and describing appears in other textbooks on historical theory written by professors during these years. In the exactly contemporary *Essay of a Systematic Encyclopedia of the Sciences* (part I, Leipzig 1796; part II, Jena 1797) W. T. Krug, an adjunct in the Philosophy Faculty at the University of Wittenberg, also divided historical subject matter into the "describing sciences" (*beschreibende Wissenschaften*), which included geography, chorography, ethnography, *Statistik*, and the "narrating sciences" (*erzählende Wissenschaften*), which included the history of sky and earth, mankind, religion, and the state. Slightly earlier, a less elaborated version of this distinction between "describing" and "narrating" historical sciences was also found in Christian Jakob Krauss's University of Königsberg lecture notes from 1789, posthumously published in 1809 with the title *An Encyclopedic View of Historical Erudition*.[67] This late eighteenth-century division between describing and narrating is, like some of Gatterer's and Schlözer's formulations, another demonstration that the distinction between antiquarian and historical modes was still generating light.[68]

For Maier, just as natural history was not really history but the description of nature, the study of people, too, was not always to be written as a "narrating historical science." Sometimes it took the shape of a science of description. He gave some examples: describing humans was "Anthropographie"; describing the soul was "Psychography"; describing the human spirit in its development could be approached either through describing human institutions, which could be called "Statistik," or by describing "contemporary humanity," which was *Völkerkunde.*[69]

This taxonomic innovativeness reminds us of Spon a century earlier with his *Archaeographia* and its eight subordinate parts. In both cases, I think, it reflects knowledge bursting at the seams and an effort to contain it through changed epistemic framings. In the case of Spon, it was about re-describing antiquarianism for a wider and more self-conscious range of material approaches to the ancient world. For Maier, it was about history and the *Hilfswissenschaften* in the age of the French Revolutionary upheavals. He described his work as depicting everyday life in a comparative frame, an approach that would reappear in the new cultural history of the next generation.[70]

The "narrating historical sciences" were about change. This vision could be applied to the history of the earth—Maier talked about a "political history of the earth," something very relevant in our age of rethinking climate history, to be sure—but also to human life. In this context, it could refer generally to intellectual and cultural history, as in his "progress of the human spirit" ("Fortschritte des menschlichen Geistes"),[71] but also to histories of speech, religion, states, counsel, trade, or literature (*historia literaria*).[72]

We can follow the thread connecting antiquities, *Hilfswissenschaften*, *Statistik*, and the describing sciences. Histories of learning seem to fall into the category of the diachronic or narrating histories, those of daily life into the synchronic or describing sciences. Art faced in both directions. Winckelmann had shown that art could be presented as a narrating science, but when treated in terms of its genres or materials it could also take the form of a describing one. A century later we find Jacob Burckhardt navigating between these same two poles of a "narrating art history" and "a representation by things and categories." A century later, histories of events still tend to be written as narratives, while daily life and its structures tend to be written thematically.[73]

Political history was, uncontroversially, presented as a narrating science. And this is where we find Maier discussing the *Hilfswissenschaften*. As with Gatterer, Maier did not conceive of the auxiliary sciences as a new kind of history or as suggesting new subject matter for a historical account—this would only begin in the work of the historical associations to be discussed in chapter 6. But unlike Gatterer, Maier was already breaking down the notion of a single set of auxiliary sciences. Instead, he divided them into those that applied to the study of all political forms, such as numismatics, diplomatics, genealogy, heraldry, and those that were specific to certain states.[74]

If we turn now to Gatterer's direct heirs, to those who taught the *Hilfswissenschaften* at Göttingen in the next generation, we will see a widening horizon. K. T. G. Schönemann (1765–1802) studied, did his *Habilitation*, and, eventually, lectured at Göttingen on the *Hilfswissenschaften* from 1799 until his early death. He began his *Outline of an Encyclopedia of the Historical Sciences* by identifying history "in its narrow sense" with the succession of events and in a broader one with the study of static subjects such as a land or a people or a state.[75] The *Hilfswissenschaften*, in turn, were defined as bodies of knowledge that validated the truth claims of those two kinds of history. Schönemann explicitly identified two sorts of basic questions and two groups of subjects that corresponded to them. The first—when? where? and by whom?—established basic framing facts and referred to chronology, geography, and genealogy. The second focused on the questions "what?" and "how?" and underpinned diplomatics, epigraphy, numismatics, heraldry, and the knowledge of authors (*Schriftstellerkunde*).[76] Schönemann offered further precision about the content of each of these; original to him is the division of diplomatics into the outer form of a document, which broke down into knowledge of linguistics, paleography, and iconography (for its seals), and of its inner form, which included knowledge of how documents were used at the time, with a special and separate section on chancery forms—understood in terms of style, formulae, and dating.[77]

The Bavarian jurist and, for a time, professor at Landshut Johann Georg Fessmaier (1775–1828) published his *Foundations of the Auxiliary Sciences of History* in 1802, acknowledging in its subtitle that it would follow Gatterer's own lecture notes.[78] Like Schönemann, Fessmaier defined the *Hilfswissenschaften* as the sciences of authenticating evidence.[79] He was, however, especially attentive to the material forms of evidence. In discussing genealogy, for example, he paid careful attention to the format of the genealogical tables and the way imagery and text interacted in source documents.

He enumerated seven kinds of possible genealogical representations, each designed to capture family descent in a different way, including biography and population history.[80] For heraldry, Fessmaier followed Gatterer in dividing the practice into the three functions of "blasoniren," "historisieren," and "kritisieren." The former described the blazon, the second explained the connection between each aspect of its appearance and the historical events it represented, and the third evaluated the authenticity of the blazon part by part.[81] Fessmaier also organized diplomatics into three parts: writing studies (*Graphik*), sign studies (*Semiotik*), and rhetorical studies (*Sprach- und Formelnkunde*). The first covered all that went into writing, from pen and ink to paper, as well as scripts and characters.[82] The second was devoted to the imagery found in and on documents, including monograms and seals. The third part focused on the language and literary style of charters.[83]

Fessmaier also introduced a new term of analysis into the discussion of *Hilfswissenschaften*: archive studies. He did this a generation before Ranke put archives at the center of the historian's practice. With this, Fessmaier shifted the discussion away from verifying specific pieces of evidence to seeing the broader picture. Archives existed, he wrote, for preservation, for information, and for polemic. Looking backwards to the seventeenth century's sensibility and forward to that of the nineteenth, Fessmaier concluded that "the archive is nothing like a cabinet of antiquities; it is an institute for the most varied and fruitful uses."[84]

Talking in terms of the archive provided a framework for Fessmaier to introduce yet another novelty to discussions of the auxiliary sciences: an evaluation of the historian's management of his sources. Talking in terms of an "institute" was a way of suggesting the potential power of a new kind of historical training in which teaching and research came together in the source. It was also, surely, a way of paying tribute to his teacher, Gatterer, and the historical institute he established at Göttingen.

Fessmaier created a checklist for evaluating the relationship between a historian and his archive. The catechism began by asking if the historian actually worked from original sources. If so, then a whole series of other questions followed:

a. Was he himself an archivist? . . .
b. Was he given access to archives? . . .
c. Were the necessary documents communicated to him?
d. Or did he use previously published collections of documents?[85]

If he used already-printed sources, then there was another set of questions to answer:

 a. Did he record things diligently and precisely?
 b. Did he have a respectable library, or was he far away from one? Did he only use secondary citations?
 c. Did he employ judicious good sense in the choice of his citations?[86]
 d. Did he work from "trivial" sources such as old travel reports?[87]

Bringing the archive into the discussion enabled Fessmaier to gather the *Hilfs-wissenschaften* together—the archive was where all the materials needed for the auxiliary sciences could be found. Still, an "archive" was not a "museum" and so even this broad vision was still inflected toward the textual.

Of the followers of Gatterer, Johann Ernst Fabri (1755–1825), who taught at Göttingen in the early 1780s before taking up chairs at Jena and then Erlangen, moved furthest from the traditional scope of the *historische Hilfswissenschaften*. As a result, his textbook offers a model for how these preliminary studies could in fact be reimagined as a manifesto for a new science. Fabri habilitated in 1781 at Halle in geography. By the time he published his textbook, in 1808, the intellectual and political landscape had shifted. The difference was reflected in the number of subjects that crowded the book's title page: *Encyclopedia of the Chief Historical Sciences and their Auxiliary Teachings: Archaeology, Antiquities, Chronology, Diplomatics, Epigraphy, Genealogy, Heraldry, Hieroglyphics, Mythology, Mythography, Numismatics, Sphragistics, Toponomy, Political Arithmetic.*

Fabri began by explaining that he taught history, geography, and *Statistik* for over twenty years and that the idea of a "universal," or totally integrated, history was simply impossible.[88] So much for Gatterer's aspirations. He then reordered the various auxiliary sciences in terms of their relationship to space and time. Those organized around their relationship to space he also called "homochronistic"—what we would call synchronic, that is, in which time stands still—and the second, based on succession in time, he called "heterochronistic"—our diachronic.[89] The synchronic sciences were organized around space, viz. geography, ethnography, *Statistik*, and the diachronic ones around time, including world history, cultural and national history, and politics.[90] This more familiar emphasis on time differs from Maier's and Will's distinction based on mode ("describing" versus "narrating").

Fabri's chief contribution was in bringing *Statistik* together with geography and ethnography. Geography he defined as the space in which men interact.[91] Many placed it as either an auxiliary to *Statistik* or to the diachronic historical sciences; Fabri sharply disagreed. "Geography is, rather . . . a sovereign, independent science."[92] By ethnology, Fabri meant the "scientifically organized synchronic content concerning the supposed relationships between the classes of various peoples and within humanity as a whole."[93] Thus, an "ethnographic" approach was precisely the opposite of what contemporary German historians would have defined as "history." For them, an attempt to do synchronic *history* would have been seen as a contradiction in terms—exactly like being an antiquarian-historian.

Fabri's *Statistik*, like Schlözer's, was to be based on material sources:

> *Statistik*, as a historical science, is charged with drawing its material not from the principles of reason, but from real experience—in other words, not from *possible* means, not from *possible* forms of constitution [Konstitutions-Formalien], but rather from means and from constitutions that are found in *real* [wirklichen, reellen] operation in one or more states, in how states are *really* organized, *really* administered, in how they *really* utilize their strengths; *not* how this all *could be*, or should be.[94]

Fabri insisted on the equality of the hetero- and homochronic, on the equivalence of the logic of Newton and Kant and "the cumbersome fishermen of Tierra del Fuego and the ham-fisted eskimo in northern Labrador."[95] This kind of full-blown anthropological perspective on human history would be developed further, and perhaps completely, two generations hence in the work of Gustav Friedrich Klemm (see chapter 7).

Fabri also re-sorted the *Hilfswissenschaften* themselves based on subject matter. Chronology, toponomy, and political arithmetic fell under the mathematical-historical, while epigraphy, diplomatics, hieroglyphics, numismatics, sphragistics, and heraldry came under the graphical. The nomenclature is his own and moves away from both temporal (diachronic/synchronic) and stylistic (narrating/describing) categories. Content established structure. Still following Gatterer, he excluded archaeology and *Altertumskunde* from the list of auxiliary sciences because he viewed them as already autonomous fields in themselves.[96] In terms of content, while acknowledging imprecise usage, Fabri sought to define "Antiquitäten studium," or antiquarianism, as the study of the technical and mechanical productions of the past and archaeology as the study of the objects of public and private life.[97]

Fabri's reform of the curriculum for material evidence stands at three generations' remove from Gatterer's beginnings. The articulation and elaboration of the *historische Hilfswissenschaften* in the German universities from 1760 to 1810 reflected an attentiveness to questions of how historical evidence functioned. That much of this evidence was material lets us read these textbooks as sources themselves, as a way of discovering how scholars were thinking about objects as evidence. We should note that, by contrast, the French equivalent of this intellectual institutionalization did not come until 1821 and the foundation of the École Nationale des Chartes. Until then, in France, it was still the age of the great polymaths, only now they were named not Peiresc and Du Cange but Barthélemy and Millin.[98]

Fabri was already making a distinction between "antiquities studies" and "archaeology." If antiquities came to the men of 1800 from the Renaissance and the seventeenth century, *archaeology* was a word very much of the times. To understand this distinction, and what contemporaries meant by *archaeology*, we need to turn to the contemporary study of ancient physical remains. Only then will we be able to assess the impact of the new curriculum of material culture based mostly on postclassical materials. This, in turn, will enable us, in successive chapters, to assess the connection to the new cultural histories of the earlier nineteenth century. But to begin, we won't have to go very far. We will stay at Göttingen, only moving from the lectures of Gatterer and Schlözer to those of their colleague in the faculty of philology, Christian Gottlob Heyne.

❡ CHAPTER 5

Archaeology as a Way of Talking about Things, 1750–1850

The historians at Göttingen were the first to systematize the study of a certain set of material remains as historical evidence. But to grasp fully the sources for the next generation's rich understanding of material evidence, we need to add to the historians' conversations those of the archaeologists. We also need to switch buildings, as it were, and immerse ourselves in a different set of disciplinary discussions, because those thinking about what archaeology was doing so within faculties of philology.

The eighteenth century saw a revolution in archaeology and in the awareness of it. The discoveries at Pompeii and Herculaneum c. 1750 stand at the center of this turn. But it was amplified by the spread of learned journals and institutes of higher learning, by the huge expansion in learned travel that we term the "Grand Tour," and by the trickle down of ancient and archaizing style in art, architecture, and design from the highest social ranks to the lower. *Archaeology* as a term, however, remained unstable. Aubin-Louis Millin (1759–1818), inspired by Jacob Spon, improvised his own plastic definition. "Archaeology," he wrote, "is . . . the knowledge of all that has to do with the customs and morals of the ancients. He who works in this way is called an Archaeologist or more frequently an antiquarian; indeed, the first title is widely used for one who studies customs and morals, and the other for those who deal with monuments."[1] By the middle of the next century, Millin's definition had spun around 180 degrees: by then it was the archaeologist who was described as the student of physical remains, as, indeed, he still is (at least for "Old World" archaeology). This suggests that something significant had occurred between 1800 and 1850.

In fact, this confusion between archaeology and antiquarianism reflects the ambivalence of all "historical archaeology," that is, the study of artifacts from periods that also left textual remains. While that term is generally used now to refer to archaeological work on the nineteenth and twentieth centuries, in fact, "classical archaeology" is no less historical. By the same token, the antiquaries of the Renaissance were actually the first historical archaeologists, since they worked back and forth between texts and artifacts from the Roman world. Archaeology as a discipline began as historical archaeology. Only the advent of prehistoric archaeology in the early nineteenth century challenged the model in forcing the birth of an object-only hermeneutic. This, in turn, became the foundation for the modern scientific discipline, which relegated historical archaeology to second-class status and antiquarianism to oblivion.

The standard narrative at this point would emphasize the importance of pre-Roman northern Europe, where there simply were no texts to accompany the excavated objects. Explicit formulation of time in terms of the three ages—stone, bronze, and iron—was made in Denmark, by Christian Jürgensen Thomsen. He was the founding director of the Museum of National Antiquities (later the National Museum), and in studying its collection and planning its installation, he developed the idea that artifacts could be dated solely by their material. By the middle of the 1820s he was talking about the idea with colleagues, and in 1836 the museum published his guide to its collection.[2]

Thomsen's guide was translated into German in 1837 and English in 1848, arriving on the scene between the founding of the British Archaeological Association (1843) and the establishment of the first chair in archaeology, at Cambridge (1852).[3] John Aubrey and William Stukeley had, over a century earlier, studied the ancient and text-free complexes at Avebury and Stonehenge.[4] Archaeological interests were at the heart of the spread of independent learned societies in Victorian England. The persistence of the old Society of Antiquaries and the vigor of the newly founded British Archaeological Association, as well as its rival splinter the Archaeological Institute of Great Britain, testify to the vitality of the subject. But 150 years after Spon, the English still had not been able to mark the frontier between the antiquary and the archaeologist: "By the exertions of the modern school of antiquaries," so proclaimed the lead article in the first number of *The Archaeologist and Journal of Antiquarian Science*, "a new face has been put on archaeology."[5]

The situation in France was no better. As we have just noted, Aubin-Louis Millin, who has only recently been reclaimed as responsible for "the renaissance of Peiresc" in France used the terms *archaeology* and *antiquarian* interchangeably.[6] Similarly, Arcisse de Caumont, a provincial Norman organizer of archaeological learning (he founded the Société des antiquaires de Normandie in 1824, the Association normande in 1831, and the Société française d'archéologie in 1834) did not distinguish between "archéologie," "histoire monumentale," "science des monuments," and "science des antiquités."[7] He did, however eventually identify the archaeologist as someone who worked in the field, while the antiquarian worked from the objects in his cabinet. If Caumont led, François Guizot, historian and minister of education, soon followed, creating in short order the public rubrics under which archaeology was conducted: in 1834 the Comité des travaux historiques et scientifiques, and in 1837 the Comité des arts et des monuments and the Commission des monuments historiques. A decade later, in the first number of the *Revue Archéologique*, the inaugural article distinguished the archaeologist from the historian by his knowledge of the figural monuments of antiquity, and from the antiquary by a body of knowledge based on comparison, critique, and art, which were seen as the basis of all archaeology. Moreover, unlike the antiquary, the archaeologist worked by "explaining the monuments by way of the books and the books by the monuments." Both of these are completely wrong as accounts of early modern antiquaries, suggesting, as with Millin's definition of archaeology, the kind of fluidity that marks a period prior to conceptual consolidation—and therefore a rich mine to delve.[8] Finally, archaeology in France spun off a literary genre, the "archaeological novel," the best examples of which are Théophile Gautier's *Roman de la momie* and Flaubert's *Salammbô*, but includes also Maxime du Camp's *Le Nil* and Baudelaire's *Le Jeune enchanteur*. Behind them all stands the ineluctable *Voyage du jeune Anacharsis* (1789), the book the young Charles Bovary is reading many decades later when we first make his acquaintance.[9] As we plunge into the German literature on archaeology we will want to keep thinking about what it means that while the Germans were making *Handbücher* about archaeology, the French were writing novels about it.

The Problematic Category of "Archäologie der Kunst"

In Germany, in the last third of the eighteenth century, the history students who were taught the *Hilfswissenschaften* were mostly trained up on postclassical artifacts, while those studying ancient texts began to be exposed to a serious course of study of classical artifacts. It was with Christian Gottlob

Heyne's lectures at Göttingen that study of antique literature (philology) came to include the study of antique art, with attention to its materiality. This mix Heyne called "Archäologie der Kunst," or "archaeology of art." Alongside of the work of Gatterer and Schlözer, Heyne's "Archäologie der Kunst" was a parallel focus for discussion of how objects functioned as evidence. For us, it is a puzzling term, as it has thoroughly fallen out of use. It also does not translate well. Are we to understand it as art archaeology? The archaeological part of art history? Or simply the history of ancient art? Nevertheless, it is the term that was used for about a century to designate the study of objects from the deeper past, so we must try to understand it.

If Gatterer excluded antiquities (*Altertumskunde*) from the *Hilfswissenschaften* it might have been, at least in part, because someone else was teaching the subject. Gatterer arrived at Göttingen at almost the same time as Heyne, who from 1763 taught classical philology. He stands at the beginning of all histories of the study of classics and classical philology in late Enlightenment Germany but also of ancient art and mythology, to which he made an outstanding contribution. Here, I would like to focus on Heyne's thinking about the material culture of antiquity. It constitutes something of a parallel to Gatterer, though perhaps with less attention to how the artifacts were to be mobilized.

Immediately upon his arrival at Göttingen in 1763, Heyne offered lectures on "Ancient Monuments and Artists." A year later, his course was devoted to "Ancient Gems and Coins." By 1767 the scope of the course had expanded to "Archaeology, or Information on Ancient Monuments and of Their Comparison with, Above All, the Fine Arts." By 1772, the title had been refined and translated from Latin into German as "Archaeology, or the Knowledge of the Art and Artworks of Antiquity." There is a whole dimension of Heyne's turn to the remains of ancient art that is directly part of his relationship to Winckelmann, which was one of admiration but also of the academic's distance-taking from the passionate but unscientific popularizer.[10]

Heyne was not, however, the first in Germany to use the term *archaeology*. In fact, he came to it via his teachers at Leipzig. Johann Friedrich Christ (1700–1756) was professor of history and then of poetry. His teaching program focused first on monuments and then on "Literatur oder Archäologie der Literatur." Archaeology by way of literature included epigraphy, numismatics, diplomatics, printing history, and engraving as well as ancient art. His contemporary, Johann August Ernesti (1707–1781), was also a professor at Leipzig (of ancient literature and rhetoric) and also delivered a series of lectures that were later published under the title *Archaeologia Literaria*. He explained that the term referred not only to works of great artistic intentionality but also to what allowed for the better explication of literary texts and, by implication, were not in themselves works of art.[11] Ernesti explained that he used the term *archaeology* to indicate that he was speaking to students of the liberal arts and not artisans, painters, architects, and assorted other makers.[12]

When Heyne lectured on ancient art from the chair of philology and called it "archaeology" he brought these associations with him. In this choice we can find all the tensions associated with the study of ancient material culture for the century that followed. It is not that Heyne had no patience for objects; quite the contrary, he came to the subject from the study of ancient gems, an antiquarian formation he shared with Winckelmann. On the other hand, as he was painfully aware, he had never traveled to Italy and so his relationship to the monuments of antiquity, as opposed to the small pieces, was fundamentally literary. Unlike many contemporaries who were less interested in ancient material culture, he never seems to have taken the measure of the discoveries at Pompeii and Herculaneum. His was, as Ernesti called the title of his lecture course, mostly an "Archaeologia Literaria."

Within the problem of text versus monument another lay nested: What kind of monument? Was the proper subject of this new archaeology artifacts of all sorts or only artifacts identified as art? To Heyne, it seemed that his great predecessors Caylus and Winckelmann—and he did not deny them this honor—were more concerned with artifacts of all sorts. He, by contrast, was more interested in the "fine arts" even if he acknowledged the need to put "the antiquarian knowledge" of artworks on firmer footing.[13] In his path-breaking *Introduction to the Study of Antiquity*, Heyne made the study of artifacts and remains important as a means to the historical understanding of antique imagery. He did think it possible to study the visual culture of antiquity from the perspective of the already collected monumental, and to use it to understand better "the old customs, habits, notions, religious and ethical terms, and even historical circumstances and facts," as well as ancient literature more generally. This method he called, variously, "antiquarian studies, studies of antiquities, archaeology."[14] When Heyne came to publish two volumes of his learned short writings on antiquity he called them "antiquarian essays" and introduced them with a history of antiquarian scholarship that culminated in assessments of the earlier work of Christ and Ernesti and the near-contemporary contributions of Winckelmann and Caylus.[15] But in another work he made clear that for him "the antiquarian part of art" ("das Antiquarische der Kunst") referred precisely to the marginal historical details in an image or object and not to the subject as a whole.[16]

This "antiquarian part of art" Heyne came to call "Archäologie der Kunst." This is how his lectures on ancient art were titled when they were posthumously published in 1822. "Archaeology of art" also retained, for Heyne, an element that was closely associated with philology. It was a bridge between the primacy of the text alone and the primacy of the object alone. Philology had, by Heyne's time, largely recognized the importance of objects, but archaeology was a way of speaking about the past, not an independent discipline, and would not become one until the middle of the next century.[17] Heyne's chapter on auxiliaries to the study of archaeology ("Hülfsmittel der Archäologie") offered a history of scholarship on antiquities, beginning with the Renaissance and its philologists and princely collectors and then jumping over the seventeenth century to the early eighteenth century and Bernard de Montfaucon and Joseph Addison. The chapter entitled "Archaeology Alone" ("Archäologie Selbst"), by contrast, refers to specific works of art and the history of these works. Heyne is, however, not calling his work a history, as in the obvious "History of Ancient Art," which was Winckelmann's title, in order to differentiate his own project, which he felt was more grounded in knowledge of the artifacts. This artifactual foundation was to be conveyed by the word *archaeology*. What was most missing, he wrote, was "a repertory" of ancient art, by which he meant an "annotated list." Winckelmann's history was simply too error-filled to suffice, and there was no introductory account of the objects that had come down to the present and the facts of their survival.[18]

"Archäologie der Kunst" was not about stratigraphy, nor was it about excavation. Its objects were already collected. It was, to put it in our own terms, a kind of "museum," or "theoretical archaeology"—where theories about already collected objects and materiality could be presented and discussed before a large audience. Hence the notion of an "archaeological discourse" in the early nineteenth century.[19]

Archaeology remained treated within the context of philology, and its questions emerge out of the discussion of philology's questions. Christian Jacob Kraus (1753–1807) lectured on history and philology at Königsberg. He had studied there with Kant before moving to Göttingen where he studied with Gatterer, Schlözer, and Heyne. His *Encyclopedic Views of Some Branches of Learning* spread over two of four posthumously published volumes of essays on humanistic subjects (1809). In the essay on philology, Kraus groups archaeology with literature and criticism. Because the ancients wrote for their own time, the understanding of ancient literature required an understanding of that time. One did that by pulling meaning from the small things that remained. He sorted this aspiration into two approaches.

"Philological archaeology" (*philologische Archäologie*)—like the *archaeologia literaria* of Ernesti—was about understanding authors from "monuments" (*Denkmäler*) whose subject matter spanned writing, art things, statues, coins, buildings, painting, inscriptions, and documents, or *Urkunden*, but also antiquities or *Altertümer*. These he divided, classically, into public (*antiquitas rerum publicarum*) and private (*antiquitas rerum privarum*). "Pragmatic archaeology" (*pragmatische Archäologie*) was about taking from the past to benefit the present, whether in the realms of politics, economics, or the fine arts. This approach elevated the study of the small, broken remains of the past because it showed their important contribution to the present. He contrasted this approach to ancient art, which he identified with the person of Winckelmann, with that of the Dutch, for whom it was all "antiquities." In this entire discussion Kraus never once uses the term "Archäologie der Kunst"—for him it was subsumed within "pragmatic archaeology."[20] Where it does appear, as one of the least discussed of the *Hilfswissenschaften* in the parallel essay on "History," it was shoe-horned into its final pages and its content limited to works of art and not history.[21]

Christian Daniel Beck (1757–1832) followed in the footsteps of Christ and Ernesti at Leipzig, appointed first to a chair in Greek and Latin literature in 1785 and then to one in history in 1819. His lecture course, published as *Foundations of Archaeology* in 1819, made clear in the subtitle—*Introduction to Knowledge of the History of Ancient Art*—that for him archaeology was about art. While Beck acknowledged that archaeology could refer to the wide array of ancient material culture, he, like Heyne, preferred to focus just on art objects: "Archaeology of art in the narrower sense."[22]

Johann Philipp Siebenkees (1759–1796) was a professor of philosophy and European philology at Altdorf who also wrote about Venetian history, ancient Roman *Statistik*, and classical Greek architecture. His *Nachlass* gave birth to a *Handbook of Archaeology or, Introduction to Knowledge of the Artworks of Antiquity and the History of the Art of Ancient Peoples* (1799). This might be the very first book with the title "Handbook of Archaeology." Siebenkees distinguished the broad subject matter of antiquarianism, which he called by the Latin *antiquitates*, namely, manners, public institutions, social constitution, religious rituals, law, and political and private life, from a focus on the physical remains of antiquity, its "Denkmäler," or monuments.[23] This latter only, he thought, marked off the domain of "archaeology."

But what did it mean to Siebenkees to study monuments? First off, he distinguished between two classes, the written (whether on papyrus or stone) and the artistic. Paleography and diplomatics were the tools used on the former; for the latter class, it was archaeology "in the narrower sense," whatever that meant. Artistic monuments, he noted, had since the Renaissance typically been reduced to illustrations of the antiquarian categories of events, people, ideas, manners, or practices. For this sort of inquiry—and this sort of inquirer—the artistic per se "lay outside of his field of vision." That these ancient remains were also art objects had been forgotten and they were seen "as mere documents, which communicated a specific history or a ritual; no one went beyond that."[24]

The contrast could not be clearer: If for the previous two centuries antiquarians had treated monuments as the means, archaeology would now treat them as ends in themselves. Change had come only recently, in the person and work of Winckelmann. More academically oriented, Siebenkees noted that ancient art was appreciated by amateurs for its luxury and pleasure, by artists for its instruction, and by the learned for both of these, combined with "a great antiquarian erudition."[25]

For anyone influenced by Heyne, material sources could not be ignored. Friedrich August Wolf (1759–1824) was the greatest philologist of his age, equally famous for his work on the authorship of Homer and for his expansion of the reach of classical philology. In the 1780s and 1790s, from his chair at Halle, Wolf shaped a generation. His epochal work on Homer fed the culturally transformative neo-Hellenism of Goethe and Wilhelm von Humboldt. As a teacher, he taught Germany's teachers, including the leader of the next generation, August Boeckh.[26] In the seminar room, Wolf ambitiously sought to transform classical philology into a kind of historical study. His *Darstellung der Alterthums-Wissenschaft* was published in 1807 at the encouragement of Goethe, to whom it was dedicated, and resumed the lecture course that he had delivered eleven times between 1775 and 1806. In it, Wolf proclaimed that his goal was to grasp antiquity as a "whole": "The political, learned, domestic situation of the Greeks and Romans, with their culture, their languages, arts and sciences, customs, religions, national characteristics and ways of thinking."[27]

Doing this meant paying attention to *everything*. Wolf began by dividing study of the past into events on the one side and conditions (*Zustände*) on the other. This distinction, and this term in particular, would have a huge impact over the next century. For Wolf, the diminutive "mere" is attached to events ("nur Begebenheiten und Ereignisse").[28] Like Francis Bacon, who described antiquities as the battered remains of the shipwreck of time, Wolf's science of the past worked with remains of all sorts. The first class of remains were textual; the second were artworks that consisted of drawing or images; the third class was more varied. Puzzlingly, Wolf, like Siebenkees, did not elaborate on its contents. He then divided the literary and artistic monuments (groups one and two) into those that spoke about the society out of which they emerged and those which spoke only to and of themselves.[29] When Wolf presented the remainder in terms of politics, military, religion, or household, he was following Biondo. This took Wolf well beyond artworks.[30]

As he stumbled around looking for a conceptual framework for dealing with these sources, Wolf reached for Spon's rethinking of this space a century before.[31] In his published lectures, Wolf cited the details of Spon's eight sub-areas (*Glyptographia, Toreumatographia, Ikonographie, Angeiographia, Bibliographia, Numismatographia, Architekonographia, Epigrammatographia*). Where Spon had called the overarching category *Archaeographia*, Wolf used *Archäologie* or *antiquitates*.[32] For Wolf, material remains, like textual ones, were a means to an end, and the end was "knowledge of ancient humanity itself."[33] This defined the inquiry he called "Altertumswissenschaft"; in Latin, he spoke alternately of "litterae antiquae," "studio antiquitatis," "doctrina antiquitatis," and "doctrina graecae latinaeque antiquitatis."[34]

The specter lurking over this quest for wholeness was well described by Wolf's contemporary Friedrich Ast. Commenting specifically on the idea of *Altertumswissenschaft*—Wolf's idea, after all—Ast wrote that it could be neither true nor valuable if it engaged with antiquity piece by piece, whether as "historical and antiquarian learning" or as "erudite study of language." This "factual and empirical" approach tended to "atomistical singularity" and made it impossible to recognize the remains as "organ of the *Geist*" and its actual being.[35]

August Boeckh: Impact and Influence

Wolf's most careful reader became his greatest critic, August Boeckh (1785-1867). He had trained with Wolf and arrived via Heidelberg in Berlin just after the founding of the new university in 1810 (and thus around the time Wolf, too, came to Berlin). Boeckh presided over the philology seminar at Berlin for fifty-six years, was a colleague of Hegel and Ranke, taught the academic stars of the future including Burckhardt and Droysen, was president of the Academy of Sciences, and lived in the same house on Leipziger Straße as Felix Mendelssohn-Bartholdy. Boeckh delivered his lecture course on classical philology twenty-six times, first at Heidelberg in the summer semester of 1809 and then in Berlin from the summer of 1810 until the summer of 1865. The title of the course changed over the years, until it was finally published, posthumously, as *Encyclopedia of Classical Philology* (1877). But the goal never deviated from that formulated by Justus

Lipsius two centuries earlier: to make philology into philosophy, or at least to make it philosophical. Because it is as yet impossible to date precisely the different states of the argument in what is generally read as a 900-page tome compiled posthumously by an interventionist editor, we will treat Boeckh here and intersperse the arguments of students, colleagues, and rivals amidst his own, since he served as a scholarly touchstone for over fifty years.[36]

On the main point, Boeckh and Wolf were in agreement: The scope of philology was total. As he explained in an oration given at the University of Berlin in 1822, philology took in the whole of the ancient knowledge of history and philosophy. He noted that while history ordered its information by time, philology aimed at comprehending "the parts" of the whole life of ancient peoples.[37]

What was philology? Boeckh famously defined it as "the knowing of the known"—more precisely, the re-knowing of the already known: "Erkenntnis des Erkannten."[38] That immediately cast it as a science of past cultural accomplishments. Comprehension meant reconstruction—indeed, Boeckh included this word in several of his pithy definitions of philology.[39] For Boeckh, the philologist's reconstructive power was nothing less than a secularization of the divinatory art of the ancients.[40] For how reconstruction actually worked, Boeckh referred to a lecture published by the philosopher Friedrich Wilhelm Joseph Schelling in 1803. Schelling suggested that the philologist was closely related to the artist and to the philosopher—or rather, both were in him. That is because historical reconstruction "required him to comprehend and represent history in a living vision," and this called for imagination of the sort found in artists.[41]

But the young Friedrich Nietzsche saw Boeckh's effort as compromised. This might have been because his approach too closely linked understanding aesthetic documents to understanding historical ones. Nietzsche wrote: "Boeckh's concept is too broad. The difference between philology and history disappears." But he then continued: ". . . and too narrow." The example was the Homeric poems, and the point was that art could not be fully grasped by a narrow kind of textual interpretation. For Nietzsche the "key" counter-example was that of Goethe, who brought a whole person's sensibility to whatever scientific work he chose to undertake.[42]

In 1873, Boeckh's nephew, Karl Bernhard Stark, himself a leading archaeologist, argued in the same vein as Nietzsche for the importance of the imagination for science and of science for the imagination. Far from the artist and the scholar needing to be kept apart, they actually needed to be brought together. What philologist, he wrote, could make sense of an ancient poem without "instinctive tact, vitality of re-enactment, and creative supplementation"? What historian could make sense of a chronologically distant person or a social world without the "fantasy" capable of bringing the dry material of the past back to life? Nor, Stark thought, could science be kept from art: Materials, industry, and modes of production all affected art making.[43] John Marsden, first Disney Professor of Archaeology at Cambridge spoke of "the close connexion between the antiquary and the poet" in his inaugural lectures, published in 1852.[44]

The philologist was also related to the philosopher because of a shared interest in knowledge. But philology was about re-knowing, whereas philosophy was about knowing, period.[45] Moreover, it was the philosopher's attentiveness to the general or whole that saved philology from being just another form of polyhistory, which Boeckh defined as "pure, raw empiricism without any clear limits and without ideas."[46] In shaping this definition, Boeckh marked the difference not just between philology and antiquarianism but, more generally, between a "science," or *Wissenschaft*, and the pursuit of information for the sake of accumulating information.

For Boeckh, *Altertumskunde* was about the re-knowing of *everything*. It was not history of literature, or of art, or of religion, but "the history of the life of a people." He offers the image of a circle any point of whose circumference can be connected back to its center. "Philology," he writes, "gathers all these lines together and separates them out like the rays of a circle stemming from a center, the spirit of the people."[47] This is the same image that Ernst Gombrich used to explain Hegel's approach to cultural history, suggesting the importance of philology for understanding cultural history, but also for understanding the history of cultural history.[48] And Boeckh, in fact, saw cultural history as comprehending all the "real disciplines of philology," invoking Benjamin Hederich's *Real-Philologie*, though he preferred to call it *Sach-Philologie*—*real* and *material* being synonyms—as opposed to a philology that was closer to purely literary studies (*Wort-Philologie*).[49] In a speech of 1850 opening an assembly of philologists and orientalists, he called for a "comparative cultural history of all antiquity."[50] Burckhardt, who audited Boeckh's lectures on "Greek antiquities" in 1839/40, got the message: He described them as "the cultural history of a particular people."[51] At the start of his own lectures on "Greek cultural history" Burckhardt described the subject of Boeckh's "great lectures" as "Greek antiquities." These were all "treated by the antiquarian method," which he defined as "with a predetermined and constant degree of factual detail and completeness of each separate aspect of ancient life, as the ground work for future specialized study." (His own approach, which he contrasted with that of his teacher, was to seek out the "habits of mind" of those who lived in the past rather than aim at a material reconstruction of their world.)[52]

One of Boeckh's contemporaries focused on the problem of what it meant to bring all these different directions together. Eduard Platner (1786–1860) studied Greek and Roman law and was called to a professorship of law at Marburg in 1811, just around the time Boeckh took up his chair in Berlin. A year later he published a book about how to treat Roman antiquities as a science. The project was based on his experience trying to lecture on this subject. The absence of any system for making sense of antiquities made it easy for students (and studies) of the Greek and Roman past to slip into pedantry, a "spirit- and taste-less long-windedness of thick quartos and folios about the houses, articles of clothing, food, and other conditions of these peoples."[53] He mocked the learned debates about whether the Romans wore hats over their right ear or their left, or those who claimed that they could find their way around the streets of Rome better than they could their own homes.[54]

Platner focused on the problem of context. Like Siebenkees's turn to the inquirer's goal, Platner argued that it was the lack of system in the study of antiquities, rather than the defectiveness of the antiquities themselves, that was at issue. As long as objects and questions appeared idiosyncratically chosen, the specifics would appear trivial. Though philosophy, he wrote, had in his era made a close association with history, it had not yet extended to antiquarianism. Platner wanted to provide this. The key idea was "totality," as in grasping the totality of any thing. This presupposition made the antiquarian focus on small things a necessary part of the chain of knowledge, even a considerable part of it. Far from positing a merely theoretical connection between things, Platner argued that there was "an inner, real connection" that illuminated the individual pieces and made sense of their relationship to one another. But this was a connection that could only be discovered by careful and patient examination of the surviving pieces. This re-grounding of the study of antiquities upended the widespread and "serene" neglect of the specifically "antiquarian" contribution to the study of antiquity.[55]

It was this ability to connect the little to the overarching that led Platner to conclude that "antiquities contain less and more than history."[56] The "antiquarian writer," when studying the clothing, shelter, and tools of the ancient Romans, was also studying something very intimate, since "all that a man makes with strength and will mirrors his interior."[57] The "antiquarian researcher" had to know all the particular details in order to be able to recombine them to make a "whole." It was the move from part to whole that generated interpretative light.[58]

In this quest for "wholeness" or "total history," texts could become a means to an end, read not only for what they were intended to say but also against their grain as sources for details about life in the past. The quest for wholeness also takes us beyond texts, because not everything gets written about, especially not things considered so much a part of daily existence as to go generally unmentioned. Seeking wholeness, therefore, also meant seeking things and seeking ways to make those things talk.[59] If Boeckh began with a section on the "Philological Reconstruction of Antiquity," he then turned to the "Material Disciplines of Ancient Studies." He also called these the "real disciplines of Philology."[60]

Taking the study of *realia* seriously led Boeckh to take seriously the history of its study. Nevertheless, the account he provides of Renaissance and early modern antiquarianism is thin. He is much more closely engaged with the theoretical position of archaeology. In the narrowest sense, he writes, archaeology had for a long time referred to "antiquarian studies." But since the history of ancient art was derived in part from material remains and included knowledge of technique as well as economics, archaeology had, in fact, been talking all along about the art of the ancient world. This overlapping area was how Boeckh described the field of "Archäologie der Kunst" or, less frequently, "Kunstarchäologie."[61] Boeckh treated Winckelmann as its pioneer, uniting "philological erudition with taste and sense for the ideal."[62] But Boeckh was quick to note that the study of material remains per se, which he called *Denkmälerkunde*, did not belong to this new category. As much as he pushed beyond Heyne's attachment to art, he could not free himself from the gravitational pull of the aesthetic.[63]

The question of the aesthetic lurks in the archaeological discourse of the 1820s and 1830s. In Denmark, where Thomsen was creating the tools for a prehistory that was formally agnostic about the primacy of both texts and aesthetics, Frederik Christian Petersen was unequivocal about archaeology being nothing other than "the Art History of Antiquity." His 1825 *Introduction to the Study of Archaeology* was translated into German in 1829 and had an immediate impact. Nevertheless, Petersen noted that in Greek antiquity archaeology had denoted the narration of early times and that Varro had actually translated it, not only into Latin (*antiquitates*) but also into specific categories. Perhaps inspired by Varro's fourfold taxonomy (peoples, places, things, times), Petersen systematized the archaeologist's line of inquiries into critical, historical, aesthetic, and technical.[64]

Petersen and his immediate German reception testify to the flourishing of an archaeological discourse around 1830. One of its prime agents was Karl August Böttiger (1760–1835), a colleague of Goethe's in Weimar who then moved to Dresden to direct the museum of antiquities. He edited the art journal *Amalthea*. But he was also in sympathy with Boeckh's extension of the realm of the archaeological toward the material culture of antiquity. (It was Böttiger, for example, who in the preface to the first number of *Amalthea* proclaimed Peiresc "the first archaeologist" and Spon his heir.) He defended this position against those who wished for it an explicitly narrower mandate. In the 1820s and 1830s he was at the heart of a series of bilateral Franco-German correspondences about the scope of archaeology which have been recently studied.[65] Even as he encouraged his French friend Desiré Raoul-Rochette to take a broad view of the sources needed to understand ancient art, there really was no equivalent to the German debate on the other side of the Rhine. In France, for example, *archaeology* was a more marginal term. Neither the 1835 *Dictionnaire de l'Académie française* nor the 1857 edition of the *Dictionnaire Universel des Arts et des Lettres* included an entry devoted to it.[66] In France, classical antiquity was, instead, accessed through the lenses of philosophy and history.[67] It took the exploration of French national antiquity—not just the Gauls but their prehistoric predecessors too—to finally liberate the study of the artifact and galvanize support for a collection. This took a generation, bearing fruit only in the 1860s when the Museum of National Antiquities opened its doors in Saint-Germain-en-Laye (1867).[68]

Another problem that arose from broadening the scope of inquiry to the world beyond texts was that of micrology. This problem was already present in Boeckh's (and not only Boeckh's) low estimation of *Denkmälerkunde*. Boeckh viewed micrology as the opposite of philology, "small" here being the equivalent of "small-minded."[69] As a discipline, he wrote, philology was vulnerable to micrology because it cultivated a commitment to precision that was necessary in order to avoid erring in even the smallest thing, and this would always verge on pedantry.[70] "Superficial pseudo-critique," "grammatical trivia," "risible conjecture-mongering" were all associated risks.[71] So too was philology's tendency toward the "history of everything."[72] Boeckh's rejoinder was that, in fact, one could plunge into a particular problem and through it "grasp the macrocosm." "Every single idea," he wrote, again sounding a bit like Hegel, "touches on the whole."[73] No detail was in itself too small. They key was to keep sight of the larger interpretative goal for which all this intellectual firepower was needed.[74] And then, in a startling comment, the Berlin professor looked back to the late Renaissance and acknowledged that what was missing in the contemporary research on "real" philology in particular was "the great spirit of erudition of the sixteenth century."[75]

Boeckh's theory of philology as a study of things was set forth in his lecture course; his practice of philology as a study of things is best seen in a book he published just a few years after arriving in Berlin. *The Public*

Economy of Athens (1817) demonstrated, along with the works of Savigny and Niebuhr, what the Berlin historians were capable of. It offered, among other things, a detailed examination of mines, houses, slaves, cereals, cattle, wine, oil, salt, wood, dining, clothing, shoes, and weapons in ancient Athens. All of this was the foundation for equally detailed discussions of prices, wages, and interest rates. Boeckh dedicated the book to his new colleague at Berlin B. G. Niebuhr, the Roman historian, with a preface declaring not just the importance of studying the parts and the whole together, but also the inadequacy of studying the parts without a sense of the whole.[76] We have here Boeckh's entire vision of what philology could achieve, and how. He would later locate economics on an individual level—food, clothing, shelter—within the study of *Privataltertümer*, which was, in turn, part of *Real-*, or *Sach-*, philology.[77]

And even if Boeckh's English translator, the philologist, man of letters, and diplomat George Cornwall Lewis, mocked his inadequate understanding of economics after Adam Smith, the simple fact of the translation and the perdurance of the volume (how many books get a second edition more than thirty years after their first?) suggests its staying power. Rather than emphasize the book's inevitable inadequacies we might, instead, marvel at the extension of philology's mandate to the reconstruction of ancient economics and at the historian's awareness that economics was a part of history: "The intellectual faculties, however, are not of themselves sufficient: to produce external action they require the aid of physical force, the direction and combination of which are wholly at the disposal of money; that mighty spring by which the whole machinery of human energies is set in motion."[78]

This daring reach deep into the material world of antiquity was laid out again on the first page of Boeckh's edition of the corpus of Greek inscriptions, published in 1825. The "matter of philology" (*res philologica*), Boeckh wrote, was divided into four parts. The first was public, and related to events and institutions of the city, or government. The second was private and included all economic and commercial things. The third concerned ritual and the symbolic arts. The fourth took in all learning, whether historical, philosophical, or mythological. The ambivalence of inscriptions, simultaneously both textual and material, made them apt vehicles for this broad view. "As with writers, so with inscriptions," Boeckh wrote.[79] These four parts of philology follow from Biondo's reworking of Varro's vision of antiquarianism and reappear in Boeckh's textbook as the first chapter in the section devoted to the "Material Disciplines of Classical Studies."

Boeckh's work showed how one might begin from philology and wind up doing economic history, all via a concern with recapturing the wholeness of the ancient world. This reflects on the history of philology, of course, but also on the historical culture of the University of Berlin, home of Hegel and Ranke, in the 1820s and 1830s. Boeckh's star student, K. O. Müller, would write the first history of ancient art, but it was another Berlin student, Wilhelm Roscher, who drew even more threads together. Roscher, whom we have encountered already as Lamprecht's teacher, came to Berlin in 1840 from his studies with Boeckh's student Müller at Göttingen. He had worked on the sophists and would, in Berlin, study with Ranke and Boeckh before returning to Göttingen in 1842 to teach *Statistik* and national economy. That same year he published his dissertation on Thucydides, which he dedicated to his teacher, Ranke. Its "Prolegomenon" laid out his vision of history, one that would underpin the work he would do on on the history of economic activity in antiquity and the German Middle Ages.

Roscher began by sharply distinguishing the sciences of experience, whether natural or human, from those that depicted or aspired to a truth higher than experience. On the one side were history and the natural sciences, on the other philosophy and art. This division enabled him to envision the possibility of a historical social science. It also enabled him to reclaim for the historian the scientific instrument whose use had been viewed, even in the work of Boeckh, as the mark of bad history: the microscope.[80]

For the microhistorical lens could be wielded by the right sort of historian. Roscher tried to define him by distinguishing between two types of historical scholars, the "craftsman" (*Handwerker*) and the "artist" (*Künstler*). The craftsman could collect but not create, transmit materials but not interpret them. He was obsessed with names and dates but was unable to put them together to make a whole. Like a true pedant, he could be counted on to mistake the trivial for the significant and miss the significant for the trivial. He was like a "miner" or an apprentice builder ("Handlanger der Baukunst") rummaging about in the warehouse for construction materials. In this we can hear Theodor Mommsen's later criticism of antiquarian scholarship as a kind of ant-like construction site: "der antiquarische Bauplatz."[81] Not for him the microscope.

The main parts of Boeckh's magnum opus were devoted to two practices with origins in the study of literature: hermeneutics and critique. Critique stood for the work of the *Hilfswissenschaften*, namely, verification. But hermeneutics, which Boeckh took from his teacher Friedrich Schleiermacher, went much further. First, it represented the principles by which humans understand, principles that Boeckh claimed were more or less universal. Then there was an objective element, insofar as all the users of the same language employed a common grammar, and also an individual one, in that every person used language somewhat differently. Humans also used language in specific historical circumstances. Boeckh argued that this required the interpreter to "transplant" himself into that context in order to grasp the full import of the words. Finally, the artistic manipulation of generic conventions constituted yet another field of interpretation, as closely related to the subjective as the historical was related to the grammatical. "History," for Boeckh, was what was needed to make sense of a text but could not be extracted from the text alone. It is the specific, most narrow definition of the historical interpretation that jumps out at us: "from out of the literal meaning with reference to material relations." In other words, Boeckh identified history with material conditions (the "real") in a way that was unparalleled among contemporary historians, even if only in an interpretative context.[82]

Boeckh acknowledged that there were also specific hermeneutics for different kinds of literature. Examples he gave were the New Testament, Roman law, and Homer. The "plastic arts," too, had their own hermeneutic. But Boeckh excluded the possibility of an "archaeological hermeneutic" on the grounds that such a thing had to be derived from the properties of the material itself, and either he did not want to do this or he did not think it possible.[83] And while some pushed him to extend his method from the domain of turning texts into sources to the world of material remains, Boeckh hesitated. The parallel between these "grammars" was closest for the non-written monuments which were works of art because inherent in their aesthetic intentionality was giving "theoretical ideas" a material form. The history of art, therefore, could be told in the same way as the histories of literature, science, and grammar. But dumb, silent objects? As open as Boeckh was to the range of *realia*, in the end he could not find his way to move his notion of hermeneutics beyond the art object (*Kunstarchäologie*).[84]

Another of Boeckh's Berlin colleagues and archaeological interlocutors was the scholar and curator Konrad Levezow (1770–1835). In November 1833 he delivered a lecture to the Royal Academy of Sciences that aimed to fill in the gap that Boeckh had left when he declined to discuss the possibility of an archaeological hermeneutic. He acknowledged that archaeology was about ancient art, but he insisted that its materials were "purely historical." He wanted to limit critique and hermeneutics to the part of archaeology that had to do with ancient visual culture—as did Boeckh—but he then proceeded as if addressing all ancient monuments.[85]

Levezow's basic move was to build a method around the parallel between text and object. Because physical monuments came from the same world as textual monuments, he proposed that they ought to be explicable in the same ways, paying attention to things like person, nation, period, affect, the body, spiritual expression, conditions, trade, clothing, dress, and weapons, among much else.[86] The breadth of interpretative categories suggests, in terms of the debate about word *versus* thing philology, going beyond the word; in terms of archaeology, it suggests the world beyond art objects. Levezow described this as "a critical revision of our existing archaeological knowledge, and of the critical and exegetical foundations and methods on which they are based."[87]

For Levezow, the task of "hermeneutics" lay in linking the idea in the object with its external form. Doing this was a task for a kind of knowledge that took in the whole. This meant knowledge of texts—where hermeneutics came from—but also monuments and even objects of nature.[88] "Critique," by contrast, was not about the "whole" so much as it was about verification of evidence—in fact, resuming the function of the *historische Hilfswissenschaften*. In a way, the movement from hermeneutics to criticism involved a shift from the monument viewed from within to the monument viewed from without.[89] Levezow enumerated the questions of *Kritik*: Was the work entirely old or only in part? From what people did it come, and in which period of the people's development? Who was the artist? Was the work a copy? And was it imitating the idea, too, or creating a new one?[90] In doing all this, Levezow could be viewed as applying Boeckh to help grasp the meaning in mute objects. To the extent that Levezow engaged with the philosophical implications of the archaeologist's quest for meaning, he was still not superseded even a century later.[91]

Levezow's premise, that philology spoke to archaeology, reflected a commitment to the material world that was not shared by all philologists or even by all archaeologists. Among the archaeologists, Ludwig Preller, writing in 1845 and specifically responding to Levezow, rejected the parallel and with it the idea of an archaeological hermeneutic. While since Winckelmann archaeology had been associated with the visual culture of antiquity, he argued that the visual only constituted part of the art of antiquity, and the art of antiquity, in turn, only a part of what constituted "all the interests of archaeology." There were many other "historical and antiquarian goals in play." This amounted to a rehabilitation of the *Denkmal* (monument). Ancient art, in any event, extended well beyond the visual or material; Preller's discussion of music and metric made clear just how much a Winckelmann-derived historical aesthetic had omitted. More profoundly, Preller rejected the parallel between word and image on which the paralleling of philology and archaeology, and thus of their hermeneutics and critique, had been built.[92]

It is the specific nature of materiality which, once substituted as the subject matter of archaeology, defies the parallel to language and thus overthrows the structure of this argument. "The entire essence of the thing consists in the full epiphany of the corporeal." In emphasizing that knowledge of things was to come from things, Preller was prying apart words from things and narrowing to something more manageable the kind of comparative scholarship that defined the antiquarian study of objects. Just as he rejected the value of literary sources for understanding monuments he rejected the study of representations of monuments. Instead, he proposed a repertory of finds—in other words, material sources from material sources—and autopsy as a way of making sure "the material *what?*" did not get ignored.[93]

The prying apart of words from things, but this time with the opposite intent of upholding the priority of words, was the position associated with the philologist Johann Gottfried Hermann (1772–1848), who taught at Leipzig and was Boeckh's peer in training the next generation of German philologists. He believed that Boeckh and his epigones had gone too far toward context and away from text. Indeed, he tossed back at Boeckh the accusation that he had flung at the non-contextualizing philologists: micrology.[94] Boeckh's response was to insist on the material forms of philology and reject the charge of micrology. But this so-called debate about *Sachphilologie* was in fact a debate about the sufficiency of language. Hermann argued that human speech was the external form of reason, and that this gave all humans—because all humans have reason—immediate, timeless access to the past. Research of the sort conducted and promoted by Boeckh on the material context of literary remains was simply unnecessary. For Boeckh, by contrast, language was but one *Sache* among others, such as art, architecture, or monuments, each of which required effortful interpretation. For Boeckh, the circular movement between object and context offered the promise of a way forward. For Hermann, all that was needed was language.[95]

Some modern scholars have argued that Hermann's position on language was taken from Kant, who had made the link between innate reason and innate language.[96] Indeed, Hermann worked on Kant toward the end of his student years and returned to Kant's *Critique of Judgment* for the subject of his first series of lectures at Leipzig.[97] Nietzsche, who trained at Bonn with a disciple of Hermann's, Friedrich Ritschl, and who shared his teacher's distance from Boeckh's approach, very clearly identified language as the main task of the philologist, and Kant as the philosopher who most closely associated language and cognition.[98] Exactly this filiation was noted also by Salomon Reinach (1858–1932), who argued that philology as a discipline needed to be freed of its dependence on philosophy. Yes, he wrote, philosophy kept philologists looking for the forest despite their natural proclivity to see trees everywhere. But it also made them less attentive to those trees. In particular, he wrote, "the influence of Kantianism is evident in all the works of Gottfried Hermann, and explains, to a certain degree, the faults" in his work.[99] If this is so, then

Boeckh's entire argument—about the need for context, about the need to go beyond the text, about the possibility of a grammar of things—all of this had to be seen as an anti-Kantian move. More recently, however, Michael N. Forster has argued that this association needs to be narrowed to the later Kant, whose arguments resemble those associated with Herder and Hamann about the innate relationship of language to culture (and which he had rejected earlier in his career).[100] Either way, whether of the early or the late, it seems clear that the epistemological foundation for the modern study of material culture depends on a rejection of Kant.

The debate about *Sachphilologie* roiled through the German philological community of the day. The canonical internalist history from the late nineteenth century seems to have put Hermann's language-based approach at the core of the discipline (in a chapter entitled "The Grammatical-Critical Direction of Philology Under the Influence of G. Hermann") while relegating Boeckh to its margins (a chapter entitled "Historical-Antiquarian Studies since Boeckh").[101] Yet the scale of Boeckh's achievements and students, as well as the openness of his work to cognate disciplines, makes his endorsement of cultural history and knowledge of *realia* especially important.

If philology provided the cocoon in which "art archaeology" developed, this in turn created the conditions for the development of one species of cultural history. Karl Otfried Müller (1797–1840), probably Boeckh's greatest student, taught ancient literature at Göttingen and wrote about Greek history.[102] His reflection on philology and archaeology took the shape of a *Handbuch der Archäologie der Kunst* (1830, second edition 1835). This was the book that provided Burckhardt with his model of cultural history (a combination of narrative and structure)—and Müller published it when he was only thirty-four years old.[103] It will help us understand the resurfacing of the problematic term "Archäologie der Kunst." In the age of Heyne, it had stood for the history of ancient art. At the same time, it also contained both an inflection in the direction of content (broad, and so including material as well as visual culture) and method (*Archäologie*'s shared heritage with *antiquitates* pointed toward the work of antiquarians).

Müller's volume began with Greek history, supplemented by brief surveys of the non-Greek peoples. Chapters on building materials and types followed, concluding with a discussion of furniture and utensils. Those on plastic art include detailed discussions of the various soft and hard materials in use. Discussion of painting techniques follow—not of paintings—and then costume. This was an unprecedented attention to the material realities of art and architecture.[104] Only after all this does Müller turn to the subject of ancient art. Even here, he soon moves from named deities to themes.

These range from the government of the world, time, and the winds to "vegetation," "country, city, and home," "human activities and conditions," and onward to "the hunt, country life, economical occupations," "domestic and married life," "death," "amulets, symbols," and "animals, plants."

Nevertheless, Müller explained that his scope was limited to art and thus excluded many things on coins, inscriptions, or monuments that could otherwise have found their way into a manual of archaeology.[105] And art, for Müller, was something metaphysical, even spiritual. He used the term *Kunstidee*, and his editor went on to describe it by comparison to Goethe's "Urpflanze," which itself stood for the unfolding "Idea," or ideal form, of a plant.[106] Müller makes explicit reference to Goethe's treatise on color theory (*Farbenlehre*, 1813) in his discussion of color in ancient art.

It is worth asking whether the historical section of Goethe's *Farbenlehre*, with its archive-like repertory of texts, had any impact upon Müller's own presentation of the history of classical scholarship, since it would have provided one of the few extant examples of this genre.[107] Müller's introduction to the literature on the study of art objects, which includes both narrative and annotated bibliography, is brief (only six pages in the 1835 edition). But it was the most comprehensive up to that time, as well as the most influential. From 1450 to 1600 the work on ancient art was, he argued, done by artists and for the purpose of art. The second period, from 1600 to 1750, he calls "antiquarian." It was not, in fact, much concerned with art. The third period, which began in 1750 and persisted into his present tense, he called "scientific" and was characterized by the discoveries around Vesuvius, the traveler's familiarity with Greece, a wider knowledge of both Egypt and the Etruscans, and the beginning of systematic historical accounts with Winckelmann.[108]

But even with all his attention to history, and even with his own interest in techniques and materials, Müller remained primarily interested in art. He explained that "the main object of this Manual is to reduce to scientific order the materials contained in archaeological literature . . . strictly confining itself to the visual arts [*zeichnenden Künste*] of the ancients."[109] The antiquarian attention to objects as a way of answering questions from elsewhere he treated as a different endeavor, one that he called *Denkmalkunde* as opposed to *Altertumskunde* or *Archäologie der Kunst*.[110]

Müller's *Handbuch* had an immediate European reception. It was translated into French in 1841 as *Manuel d'Archéologie* and then into English in 1850 as *Ancient Art and its Remains*. It was reprinted as late as 1878, with an additional bibliography and annotations. These later editions were done without the author—he died a young man on the voyage to Greece he undertook immediately after putting the second edition of his *Handbook* to bed.

By the 1850s considered reflection on Müller's achievements led to the conclusion that he had overemphasized aesthetics. Friedrich Wilhelm Eduard Gerhard (1795–1867), August Boeckh's first doctoral student, structured his *Outline of Archaeology* (1853) as a guide to those using Müller's book as the basis of their lectures. Most of Gerhard's intellectual career happened outside of the university. After training with Boeckh, he spent his longest period anywhere in Rome as one of the founders, and then secretary, of the Instituto di corrispondenza archaeologica, forerunner of the Deutsches Archäologisches Institut. He returned to Berlin in 1833 to take up the position of archaeologist at the Royal Museum and in 1844 became ordinarius professor at the university.

Gerhard's biggest problem with Müller's book was its lack of attention to monuments, museums, "or also archaeology in the narrower sense (as opposed to art history)."[111] These three domains corresponded to the need to look at art, to examine it critically, and to interpret it, for which Gerhard proposed the terms *autopsy*, *critique*, and *hermeneutic*. These, in turn, reflected approaches focused on material, style, and narrative.[112] We should see Gerhard as sharing Levezow's aspiration to elaborate the archaeologist's way of thinking but taking it even further into practice. He complained, for example, that Müller paid no attention to the apparatus of archaeological study, such as excavation techniques. This now seemed a glaring fault amidst the explosion of guides to archaeology after 1830, the year that Müller's *Handbook* first appeared.[113]

As an appendix, Gerhard reprinted a lecture he had delivered in 1850 "On the Relationship of Archaeology to Philology and to Art." He defined *archaeology* as the branch of classical philology based on monumental works and traces of ancient "Technik" rather than on literary sources. Its scope included "the totality of monumental remains, in and for themselves, but also their implications for literary, religious, and private antiquities." The purpose was to grasp the "total view" of ancient life. Research on monuments had, however, to begin from literary monuments, as well as from art. These two types of sources informed all that archaeologists worked on. Gerhard insisted that the ancient monuments were not only aesthetic but also "indispensable sources of antiquarian knowledge." If some struggled with their difficulty as mere *Hilfsmittel*, or means to an end, he insisted that they were as accessible as they were rewarding.[114]

Others, too, were thinking about archaeology with Müller as their point of reference. Gerhard refers to a review of the new edition of Müller by Karl Bernhard Stark, then a youngish professor of archaeology at Jena, recently published in the *Zeitschrift für die Altertumswissenschaft* in 1852. In this review, which stretched over a whopping nine parts, Stark demonstrated how seriously he took Müller's work by arguing with it detail by detail. But his main point was that Müller too sharply divided art history from the study of artifacts. His emphasis was on the neglected "Denkmalkunde." Stark proposed a re-structuring of Müller's *Handbook* into three parts, a general overview of the history of art history and "a real hermeneutic and critique of monuments," an overview of the relationship of archaeology to questions of geography, technology, and art, and then a review of the objects themselves. Müller, he wrote, devoted himself less to the monuments than to the literary study of them, whether poetical, religious, or philosophical.[115] Stark also argued that Müller's blind spot affected his treatment of the past. He had worked exclusively on Italian antiquarianism and ignored the many others across Europe who had studied the material culture of antiquity.[116]

All of these criticisms—lack of attention to monuments, to archaeological method, and to the history of archaeology—would be corrected by Stark in his own *Handbook of the Archaeology of Art* (1878, expanded 1880). This was the book Momigliano described in 1950 as the best extant history of antiquarianism, an attempt to connect antiquarianism and archaeology that would be fleshed out a century later by another historian of archaeology, Alain Schnapp.[117] In this remarkable volume, Stark concisely re-presented a century's discussion of archaeology's emergence out of the spirits of philology and art history.

Stark very clearly defined "Archäologie der Kunst" as ancient art history.[118] He followed in the footsteps of Boeckh, whose biography he planned to write but never did, by positing as its goal reconstruction of the whole life of antiquity.[119] More than his predecessors, he poked at the fault lines concealed by the term. Reconstruction, he wrote, could be based on the textual remains found on all kinds of material supports, whether stone, metal, papyrus, or anything else. However, archaeology could also refer to monuments whose communication took place not through text but through placement, or chemical signature, weight, or color. This was a vast field, including the biggest and the smallest buildings, and also the transformation of the earth's surface on land and in water, objects both high and low—jewelry, for instance, but also tools and instruments and weapons. Counterposing a literary to a monumental philology was one way of putting this distinction; seeing it as a difference between philology and archaeology was another. "The philologist critiques and interprets his texts," Stark wrote, "the archaeologist investigates and specifies, like the historian of nature, its ancient objects."

This preserved for the philologist an engagement with "the core, the spiritual content of the ancient world," while the archaeologist was left to work with its external manifestations. Still a further distinction had to do with context—theoretical discussions were for philologists, practical ones for the archaeologists. A final way of slicing through the terrain turned on method, not content: The specific ways in which the literary remains on the one hand and the material ones on the other were made to yield up their fruits.[120] But even with all this precision, for Stark "Archäologie der Kunst" remained anchored to the aesthetic. Though his distinctions provided archaeology with autonomy from the textual, he did not go a step further and articulate the grounds for its formal separation from the aesthetic. On the contrary, his own vision of archaeology had three parts: art theory, art history, and the study of mostly figural objects for which he repurposed the term *Denkmalkunde*.[121]

As self-conscious as he was, Stark did not reach for "hermeneutics" to frame his thinking about archaeological interpretation. It wasn't an archaeologist who would do this but a philosopher of the next generation, Wilhelm Dilthey, who took up Boeckh's encyclopedic vision of hermeneutics and turned it into the foundation stone of what he called the "human sciences." The main part of Dilthey's career was in the chair of philosophy at the University of Berlin. He insisted that the circular motion between text and context, object and interpreter, could yield only as much fruit as the spiritual resources the scholar brought to bear. This attack on the objectivity cult associated with Rankean history could also be read as a response to Nietzsche's *Wir Philologen* but for the inconvenient facts that Nietzsche's plea for the human in scholarship remained unpublished and Dilthey seems to have shown neither an interest in nor an understanding of Nietzsche's arguments.[122]

Despite the philosophical vocation, Dilthey wrote history and thought about history. And despite not trying to provide the content of the archaeological hermeneutic that Boeckh imagined but did not supply, Dilthey included material evidence within the scope of his human sciences. "What is available to us," he writes, "is remnants, parts of the historical events of the past. We have heaps of ruins, fairy tales, customs, and a few reports about political affairs."[123] Understanding (*Verstehen*) was the name for the process whereby a given individual got inside another person or human-made thing: "Through stone and marble, musical notes, gestures, words, and texts, actions, economic regulations and constitutions, the same human spirit addresses us and demands interpretation." Insofar as these objects to be understood remained for us to return to them, the process of rule-guided interpretation can be called exegesis.[124] These perduring works of the human spirit he called "objective." The encounter—or re-encounter—with them was central to the making meaning he called hermeneutics:

> The distribution of trees in a park, the arrangement of houses in a street, the handy tool of the artisan, and the sentence propounded in the courtroom are everyday examples of how we are constantly surrounded by what has become historical. What the human spirit is today projecting into some manifestation will tomorrow, when it stands before us, be history. Through the passage of time we become surrounded by Roman ruins, cathedrals, and the country palaces of autocrats.[125]

Dilthey's way of talking about the world is actually full of things. If he seems to select his examples almost randomly, even unselfconsciously, he also unerringly crafts his argument so as to suggest, on the contrary, that he had put a great deal of forethought into his choices. "In this sense," Dilthey concluded, "there is also an art of interpretation whose objects are statues or paintings, and Friedrich August Wolf already called for archaeological hermeneutic and critique."[126] One hundred years later, Dilthey was still organizing his own argument around Wolf's problematic. Moreover, Dilthey saw archaeology as an answer to a question emerging organically from the general challenge of studying the past. Wolf, he wrote, "proposed a new ideal for philology in accordance with which, it, while firmly grounded in language, would encompass the entire culture of a nation in order to attain on this basis an understanding of its greatest cultural creations." This, in turn, was the philological heart of the historical operations of Niebuhr and Mommsen, Boeckh and Müller.[127]

Nevertheless, as profound as Dilthey's understanding of this line of thought was, he viewed it as if from the other side of the river. For him there could be no independent archaeological hermeneutic because the "interpretation of mute works is everywhere dependent on literature for its elucidation." With this flourish, Dilthey turns his back on material culture, reserving a deep, world-making kind of understanding for literary sources only.[128]

"Archäologie der Kunst" sank beneath the interpretative horizon. As it went down it took with it access to the nineteenth century's intense conceptual reflection on antiquarianism and the archaeological hermeneutic. When the archaeologist Otto Jahn gave a series of lectures in the summer semester of 1865 at the University of Bonn, he gave them the title "Foundations of Archaeology." One of his student auditors wrote down "Archaeology" as the course title. His summary notes, however, described the course as an "Introduction to Art History." "Archaeology" and "Art" had pulled in different directions for a century, and for a century they been held together, however loosely, by "Archäologie der Kunst." One wonders whether it was an aestheticizing impulse that most shaped that particular student's vision of archaeology or simply discomfort with the old term that led him to abandon it. In either case, within the next decade, that student, Friedrich Nietzsche, would select just this foundation stone of German philology as the target of his explosive charge.[129]

❧ CHAPTER 6

Material Culture in the Amateur Historical Associations of Early Nineteenth-Century Germany

First at Göttingen and then elsewhere, lecturers on historical methodology presented students with a variety of material evidence. But they were still presenting this material evidence as having only heuristic value, as a means to an end—verification—rather than an end in itself. Indeed, Gatterer himself made clear that the acquisition and mastery of these bodies of evidence would help engage readers in the "old-fashioned" subjects of history: politics, rulers, wars. Having mastered the *Hilfswissenschaften*, the newly minted historians would be able to ascertain the authenticity of the names, dates, and events on which scaffolding they would arrange their histories. It was only with Schlözer's new structural contextualism (*Statistik*) and the later emphasis on geography and ethnology that material evidence broke through to broader historical horizons.[1]

In addition to the historians, philologists also paid attention to objects. Making ancient texts fully intelligible meant identifying and explaining the objects referred to in those texts. Hence the close relationship between philology and antiquarianism. We might, then, view the birth of archaeology within philology faculties as the culmination of a long gestation period. Yet something changed between the old antiquarianism and the new archaeology, and it had to do with the tendency to reduce the scope of what one studied. Archaeology, in its infancy, was really antiquarianism applied to art objects. The early archaeologists didn't excavate new objects so much as categorize existing collections. The literature of "Archäologie der Kunst" provides us with a rich selection of early nineteenth-century historical thinking about how to work with objects. The very question of whether philologists ought to work with artifacts generated some theoretical discussion of how to make meaning from objects. If this literature doesn't quite yield a full-blown argument for history-through-things, it is because of the residual gravitational pull of the art object, always tugging scholars toward the history of ancient art as opposed to the history of ancient society.

The part of the spectrum left abandoned by the university professors was, however, taken up by amateurs: the local erudites, either *Gymnasium* teachers, or librarians, or archivists, who had been exposed to the *Hilfswissenschaften* in university but who had not gone on to become professors. Because the ancient Germans did not leave written remains and the German climate destroyed much of whatever else had survived, the national history that could be written from sources was almost entirely medieval and post-medieval; as common as relying on text was reference to coins, inscriptions, charters, seals, coats of arms, structures, sculptures, and costumes. German history, in short, was being written from the type of material remains studied up to that point in the *Hilfswissenschaften*.

The French Revolutionary invasions of Germany initiated a shift of perspective. The decline in the appeal of political history coincided with the decline of Germany's political fortunes—during the first decade of the nineteenth century Germany became for a time a mere geographical description. Under these circumstances, writing German history seemed like a form of resistance, and one that could also be conducted by those not bearing arms. But the kind of German history that now seemed worth writing was no longer that of rulers or wars but rather the life of the people. Schlözer's textbook on *Statistik*, published in 1804, made the point that *"le Peuple est tout."* (That his call to a form of national resistance was made in French is something of which historians of German national identity must make sense, as is the relationship between Napoleon's extinguishing of the Holy Roman Empire in 1806 and the rise of regional history.)

Beginning in the first decade of the nineteenth century as a patriotic gesture and continuing for another fifty years, a new genre of German history flourished. It was often conducted at the scale of the region or territory, not the state, under the auspices of local historical associations and published in their newly created journals. In these regional associations, what had previously been a means to an end—material sources—became an end in itself: the subject matter of German history. And because artifacts were now venerated as subjects rather than just objects, they began to be collected.

Local historical associations begat local museums. Objects that had been relegated to the footnote, the basement, or the cupboard now emerged as important documents of German culture.[2]

Something similar was happening at the same time in England and France. Mark Phillips and Stephen Bann have shown how historical knowledge informed a range of "para-historical" genres that matched the broadening readership of a newly commercial, or civil, society. The founding and proliferation of regional archaeological and antiquarian societies in the middle decades of the nineteenth century belongs to this same phenomenon. François Lissarrague and Alain Schnapp have argued that in France the destruction of monuments during the Revolution generated a salvage impulse that made historical monuments urgently important in a way they had not been even a generation earlier.[3] Destruction of the past in France, as in Germany, was a catalyst for the public prestige of archaeology (much as it had been in sixteenth-century Rome).[4] The first regional French archaeological societies included the Commission permanente des antiquités of the Académie des sciences, arts et belles-lettres de Dijon (1824), the Société des antiquaires de Normandie (1824), and the Société archéologique du Midi (1831).[5] The English looked across the Channel with admiration and some envy for the proliferation of this kind of provincial intellectual vigor.[6] Soon archaeological societies in both countries began to create collections related to local history.[7] As Philippa Levine has made clear for England and Charles-Olivier Carbonell for France, the emergence of local history was directly tied to the evolving status and rules of disciplinary history and archaeology. Stark documented this concurrent nineteenth-century development in his handbook on archaeology.[8] Tim Murray has argued that the persistence of these societies reflects the breadth of the antiquarian engagement with the past, going beyond the scope of what archaeology was licensing itself to study.[9] The role of these amateur associations as incubators of new thinking about how objects could tell stories is what we shall now explore, availing ourselves of the dense and highly self-conscious publications of the German historical associations.

History and Material Culture in the University: The State of the Question at the Beginning of the Nineteenth Century

Friedrich Rühs, one of August Boeckh's colleagues, was called to Berlin in 1810 to serve as ordinarius professor of history around the same time that Boeckh arrived. He had trained at Göttingen and had taught medieval history. Since most of the *Hilfswissenschaften* referred to medieval (and later) sources, he was responsible for their instruction. They were not popular. For comparison's sake, in the winter semester of 1811, B. G. Niebuhr had 200 students, Fichte and Savigny 90 and 46, respectively, Schleiermacher 17, and Rühs 5. (August Boeckh averaged 65 auditors over the twenty-six times he offered his survey course.) It is for this course that Rühs published in that year his *Plan for a Guide to Historical Study*.[10]

Before turning to Rühs's textbook, however, we ought to consider a memorandum he wrote in 1814 reviewing the proposal to establish what became the Monumenta Germaniae Historica (MGH), the vast and still-ongoing project to publish all of the sources of German history.[11] Rühs lent his voice to establishing a "Learned and Patriotic Society" with the goal of "Collection, Production, Checking and Explanation of all Relevant Sources." But, as Prussia had no antiquities, he proposed that its geographical scope be extended to the rest of Germany. And instead of limiting its chronological targets to ancient history and antiquities, he suggested concentrating on more recent German history. In other words, Rühs advocated a shift in prestige from "Archäologie und Antiquitätenkunde" to a German "Altertumskunde."[12]

The terminological sensitivity is fascinating. It marks the explicit extension of the concept of *antiquitates* to a non-classical people and a non-antique period (the German Middle Ages). This is the conceptual shift at the foundation of the local history associations (*Geschichts-* or *Historische Vereine*), and it makes sense that this proposal came at the planning stage of the first real association project, which became the MGH.[13] But just as interesting is that Rühs saw the articulation of a German *antiquitates* through the lens of the *Hilfswissenschaften* (their description took up 220 of the 275 pages of his *Plan*). Nothing could more clearly mark out their transformation from means to end.

The fourth section of Rühs's textbook is devoted to "Historical Research, or Criticism." These are terms generally associated with Ranke's achievement, but in Rühs they refer to monument studies, historical numismatics, epigraphy, medals, diplomatics, and literary studies—more or less the classic Göttingen curriculum. Rühs, however, rejected the notion of subordination that for Gatterer was implied by the term *Hilfswissenschaften*. Rather, for him, they referred to "only those disciplines, the content of which is not immediately historical in nature, but which are necessary and essential both for procuring materials and for properly evaluating them."[14] The crucial words are "not immediately historical"—for this opens up the possibility of their at some point becoming historical in the hands of a more imaginative researcher, one able to ask of them the right questions.

All monuments (*Denkmäler*), Rühs wrote, fell into two main classes. There was what remained from earlier times, which would include ruins of big cities like Palmyra, Persepolis, and Madjar-on-the-Volga. There were also "individual antiquities, machines, weapons, cut stones, coins (which differ from medals, which belong to the following class), etc." Rühs did not distinguish between classical ancients and non-classical moderns.[15] "To the historian," he continued, "all of these things are of equal value, and to him, the remains of the Indians, and Slavic and Germanic peoples are just as noteworthy as those of the Persians, Greeks, and Romans."[16]

Material evidence itself, however, was full of puzzles. For instance, sometimes one found objects from very distant peoples and places in unexpected locations, like Islamic coins on the shores of the North Sea—later noted by Pirenne in his great *Mohammed and Charlemagne*.[17] Coins might have been the most important material form of historical evidence, but when they turned up where they didn't belong, many of the attendant questions extended well beyond the remit of numismatics. The second class of monuments were those that were made as monuments; these therefore enabled later viewers to decode a whole belief structure. Examples included the Pyramids, or Stonehenge, before which, Rühs writes, the critic had to stand with modesty and impartiality. Monuments themselves, even if rightly ascribed to the correct person, often came from a later period—like the one to Kepler in Regensburg—and this was no different in antiquity, when great figures were often honored long after their demise.[18]

There was one further point to be made. Monuments needed inscriptions to be complete: "Mere monuments fulfill their goal only very imperfectly; only when an inscription gave voice to its purpose could one be certain that the monument could communicate why it was erected to future generations. Thus, writing has the most important and definitive consequences for the preservation of historical objects."[19] Here is the enduring textual bias of the historian and antiquarian on which Francis Haskell insisted upon long ago. Even Rühs, charged as he was with the curriculum for material culture—or as close as it would come to a curriculum for nearly two centuries—acknowledged that the literature on how to handle monuments-as-evidence was limited.[20] A historian's guide to the history of material evidence c. 1810 remained to be written.

Rühs identified narrative history with the historian's art ("historische Darstellung" and "historische Kunst") and the historian's work with arranging the material presented by historical research.[21] Herein, it would seem, lies an origin, if not *the* origin, of the distinction drawn by Roscher a generation later between the historical "artist" and "artisan." Rühs ends his

Plan, appropriately, with a sketch of the history of history writing in Europe, which included the Reformation-era turn to monuments and the Göttingen circle's work on chronology and geography. France, by contrast, had produced "admirable critics," who "if they often lost their way in *Micrologien*, still provided much foundational information, such as Ducange, Duchesne, Mabillon, etc."[22] Antiquaries remained those who did research, and historians remained those who wrote up the research.

Archaeology and Material Culture in the Associations

The Monumenta Germaniae Historica, whose establishment Rühs supported in 1814 and which came into being in in 1823 with the appointment of G. H. Pertz as editor, was the standard bearer for a movement that spread across Germany.[23] Over the next three decades there was an explosion of regional historical associations.[24] A Hessian bureaucrat in 1846 estimated that there were sixty archaeological and historical *Vereine* with about nine thousand members.[25] A bibliography of association scholarship published in 1845 extended to 654 close-packed pages of titles.[26] The founding of new associations restarted after 1848. A third wave of association-making occurred in the 1890s. It is in these associations, outside the hardening boundaries of discipline-driven university departments, that a fascinating mixture of art history, archaeology, philology, geography, and folklore was concocted. Most of all, models and language drawn from the study of the ancient world's culture were being adapted for the study of the more recent past.

In this bibliography we can chart the relationship between using objects as evidence and asking new kinds of historical questions. The associations were asking new questions and so they had to find new kinds of sources with which to answer them. We can also observe the connection between the old but still living antiquarianism, the *historische Hilfswissenschaften*, and the new history. In the section of the bibliography devoted to "History and its *Hilfswissenschaften*" we find, in addition to a list of publications, a lengthy review of contributions in the specific category of "Archaeology-Ethnography-Statistik." In this chapter we find titles on subjects such as population, education, clothing, dwellings, baths, tools, food, festivals, tournaments, funerals, trade, seafaring, and the like.[27] This is Spon's *Angeiographia* expanded, or Schlözer's *Statistik* read backwards, or Wolf's *Altertumswissenschaft* extended.

An example of modeling contemporary history on *antiquitates* is provided by Friedrich David Gräter (1768–1830), collector, sometime Norse philologist, journal publisher and correspondent of Jacob Grimm. In his journal he

discussed different kinds of evidence. "Antiquities" he subdivided into religious, political, military, and private *Altertümer*, which last category included
dwellings, food and drink, clothing, work, public festivals, marriage, and
family.[28] In this same hothouse world of neo-humanism, Christian August
Vulpius, a Weimar librarian and brother-in-law of Goethe, explained in 1811
in the first number of a journal that he edited that an interest in all these
daily details was needed if one wished to bring back "the life of the past with
its forms and mix of colors." In the anonymous "Plan and Announcement
of this Journal," Vulpius identified five focal points for study: (1) "Special
customs and uses of our past, courts and community," (2) the same for other
peoples, (3) superstitions and mysteries, (4) character sketches of important
individuals, and (5) marvels.[29]

If interest in capturing a broader spectrum of the life of the people helped
encourage a new recourse to the old model of *antiquitates*, so too did a conviction that the land or region helped shape its population. Let us take the
example of Westphalia. Paul Wigand's "Plan of the Society for the History
and Antiquities of Westphalia" of May 25, 1819, and again of January 1820,
adopted the perspective of a German *antiquitates* for study of this frontier
land.[30] As he wrote, "We will collect antiquities of all kinds and dedicate
special effort to researching the life and character of the people, their civic
economy and institutions, their private economy, architecture, and utensils
for land, home, and labor, which often bear the traces of a Germanic type
and origin even today."[31] This cultural geographic perspective on the Rhineland was still alive enough half a century later to be revived by Karl Lamprecht, as we have already seen.[32]

It was in the regional historical associations that these twin concerns, daily
life and the region—each in fact a different side of what it meant to study
a people's formation *in situ*—came together. In 1818, for example, Johann
Gustav Gottlieb Büsching (1783–1829), royal archivist and then professor of
archaeology at Breslau, began to build a collection of Silesian antiquities for
local but also "scientific value." In his *Summary of German Antiquities Studies*
he emphasized the importance of describing the situation of the finds as they
appeared in the ground: "For there to be any clarity in these studies, I needed
to create a structure [*Fachwerk*] that allowed each and every discovery to have
its place; in which every relationship was, to the greatest extent possible,
observed and weighed."[33]

Büsching divided his essay into two parts, the first organized by geography and population and including forms of social organization, law, religious
worship, domestic life, art, and knowledge. The second section focused on

funerary rites, graves, and grave goods, organized by type as well as by material. All these, and how they changed, could be documented through archaeology.[34] More poetically, Büsching looked at early German history and observed, "It is not solely the conflicts between kings, battles and wars that give us our history; and they almost never account for a people's true and actual history; they are merely the bloody veil that until recently concealed the actual lives and activities of people, a veil behind which, in quiet solitude away from this deafening din, far from the clattering of war that deafens the observer standing behind the veil, the true lives and inner history of peoples unfold, hidden from us."[35] The explicit repudiation of the political dimension and its presentation as a "veil" concealing the real history, which concerns the lives of ordinary people, is offered matter-of-factly but marks a decisive turn.

There was a dramatic increase in the volume and sophistication of the discussion of German antiquities in the late 1820s. In fact, it parallels that of the archaeological discourse we have just examined. In 1827 Ernst Hermann Joseph Münch (1798–1841), professor of the *historische Hilfsfwissenschaften* at the University of Freiburg and later royal librarian at The Hague, addressed head-on the meaning of a German *antiquitates*. His outline form, like Büsching's, identified its content with the world that people made for themselves. The chief objects of this German *antiquitates* were "geography, statistics, political and domestic organization, the religious and cultural history of Germania in the most ancient times, and of the German people in the Middle Ages, including the monuments that comprehend these periods." For him, "Altertümer" ended with the Crusades.[36] Sources for this type of work included ancient literature, German literature, and archaeology.[37] From these he made observations about their "fundamental character" and "virtues," their "civil society," "military organization," "crafts," "trade," "art," "science," "religion," and "private law."[38]

One of the most important—and telling—documents of this turn to the material is a prize competition in "German and Nordic Antiquities" announced in the periodical *German Antiquities* for the year 1827.[39] The question had been posed initially by the Academy of Sciences (Historical-Philological Class) of Göttingen for the year 1823. The subject was old German tumuli, and the deadline for submission was December 6, 1826. When no one responded, the Thuringian-Saxon Association for the Study of National Antiquities stepped in to fund the prize and extended the deadline.

The original question asked for an "overview" of what was already known of these graves, a "comparative description" of them, and a proposal for how this information could be applied to the study of other ancient peoples.[40]

The hope was to stimulate work on the prehistory of the far north. The gaps in the written record were so great, and the extant record itself so imperfect, that there could be no hope of reconstruction from texts alone. The physical remains of Germanic, as of Scandinavian, antiquity had to do the talking.[41] The elaboration of possible lines of inquiry and the resources appropriate to resolving them offer us a very clear sense of how sophisticated was the understanding of the sources, especially material ones, needed to study culture historically. These research foci included (1) linguistics, (2) what we might term social history, (3) history through monuments, (4) literary and musical monuments, (5) art and architecture, (6) agriculture, and (7) manners of the people.[42]

Karl Preusker (1786–1871), founder of the first public library in Germany and a serious amateur archaeologist, may have been the most incisive exponent of this concept of a modern *antiquitates*.[43] German antiquities, Preusker wrote in 1828, had been little studied, rarely admitted to the cabinets of collectors, and sparsely represented in scholarly bibliographies. It was only "the important changes in recent times in political and spiritual respects"—again the French Revolution and its after-effects—that had elevated its status.[44] His published works from the late 1820s and 1830s focused attention on prehistoric Germanic remains. He also collected what he wrote about, and seven hundred pieces were left as a bequest to the antiquities collection at Dresden in 1853.[45] Toward the end of his career he characterized his work as "cultural history," as displaying a "historical-antiquarian tendency," and as having "cultural historical results."[46]

In an address to the Society of Sciences of Görlitz in 1829, Preusker analyzed the various contemporary meanings of *Altertumskunde* and their implications. History, he began, placed its objects in a sequence ("in zusammenhängender Reihenfolge"), while *Altertumskunde* closely examined each object of study in turn.[47] Yet, *Altertumskunde*, he acknowledged, meant many things to many people. At its most capacious, it referred to the comprehensive knowledge of early times, or of one particular people. Sometimes it focused on one age only, sometimes on a particular set of circumstances relevant to that people. Sometimes it focused on monuments and sometimes on visual arts in particular.[48] More narrowly, it referred to "knowledge of the institutions, offices, customs, and basic principles of the state's constitution and administration, the waging of war, the administration of justice, literature and languages, arts and commerce, and religious, moral, and domestic life and the geographic distribution of our ancestors, as shown by the surviving remains of literature, language, morals and customs, legends and myths, and names of persons or places."[49] And in its narrowest sense *Altertumskunde* meant "material remains from the hand of men, whether higher or lower art products, construction or art works of all sorts, coins, costume, tools and instruments in every form and measure."[50]

Preusker remarks that *historian* and *antiquary* were used interchangeably, sometimes with confusing consequences. Often answers were sought from historical narration that could only come from research (*Alterthumsforschung*). Here Preusker insists on a distinction that eluded Gatterer and Schlözer, identifying the research component with the antiquarian. Drawing together the work of researcher and writer did not mean overlooking their specific differences, however.[51] The wide scope of *antiquitates* led to the subdivision and development of particular parts of it as "doctrines" or disciplines or fields. Preusker offers, matter-of-factly, that these material-based carvings-up of the antiquaries' field defined the various *"historische Hilfswissenschaften."*[52] They included "diplomatics," which he defined as the study of medieval sources, numismatics, epigraphy, and mythology, this last, in turn, including knowledge of religious teachings, ethics, and the practice of paganism.

But just as Preusker thought about the boundary between history and antiquarianism, he also distinguished these from "actual antiquities or archaeology" ("eigentliche Altherthümerkunde oder Archäologie").[53] This specifically referred to "knowledge of the remains of ancient literature and art and indeed architecture, images, painting, stone and stamp-cutting art." Thus far, Preusker's categories coincided with that of "Archäologie der Kunst." But he went on to note that tools, weapons, and costumery had been ignored up to now "because they lacked high artistic value."[54] In short, Preusker, like his exact contemporary K. O. Müller, saw archaeology as a form of historical inquiry in which objects provided access to a past culture. But unlike the university-based Müller, Preusker pushed to admit a broader range of surviving unaesthetic remains into the category of archaeology.

Just what kind of sources were there for studying national history and antiquities? Preusker divided them into four categories: (1) written or literary monuments, including books, manuscripts, diplomas and inscriptions; (2) images, architecture, and sculptural forms, of whatever material and on whatever surface; (3) products of nature in their "historical-antiquarian relation"; and (4) linguistic remains, including folk sayings, old dialects, toponyms and homonyms, religious ceremonies, popular festivals,

> and similar objects which the attentive observer will not leave aside, but will rather seek to preserve for posterity . . . as it is often the simple inscription, the most worn-away gravestone, an insignificant and

unsullied portion of a carving or coin, a half-ruined building, etc. that is of historical importance and will provide the historical researcher with welcome proof.[55]

Finally, showing his acuteness, Preusker observed that many of these objects were typically treated under the heading of "Fine Arts" even though in regard to their origins, goals, and representation they were much more closely related to "national antiquities" (vaterländische Alterthumskunde).[56] By the same token, Preusker noted, as he had earlier, that weapons, tools, and costumery were often ignored because in terms of aesthetic standards they "counted only as curiosities."[57] By flagging and then going beyond the problem of aesthetic origins, Preusker was moving toward a more coherent category of the archaeological than what was denoted by "Archäologie der Kunst."

In the second half of the volume, Preusker laid out possible types of objects that could be collected by the society for scientific purposes. His model was provided by the inventories in Büsching's Outline of Antiquities Studies and Münch's Foundations of German Antiquities Studies; the impact of his work on the study and collecting of regional German antiquities will be the subject of the next two chapters.[58] Preusker's description of proper excavation practice shows that he took seriously the entire continuum of the artifact's existence, from its place in the dirt to its place on the study table to its place in the display cabinet.[59] Even the broken and the seemingly worthless had to be collected, "because only the scientific expert can distinguish what is interesting and worthy of being saved."[60]

A few years later, Preusker returned to the subject of the nontextual sources for a modern antiquitates. "To the researcher into German history," he wrote in the first issue of a new journal devoted to the history of Germanic peoples, "the actual scientific sources, documents and other textual monuments of earlier times stand still higher. . . ." The artistic monument, Preusker argued—in the spirit of Ligorio and Winckelmann—was one of these authentic sources.[61] And, in this context, he again affirmed the connection between anthropology and antiquarianism, speaking of a Statistik and a "folklore of spirit and manners" for living peoples that paralleled Alterthumskunde for dead ones.[62]

The full measure of Preusker's innovations can be grasped by even the briefest of comparisons with Christian Jürgensen Thomsen—director of the National Museum in Copenhagen from 1816 to 1865. His Guide to Northern Antiquities Studies (1836, German translation 1837), published as a guidebook to the museum, has been described as one of the two "most important archaeological works produced in the first half of the nineteenth century."[63] Thomsen began with the question of evidence and then turned to compare Icelandic and classical history.[64] Dumb monuments, Thomsen thought, gave a more living image than the words of ancient writers.[65] He lamented how much had already been lost, even in the last century, despite the work of the antiquaries Worm and Bure, Resen and Rudbeck.[66] Thomsen then proceeded from graves and stones through the various sorts of things that survived, including scripts and their evolution in the Middle Ages and the Byzantine and Abbasid coins that were found in the Baltic region.[67]

The Danish "breakthrough" was in the development of a dating scheme for prehistory, the famous stone, bronze, and iron ages by which everything has since been dated. But when we reflect that in Copenhagen by 1850 there was a Museum of Northern Antiquities, a Cabinet for American Antiquities, an Ethnographical Cabinet and an Antique Cabinet, we perceive the breadth of the Danish turn to material evidence. Why did this occur there? J. J. A. Worsaae, Thomsen's successor at the National Museum, speaking to the Royal Irish Academy in 1846, explained it in terms of the upheaval of the French Revolution. Like Schlözer, he believed that "there awakened in the nations themselves a deeper interest in their own history, language and nationality . . . as a time from the contemplation of which their spirit of nationality might gain support, and in whose memories they found the hope of a new and equally glorious era again."[68]

It was in the context of national, not classical, antiquities that in France, too, arguments were first made clearly for the value of the non-aesthetic object. In 1861, Alexandre Bertrand (1820–1902), founding director of the Musée d'Archéologie Nationale in Saint-Germain-en-Laye, wrote that that crudest pot or knife was a kind of "depot of precious documentation on the manners and customs of primitive peoples."[69]

The literature produced by and around the historical associations devoted much more attention to things than did historians of the period, and they talked much more about the nature of these sources as well. But behind this scientific purpose lay also an older relationship to things, signaled in the epigram selected by Christoph von Rommel (1781–1859), a historian who trained at Göttingen before teaching in the Ukraine and then at Marburg, to introduce "On the Sources and Supporting Materials of Hessian History" (1837). It is none other than the lines from Ovid's *Metamorphoses* (XV.234–38), the "Tempus Edax Rerum" of Posthumus's great painting, that were so closely linked with the practice of antiquarianism:

Devouring time and you envious age
Destroy all, and the grinding teeth of time

Slowly consume everything.
Even what we call the elements do not endure.[70]

Rommel was a member of antiquarian societies at Cassel, Darmstadt, Nuremberg, Frankfurt, and Leipzig as well as the Moscow society of naturalists. Like Leibniz a century earlier and like so many of his own contemporaries, Rommel insisted that any local history had to emerge from the nature and formation of the land: "The influence that land and soil, that nature and the formation of countries, exercise upon their inhabitants is a physical and moral interplay that . . . justifies linking the most ancient history of a country with natural history."[71]

But Rommel, also typically for this group, was not a geologist, and his interest in landscape was directly linked to his interest in what humans did to the landscape. Whether one called it "cultural history," as Rommel did, or "cultural geography," as we might today, the function was the same: "In which reciprocal interaction of not only mining and road development, but also agriculture, farming, and industry in general with our mountains, our masses of stone stood and stands—we leave that to the geologists, who are also familiar with our cultural history."[72] For example, referring to the local importance of basalt, Rommel let it be known that "the influence of this formation on road development, the building of the oldest forts, and other cultural icons certainly deserves special attention."[73]

One of the most striking things about Rommel's formulations is how often his picture of the goal of association practice is expressed in terms of "cultural history," a term largely absent in the first generation of association historians (that is, roughly 1800 to 1825). It is indeed precisely in the 1830s and 1840s that *Kulturgeschichte* emerges as a theme at work in discussions of studying the national past in a more inclusive form. The content of this new *Kulturgeschichte* is the old *antiquitates*: customs, laws, clothing, construction techniques, and the like. Some sources survived from the recent past, almost none from much earlier. In explaining what was difficult to find, Rommel ended up providing an ideal repertory of the sorts of evidence he felt were important. "Many customs of the fifteenth and sixteenth centuries, village celebrations, and changes in traditional dress have been recorded by our annalists. It seems almost too late to attempt to recover a characteristic description of the particular archaic clothing (*alterthümlichen Kleidung*), way of life, games, and architecture of our countrymen. . . ."[74]

By the 1840s it was possible to begin reflecting on a historical circle nearly closed. Karl Wilhelmi (1786–1857) was a minister based in Baden who wrote on prehistoric finds in Germany. In a lecture he delivered at the first General

Assembly of the Antiquities Society of the Duchy of Baden, he began by noting that the German response to Napoleon lay in seeking the origins of the nation in the deepest possible past. That this required no special justification suggests that the link between the French Revolution and the turn to study of the "Nation" was already taken for granted.[75] Wilhelmi then provided a roll call of foundings of historical associations, beginning in 1818 in Thuringia and continuing up through 1844. He noted also the existence of other "historical and antiquarian" societies in Berlin, Moravia, Brno, Leiden, and so on.[76]

What kinds of things were there to find? Relevant materials included metal objects, grave goods, images, jewelry, wood, glass, stone, weapons, words, place names, and even written texts.[77] Wilhelmi encouraged civil servants, builders, and engineers to make the population attentive to things so that found objects would not be discarded or destroyed. He also suggested some organizing principles for these discoveries. He wanted to know when things were found, to depict them as they were found in the ground, and to map out the finds of others.[78]

Finally, and following from this last point, Wilhelmi urged that what was found together in the ground be kept together in collections. They could of course be organized by type of object, but Wilhelmi preferred the culture group instead: "[Organizing by type] would be most interesting in terms of the comparison of individual objects, but would provide no insight into the overall culture of a given group."[79] Insofar as Wilhelmi was aware that *telos* inevitably shaped display, his insistence on the "total cultural conditions" of a people led him to non-typological modes of display. There would be a long after-life of this idea, most famously involving the German-trained Franz Boas at the American Museum of Natural History in New York.[80]

Another reflection on the workings of the historical association movement was produced two years later by J. F. Knapp in the *Archive for Hessian History and Antiquities Studies* (1846). The usual admonition to preserve what had survived from the destruction of the past was quickly followed by a defense of association history as an archival and source-based practice.[81] "It has also been said," he wrote, "that the activity of the associations is being lost in dilettantism and the hoarding of curiosities."[82] Knapp deployed the obvious answer: One could never know what trivial-seeming piece of evidence might contain the answer to the really big question. Moreover, and this was extremely perceptive, he noted that the determination of what was interesting (or trivial) was always positional. From the point of view of national politics, artifacts might be useless. "Fragments, rings, and weapons retrieved from graves may be of little or no worth to the researcher in the faculty of political history; but," Knapp continued, "someone researching customs, art, taste, and ancient metallurgy would gladly devote his full attention to such objects."[83] The associations represented the survival of curiosity in an age of the primacy of politics. Nevertheless, as Bonnie Effros has shown, looking across the Rhine, even prehistoric cultural goods could be recruited to national political debates.[84]

Knapp observed that association scholarship had its own style. It lined up with the auxiliary sciences but also with antiquarianism: "The nature of the organism tends to lead them there through local and other special histories, through discussion of individual historical events, antiquarian discoveries, genealogical objects, myths and legends, legal customs, and other monographs."[85] He contrasted this breadth with the narrowness of a pure, politically defined notion of "history."[86] Knapp presented *Altertumswissenschaft* as the model: "Classic antiquarian studies involve the system of disciplines that belong to the understanding of the works surviving from the two classical nations, Greece and Rome, and give us a clear knowledge of their achievements on various levels, including the sciences, and the arts."[87]

The range of antiquarian research projects that the historical associations were conducting across Germany did, however, make it necessary to begin thinking about a central organ for assembling information and *realia*. Knapp's plea for centralization is almost overwhelmed by the centrifugal quality of the evidence that organ or institution was to collect:

> The searching out of Germanic and Celtic antiquities, finding the old sites of the religious cults of the Germanic tribes, the tracing of Roman roads, fortifications and settlements, the study of old building construction, district, diocese, dominion and jurisdictional borders, legal customs, myths and legends; the collection of official documents regarding countries and areas that are now distinct, as well as the lineages of people who settled in various areas and many other items with which the associations were concerning themselves, extend into the sphere of several of these associations, and can be discussed by individual associations only in unsatisfactory fragments.[88]

Any such central association would have the task of "searching for and shedding light on everything of antiquarian and historical [*antiquarisch und historisch*] interest in the Fatherland, and doing it justice to some degree."[89] A journal to publish this information would, he thought, be very desirable. In all this we can hear the program developed at the very same time by Hans von und zu Aufseß that would be realized at the Nuremberg museum he would found in the next decade (see chapter 8).

The "Association for Hessian History" provided a platform for a contribution to this conversation. J. F. Lange's "Sketch of a Historical-Artistic Representation of Hessian Art Monuments" (dated 1844 but published in 1847) went one step further in separating history-politics from antiquarianism-culture. He argued that political history was actually "external" to the life of the people, while the study of speech and literature, customs and art, agriculture and commerce took one into its very core.[90]

Art objects provided crucial evidence for this domain of experience. Works of art, he argued, were "created from the depths of a culture's soul and embodied in its external material and technical means, springing from the unique thrust of thought of an age, from its moral and commercial makeup, from the enormity of its productive power in various periods following from the oppressed or freely developing spirit of the people."[91] We could read this as trying to reconcile Winckelmann the antiquarian with Winckelmann the rhapsode: favoring the art object as the privileged way into the soul of past people, but always remaining committed to the scholarship that collected and studied the artifacts.

When defining the kind of skills required for gaining access to the soul of the past through its remains, Lange pointed directly at the auxiliary sciences. They were no longer subordinated to political history but were treated as evidence in their own right. It was in this way that a new kind of art history of the German Middle Ages could emerge, in which art objects could function as sources in the same way that diplomatics or paleography had become sources for the association scholars, and not mere prooftexts.[92] Lange went on to provide a list of the kinds of material sources that could count as evidence in an art historian's examination of the inner life of the medieval Germans. The first group was church-related: buildings, churches, chapels, cloisters, with all of their ornamentation and objects pledged for divine service, including wall hangings, curtains, altars, tabernacles, shrines for relics, christening stones, church pitchers, choir stools. The second was military: Roman roads, walls, fortresses, guardhouses, municipal fortifications, towers, and watchtowers. The third included civic things such as town halls and public rooms, wells, and wooden dwellings. He stressed that it was important to survey these objects immediately because the peacetime building boom had imperiled a great many of them. The fourth class included small private things, engravings and stone monuments, statues and sculptures of all kinds, paintings and drawings, machines and weapons, jewelry and decorative items. Again we see how Biondo's public, private, military, and sacred antiquities provided a foundation for the later development of material culture studies.[93]

With Preusker, Knapp, and Lange, then, we can survey the entire trajectory of the shift from the seventeenth to the nineteenth century at issue: from antiquarian scholarship, through the *Hilfswissenschaften*, to the historical associations and on to the founding of a cultural-historical museum. In the chapters that follow we will examine in greater detail the state of cultural history in the 1840s in and out of the university and the museum. In the work of Gustav Friedrich Klemm, the most important of the cultural historians of the 1840s and 1850s, we see the way in which antiquarian and ethnological visions could together inform a new kind of historical vision. In the work of Hans von und zu Aufseß, founder of the Germanisches Nationalmuseum, these issues are formally synthesized into a new institutional model. These chapters could be viewed as a contribution to the history of cultural history before Burckhardt or to the process of seeing Burckhardt in context.

CHAPTER 7

Gustav Klemm, Cultural History, and *Kulturwissenschaft*

If we stepped back from the body of historical scholarship produced in the regional associations, we might regard it as the historical study of medieval and early modern German culture with an emphasis on everyday life. Many of those active in the associations began to write books with the words *cultural history* in the title.[1] The sense of peoplehood inspired by the late revolution in France had created a powerful argument for the viability of historical accounts not oriented around great events or great lives. Indeed, their experience of the fragility of the political led Germans, especially, to devote scholarly energies to the study of culture instead. For the reformers of the 1840s, writing cultural history was politics by other means: an argument for the role of Everyman (and even Everywoman) in history.

In the literature of the historical associations the content of the academic curriculum of the *Hilfswissenschaften* was transformed—liberated, really—to serve as the substance of a new material-based history of culture in Germany. "Cultural history" was the context in which "antiquarian" (*antiquarisch*) methods and the studies of antiquity (*Antiquitates; Altertumskunde; Altertumswissenschaft*) were brought to bear on present history.

In the concluding two chapters we will explore two different ways in which the study of material culture was presented as cultural history in Germany. We might better grasp the distinctiveness of this German story if we set it against the path taken in France.

When the historian Augustin Thierry complained about the state of French history writing, he singled out the "writers without imagination, who were unable to describe."[2] The conjunction of imagination and description follows directly from Gatterer's proposal that detailed research was necessary in order to create imaginative, attention-grabbing prose. This provides insight into how, in an age of a widening reading public, the new para-historical genres (fiction, memoir, and so on) could perpetuate *what* antiquaries did while creating a new *how*. We have already mentioned Mark Phillips's argument about the unfolding of this process in eighteenth- and early nineteenth-century England. We could add Michael Shanks's close examination of Sir Walter Scott's antiquarianism.[3] "Thick" descriptions may have been developed by antiquaries, but by the 1830s such texts were seen as the province of the prose writer. During this decade, Honoré de Balzac launched his *Comédie humaine*, a series of nearly a hundred novels and essays that self-consciously and programmatically described the society around him.

Like Aubin-Louis Millin a generation before, Balzac used the terms *antiquaire* and *archéologue* interchangeably, though he did so during the very years archaeology as a discipline was defining itself as a science based on "positive certitudes" rather than "mere curiosity."[4] His contemporaries were trying—haltingly—to define for themselves the nuances that separated the antiquary from the archaeologist. The former was in the process of being redescribed as a collector of objects, a person of taste and eye; the latter, their interpreter.[5] Balzac the novelist had an eye for *realia* as keen as any antiquary's and a commitment to interpretation to match any archaeologist's. Yet, at the same time, he insisted on the importance of imagination, speaking of his role as an "observateur-poète" who joined imagination to archaeology. Balzac hailed the French naturalist Georges Cuvier as "the greatest poet of our century" in *La Peau de chagrin* and saw his own time as "swiftly becoming antiquity."[6]

From Balzac, we can see the path stretching out in one direction to the imaginative works of observer-artists and in the other direction to the archaeologists of daily life. The novelists and poets we might describe as retaining the spirit of the antiquary but using different methods to prospect in different landscapes. Think of the chapters in *Moby Dick* devoted to cetology and the business of whaling. The archaeologists of daily life employed many of the antiquary's questions but put them to a different end. These would include people like Eduard Fuchs, an amateur historian of popular culture through caricature, but also a publisher of volumes on porcelain and Chinese roof ornaments who owes his immortality as the subject of one of

Benjamin's most brilliant essays.[7] These local, amateur historians were sometimes extremely interesting—and more willing to stretch the boundaries of
what university-based historians considered "history."[8]

The History of Culture in Early Nineteenth-Century Germany

Kulturgeschichte flourished in the 1830s and 1840s. There was "cultural history"
that was written in the 1780s but, as in so much else, the French Revolution
and the Napoleonic wars marked a caesura. On the other side of the divide
people felt that they occupied a changed world. In the decade before the revolution, Voltaire was for many, on both sides of the Rhine, the pioneering cultural historian. Investigating works produced in the later eighteenth century,
Jörn Garber was able to identify ninety-three titles related to the history of
culture (although not necessarily with the word *Culturgeschichte* or *Kulturgeschichte* in the title).[9] The focus on culture and history in the generation of
Johann Gottfried Herder, Christoph Meiners, and Johann Christoph Adelung
has been studied by Donald R. Kelley, Hans Schleier, and Michael Carhart,
among others.[10] But by the first decades of the nineteenth century, everything
had changed. The work of the historical associations was one part of this and
fed into a different kind of cultural history, one less preoccupied with using
facts to define the nature of mankind in the abstract and more focused on
people living at a particular time in a particular place.

One consistently puzzling aspect of cultural history in the nineteenth
century, and into the twentieth, has been the capaciousness of the category.
Encompassing both high culture and low, the popular and the elite, cultural
history has often seemed borderless and indefinite—leading even its admirers to "search" for it or to see it as a "problem."[11] The origin of this problem,
which at its core has to do with the ambivalence of the term *culture* itself, has
been convincingly explained by Istvan Hont in an unpublished paper devoted
to the seventeenth-century political thinker Samuel Pufendorf.

Hont's discovery was that for the Latinate authors of the late eighteenth
century who talked about "cultura," whether in Scotland or in Germany,
there existed a living semantic field with a plenitude of current uses of the
term, all of which could be traced back to the work of Pufendorf a century earlier. In his *De Officio Hominis et Civis juxta Legem Naturalem* (1682),
Pufendorf had offered a taxonomy of "cultura." There was *cultura animi*, or
"culture of the mind," which he defined as the development of judgment
and rationality. But there was also *cultura vitae*, or "culture of life," which
referred to the effortful human shaping of the world in its most general

sense. Anything that was the "specific product of human labor" could be described in terms of *cultura*. According to Hont, it was this latter category that Pufendorf connected to the "four stages" theory of cultural development, from hunter-gatherers to pastoralists to farmers and finally to industrial city-dwellers. But the ambivalence of those two different visions of culture was bred in the bone of language. Was cultural history about the attainments of "cultura animi" or "cultura vitae"? About the "arts and sciences" or about everyday life and material development? We are still asking these questions; in the nineteenth-century they were bound up with disciplinary and institutional legitimation as well.[12]

Wilhelm Wachsmuth, for example, was a classicist who shifted his focus to modernity as a result of the French Revolution. He began his career writing a textbook on method in the style of Rühs, also entitled *Plan of a Theory of History* (1820). Wachsmuth sought to advance the cause of studying everyday life in its concreteness from "within" the academy. Unlike Rühs, however, Wachsmuth was much more uncomfortable about linking the word *Wissenschaft* to the evidentiary sciences, which were "better called auxiliary, preliminary or elementary knowledge for historical research and art." Such "simple knowledge of materials" he considered but "a lowly servant."[13]

Despite this, Wachsmuth's *Plan* presented the subject matter of history as humanity in its full concreteness. And even though he was then emphasizing the role of the state as a focus of that concreteness, it was the inclusiveness that stood out.[14] Only a decade later, in his *History of European Manners* (1831), he had moved from the state to the *Volk* as the organizing principle, and therefore the object, of history. Yet Wachsmuth, alive to the fact that a historical approach to the life of the people had already been described as "ethnological" by scholars of the previous generation, such as Fabri, introduced a new distinction, reserving "history" for the study of those capable of acting independently of nature and ethnography for those who lived in nature as if by necessity. By this definition, the European peoples alone had "history."[15] Within that grouping, Wachsmuth's distinction between states and peoples framed the latter in terms of conditions and processes (*Zustände*), not events.[16] This was a very important distinction as it licensed history, at least insofar as it studied the masses, to return to the synchronic studies associated with antiquarianism while still being called history.

But if Wachsmuth is remembered at all today, it is for his *History of France in the Age of Revolution* (1840–1844 in 4 vols.), which Ranke praised and Marx read, in the latter case precisely because of Wachsmuth's commitment to studying the social.[17] By 1850, when Wachsmuth published the first volume of his *General Cultural History*, his evolution was complete. Politics was now viewed as an expression of culture and the universal, with humanity as a goal replacing the particularity of a single people. With it disappeared his prior distinction between ethnographic and historical peoples.[18] Addressing in a footnote the existing literature on cultural history, Wachsmuth placed Herodotus at the top of the list for his attention to the "manners of Peoples." Wachsmuth's turn had the effect of subordinating ethnology to cultural history as a kind of *Hilfswissenschaft*.[19] And while Wachsmuth rejected the idea of casting his history from a material perspective, he did suggest that it be wholly integrated into a narrative of progressive human development through chapter sections devoted to constitution, law and economy, state commerce, foreign affairs, war, family and education, crafts, trade, and seafaring. Beyond these, the "higher" culture was fulfilled through treatments of religion, learning, and art.[20] How the material and the spiritual dimensions were to be fit together in a single account Wachsmuth thought still puzzling, though he tried to do just this, using *Statistik* as the model.[21] In later volumes of his cultural history, as Wachsmuth's focus approached the present and information multiplied, the investigative units grew ever more detailed.[22]

The flowering of the historical study of culture in the 1830s and 1840s, likewise understood in terms of context rather than events, occurred outside of the university. First with Johann Georg August Wirth, *Fragments towards Cultural History* (1836) and then Georg Friedrich Kolb, *History of Mankind and Culture* (1843), Karl von Rotteck, *General History* (1843), Gustav Friedrich Klemm, *General Culture-History* (1843), Ernst Friedrich Apelt, *Periods of the History of Mankind* (1845), and Wilhelm Drumann, *Foundations of Cultural History* (1847). The editors of the *Zeitschrift für deutsche Kulturgeschichte* in 1856 gave 200 as the number of cultural historical publications between 1850 and 1855 alone.[23]

There is, as James Ryding and Heinrich Dilly have persuasively argued, a clear link between the political situation in Germany and the proliferation of cultural histories. Cultural history was a specimen of the *Vormärz*—the period of liberal anticipation that led up to the failed revolutions of March 1848.[24] Many of those who wrote cultural histories were liberals who acted out their political commitments in their writing. Kolb, for instance, was a journalist who became the mayor of Speyer; his *Neue Speyerer Zeitung* was closed down in 1853 and he and his family were forced to flee to Switzerland, where they were obliged to remain for six years. Karl Biedermann was a journalist and vice president of the National Assembly as well as a professor at Leipzig. He was a true liberal revolutionary, a status that led to his losing his professorship in 1853. He supported himself as a newspaper editor in Weimar while he founded the Association for German Cultural History in 1857. Wachsmuth himself, on the first page of the preface to his *General Cultural History* of 1850, explicitly states that his own turn to cultural history was a search for progress in the face of the frustrations and dead ends of politics. "In it," he wrote, "we find again the lofty mission of humanity."[25]

Like the historians of the generation of 1968, those of 1848 emphasized study of the life of the people as a form of political action. Just as those who supported the politics of the nation (Prussia, that is) saw history as being about politics, those who rejected this politics rejected also the primacy of politics in writing the history of the nation. Instead, economy, society, and lifestyle became central. In 1856, a journal devoted to just this part of the historical spectrum sprang into being. We will discuss the *Zeitschrift für deutsche Kulturgeschichte* in greater detail in the next chapter. Its editors argued that "'cultural history' strives to present a picture of the development of all the other forces of a people with the exception of the political."[26] The curiosities that once upon a time could not be accommodated into the schema of political history now served to tell the story of those left out of that history. This was cultural history in fighting mode, truly the "Oppositionswissenschaft" of Thomas Nipperdey's turn of phrase.[27]

Gustav Friedrich Klemm

In this generation of cultural historians, Gustav Friedrich Klemm was the most important, and he remains, a century and a half later, the most interesting. His *General Cultural History* (1843–1852, 10 vols.) and *General Cultural-Science* (1855, 2 vols.) are significant works of scholarship. Born a generation after Wachsmuth, he did not have to unlearn the primacy of the political and began at more or less the place that Wachsmuth reached only at the end of his life. Reviews in the cultural historical literature published in the 1870s were admiring of the breadth of his research but sometimes also uncomfortable with his unabashedly ethnological perspective.[28] Braudel, a century later, thought enough of him to suggest that Burckhardt's cultural history was best understood alongside of Klemm's.[29] But by and large he has not been much studied. Before 2012, the most recent treatment tried to present him as a prophet of Nazi racial theories.[30]

Most of what is known about him is what he himself tells us. There is an autobiographical account in the introduction to his *Allgemeine Culturwissenschaft*. Klemm explains that his intellectual awakening was caused by the sight of the different armies passing back and forth through his hometown of Chemnitz during the Napoleonic invasions, with their different faces, different weapons, different gear, and different uniforms. Klemm fell in love with

Figure 12   Gustav Friedrich Klemm, oil on canvas portrait by Karl Gottlieb Rolle (1814–1862).

Greek and Latin at the local *Gymnasium*, while the tercentenary celebrations of Luther in 1817 re-focused his attention on to the German Middle Ages.[31] He read Herder and Voltaire and it was because of them that he took for himself the "goal of studying human conditions in family, state, war, religion, science and art." He was especially inspired by Friedrich Adolf Ebert's *Bildung des Bibliothekars* (1820). Klemm's intellectual maturity began by excerpting the historians and travel writers of the Middle Ages, after which he turned from books to things. During his school vacations he wandered through Saxony and Thuringia with a sketchbook, drawing weapons, tools, buildings, and tomb-stones. With help from "Montfaucon and Moller," when necessary, he turned his own drawings into the basis of "a collection of antiquarian illustrations." By 1825, the year he obtained his doctorate, his collection was already giv-ing him a general sense of the history of human conditions.[32] He also began excavating.

In the summer of 1830 Klemm worked in Leipzig with the famed natural-ist Wilhelm Gottlieb Tilesius (1769–1857)—and then returned to the archae-ology of old German monuments, comparing them just as an early modern antiquarian would have.[33] By the end of the year he had a position at the Royal Library in Dresden as second secretary. He went to Nuremberg to take up the job as editor of the *Friedens- und Kriegs-Courier*, a local newspaper. But the very next year he was appointed to a position in the Royal Porcelain Collection in Dresden and charged with reorganizing the holdings.[34] In 1834, while holding the post of "Inspector," Klemm published a guide to the collection on the occasion of its reinstallation.[35] He began, however, not with its contents, nor with its history, but with a brief account of porcelain and vase-making from antiquity up to the present.[36] He focused on porcelain: its origins in China and its arrival in Europe.[37] Only after all the history did he offer a room-by-room tour of the collection.

We have Klemm's reports of his excavations around Saxony in these years. While his techniques seem to have as much in common with those of the opportunists as with those of the scientists—cutting trenches with-out measuring them, cutting them with little logic—the practice taught him something: Excavation was only a means to an end. To get to knowledge, artifacts needed to be collected in great number and published. Only then could comparison do its work. "Consequently," he wrote in his *Handbook of German Antiquities* (1836), "collections should be regarded as the proper focus of archaeology."[38]

And not only archaeology. The *Handbook of German Antiquities* marks that moment when Klemm found his *métier*. The title page identifies him as the Royal Saxon Librarian—he seems to have replaced Ebert—and Inspector of the Royal Saxon Porcelain Collection. He was also secretary of the Royal Saxon Antiquarian Association from 1835, rising to vice-director and then to director (1855–1863). Just as interesting are Klemm's memberships in four-teen other regional historical associations, for they tie him into the wider world we examined in the preceding chapter.[39] More important, Klemm also links himself personally to some of the key figures who placed the historical associations at the crossroads of the *Hilfswissenschaften* and cultural history: Busching and Preusker.

This points us to the Dresden context. For Karl Preusker, whose thinking about German antiquities and archaeology was very close to Klemm's, lived only nineteen miles from Dresden and eventually donated his collection of finds to the city. Forty-seven letters from Klemm to Preusker survive in the Saxon state library, documenting a close intellectual conversation.[40] When Klemm first arrived, his boss at the library was none other than his intellectual hero Friedrich Adolf Ebert. Some correspondence between them is also preserved.[41] Another hero of the age then in Dresden was K. A. Böttiger, Goethe's collaborator on the art and archaeology journal *Amalthea*. Around 1800 he had left Weimar for Dresden, where he developed his thinking about the meaning of archaeology. We can easily imagine Böttiger and Klemm talking across the generations about objects and how to study them. Theirs is one of the fascinating unexplored conjunctions in the early entangled history of archaeology and anthropology.[42] Finally, one of the younger members of Klemm's Dresden circle, if not exactly an antiquary, was Gottfried Semper.[43] Klemm was an important local resource for Semper's interest in anthropology. They were members of the same local antiquarian society after 1837. However, that Semper did not refer to Klemm in print when discussing prehistoric objects in his book on *Style in the Technical and Tectonic Arts* and only once altogether, citing Klemm's *Cultural History* as a reference work on the Pacific islanders, suggests that their relationship was not close.[44]

In the preface to his *Handbook*, Klemm explained that in his "antiquarian studies" he had been looking for source material on "the most ancient cultural history" of Germany.[45] The influence of Busching and Preusker is evident already in the table of contents, which moves from "The land and its products" to "The physical and moral situation of the Germans" to "Ways of living," "Life course and customs," "Knowledge and achievements," Public life in peacetime," "War stuffs," and "Worship."[46]

With his next publication the following year, Klemm distinguished himself. *Towards a History of Collections of Art and Science in Germany* is one of the pioneering treatises in the history of early modern learned collecting—or would be were it better known. It could have been the authoritative history of early modern collections that Julius von Schlosser's *The Cabinets of Art and Curiosity of the Late Renaissance: A Contribution to the History of Collecting* (1908) eventually was. It offers a history that ranges from the church libraries and collections of the Middle Ages through the founding of museums in the eighteenth century. The main thrust of the argument about the early modern cabinets establishes a link between the study of antiquities and the study of nature. Travel plays a central role here. Klemm emphasized the triangular relationship linking *antiquitates*, natural history, and ethnography.

Ole Worm's *Musaeum Wormianum* (1653) represented for Klemm, as it does still for historians of collecting, the moment when a mature literature on collecting the man-made met a mature reflection on the study and collection of nature. Ole Worm was a doctor as well as a naturalist and also a pioneering archaeologist and anthropologist (his queries about life and literature on Iceland remain a classic).[47] The *Musaeum* represents the fruit of this comprehensive vision. But its frontispiece has made it famous: a stupendous vision of a chamber in which naturalia and artificialia are mingled together, not indiscriminately but with an order that cuts across the obvious differences to display deeper convergences. (The power of the image still inspires: There is a full-scale reconstruction of the frontispiece in the Danish National Library by Rosamund Purcell, who has also recreated it in Santa Monica and Cambridge, Massachusetts.)[48] More to the point, Worm's principle of inclusiveness puts the human inside the natural, seeing human history as part of nature's history. Klemm took this as the organizing principle of his *General Cultural History* and then devoted a long passage to ekphrasis of Worm's frontispiece.[49]

Klemm focuses on the princely *Wunderkammern*, beginning with that of Augustus I of Saxony (1553–1586) in Dresden. The Saxon collection, he notes, contained antiquities, naturalia, and later also ethnographic materials, much of which was captured from the Turkish camp around Vienna in 1683. Augustus II the Strong (1670–1733) remodeled the Grünes Gewolbe and built the Zwinger to house his collections. Klemm, like the historian of scholarship that he was, contrasts the more "practical" Saxon collection with Habsburg exotica lodged at Schloss Ambras—whose room-by-room disposition he also provided.[50]

Klemm knew the literature on the history of collecting, and not just retrospectively through compilations such as Caspar Friedrich Neickel's famed *Museographia* (1727). Klemm devoted much attention to Samuel Quiccheberg's description of Duke Albert of Bavaria's collection at Landshut and Munich, and to Adam Olearius's trip to Persia. He also surveyed sixteenth-century private collections in Augsburg and Nuremburg and devoted significant space to Friedrich Lorenz Hoffmann in Halle, whose Latin catalogue was published in 1625 and contained a great deal of foreign ethnographic material.[51] He saw the Dutch opening of the East as a key moment in the history of cabinets.

In Klemm's survey, the eighteenth century marked the great leap forward in museum organization and content, especially in the natural sciences. Only then was the unsystematized disorder of Worm or Hoffmann finally brought under control. Klemm was deeply committed to the details of this history: He even provided the opening hours for the Berlin Museum, as if recognizing that access—and sensitivity to the importance of access—denoted a wholly changed attitude to the purpose of collecting and its audience. While natural science collections had existed in the sixteenth century, it was only from the beginning of the eighteenth that there was more emphasis on technological and ethnographic materials. Klemm ends his remarkable survey with gardens and zoological collections broken down by type: fish, birds, and so on.[52]

Turning from the history of collections to their taxonomy, Klemm broadened out to include collections for "history and folklore." In this section his keywords, following the turn initiated by Schlözer, are "history, antiquities, and ethnography." The oldest collections, he wrote, placed tools and scientific instruments alongside natural, artistic, and historical materials. They were, in effect, "technological" collections in the sense employed by Leroi-Gourhan in the twentieth century, of objects understood through their use.[53] Art collections, by contrast, tended to reside in churches, then in princely residences, and finally, by the eighteenth century, in galleries and museums. These, in turn, often became art academies. The book concludes with an overview of the Dresden collections of which Klemm himself was caretaker.[54]

While writing this book, Klemm was selected as tutor to accompany the Saxon heir on his Italian trip in 1838. As with Johann Jacob Bachofen of Basel a few years later, travel to Italy would trigger in Klemm an explicit shift (though not a break) from antiquarianism to cultural history and from archaeology to ethnology. A few months after completing his travels, Klemm had outlined "the plan of a Cultural History and a Cultural Science."[55] It was at this point that he began to organize his own collection. He purchased South Sea materials, followed by objects from Africa and the Arctic, and worked diligently on their disposition.[56] By 1840 this collection numbered 1,257 objects and was distributed through five large rooms sorted into thirteen sections by function: tools and weapons, jewelry, clothing, vessels, dwellings and furniture, writing materials and writing, coins, weights and measures, vehicles, musical instruments, the sacred, the arts, and the history of writing. The objects came from all over the globe and continued coming: 700 were from Africa, 500 America, 600 Russia, 350 Arctic, 600 the Far East, 600 the Near East, 500 Greco-Roman, 400 early German, and 1,200 from medieval Europe.[57] Klemm's collection reflected an object-based vision of knowledge-making: "As in mineralogy, zoology, botany, archaeology, numismatics and paleography, so too in history, direct perception of objects is the best aid to correct understanding."[58]

In 1841 the first volume of that *The General Cultural History of Mankind* was ready for the press. Klemm's introduction to the project took the form of the prehistory to what he was calling "Cultural History." While beginning, conventionally enough, with the Greeks and Romans, his story kicked off with a long discussion of the revival of the study of antiquity in the sixteenth century. He then surveyed the practice of antiquarianism before turning to the mass of historical critique in the eighteenth century. Voltaire is presented as the first to make cultural history important. With the French Revolution, politics reasserted itself as the centerpiece of universal history. Against the political tendency of the age, Klemm enlisted science as a way of bringing the cultural world back into the story. It was this scientific perspective, Klemm asserted, not the political nor even the literary, artistic, antiquarian, or technological ones, that was reflected in his argument. He would follow the development of mankind from wild childhood to the division into social bodies with reference to the specific conditions of existence.[59]

The sources for such a project were as comprehensive as the project itself. What distinguished them was not their content but how they were examined: namely, as historical evidence. "Coins, coats of arms, medals and reliefs, statues and figural groups, entire buildings dedicated to war or peace, for sacred or profane use," wrote Klemm, "are, like all art objects, important sources for historians, above all if they contain information about the time or the place of their creation or creator."[60] By designating the "art object" as the other, Klemm was identifying everything else as, if not antiquarian per se, then as non-art objects, as "things," whose value were as documents of time's passage. Klemm did not speak in terms of "Archäologie der Kunst" but also seemed to be grappling with the ambivalence of the art object.

Because Klemm was living in the 1840s and not the 1740s, he insisted that the source base for understanding the past needed to move beyond the art object, but also the confines of the old *Hilfswissenschaften*: "Those image-less, often style-less things; tools, clothes, weapons, models of vehicles, buildings etc. which managed to survive to us from a distant time or space, are of no little worth." With these materials one could do comparative work and cast light on the "relationships of peoples." This was Klemm's *Statistik*, his attempt to mobilize the plenitude of historical artifacts to make sense of the contemporary state of the planet.

The table of contents says a great deal about Klemm's ambitions. It begins with a section on the Earth as a body ("Die Erde als Weltkörper") and contains chapters on the products of the earth and on "Man" in the abstract before moving on to natural man as defined by ethnographic reports from the most miserable and difficult places to access, including the "wild men in the primeval forests, on the sea coasts or the arid plains." This second, long section is devoted to the world of the hunter-gatherers. The categories that he proposes to use as analytical and descriptive reflect a historical sensibility that moves a step beyond what even Schlözer and Fabri had sketched out.

Taking the American Indians as his model, Klemm proceeded to lay out an inquiry that took in food, its acquisition and preparation; hunting weapons; hunting of animals and birds; clothing and its manufacture; jewelry and ornamentation; domicile and resting place; tools, devices, and containers; vehicles; marriage and family life; death and the funerary; conviviality; games and festivities; dance; public life in peacetime; warfare; religious concepts (faith, religious services, magic); culture (language, songs, stories, hieroglyphics, letter by a Mandan, painted robe, numbers, division of time); history.[61] Because the people under examination were without written culture, this is, by Klemm's own definition, an ethnographer's inventory—or an archaeologist's. But harnessed to an evolutionary, diachronic account of the human species, it could also function as the skeleton of a historical account. Fabri, for whom archaeology was so closely linked to the ancient world that he did not see a connection to the material culture of distant peoples, had already defined ethnology as the "scientifically organized synchronic content concerning the supposed relationships between the classes of various peoples and within humanity as a whole."[62] This synchronic approach was the opposite of what contemporary German historians defined as history. For them, an attempt to do synchronic *history* would have seemed a contradiction in terms. Yet this crossing of the synchronic and the diachronic was exactly what Klemm meant by "cultural history."

These same ethnographic categories served Klemm also for the wild men of the forests and deserts and then for nomads and mountain peoples. From them, Klemm turned to the historical peoples and the states of Anahuac and Egypt. But—and this sheds crucial light on how Klemm had come to think about history too—the categories of "primitive" folks repeat at all subsequent stages. "Food, clothing, jewelry, housing, devices, handicrafts, family life, conviviality, commerce, public life, war, religion, level of culture, history" never stop being important. For Egypt he added one more: "trade."[63]

The major expansion of categories comes with the discussion of China and Japan (vol. 6). Here Klemm introduces after food: drink; after housing:

navigation; after trade: cattle breeding, farming and horticulture, handicrafts, mining, ceramics; after family life: actors, constitution of state, government, provincial administration, urban culture, finances, legislation, punishments, public transportation; after religion: Kung-tsen or Confucius, science and literature, art. Even the pattern of insertion is telling, as it shows us how Klemm construed the inner connections of field and sub-field. It is in China that Klemm first locates the practice of *history* in a human community.

The categories of analysis become more detailed and ramified as we move closer to the present, through chronological-geographical chapters entitled "The West," "Old Europe," and finally "Christian Western Europe, or the Germanic-Roman Peoples." This chapter marks a crucial moment in which classical history, which had been studied as its own entity, was joined to a history that could only be studied as material culture. The categories here are plainly delineated: Physical conditions; clothing, living quarters, domestic furnishings; means of locomotion; industrial activity; family life; social life; games; funerals; public life; constitution of state; estates; constitutions; state administration; head of state; laws and administration of justice; warfare; defensive weaponry; attacking weaponry; religion; sacred places; religious service; sciences; history.[64] This vast tableau concludes with a volume (no. 10) on "Christian Europe or the Slavic-Finnish Peoples," very much reflecting the influence of Schlözer and his school on the importance of Eastern Europe and the later migrations to it for defining the character of modern Western Europe.

Perhaps the most important thing about this entire project is that it is an example of history being built out of things. For the arc of the ten volumes reflects the shape of Klemm's own collection. The example that establishes the connection between the autobiographical and the historical projects is introduced only as an aside, in an appendix to the larger work. But it is eye-opening. "Fantasy of a Museum for the Cultural History of Mankind" is a room-by-room guide to human history as if laid out in space. Each room of this museum happens to correspond to a volume of the *Cultural History*.[65] This "fantasy" is no daydream but the blueprint for the actually completed project.

Klemm noted that ever since Buffon people acknowledged a connection between museums and *Bildung*, and between the sixteenth- and seventeenth-century cabinets of curiosities and modern scientific collections. But no one had tried to put the museum to work. Klemm located his own project in the history of early modern collecting, alongside the category-busting projects of Samuel Quiccheberg and Friedrich Lorenz Hoffmann of Halle. His vision only came into focus with Cook's voyages to the Pacific and Napoleon's invasion of Egypt, both of which brought much non-European material into European collections. "From now on," he wrote, "fundamental historical research no less than the natural scientific can be based on the contemplation of monuments through which comparison and evaluation of the evidence is possible."[66] Those who were more skeptical of Klemm's achievement saw him as regressing to the "old-fashioned," "rococo" pre-Enlightenment encyclopedism of the *Wunderkammer*.[67]

The scientific model underpinned the proposed cultural historical museum as it did Klemm's own collection and the *General Cultural History* itself. It, too, began with the earth, its history, natural products, flora and fauna. Only "the last division of the natural historical collection" introduced "anthropological portraits"—the peoples of the earth treated as naturalia. The result was an "anthropological collection from a historical perspective."[68] And then, as in the *General Cultural History*, Klemm moves from fisher-folk through the Meso-American and Egyptian theocracies and on toward the present, object by object.

At the heart of this project lies the argument that static artifacts contain within themselves information relevant to dynamic change. Klemm acknowledged that the "embodiment of cultural history" (*Verkörperung der Culturgeschichte*), as in a museum, makes the choice of illustrative objects of paramount importance. Because every step could not be illustrated, the selection principle had to be biased toward showing change—which also meant that if there were periods of little evident movement, they would not be illustrated. Klemm's vision was of a museum as a "book of proofs" of human knowledge, borrowing a term from diplomatics (*Codex probationum*).[69]

And thus Klemm comes to his next extraordinary point: Oftentimes smaller and well-chosen private collections could function as more powerful *scientific tools* than fancier and grander public cabinets of curiosities. It was essential, he argued, that museum curators and administrators not treat their collections as a "dead treasure" but as a living intellectual project. They must, therefore, strive for a sense of "wholeness" as a result of which the collection itself sometimes had to make do with copies or reproductions of lost originals. There was no aura of the original for Klemm. His purpose was entirely scientific, and issues of authorship and authenticity did not much concern him. The new technologies of lithography and printing existed in order to be used to reproduce the "many monuments of public and religious life" that had fallen to "barbarism and fanaticism."[70]

If there was danger in having too many individual pieces, there was also danger in having too few. The curator could not omit what he did not like or was not interested in. Paraphrasing (and perhaps poking fun at) Ranke, Klemm declared that "this is the true impartiality and justice of the historian" (*Dieß ist die wahre Unpartheilichkeit und Gerechtigkeit des Historikers*). This commitment separated him from the "Kunst-dilettant," who, for instance, would never include the carvings of the Eskimos or images of the Mexicans and Chinese alongside the Medici Venus or a Raphael Madonna. Just like the student of nature, the student of the human past could not treat some artifacts with more seriousness and care than others. They were all evidence.[71]

Klemm brings the "fantasy" to a close, after traveling through the ten rooms, by declaring that it would not be so difficult to create such a museum. "In places, where, like Paris, the greatest ethnographic and antiquarian treasures are divided up amongst many museums, these indigestible fragments could in the same way serve as a central, or crystallization point."[72]

We can compare Klemm's vision of a cultural history museum of mankind with the slightly later one of his fellow Dresdener Gottfried Semper, for in between stands the World Exposition of 1851. A political exile from Saxony, Semper was living in London at the time. The exposition looked like "a culture-museum of mankind" and prompted Semper to reflect on the organization of things. He proposed an alternative taxonomy divided instead into ceramics, textile, wood, and brick. Here lay the origins of the decorative arts museum of the later nineteenth century. But Semper continued thinking and offered yet another taxonomy, dividing materiality into hearth, roof, mound, and fence. These were parts of building but also stood for a way of addressing different human activities. Where Klemm's approach was encyclopedic by general human practice, Semper's was typological, in the sense of Christian hermeneutics, finding in building forms a way of accounting for general human cultural development.[73] But, like Klemm, Semper wrapped his intervention in a history of collecting. Prehistory got short shrift, but the antiquarian collections of the early Chinese emperors were front and center. At once less comprehensive than Klemm and more incisive, Semper's quick survey led to the following conclusion:

A Complete and Universal Collection must give, so to speak, the longitudinal Section, the transverse Section and the plan of the entire Science of Culture; it must show how things were done in all times: how they are done at present in all Countries of the earth: and why they are done in one or another Way according to Circumstances; it must give the history, the ethnography and the Philosophy of Culture.[74]

This is exactly what Klemm was himself thinking. For in the very same year of Semper's "plan for a cultural historical collection" he delivered a lecture in Vienna to the Anthropological Society entitled "The Foundations of a General Cultural Science." This *Kulturwissenschaft* was his next step beyond cultural history.

Klemm set up his argument in terms of the opposition between nature and culture. *Cultura*, for the ancient Romans as for the readers of Pufendorf, was what humans did to change the world. A cultural science would, therefore, have to do with food, clothing, and shelter but also with vessels, tools, and machines. These constituted the "thing-ly foundations" ("sachlichen Grundlagen")—later in the same essay he refers to "material foundations"— of human existence. Studying their origin and development, he wrote, constituted the first axis of a future cultural science.[75] The second lay along the human vectors: from man and woman to child, family, clan, tribe, city, and state. The third line would examine the spiritual life of man through his creation of art and science. In so doing Klemm succinctly plotted the outline of the cultural sciences: archaeology, anthropology, history of religion, and art history. Klemm summarized this very clearly:

> Cultural Science [*Kulturwissenschaft*] begins with the material foundations of human life, with the representation of bodily needs, the means of their satisfaction and the products arising from that. It then represents human relations within the family and their extension into the state. The task of its final section of it, however, is to elaborate on the results of human exploration and experience, as well as the spiritual creations of mankind in science and art.[76]

That key first phrase of this passage recurred in the subtitle of Klemm's next work, *General Cultural Science: The Material Foundations of Human Culture* (1854–55). One volume was devoted to tools and weapons, the other to fire, food, drink, and drugs. In the introduction, Klemm contextualized his own work within the history of encyclopedism, insisting that the organization of knowledge for its transmission was of universal importance. South Sea Islanders used knots, Peruvians the quipo, Mexicans hieroglyphs. But for all of them transmission was linked to the need to communicate knowledge.[77] The history of collecting was both a prerequisite for this communication and in some way itself a form of communication.

Klemm began in ancient Greece, worked his way through Rome and the Scholastics of the European Middle Ages up to the early modern pioneers of collecting he had written about twice before.[78] Klemm's connections are exciting but also sure-footed. For instance, he moved from encyclopedism to collecting and then from collecting to cultural history via a survey of the late seventeenth-century genre of *historia literaria*. Voltaire—whether for the *Age of Louis XIV* or the *Essai sur les Moeurs*—was hailed as making the break-through to cultural history.[79] The subsequent step forward was driven by the work of Linnaeus and Buffon on the one hand, and the arrival of new materials from the South Seas, America, China, and Siberia, on the other. Only then did it finally become possible to envision a truly global human science.[80]

It is at that point, between 1819 and 1823, Klemm writes, that *moeurs*, family life, religious forms, art, and science began to become independent subjects for inquiry, edging out politics. With politics receding, Klemm commented that young people were stimulated by historical and antiquarian scholarship to engage with the natural sciences.[81] As we know, he was him-self one of those young men.

"Culture" meant for Klemm something like a "civilizing process": "the improvement or refining of the entire spiritual and bodily force of men or of a people." But it also referred to the broadest range of human interventions in nature, when someone turned a tree branch into a spear to throw at an animal, or rubbed two branches together to make a fire to cook that animal, or painted his body for war or decoration, or used fire to burn down the hut once inhabited by his father and now housing his father's corpse. "These are all signs of drives and properties that distinguish him from animals," Klemm wrote.[82]

"Cultural History," for Klemm, was the collection of such data, "Cultural Science" the theory based upon it.[83] The latter, he wrote,

> has the goal of showing how the various physical and mental drives, temperaments, and forces, through natural products and natural phe-nomena, bring forth a new array of products and phenomena in the individual as among men united into family, tribe, people, and state, and the laws according to which this occurs across the globe. Culture is the result of the interaction between people and nature and, subse-quently, the commerce among peoples.[84]

Kulturwissenschaft was a "science of experience" (*Wissenschaft der Erfahrung*) based on the appearances of things—just like the natural sciences. Their object was not one part of the human race only, nor one state, nor one part of the earth, nor one of the many activities and achievements of man, such as commerce, war, law, or literature. *Kulturwissenschaft*, according to Klemm, "had the task of representing human nature as a whole." Whereas cultural history treated this individual in his developmental aspect, marking progress in his circumstances, cultural science showed him in his varied fundamental postures, in family life and society, in war and in peace. As Klemm explained, "*Culturwissenschaft* has the task of bringing into view the whole of human activity and its monuments at all times and places."[85]

In the book, Klemm expanded upon the three axes laid out in his Vienna lecture. This meant starting with the fundamental transformation of natural into human products: "Food, clothing and ornament, tools, shelter, vehicles and vessels, these are the material foundations of human culture." Explaining their origin and development constituted the first task of a *Kulturwissenschaft*.[86] The second focused on the relations between people as mediated by objects, such as in the family, the state, religion, commerce, or the army. The third and final task was to narrate the "achievements of human inquiry and experiment, as well as the spiritual creations of peoples in science and art."[87] Thus, what his younger contemporary Burckhardt regarded as defining cultural history was for Klemm but the final part of a much bigger project.

The first volume of the *Allgemeine Culturwissenschaft* (somewhat puzzlingly, Klemm's introduction appears at the head of volume 2), reprinted separately in 1858, was devoted to "Tools and weapons, their origin and development." It surveys classes of objects, such as knives, clubs, needles, axes, bows, and spears. Klemm's point is that these kinds of objects are universal and exist at all levels of culture. "Tools," he writes, "belong among the most important monuments of human cultural conditions." As such, they provided insight into the "material foundations" of culture.[88] Klemm's survey leaves him on the brink of industrialization, with the transition from tools as discrete artifacts to machines as compound artifacts. Studying this was the task, he writes, of "technology." It is no surprise, then, that this was the one of Klemm's works that could be found in the library of Karl Marx, whose copy was, indeed, heavily annotated.[89]

Never-completed volumes of the *Allgemeine Culturwissenschaft* would have discussed clothing (vol. 3), dwellings (vol. 4), and vessels (vol. 5). But separate studies of clothing and hats offer insight into what the whole project might have looked like. Thus, in 1854 Klemm delivered a lecture to the Chamber of Commerce of Dresden on its twentieth anniversary, with the title "Human Clothing: Cultural Historical Sketches."[90] Beginning with the Greek love of the body and then the unformed clothing of the early and high Middle Ages, Klemm's story begins to get interesting in the fifteenth century—clothing for Klemm marking what Burckhardt was about to identify as the kernel of the

Renaissance, namely, the idea of the individual. Klemm even linked it to the rise of mathematics.[91] Clothing was common to men but also the greatest of individuators. Not for nothing, he concluded, did the old saw proclaim that "clothing makes the man."[92]

Klemm ended with a long discussion of shoes and hats—explicitly paired as covering the antipodes of the body. The importance of the head explained that of the hat. Klemm posited that the extraordinary headdresses of the North American Indians had their match only in the elaborate hairstyles found at the court of Louis XV.[93] He then undertook a survey of headgear amongst the ancient Egyptians, the ancient Greeks, the ancient Romans, the Oriental peoples, and the later Muslims, drawing from numismatic, sculptural, and iconographic sources. Klemm records the use of straw hats in China and Germany and wooden hats from Asia and the Northwest of America. Russian hats were discussed separately. The perspective was avowedly global and comparative. He concluded with a similarly wide-ranging, though brief, survey of military headgear. And we can even catch echoes of the child's fascination at the panoply of colors and shapes that he saw as the troops marched back and forth through his hometown of Chemnitz.[94]

Signaling its importance and his own fascination, Klemm returned to the hat (*Der Hut*) in a stand-alone piece of 1854. In it he focused on the ancient and medieval periods and began from the anthropological present: the hat follows the shape of the head. Climate, occupation, and social standing were other contributing factors. What followed was a whirlwind tour of hats from across the geographical and visual spectrum.[95]

During these highly productive years Klemm also published a six-volume encyclopedia of women's history, *Women: Cultural Historical Sketches of the Conditions and Influences of Women in Different Places and Ages*. The subtitle signaled its family resemblance to the recently completed *Allgemeine Culturgeschichte*.[96] He began with the women of the "passive races" proceeding from hunter-gatherers up through Americans, Asians, and Middle Easterners (Turkey, Persia). This was the first volume; the remaining ones were devoted to women in Europe, divided up in terms of their position in family and society, public life, the Church, and art and also as represented in literature. In addition, Klemm was sensitive to changing attitudes toward women, from the Mariolatry of the twelfth century to the beginnings of serious misogyny in the sixteenth. It makes perfect sense that one of the first to write an inclusive anthropological history was also one of the first to do women's history.[97]

In the 1860s, Klemm's eyes began to fail. His final work was a memoir, *Fifty Years Ago: Cultural Historical Letters*. It is an account of a world before it had changed, written from the perspective shared by other contemporaries, such as Burckhardt and Balzac, that the nineteenth century constituted a historical watershed. Through this looking glass Klemm examined his own distant childhood as if it were a far-off, even extinct, civilization.

He described the world of his youth, its houses and domestic arrangements, childhood and marriage, food and drink and decoration. His goal was, through these descriptions, to provide a "clear picture of the old times from 1800 to 1830."[98] Only after the July Revolution (1830) could one speak of "a public life" in Germany. The number of festivals, parades, processions, and theaters accelerated after 1848.[99] Turning in the second part from family to *Volk*, Klemm discussed his hometown, Chemnitz, its origins and professions, and then Dresden, where he lived when he was older.[100] The 1830 revolution was a real turning point: The palace in Dresden was burned, and he described it as the "entry to a new age." In the third book, "Popular Movement," Klemm linked communication with development. When he came to his experience of Leipzig in 1830, he used it as an opportunity to talk about the history of the city and its development.[101] In the fourth book, on the state, Klemm took the *Zopf*, or ponytail, as the characteristic mark of the late *ancien régime*, ending in Saxony in 1806.[102] Again, as in Burckhardt, there is a real sense of modernity encroaching upon and forever altering older ways of doing things. The railroad was one such novelty, the telegraph another. Thinking in terms of *la longue durée*, Klemm tried to imagine the impact of additional new technologies: "In the geological chronology a millennium is about as much as a week in the cultural historical, yes, maybe even just like a day or a telegraph second."[103] We can see why Braudel might have felt some kinship with Klemm—or the Warburg who worried about "the distance undone by the instantaneous electric connection" in the final paragraphs of the lecture on the Snake Dance.[104]

Kulturwissenschaft and Material Culture

Klemm's autobiographical effort frames his own life as a cultural history. But what of his other keywords, *Kulturwissenschaft* and *materielle Kultur*? These take us into a borderland in the generation after Hegel where culture was one of the ways in which spirit and matter were reconciled. In the second volume of his largely forgotten *General Outlines of Social Science* (1838, 1841), for example, Moritz von Lavergne-Peguilhen devoted an entire section to what he called the "general laws of culture" (*Allgemeine Kulturgesetze*). It begins with a section devoted to *Kulturwissenschaft*—as far as I know, the first use of the term. He explained that it had nothing to do with the formation of artists or scholars or individuals in general but with the discovery of social laws for treating the population as a collective entity.[105] The goal was the integration of "economic and political activity" for the perfection of the "mass of the population."[106] This could only be achieved through what he called "Kulturwissenschaft."[107] Lavergne-Peguilhen's "science of culture" would soon be called a "science of society."

Another work of the 1830s—when Klemm was making his turn from the history of collecting to the history of human culture—by the equally forgotten Karl Arnd helps locate the origins of Klemm's "material foundations." Arnd (1788–1877) was by day a road and bridge inspector and by night an autodidact. His earliest publications date from the 1820s and reflected his vocation, those from the 1840s onwards his avocation. But right in between, indeed the pivot from the one to the other, was an essay on the phenomenology of political economy entitled *The Material Foundations and Moral Claims of European Culture* (1835).[108] He aimed to lay bare the full spectrum of connections between what nature presented to man and what men did to nature. While grounding his study in what was readily understood as material—food, clothing, and shelter—Arnd also generalized the material to describe the foundational layer of existence upon which humans acted.[109] These workings he identified as "natural laws." Unlike Smith, whom he discussed at some length, Arnd insisted that the material dimension could not circumscribe the goals of human existence.[110]

Beginning with production in the most primitive stage of social life and accounting for inequality as the basis of exchange as well as for the difference between "use-value" and "exchange-value," Arnd came to the issue of "capital." He identified it with the value in objects, such as food, clothing, shelter, land, animals, tools, coins, and so on.[111] In other words, like his exact contemporary Karl Marx, Arnd was trying to generate a phenomenology of social life that accounted for its material dimension. Unlike Marx, he did not begin from Hegelianism but from the more anthropological side of Enlightenment philosophical histories, such as Isaak Iselin's *Geschichte der Menschheit*—or Schlözer's *Statistik*.[112]

Arnd also came to distinguish between "material" and "immaterial" goods. The former included basic things like food, clothing, and shelter as well as sophisticated social constructs such as cities. But objects made by men for use could be both material and immaterial. Tools, for example, could produce other material goods. But they could also produce an image, which was an immaterial good. By introducing the question of art in this context, he pointed directly to the ambivalence of the art object—of the world but not always in it.[113] This allowed for the possibility of cultural history being oriented toward either material or immaterial objects (as with Lamprecht, for example, or Burckhardt). We might see this positioning of the artifact at the crossroads as an exact parallel to the contemporary discussions within "Archäologie der Kunst."

In 1843, Arnd gathered these thoughts into a more conventional package and published a textbook on political economy. It began with material goods and had introductory sub-sections devoted to "exchange value," "production," "prices," and finally "capital." The discussion of "labor" that came next enabled Arnd to make the point that as a category it followed the development of society; in primitive conditions the labor was animal-like, but in productive ones it diverged more and more from that of base animals.[114] Thinking about economic life led Arnd, in turn, through the different stages of production, from hunter-gatherers to fisherfolk, pastoralists, agriculture, forestry, and mining. Only then did he come to trade. By anatomizing "every material good" into two components, a physical substance derived from nature which was then transformed by human labor into something with exchange value, Arnd provided a material foundation of economic life but also a cultural account of how economic life transformed matter.[115] Arnd shows us what Klemm's *Kulturgeschichte* might have looked like had it been written by someone interested in economics.

Klemm and Arnd developed their thinking about culture, history, and material life outside of the university. Wilhelm Roscher's exactly contemporary work on economic history, *An Outline of Lectures on Political Economy* (1843) came from within the university world. He began by declaring that the "historical method," which he had detailed in his book on Thucydides, published the previous year, was not only about chronological narration. Applied to questions of national economy, history meant describing what people had done and how they had lived. And this, in turn, was only possible with the closest contact to the other "sciences of the life of the people, specifically, legal, political, and cultural history." In Roscher's hands, these relations had to be pursued not only from a contemporary perspective, no matter how difficult this was to achieve, but also historically, through the study of preceding "cultural stages" (*Kulturstufen*).[116]

Roscher began with need, not far from where the modern heroes of natural law theory began, and concluded that "with the progress of culture, the realm of goods also expanded." These goods included things, personal services, and relationships.[117] This made a history of economic activity into an arena for the study of the development of a people, that is, its character and cultural attainments.[118] Like Klemm, Roscher's outline history of national economics began with the lowest cultural level, that of hunters and fisherfolk, and then moved to pastoralists and agriculturalists.[119] Unlike Klemm, Roscher plugged this history of economic life into a narrative of political development in seventeenth- and eighteenth-century Europe.[120] Corn laws, forestry, and mining all were approached as economic, political, social, and cultural functions.[121]

But it is when Roscher turned to "industriousness" and explored its rise in medieval city cultures that the line between economic and cultural history blurred completely. Trying to explore an attitude, or behavior, through external activity meant developing a historical framework that did not yet exist. We are, after all, more than sixty years away from Weber's *Protestant Ethic and the Spirit of Capitalism* (1905), though we do know that Weber was one of Roscher's most careful readers (as we have seen, Nietzsche was another).[122] "Communications" was one of the categories Roscher identified as uniting economic and cultural history: "The situation of the means of transportation is an important symptom of economic culture." This was true of all times, though Roscher focused on the modern era.[123] Finally, "population," the subject of chapter 4 and the direct continuation of Schlözer's work on *Statistik*, raised a series of questions about happiness, cultural diversity, and economic life.[124]

Lorenz von Stein (1815–90), like Roscher, thought about economics. And like Lavergne-Peguilhen he thought about economic life in terms of society. The first volume of his *System der Staatswissenschaft* was devoted to *Statistik* and the second to the neologism "social theory" (*Gesellschaftslehre*). While he did not use the Lavergne-Peguilhen's "Kulturwissenschaft," Stein shared the latter's conviction that the social was the most meaningful unit of measure. If many of those who wrote *Kulturgeschichte* were "1848 liberals," then von Stein's political basis was "France 1840," which led him, instead, to publish *Socialism and Communism in Contemporary France* (1842). It was the novum of the proletariat that led him to call for a "Wissenschaft der Gesellschaft." His way to social theory started from society. The experience of 1848 led him to write *The History of the Social Movement in France from 1789 to Our Day* in three volumes—a blend of history and social theory comparable in method to *Democracy in America*.[125] It was deep into its 150-page introduction that he proclaimed that the solution to the social question lay in "the relationship between capital and labor."[126] Finally, refining his argument still further, he wrote *Social Theory: The Concept of Society* (1855), though only its first part was ever written.

The insistence on the originating force of material existence by Klemm, Lavergne-Peguilhen, Arnd, and Roscher in the 1840s, whether called *Kulturwissenschaft, Materielle Kultur, National Oeconomie,* or *Gesellschaftslehre,* brings us directly to the concerns of the middle-aged Marx. In the exactly contemporary *German Ideology*, for example, Marx emphasized that his theory focused on the real, not the imaginary: "They are the real individuals, their activity and the material conditions under which they live, both those which they find already existing and those produced by their activity. These premises can thus be verified in a purely empirical way."[127] It was just then, Keith Tribe reminds us, that Marx began reading the literature on political economy, but since he seemed to read only what had been published before the 1840s, it is unclear how much he would have known of what these authors wrote. His reading, insofar as it can be reconstructed, also seems focused entirely on French and English writers.[128]

Indeed, if we follow Marx's argument we see a similar awareness of the anthropological, but inflected toward an economic teleology, in a break from Klemm's naturalism. One could say, perhaps, that Marx introduced a theoretical sophistication to the realm of modern social study that Klemm's argument lacked, focused as it still was on the early modern antiquarian model of collection, description, and comparison. The way in which men lived—Klemm's approach—for Marx depended rather upon their actual means of subsistence and mode of production. Going a step further, Marx suggested that mode of production

is a definite form of activity of these individuals, a definite form of expressing their life, a definite *mode of life* on their part. As individuals express their life, so they are. What they are, therefore, coincides with their production, both with *what* they produce and with *how* they produce. The nature of individuals thus depends on the material conditions determining their production.[129]

Marx can also serve as a prism to help place Klemm more precisely alongside his contemporaries. For example, if we look at Georg Friedrich Kolb in his *History of Mankind and Culture* (1843), later retitled *Cultural History of Mankind* (1869–1870), we see how much closer his version of cultural history is to Marx than to Klemm. As Friedrich Jodl writes, commenting on Kolb's approach, his is a history of the masses.[130] The masses provided Kolb with his frame of reference and even his notion of culture. In 1843 Kolb declared that "true culture exists within each People to the extent to which all of its social institutions and relationships promote and conduce to the development and elaboration of all available mental and physical powers for the permanent foundation and reasonable application of the intellect and the material well-being of the totality of society."[131]

Marx's own particular contribution was, of course, to emphasize not just the connection between individuals and their material lives but also the connection between those material lives and political conditions. This boldly went where Klemm hesitated: "The social structure and the State are continually evolving out of the life process of definite individuals, but of individuals, not as they may appear in their own or other people's imagination, but as they *really* are; i.e. as they operate, produce materially, and hence as they work under definite material limits, presuppositions and conditions independent of their will."[132] Marx even suggested—notoriously, for the history of ideas—that high culture, too, was a function of these material realities:

> The production of ideas, of conceptions, of consciousness, is at first directly interwoven with the material activity and the material intercourse of men, the language of real life. Conceiving, thinking, the mental intercourse of men, appear at this stage as the direct efflux of their material behaviour. The same applies to mental production as expressed in the language of politics, laws, morality, religion, metaphysics, etc., of a people.[133]

The early Marx reached these conclusions based on a philosophical reading of history. He makes more sense, or at least becomes less unique, if read against the background of works like Stein's *Gesellschaftslehre* (Marx was himself a reader of Stein and seems to have gotten from him the terms *class* and *proletariat*).[134] Stein had connected Klemm and Arnd's notion of "material foundations" to the idea of property. He even called it "the material foundation of society." It was property, he wrote, "through which the material world came to intervene in personal life." This intervention turned an "ethical order" into a social one and led to the clear conclusion that property was "the material foundation of society."[135] "Things," Stein writes, "which happen in society, come to be realized through the relationship to property and so create what we call the form of society."[136] That Stein's discussion of property is immediately followed by its relationship to "labor" helps us understand that though his argument may seem to play out at a too-great level of abstraction, this was actually a post-Hegelian generation's way of talking about the impact and workings of material culture.[137]

Marx may have shared these terms, but his insight into the relationships linking human beings, objects, and history goes well beyond them. In an analysis of his notion of "use value" in the first chapters of *Capital*, Istvan Hont shows how our contemporary conversation about writing history from things is coded directly into Marx's argument. Marx—and Hont—begin from the thing or object in its "natural particularity," in its "physical palpable existence." The commodity, or use value, is a way of thinking about that object as a thing that satisfies another person's needs. The "usefulness" in some sense follows from "the physical properties of the commodity. . . . It is therefore the physical body of the commodity itself, for instance iron, corn, a diamond, which is the use value or useful thing." But since most objects are made or transformed by men, that transforming labor is preserved, somehow, in the object itself. And so the outcome of the objects produced by men contains in it all of that human effort. Wealth, or use value, is therefore, according to Marx, "historical" since discovering and disinterring all of the impacted use value is "the work of history." From the point of view of its consumption, however, that use value is "dead" since it is completely irrelevant to the fact of its consumption. The consumer, to put it bluntly, is not interested in the history in the object. Marx's political insistence that there is no unmediated relationship between man and object is, therefore, also an insistence on the ineradicable presence of history. The history of the world in a hundred, a million, or a billion objects follows directly from this conceptual foundation.[138]

It is at this point that Marx's ontology of the object, motivated by revolutionary politics, meets up with the antiquarians' deep history of objects, motivated by conservative politics (with a small *c*). Marx's ventriloquism of the consumer's disdain for an object's use value as "dead" history perfectly parallels his contemporary historians' disdain for "dead" antiquarian learning.[139] Both Marx and the antiquarians, though for different reasons, are committed to the task of archaeological excavation. Where they part company, significantly, is in their interest in the historical *per se* and in their attentiveness to the individual thing. For Marx, history was studied for a purpose beyond history, and always toward the collective, as in the *Theses on Feuerbach*; for the antiquarians, research was a pursuit both pleasurable and ethical, and the individual documents, lives, and stories were in themselves worthy objects of this study.[140]

The very late Marx, however, turned strikingly toward history and, in particular, the latest work on prehistory. His *Ethnological Notebooks* document an intense engagement with Lewis H. Morgan and John Lubbock, among others, between 1880 and 1882. Marx was looking for communism in prehistory, and he found what he was looking for in Morgan. Engels, who was to incorporate much of this Marx into his *Origin of the Family* (1884), began his commentary in the 1888 edition of the *Communist Manifesto* by noting, "That is, all *written* history. In 1847, the prehistory of society, the social organization existing previous to recorded history, was all but unknown."[141] Like

Nietzsche at roughly the same time (1878–1879), Marx grasped that the vast depth of prehistory altered the kind of generalizations that historians and philosophers routinely made about the natural condition of man.

If we think that Klemm would have been an obvious source for Marx and are therefore puzzled by his absence, the fact is that Marx agreed. In a letter of 1869 to Engels he lamented not knowing of Klemm's work, specifically, *Die Werkzeuge und Waffen*, before completing the first volume of *Kapital*. He specifically mentioned that his discussions of the labor process and the division of labor would have been aided by the rich evidence that Klemm provided. It was Marx's late-developing interest in ethnology that had kept Klemm from him until then.[142]

Marx's English ethnographic sources, however, were familiar with Klemm. Edward Tylor, for example, introduced Klemm's conception of "Culture-History" on the very first page of his *Researches into the Early History of Mankind and the Development of Civilization* (1865).[143] Augustus Henry Lane-Fox Pitt Rivers was another attentive reader of Klemm. In 1867, while Klemm was still alive, Pitt Rivers delivered a lecture on "primitive warfare" at the Royal United Services Institution that may have been inspired by *Werkzeuge und Waffen*.[144] In fact, Pitt Rivers borrowed Klemm's approach of classifying by forms. The visitor to his museum, even today, could feel that she was strolling through Klemm's fantasy of a cultural-historical museum of mankind made real in Oxfordshire—assuming, of course, that Klemm was known to her in the first place. It is Pitt Rivers who is generally given credit for the coinage "material culture," though it appears that it, too, may have been borrowed from Klemm.[145]

After Klemm's death on August 25, 1867, his son J. Gustav Klemm tried to sell the collection.[146] In 1868 the British Museum bought his German antiquities.[147] The University of Leipzig decided against buying the rest, saying it was not of scientific worth. The materials ended up in private hands, with a physician who created a committee of thirty-eight well-known Leipzigers. On November 24, 1869, the committee published in the *Leipzig Daily Journal* a "Call for Contributions for the Acquisition of the Cultural-Historical Collection of the late Councillor Dr. Klemm for the Founding of a General Anthropological Museum." Their call was answered. In 1870 negotiations for the purchase went ahead and in 1871 the collection was bought for what became known as the German Central Museum for Anthropology of Leipzig. This was the first ethnological museum on the Continent. In 1904 the museum in Leipzig changed its name to the Städtisches Museum für Völkerkunde and in 1926 moved into a new building, the Grassi Palace, which was destroyed in an air raid during World War II.[148]

Der Form des Ruders nähern sich diejenigen Keulen, die wir sowohl in der Südsee, als in den Abbildungen der Ureinwohner Brasiliens bei den ältern Reisenden finden, mit denen Verbrechern oder Feinden der Schädel gespalten wurde. Der Griff war meist mit Bünden verziert. Sie vertraten bei diesen Völkern, denen die Metalle unbekannt oder wenigstens nicht so leicht zugänglich waren, die Stelle der Schwerter.

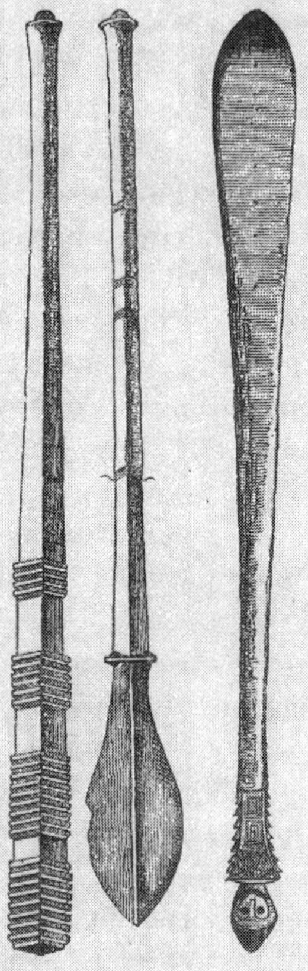

In der Südsee kommen Keulen vor, welche der Schwertform sich noch mehr nähern. Zwei Exemplare meiner Sammlung haben 40—44 Zoll Länge bei 3—4 Zoll Breite, der Querdurchmesser verjüngt sich nach unten bis auf einen halben Zoll und die Schneiden sind ziemlich scharf, das obere Ende ist ausgeschnitzt.

Das eine Exemplar (Nr. 1286 m. S.) ist aus lichtbraunem geflammten Holze, 2 Ellen 3 Zoll lang. Das was man am Schwert die Klinge nennen würde, ist mit rother Farbe bemalt, der Griff schwarz, mit Linienverzierungen und an den Seiten mit Zacken versehen, die abwechselnd roth und schwarz bemalt sind. Der Griff endet in ein ovales Ornament, das ein Menschenantlitz nachahmt und mit schwarzer und rother Farbe erhöht ist. Eine andere (Nr. 1285 m. S.) ist einfacher, nur 4 Fuß lang, aber 5 Zoll breit.

Dieselbe Form, nur bedeutend kürzer, kommt noch jetzt bei den Arowaken von Surinam vor. Ein Exemplar meiner Sammlung (Nr. 1291) ist aus dunkelrothem, schweren Holze, 29 Zoll lang, 4 Zoll breit und fast 2 Zoll dick. Die Keule endet oben in eine Spitze, unten aber wird der Schlag durch ein eckiges Ornament nachdrücklicher gemacht. Der Stiel ist mit sauberem Flechtwerk aus

Fig. 37. 38.   Fig. 39.

FIGURE 13A Klemm, *Werkzeuge und Waffen, Ihre Entstehung und Ausbildung* (1858), p. 23.

Diejenigen Spitzen, welche in eine
Holz- oder Knochenspitze gesetzt wur-
den, haben entweder gar keinen Zapfen, wie diejenigen, welche in den alten
Gräbern von Grönland gefunden wur-
den, oder aber der Zapfen ist mehr breit.

Fig. 90—92.

Die erstere Art, die altgrönlän-
dischen Pfeilspitzen, bestehen aus braunem Feuerstein (Nr. 4432)
oder aus milchblauem Chalcedon (Nr. 4433). Die Länge beträgt
1½ Zoll, die Breite drei- bis siebenachtel Zoll. Die Oberfläche zeigt
Muschelgefüge, die Schneiden sind scharf.

Die andere Art mit breitem Zapfen ist zum Theil nicht allein
breiter, sondern auch dicker.

Ueber die Art und Weise der Befestigung an Holz oder Kno-
chen gewährt das Exemplar einer oben erwähnten Harpunenspitze
meiner Sammlung belehrende Auskunft. Diese von der westame-
rikanischen Polarküste stammende große Pfeilspitze ist aus grauem
Thonschiefer, 1½ Zoll breit und 3 Zoll lang und ziemlich scharf
geschliffen; sie ist an einen fast 15 Zoll langen platten, sechsachtel
Zoll breiten, auf der einen Seite zu acht Widerhaken ausgekerbten
Schaft von weichem Holze befestigt. Auf der einen Seite liegt der
Stiel 1¾ Zoll lang an der Steinspitze an und ist hier mit Harz
fester an dieselbe geklebt, während der Zapfen
neunmal spiralförmig mit schmalem Pflanzenband angeschnürt ist. Um die Spitze gegen
Verletzungen während des Transportes oder in
der Ruhe zu schützen, ist eine Art Zwinge, die
aus zwei klingenförmigen schmalen und 4 Zoll
langen Hölzchen besteht und die ebenfalls mit
Pflanzenband zusammengehalten werden, vor-
handen (Nr. 1832 m. S.).

Fig. 93.

Solche kleine Pfeilklingen findet man häufig in den Museen
von Leyden, Copenhagen, Schwerin, Halle, Berlin u. s. w., wo
überhaupt Steinsachen aufbewahrt werden. Man hat überdem auch
in Amerika ganze Arbeitstätten solcher Steinspitzen gefunden, unter
denen die von Eaton in Pennsylvanien die interessanteste sein dürfte,
über die uns ein Bericht in der Copenhagener antiquar. Zeitschrift
(1843—45, S. 34) vorliegt. Unter den Exemplaren dieses Fundes,
welche ich der Güte des Herrn Etatsraths Rafn in Copenhagen
verdanke (Nr. 2751—2807), sehen wir alle möglichen festern

4*

Klemm's biggest impact, though, may actually have been in the United States. The Bureau of American Ethnology had its origins in an exhibition planned by the Smithsonian Institution and the Department of the Interior for the Centennial Exposition at Philadelphia. To help the agents charged with this project, Spencer F. Baird, naturalist and assistant secretary of the Smithsonian, looked to Otis Mason, a professor at Columbia University, to draw up a plan of "ethnological directions." Mason, who had read the newspaper article on Klemm's collection and had produced an English translation and abridgement, proceeded to incorporate Klemm's vision into his report. In these "directions," Mason asked the agents, many of whom were indifferent to Indians, material culture, or both, to seek out artifacts to "present savage life and condition in all grades and places," without leaving anything aside just because "they are either rude or homely."[149]

Just as Klemm's work and thought as a cultural historian was obscured by the greatness of a cultural historian of the next generation (Burckhardt), so too was his work and thought as an ethnologist by the greatness of Adolf Bastian (1826–1905).[150] Bastian was another liberal marked by the failure of 1848, though in his case it led not to some "inner" emigration but to a lifetime of wandering, exploration, and collecting. By 1873 he was the director of the newly autonomous Ethnological Museum in Berlin. From his sea of publications, one stands out: *The Pre-History of Ethnology* (1881). It is an extraordinary document: a history—or rather a prehistory—of a field written by the one who could best lay claim to be its founder. He immediately rooted ethnology in the comparative method, looking to psychology, physiology, and geography "and then to *Altertumskunde*, especially in its earliest form, and then to all the wider sciences" as they impacted upon it.[151] Just as with Hans von und zu Aufseß, to be discussed in the following chapter, the study of antiquity provided a model for this kind of totalizing attempt to recover a past culture. The expeditions of Cook and Banks in the South Seas had a decisive impact, but so too did the "discovery" of prehistory.

The biggest change, however, coincided with the breakthrough of a natural scientific worldview around 1850. This was marked by the establishment of the Ethnological Museum in Copenhagen. As an aside, Bastian observed that they possessed there Ole Worm's cabinet and then noted that the early modern *Wunderkammer* represents the modern ethnological museum in embryo. For this period, Bastian refers to Neickel's chapter on the "Raritäten-Kammern" in *Museographia* and to Klemm's history of collecting. Indeed, as an exception to his general view of the primitive and preliminary character of these collections, Bastian cited Klemm's as "the most important" of all those before his own time. Amongst the reasons he gave was its emphasis on just-post-contact items, before the natives had completely abandoned their material culture for that of their globalizing western inter-locutors. Bastian also stressed Klemm's scientific conceptualization. Here, in a note, Bastian quoted Klemm directly. It was considered "the purpose of the collection to show the emergence of the various products of arts and crafts from natural materials as well as their further development."[152]

Nor was this reference to Klemm casual. For Bastian had carefully read Klemm's "Fantasy for a Museum of the Cultural History of Mankind," and in a footnote devoted a long discussion to its organization. He observed that its ethnographic sections (roughly rooms 1 through 5) linked ethnology to the natural sciences as in geography museums. Now, however, Bastian added in conclusion, this principle of organization conflicted with the current state of thinking about the sciences.

What most separates Bastian's approach from Klemm's, however, is his insistence on psychology as a central element of cultural history. One might say that the previous century's thinking about *esprit* or *Geist* was in fact a pre-disciplinary way of talking about "collective psychology" as the core of the identity that cultural history was seeking. But it is nonetheless striking that Bastian declares that "the task of Ethnology lies in . . . the inductive side of history," and then proceeds to identify ethnology with "comparative psychology" on a collective and global level.[153] Psychology, indeed, throws a bridge across from science to philosophy: It is "rooted in individual physiol-ogy and unfolds into the thought of the *Volk*." Or, citing Théodule-Armand Ribot, it "plunges its roots into the life sciences and blossoms in the his-torical sciences." Bastian reflects, like his contemporary Lamprecht, the view of Wundt and others that social psychology could be both scientized and historicized.[154]

And so, Bastian argued, "in these museums, I should try to represent the spiritual life of natural peoples in its embodiment." This led him to make a categorical distinction between ethnological and art museums. These latter present "the ideal creations of the Muse-favored Geniuses," while the eth-nological collection tries "to represent the typical norm of the people as the starting point of study, whose aesthetic goals lift it up and whose biological goals weigh it down." And as Bastian spun out what this "normal" life meant, he sounded themes that the historical association men had broached: "the appearances of material life (in utensils, tools, weapons, clothing etc.) as well as the spiritual (in the style of decoration and ornamental jewelry, religious imagery etc.)." But by now the quarry was elsewhere and reconstruction in itself, even along these lines, was uncontroversial. What mattered was arguing that this reconstruction provided access to the *Weltanschauung* of a people and that this "circle of ideas" (*Ideenkreis*) traveled over the face of the earth. Representing all "these differences in the complete fullness of their manifoldness is the specific purpose of ethnological museums."[155]

Ethnology united the study of men with the study of things—as if anthropology with archaeology. The specific archaeology that mattered to Bastian was prehistoric. But within this general framework, he called attention to the usefulness of "art evidences to illustrate the character of Peoples." Whereas the study of art within archaeology was "esteemed only a historical *Hilfswissenschaft*, it was prized in Ethnology with the importance of a *Hauptwissenschaft* insofar as it studies literature-less peoples."[156] He wondered aloud, in a long footnote on contemporary Catholic piety, whether the primitive age of superstition was really over.[157]

Aby Warburg was then a student of Lamprecht's in Bonn. This discussion about art and ethnology resonated with him. We know that when Warburg contemplated his *Habilitation*, it was with Bastian. And Bastian's question about contemporary superstition reminds us of nothing so much as the final plates of Warburg's *Mnemosyne Atlas* (c. 1925–1929) illustrating the Concordat between Pius IX and Mussolini. And the question of the status of the art object as evidence in pre-literate times lay at the very center of his work. Could it have been, perhaps, with Klemm in mind that Warburg—who famously traveled to the American Southwest and donated what he collected there to the ethnological museums in Hamburg and Berlin, and turned Klemm's neologistic *Kulturwissenschaft* into his own keyword—formulated his own research project?

> Works of applied art have the misfortune of being regarded as products of the lower faculties of *homo faber* and of being relegated to the basement of the museum for the history of the human mind where, at best, they are shown as creations of technical interest. Who would so easily hit on the idea of responding to such precious showpieces as sensitive reflectors of the outward and inward life of their period?[158]

🍂 CHAPTER 8

The Germanisches Nationalmuseum: *Antiquitates* and Cultural History in the Museum

The founding of the Germanisches National-museum made good Spon's old claim that a historical argument could be told through artifacts at least as well as it could through books. It followed Klemm's vision of a museum of cultural history, albeit devoted to a single nation and not the entire world. There was also a political argument: The museum was a place of learning that was open to the people in a way that a scholarly literature was not. How to make learning accessible without compromise was a challenge that some—usually within the university—thought impossible to resolve. Others thought it not even worth addressing. But after the French Revolution the challenge could no longer be avoided. For all these reasons the story of the museum's founding and early years is an important subject for historians of scholarship and the museum alike, but also for museum practitioners thinking about the nature of their enterprise.

The Germanisches Nationalmuseum was the brainchild of Hans von und zu Aufseß (1801–1872). Inspired by the work of the historical associations in the late 1820s, he began his efforts to create a national historical museum in the early 1830s. We should see him alongside of the Norman aristocrat Arcisse de Caumont in France or his fellow German Ludwig Joseph Linden-schmit, who founded the Römisch-Germanisches Zentralmuseum in 1852, around the same time and as part of the same process that led to the founding of Aufseß's museum in Nuremberg.[1]

FIGURE 14 Hans von und zu Aufseß (1801–1872) in armor. Germanisches Nationalmuseum.

In the context of my argument, Aufseß is especially important because he self-consciously organized his historical museum on the lines of the old *antiquitates*. The bureaucratic needs of institutional organization combined with an obsessive tendency toward taxonomy mean that the creation of this museum has left us with an array of self-conscious discussions of many of our themes: antiquarianism, modern antiquities, philology, ethnology, and cultural history. Aufseß thought very hard about sources and was as open to material as to textual forms. He used *Altertumskunde* and *antiquarisch* inter-changeably to describe the field he was in and *Zustände* (conditions) to refer to the kinds of things these modern "classicists" or antiquarians actually studied.

To the Founding (1852)

The idea for a national cultural-historical collection, which became the Ger-manisches Nationalmuseum (GNM), germinated in the soil of the historical association movement of the first decades of the nineteenth century. For instance, in 1816 K. A. von Hardenberg mapped an encyclopedic collection of sources relating to national history that would take in all kinds of art-works as well as evidence for customs and manners, music, dance, agricul-ture, and tools.[2]

Aufseß was a Bavarian aristocrat who had studied law and worked on the family's archive.[3] From this he understood that an archive was not only com-posed of paper but also of things. It was this family collection that provided the kernel of the later museum. He persuaded King Ludwig I of Bavaria in 1832 to put him in charge of setting up something like the already-founded Bohemian national museum. The king wrote: "I have before wished that those in possession of marvelous objects should—with no prejudice to ownership—exhibit them at such a public locality in Bavaria as already exists in Prague; many a hidden and as yet unused treasure would become useful this way."[4] Bamberg was initially named as the location, but it eventually shifted to Nuremberg.

As a first step, Aufseß began publishing the *Anzeiger für die Kunde des Mittel-alters* in January 1832 in Munich. In the foreword he appealed to patriotism, honoring even its small, broken, and unheralded parts:

> Whoever loves the Fatherland, be he a duke or a subject, burger or
> peasant, poor or wealthy, must also foster a love for the history of the
> Fatherland, [and] he must willingly contribute to glorify the honor and
> continuing fame of his own hearth and home through all the beauty

and grandeur which are offered to us by art and history. This is my historical profession of faith, which I feel obliged to give here publicly, right at the beginning of my enterprise and of which I am not ashamed, even if I should suffer the misfortune of ridicule and misjudgment. The knowledge of art and history should not be the property of one specific class, e.g. the educated and the artists; rather it should, as in the old days, spread among all classes of man.[5]

Aufseß moved to Nuremberg in winter 1832. In 1833 he set up the Society for the Preservation of the Monuments of Older German History, Literature, and Art. He gathered members of the society, all of whom pledged to send things to Nuremberg. He donated his own collection and expected others to follow. From this emerged the plan to set up a central library of German historical literature and a "general German historical museum" in Nuremberg.

Already in 1833 the wags were hard at work. They zeroed in on the kind of little things that Aufseß had gathered: "old grave pots, miners' hammers, beer steins, rusty clips and distorted images of saints."[6] The director of the local Bavarian historical association mocked the idea of centralizing all of this junk in a single place.[7] Jacob Grimm was more subtle, but the point was the same: Real work was furthered by real sources, not these trivialities and vanities:

> Our studies can only be helped by honest industriousness carried out in our small corner and in silence, not by parades, dining halls and vain collections. Why does Aufseß have trivial matters printed on beautiful paper? People will buy it for the sake of single notes as long as he is able to continue but nobody will consider it any real achievement. The natural scientists are already bored by their meetings. What purpose is served by aping them so miserably?[8]

Because of political squabbles, Aufseß took back his collection and separated from the Nuremberg society, which soon became just another local historical association. The *Gazette* was also taken away from him in 1834, after being much praised by other journals.[9] The next ten years were lonely ones for Aufseß. He viewed his project as a salvage scheme for the destroyed sources of German history. He acknowledged that he was pushing at the limits of the conventional use of the word *museum* but that the alternative, *national historical academy*, sounded too pompous. Also, *academy* would have given the priority to texts whereas *museum* made clear that objects were the central resource.[10]

He and his idea resurfaced in 1846 at the Germanistentag, the annual conference of German legal, historical, and literary scholars held that year in
Frankfurt. Aufseß presented the idea of a "general repertory" of the sources
for German history, a kind of collections-based counterpart to the MGH.[11]
In the document he prepared for this meeting Aufseß resumed the history
of the project. It had begun in the 1830s with the idea of creating a historical
society and journal devoted to the German Middle Ages structured around
a collection of the monuments of history, literature, and art. He wanted to
bring together as many of these as he could, as he did in his home in the
1830s. Gaps were to be filled with copies. What one or another association
could not do on its own would be made good by an overarching national
society.[12]

Importantly, this was to be a collection for work, not show. History was its
organizing principle and purpose. "One can see from this," he wrote, "that
the plan was not to pile up a museum of precious and rare exhibits as they are
presented by chance and opportunity or even to centralize the historic treasures of Germany but rather to bring the historical material from all places,
be they public or private collections, into a large general repertory, to render
it clearly arranged and more easily accessible for the researcher of history."[13]
Aufseß acknowledged that the associations were, once upon a time, plagued
by dilettantism. But this was no longer the case. In an age when so many new
sources were available, it was a crime not to gather them up.[14]

Aufseß's goal was no less than a kind of "union catalogue" or, as he put
it, "an ideal systematic compilation made by thorough inventories."[15] Such
ordering would illuminate many existing obscurities: "How many new
inducements and motivations to examine fields of ancient history as yet dark
or unknown would spring from a complete compilation of each and every
monument or source!"[16]

The second Germanistentag at Lübeck in 1847 set up a commission to
study this idea. It was to have been followed by a third one at Nuremberg in
1848, at which Aufseß would present his full-blown project. This was can-
celed because of the revolution; it did not meet as the "Assembly of German Researchers into History and Antiquities" until 1852 in Dresden. The
board of the commission was to report to the assembly on the possibility of
a national German museum. The commission was headed by Aufseß and
included the director of the Imperial Coin and Antiques Cabinet in Vienna,
but the others were all non-habilitated professors, mainly archivists.[17]

Aufseß brought his plans for the Nuremberg museum with him to Dresden. In the audience were Jacob and Wilhelm Grimm and Georg Heinrich Pertz, director of the MGH, from Berlin. Also present were the Duke

of Saxony and Gustav Friedrich Klemm.[18] The meeting established three working areas: (1) "Archaeology of Pagan Prehistory," (2) "Art of the Middle Ages," and (3) "Historical Research and the Historical Auxiliary Sciences." Aufseß spoke, followed by representatives of the associations, who talked about the question of uniting them all into a single collection. Day three of the meeting was devoted to Aufseß's plan for a German national museum.

The proposed statutes of the museum were published as a supplement. It aimed to do three things: create a "well-ordered general repertory of all the source materials for German history, literature and art"; display these sources; and then publish them. Aufseß offered specific recommendations for the handling of sources. His first priority was to gather up all unpublished documents and inventories of documents from private and public archives. He also sought to expand the range of sources by seeking out manuscripts in private hands, by exploiting hitherto ignored monuments, and documenting living ritual, "those old customs, traditions, folk tales and songs still alive among the people which are to be specially recorded as far as they are still unknown in print."[19]

Aufseß's range of evidence takes us from the materials of the *Hilfswissenschaften*—genealogy, heraldry, diplomatics, numismatics, epigraphy—all the way to folklore and ethnology. The goal of the museum was to systematically order *everything*. This was to be linked to a publication project, with a journal or bulletin to disseminate the latest research.[20]

Founding Documents

To coincide with the museum's opening, Aufseß published a guide to his thinking and to his collection, entitled "System of German History and Antiquities Designed for the Purpose of the Arrangement of the Collections of the Germanic Museum." The text accompanied a truly extraordinary visual tabulation, which was obviously the central statement. But let us turn to the text first.[21]

The "System," he wrote, arose from necessity. "It had to be invented for this specific purpose," Aufseß explained, "as none known to us served the purpose of combining written and visual materials in such a manner that both could be fitted into one and the same system and structure as is necessary here."[22] Because he was not writing a book, nor merely fantasizing about a museum, but actually making a museum, the realms of the material and the textual had to be integrated.

Since each question determined the sources that were its answer—and "every document, chronicle, monument and image is in its own way a source"—by selecting and ordering its collection, the museum would determine the very categories of German history. Aufseß believed that the old category of *Altertümer*, or "Antiquities," could be adapted for the specifics of modern times. But because the term itself "is so wide and imprecise, like its sources," some topping and tailing was necessary. Since *history* was the term generally used to narrate what happened in time, the artifactual focus of the collection required the use of a different term. Aufseß drew on F. A. Wolf's *Zustände* (conditions) so that the first division of the inventory was into materials related to *Geschichte* and to *historische Zustände*. This amounted to a distinction between the diachronic and the synchronic.[23]

Aufseß upheld the importance of these "historical conditions." In doing so he had to liberate the *Hilfswissenschaften* once and for all from their subordinate status. "To study historical conditions systematically," he wrote, "is as important as the study of history itself, and thus they rightfully find their place next to history and not, as up to now, as a servant or helpmate to history, as auxiliary sciences." In other words, what were once mere supports were now finally to be treated as legitimate subjects of inquiry. It makes sense that this affirmation of material evidence came from a museum founder, just as it had from the private collector Klemm.[24]

Aufseß reiterated this connection between the content of his museum and the content of those methodological sciences in a report on the museum's first year. He reprints as a mission statement what was approved on August 17, 1852:

> . . . it was decided to gain an overview of German history up to the year 1640 by documenting the scattered source material about German history with all its auxiliary sciences, including literary and art history, on the one hand, and on the other hand to found a German national museum proper, a museum for German history, art and literature, regardless of Germany's existing political borders, by collecting the sources themselves in originals, copies and abstracts, as far as this can be done without damage to existing collections.[25]

Aufseß insisted on integrating specific historical facts into a larger framework, sensing already that much information was migrating to the various disciplines (*Spezialwissenschaften*), each with its own handbook. "Even material objects," he wrote, "such as coins, household effects, clothes can become very apt examples of art." But they needed to be very precisely classified.[26]

Aufseß himself thought that the greatest precision could be achieved by visual presentation. His extraordinary "Schema of German Historical and Antiquities Studies according to which the collections of the Germanic museum are ordered" translates this discussion of German historical studies—and indeed that of an entire generation—into a picture. Its fundamental division is between "history" and "conditions," but as we explore the contents of the latter it will become clear that the operative distinction remains something like that between history and *antiquitates*.

Aufseß divided the class "History" into "places," "personalities," and "events" (Varro's fourth category, "things," or institutions, being shifted to *Zustände*). "Places," in turn, he broke down into imperial or political, provincial, and then local history. "Personalities" were divided into family and biographical, and events were subdivided into church, state, war, travel, and marvels. "Conditions" took up about two-thirds of the chart, and almost four times as many of the categories were devoted to it (15 versus 58). These *Zustände* were first split into "general cultural and social conditions" and "specific institutions for the general welfare." The former, in turn, were divided into spiritual and material relations. The spiritual or creative was expressed in "literature, the arts, sciences, and education," the material in "land & people," and lifestyle. How people lived included the categories of agriculture, architecture, industry, ornament, trade, mores, customs, courtesy, and festivals. Specific institutions for the general welfare were also divided into spiritual and material, with the church in the first category and government and army in the second.

The two greatest historians of the age, Johann Gustav Droysen and Leopold von Ranke, responded viscerally to Aufseß's organizing principle. Droysen wrote to Heinrich von Sybel—soon to be the first editor of the *Historische Zeitschrift*—in 1853 describing the meetings of Mainz, Dresden, and Nuremberg at which Aufseß gained approval for his museum as "miseries." But he was happily persuaded that "they were fully played out—that the impotence—what many will say—is bigger than I had myself assumed." And Ranke, responding to a question from the Prussian government about Aufseß's plan, was even more dismissive: "The schematizing of stuff, which Herr von Aufseß organized, may have its worth for the odd rarity and curiosity: for living learning it is deadly."[27] Ranke *was* smart—he saw that Aufseß was reviving the old model of *antiquitates* that professional history in modern Germany was dedicated to killing off. To the extent that Aufseß's plan

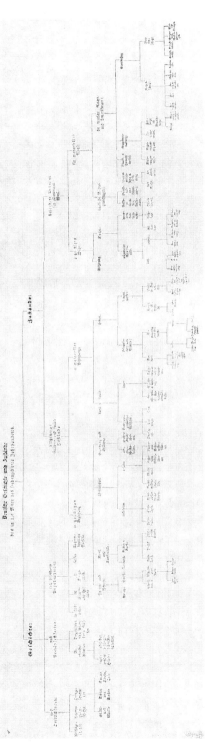

FIGURE 15 Schema der deutschen Alterthumskunde. Photo by author.

reminded him of antiquarianism, it is no surprise that the word that came to mind was "dead." This was an association made by professional historians but also by writers (Eliot) and philosophers (Nietzsche).

Aufseß, however, was not to be deterred by objections from the professoriate. In the Museum's third annual report, published in 1855, Aufseß described it as "the whole national collection for the historical sources of the German past."[28] But unlike other museums, the collection of original materials was only a means for reaching the chief goal, namely "the compilation of all remaining collections referring to German historical conditions into an orderly repertory of written as well as pictorial representations of the materials."[29] The repertoria themselves were organized "as an overview, coordinated as to both topics and chronology, of the material necessities of our ancestors from the 11th up to the 17th century (1650)." Images were filed alongside of books and papers as "sources" rather than as "art."[30]

The memoranda, or *Denkschriften*, of the museum began appearing in 1856. These constitute an important bit of institutional, but also intellectual, self-reflection. The first number, published in 1856, referred to the 1852 statutes of the museum.[31] It described the museum as an "organism" and thus as "analogous to a scientific institution of the state."[32] The biological metaphor reflected not only the current fashion but also Aufseß's view that the collection stood for the nation. Just as the latter could be hypostatized as a living entity, so could the former.[33]

The "organism" that was the GNM had the following departments:

a. pagan archaeology
b. history, genealogy and topography
c. legal, political and military
d. pedagogy, church and school
e. literature, language and bibliography
f. art and technology
g. lifestyle, necessities, culture
h. numismatics, heraldry, sphragistics

Aufseß was an inveterate taxonomic thinker. If in the "System" he represented the collection in terms of history and antiquarianism, here he presents it in the categories of *Kulturgeschichte* and what were once *Hilfswissenschaften*. For example, in the museum, the department of "Art and Antiquities" included numismatics and heraldry, geography, and genealogy. These were separate from the library and archive.[34] It is his persistence in trying to perfect the gearing of these different ways of thinking about objects and their relationship to history that makes Aufseß an important source for understanding how people thought about objects as historical evidence.

The second section of this first *Denkschrift* includes a systematic "Overview of the Contents of the Art and Antiquities Collections" in which the purely textual material is put in cursive and the material in roman letters. This memo complements, and also deepens, the "System of German History and Antiquities" of 1853. Most of all, it adds detail—52 sub-categories to the 15 in the chart on the "history" side, and a whopping 406 to the existing 58 on the "antiquarian" side of the chart. And if one looks very closely, one finds something else: Aufseß redistributes the old *Hilfswissenschaften*. He places epigraphy, diplomatics, and paleography under "the study of writing" in the section of *Zustände* devoted to immaterial cultural history ("Allgemeine Cultur- und sociale Zustände in *geistiger Beziehung*"). Public documents (*Urkunden, Akten, Notizenbücher*) and numismatics (*Münzwesen*) he puts in the category on "Commerce" in the section on "Production and Consumption." Heraldry and sigillography appear under "Honors" (*Ehrenauszeichnungen*). "Chronology" is not specifically identified as a category but as the other "eye of history." Geography is more than amply represented in History "by place" and in Conditions under "Land," itself viewed through the lenses of topography and *Statistik*. We have come far from Gatterer. The *Hilfswissenschaften* are now so fully integrated into Aufseß's vision of a wider evidentiary base that they no longer constitute an independent category.

As we look at this material, we see that Aufseß was also explicitly committed to the broadest meaning of *German* and of *nation*. The political dimension of Aufseß's ethnographic vision of German history, which is to say his interest in every aspect of the lived German experience in the years after 1848, was not to be ignored. As Aufseß himself wrote,

> The object of the assignment set before us is the history of the German lands and peoples in the widest sense, encompassing not only political life as it emerges on the outside, but also the social, family and intellectual life of the people and, generally, the entire life of the state and people in all its relations. For this purpose a central point shall be founded where everything that can pass for a source of German history in this widest sense is united—as an original or as a copy or at least an indication as to where it can be found.[35]

An article in the *Gazette* of the GNM in 1859 presented the museum as a source of spiritual unity for the nation. Aufseß may have been no social radical, but his museum made common cause with the children of 1848.[36]

This politically inspired "ethnographic" or cultural-historical approach meant paying attention to objects not because they were aesthetically worthy but because they were historically significant. The general public may, indeed, have wanted P. T. Barnum–style marvels and the well-educated fine masterpieces, but "from the point of view of cultural history the products of the common toil and commerce of an era are much more important than the works of the distinguished masters." Moreover, Aufseß added, just as the connoisseur could tease a crucial insight out of handwriting, "the 'old pots and pans' talk as loudly as the revered masterworks of art."[37] Aufseß always classified material according to function, not quality. So, for example, an expensive table cover falls into category of "household furnishings," not "artworks."

The First Cultural History Journal

Aufseß's vision also shines forth in his imagining of the museum as a publishing platform. The importance of the *Zeitschrift für deutsche Kulturgeschichte* (*Journal of German Cultural History*) as a venue for an alternative to political history cannot be overemphasized.[38] Johannes Falke, for example, who was first secretary of the GNM and one of its two editors, was an economic historian and the brother of the Jacob von Falke who would become director of the Museum für Kunst und Industrie in Vienna (forerunner of the Museum für Angewandte Kunst). He left the museum in 1862 to take up the position of state archivist in Dresden. The other editor, Johannes von Müller, was "Keeper of Antiquities" at the GNM between 1854 and 1861 and then founder and director of the Welfen Museum in Hanover and conservator of regional antiquities of the province of Hanover. He also served as editor of the *Journal* when it reappeared for a second series in 1872.

The *Zeitschrift für deutsche Kulturgeschichte* was initially published monthly between 1856 and 1859. In 1857 it became the house organ of the newly founded Association for German Cultural History run by Falke, Karl Biedermann, and Wilhelm Wachsmuth. The "Prospectus" printed at the head of the first issue defined *cultural history* as "the chief part of the life of a people, the developmental history of its physical and psychic organs." The *Journal*'s goal was twofold. First, to gather up material relating to cultural history and prepare from these materials self-standing works. Second, through this work to demonstrate the method for doing cultural history, thus far still lacking an accepted form. Its practice would follow that used in popular writing, "through cultural-historical images." These microhistories were, however, to be pursued with a "thoroughness and scientific rigor" that, presumably, would distinguish them from the popular literature.[39] Readers of the *Zeitschrift* might well have needed this insistence on difference when confronted with, for example, Gustav Freytag's exactly contemporaneous *Bilder aus der deutschen Vergangenheit* (4 vols, 1859–67)—an imagined, literary version of the collecting Aufseß had done in three dimensions.[40]

The *Journal*, the editors declared, would publish both narrative and analytical materials. In the first category they envisioned surveys of different periods, representations of particular lines of cultural development, and biographies. In the second, they emphasized the publication of source collections. As they explicitly broadened out from politics, they identified their scope in the conventional romantic language as the "organic and living totality of the national life." Finally, perhaps crucially, they viewed their audience as the general, not just learned, public.

The first article in the very the first issue was a programmatic statement by Johannes Falke entitled "German Cultural History." He praised the work of the local historical associations and stressed that, contrary to the received view, politics only scratched the surface of the history of the *Volk*. He named Ranke, Gervinus, and Macaulay as historians whose achievements he admired. But it was their ability as storytellers, rather than the specific content of their work, that seems to have drawn Falke to them.[41]

Falke wrote that while literature used to be the only available tool for getting at the life of the nation, there was now historical work on costume, farming, tools, trade, and women. Knowledge of individuals, as of the nation as a whole, was not only a matter of disciplinary mastery but also of grasping "the entire personality in the sum of its organic strength, and to determine from the conditions which generate these conditions all the rest of the inner talent of the people in its organic structure." These deeper forces he identified with the scope of cultural history because "it was in its cultural history that a people recognizes itself in its relationship to itself."[42]

Cultural history he then defined as the "history of the total organism of the people." This included its material conditions, which in turn could be written in terms of a progress from the satisfaction of physical necessities to an ascent to the ethical—the role of the family, society, and state—and, finally, to the creation of spiritual life in which were found letters, arts, and the sciences.

Most provocatively, for Falke the operation of cultural history shifted the perspective on truth. In approaching church history as a cultural historian, for example, the inquirer could sidestep the question of superstition or unbelief. Instead, every belief offered its own possibilities: "Cultural history finds in the crudest superstition truth worth remarking upon," since every opinion, whether true or false, reflected the condition of the people at a given moment in time. Thus, while church history represents "the triumph of the Church over the *Volk*, cultural history" represents "the development of the Church as the victory of the *Volk* over itself."[43]

The method of cultural history that was appropriate to the *Volk* focused on the concrete and particular, irrespective of value. Falke explicitly rejected a purely rational notion of culture—we are here in the realm of Herder and Wachsmuth, not Kant. The point is that the people's "most inward life itself is the object of this science."[44] Not chronology but the synchronic study of the relationship of agriculture and trade, or agriculture and city life, were better ways to grasp the life of a people. Chronological order simply did not suit the "organic" character of the people. Falke comes back to this time and again. Classification had to follow the *Volk* and not impose itself upon it.[45]

Other articles in that first year of publication discuss baths in German cultural history, the impact of the Thirty Years' War on social circumstances, family histories of the sixteenth century, characteristics of female reading at the beginning of the eighteenth century, military and trade routes in old Germany, executed animals and ghosts, marriage ordinances from the fourteenth century, student life in the seventeenth century, medieval anti-Semitic imagery, characteristics of fashion in the sixteenth century, the schoolmaster in the sixteenth century, medieval German pirates, autobiography in Germany at the end of the sixteenth and beginning of the seventeenth centuries, criminality and the history of manners in the seventeenth and eighteenth centuries, the age of "state-wigs," and the history of German dance forms as well as a host of local historical inquiries, sometimes with interesting foci, such as W. Strickler's investigation of Frankfurt am Main's public health ordinances in the seventeenth century.[46] While these are the kinds of subjects that could now easily find their way into respected historical journals, in the middle of the nineteenth century, in an age and climate dominated by high politics, they would have seemed irredeemably lightweight, not to mention egregiously demotic in a post-revolutionary age of reaction. It was also a problem for the journal that very few of its contributors were professional academics; most were archivists, gymnasium teachers, or private erudites. Wilhelm Wachsmuth, who published a prospectus for his 1863 study of Hildesheim in the *Journal* in 1857, was a rare exception.

Sometimes the politics that might have offended had a capital *P*. For example, the 1857 issue published an article "On the Persecution of Jews in the Middle Ages" that began by noting that the *Wiener Kirchenzeitung* had recently published an article rejecting an apology to the Jews for the blood libel. As

the author, one R. Hoder, commented, "That in the century of Enlightenment such opinions can be represented at all seriously is a symptom that the
cultural historian may not pass by."[47] That same year the *Journal* published
a sympathetic article on medieval Jewish resistance to persecution.[48] So, to
its dangerously liberal tendencies toward the masses and women do we also
need to add to the charge sheet drawn up against the Nuremberg-based cultural history an excessive sympathy for the Jews?

Nor, one needs to add, given the reception afforded this material by the
professional historians, were the editors oblivious to the danger of dilettantism. Indeed, in the very first number there was a short notice entitled by
the editors "Dilettantism in Cultural History." It acknowledged that the very
style of the subject, as well as its objects, could lend itself to a superficial
treatment. Moreover, the "organic" quality of the *Volk*, which made every
part of its life worthy of study—just as, we are told, the natural scientist
studied small parts of the whole in great detail in order to better understand
its function as a whole—could allow for detailed studies of small-seeming
matters. In a way, this was not so very different from Boeckh's concession
that philology contained within itself a tendency to pedantry and micrology.
What the philologists did not worry about, however, was that their practice as a whole would be discredited by its least able practitioners. Not so
the cultural historians. Their insecurities were more visible. Therefore their
insistence that raising the quality of popular history was needed in order
to minimize opportunities for highbrow dismissal of amateur scholarship.
They were looking over their shoulders in a way that scholars in established
and prestigious fields of study did not need to.[49]

As if responding to an offstage chorus of criticism, Johannes Falke, writing for the editors, inserted another prospectus-like text midway through the
second year of publication. It sought to defend the *Journal* from all the obvious
attacks and to clarify its purpose. Accused of merely entertaining readers, Falke
distinguished the *Journal*'s articles from those in the popular "entertainment
literature." Accused of publishing anecdotes, he insisted that cultural history
had its own "rigorous scientific laws." Accused of focusing on the odd case, he
defended study of the representative rather than the exceptional. As for the role
of narrative, Falke pointed to the examples of Macaulay in England and Biedermann at home as popular and praised models of storytelling joined to good history.[50] In all this, and perhaps especially in the last point, we can hear the voices
of the professional historians, committed so self-consciously and, perhaps, also
not a little self-righteously, to a scientific vision of their own practice.

Karl Biedermann was one of the driving forces of the *Zeitschrift für
deutsche Kulturgeschichte*.[51] He warned against the danger of dilettantism

but also thought that cultural history could stand alongside of political and ancient history. In a short contribution to a "cultural historical treatment of Leibniz's philosophy" (1856) he raised a question that still perplexes: What is the relationship between cultural history and the history of philosophy? In this, as he noted about an earlier work of his on post-Kantian philosophy "in context," he wished to suggest that there was a cultural-historical line of approach—examining origins, influences, implications, and side effects—for strictly philosophical ideas.[52] In 1857, attempting to sketch what such a cultural historical study would look like, he began with a plea for a history that was not simply a "quantitative . . . agglomeration" of work done in different specialist fields but was a multi- or even post-disciplinary combiner, qualitatively different from the sum of its parts.[53] The third part of this article bore the title "Leibnitz und seine Zeit."[54] This is a familiar kind of "intellectual history," even if it remains anchored to a prior and ahistorical commitment to the permanent reality of a German *Geist*.

But Biedermann's main contribution to the *Journal*'s life was an article entitled "The Place of Cultural History in the Present, with Particular Respect to the Idea of a Cultural Historical Association."[55] He proposed creating a new "Society for German Cultural History" distinct from all the many historical associations. He explained that however desirable the mixing of the cultural historical "with the antiquarian element," in practice they pointed in different directions. The existing associations were more concerned with the antiquity of the Fatherland, and thus with the earliest times, while cultural historians were concerned with the life of the people and thus gravitated to the present because thinking of the future.[56] Biedermann's definition provides some explanation for the ways antiquarianism and cultural history did not work together, and it reflected not a difference of sources so much as a difference of goals.

After giving a brief survey of the history of cultural history, starting from Christoph Meiners and Herder, Biedermann explained that if in the past writing national history meant writing about its rulers and ruling class, it was now "no longer simply the aristocratic ranks of society, but the whole People . . . [who] step upon the stage and help make history." The facts of the world had changed, and history had to change too. His language is forceful:

> The so-called material issues—agriculture, traffic, trade and commerce including the economic and social conditions resulting therefrom among the different classes of society—issues, which in spite of the haughty contempt with which a part of the scholarly community treated them have become not *a*, but rather *the*, social force of our

century, will hence also become the indispensable, broad and solid base
for historical scholarship and historiography, the sole foundation on
which a truly historical edifice can be erected.

Understanding the ethical (*sittliche*) life of the people required knowledge of
the material life of the people.[57]

It was precisely because the sources required for telling this story were
so extensive—almost limitless—that it was important that there be a center.
It was this, along with his sense that "cultural history" was "a new current
in the flow of German spiritual life," that explains why he thought a new
association was needed.[58] It would focus on the period after 1648, where the
Germanisches Nationalmuseum's collecting policy stopped.[59] This had the
effect of identifying cultural history with "modern history."

One of the most interesting insights that emerges from a perusal of the
four volumes of the *Zeitschrift für deutsche Kulturgeschichte* published in its
first series is the common ground between "cultural history" and "national
economy." In part this is a rediscovery of Schlözer's vision of *Statistik*, in
part a taking seriously of cultural geography in an age that was obsessed by
both culture and geography. But it also reflects the development of "National
Economy" as a university-based academic subject that paid attention to the
physical and psychic characteristics of a particular land and population. And
this, as Aufseß's chart showed so well, was an integral part of cultural history. As we will see, this alignment between economic and cultural history
becomes even more pronounced in the *Journal*'s second series.[60] Moreover,
both cultural history and national economy could be viewed as practical or
concrete sciences, opposed to the abstract and ideal. "We build up theories
and spin out systems"—all fantasies, writes August von Eye. Cultural history and national economy were instead sciences of the real, of "experience"
as Fabri, Klemm, and Roscher put it, and an antidote to the very German
tendency to idealism lambasted by Marx at the beginning of his *German
Ideology*.[61]

The principle, as it was expressed by Eye in 1853, was to create "a new era
of historical study" by "emphasizing the contextual and inner process of historical sources of various sorts."[62] Whereas some conservative interpreters,
such as Wilhelm Heinrich Riehl, were willing to sign on to cultural history
in order to study the unchanging *Volksgeist*, the Nurembergers thought in
terms of change, of a back-and-forth process between internal and external
causation that they called "Ineinander-Verarbeitung" and that Goethe had
famously called "morphology." If professional political historians couldn't
stand Aufseß's program, art historians had an easier time of it, perhaps

thanks to the old connection between Herder and Winckelmann. Thus, for instance, the director of the Berlin paintings gallery, Gustav Friedrich Waagen, was a founding fellow of the Nuremberg museum and also one of the founders of its Berlin supporters group. He wrote about the Van Eyck brothers in this same way. For the art historian Karl Schnaase (1798–1875), "the art of every period was the most perfect and at the same time also the most reliable expression of a given *Volksgeist.*" Schnaase, in turn, was a big influence on Johannes Falke's brother, Jacob, the future museum director.[63]

Speaking to the Prussian Parliament in 1860, Aufseß presented the museum's perspective on contextualism, that objects of all sorts and all qualities were needed in order to understand the past. This view underwrote the *Journal*'s editorial policy as well. Collecting, inventorying, and organizing all the surrounding materials was necessary because "only with careful attention to such cultural historical sources can living, warm and truthful representations of individual sections of the life processes of the entire German people be grasped." He noted in particular that this was long the practice with the study of Greek and Roman antiquities and had more recently become the mode of approaching Asian and African monuments. England and France had made great strides in this area. Only Germany lagged behind. This was, he concluded, the task of his newly founded museum.[64]

Droysen and Aufseß

Aufseß got support from Waagen, Alexander von Humboldt, Director of the Royal Kunstkammer Karl W. A. Freiherr von Ledebur, and the biologist Ignaz von Olfers, who was general director of the Berlin Museums. In March 1857 Aufseß founded the supporters group of the museum. In 1859 speakers on behalf of the museum included the writer Theodor Fontane. But the leading historians kept their distance: Droysen refused to speak at the museum, and Burckhardt refused to become a fellow of its society. The Prussian king solicited the opinions of the Berlin Academy of Sciences, and the committee's report, signed by Boeckh, among others, was sharply negative (fig. 16). Their verdict was that the Nurembergers were overrating themselves. They did not constitute a German historical national academy, their fellows were not good scientists, and their source collection was insufficient.[65]

Of the great contemporary historians, Droysen was in theory the closest to the museum's ambitions. He had accepted his membership in the GNM's society in 1857 at exactly the moment when he began his survey course on method ("Encyclopedia and Methodology of History"). He was, in fact,

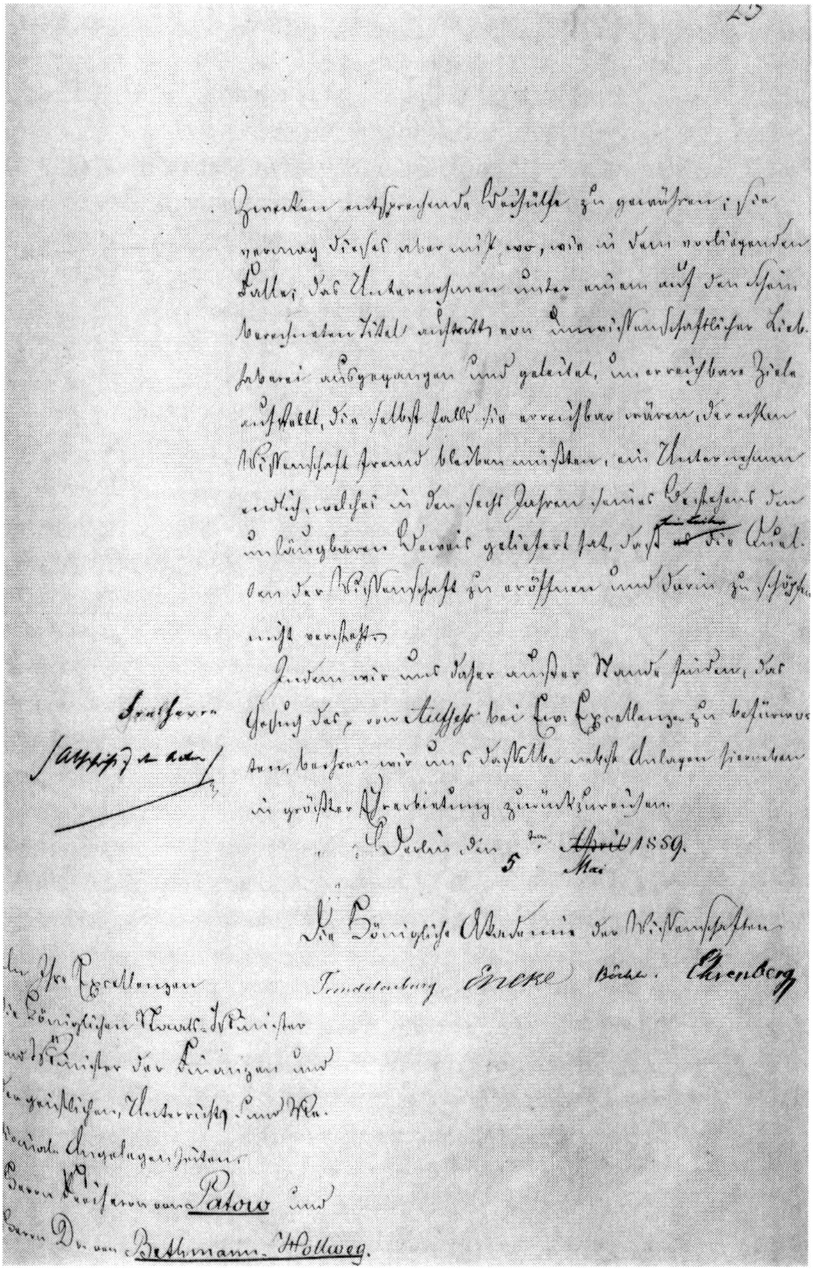

FIGURE 16 The 1859 report of the Berlin-Brandenberg Akademie der Wissenschaften. Photo by author.

deeply committed to the possibility of understanding the past through its sources and of broadening the range of those sources in order to bring more of the past into focus. In one of the appendices in the textbook that emerged from the course, the *Grundriss der Historik*, Droysen wrote that if history were only about politics, it could be written from written sources, once their truth was established. But since it was not, new methods were needed. History "has to investigate formations according to their historical connections, formations of which perhaps only individual remnants are preserved, to open fields hitherto not considered or treated as historical, least of all by those who lived in the midst of them." Just because the historian was confronted by all sorts of new sources did not mean that he was absolved from trying to write new kinds of history. Droysen tells of walking into a gallery devoted to Egyptian antiquities and all the questions it raised in him about tools, metals, color preparation, and materials. "In the way of such technological interpretation of remains, facts are made which in numerous and important directions fill up our meager tradition concerning ancient Egypt; and these facts possess a certainty so much the greater for the indirectness of the manner in which they were deduced."[66]

Droysen thought hard about the history that emerged from things. Nor did this sensitivity come at the expense of the questions that arose from the more familiar subjects. He gave as an example the relations between Dürer and the Italians, which required knowledge of painting technique but also "local and daily history" and general knowledge.[67] "The same," he wrote, was true, "in all other departments. Only deep and many-sided technical and special knowledge, according as it is art, law, commerce, agriculture, or the state and politics that is to be historically investigated, will put the investigator in a condition to ascertain the methods demanded for the given case, and to work with them. Just so, new methods are continually found out in the natural sciences to unlock dumb nature's mysteries."[68]

But as much as this amounted to an extraordinarily thoughtful argument for the importance of what Klemm called "material culture" and "cultural science," Droysen was very uncomfortable about using these terms. Writing to von Sybel in September 1857, Droysen acknowledged that economic history as practiced was "fully dead." But he was just as upset with the way in which the "dumb cultural historical dilettantism" of the Aufseß crowd was going about trying to revive it.[69]

It is in the unpublished parts of the *Historik*, however, that we see the fullest of Droysen's reactions to the contemporary discussion of cultural history. He struggled with the term: "I go with a heavy heart to broach the term Cultural History. It is a name of highly dubious scientific worth and of all too dilettantish rank. Wachsmuth's *Essay on Cultural History* [a misremembered title] and the efforts of the *Zeitschrift für deutsche Kulturgeschichte* have not done anything to pierce the fog."[70] Just because there were facts and stories did not mean that just any fact could be turned to a historical purpose. "It would be false to say that we can make out of every investigation of a given empirical occasion something called historical. But it is trivial history [*kleingeschichtlich*]. It is micrology [*Mikrologie*] which sees the big things as small and the small as big." Here Droysen joined himself to the line that went back to the seventeenth-century in which the work of the antiquary was pejoratively labeled *Mikrologie*; it was, after all, Droysen's teacher Boeckh who represented "micrology" as defective "philology."[71]

What he hoped to offer was "a sharp and fruitful concept for that to which alone cultural history can refer, if it can mean anything." Droysen concluded that "every moment of history can also be grasped as a present tense of conditions." History "is the totality of its ethical forms, its inner hanging-together, its reciprocal dependence." What this means is that a thought or a style or an idea found somewhere in that web is true also for another node in that web. Droysen gives as an example that the "proud, dark, passionate tone of Philip II's politics shows in the same way the Spanish church of his time," its painting, and its literature. Droysen suggests that the "cultural-historical image of any present," such as that of the year 1580, would be more persuasive the more facets of contemporary Italy, England, and France it included: "All these together, these cultural-historical peoples, give then an image of circumstantiality." Cultural history, in Droysen's view, was all about the connectedness (*Zusammenhang*) and resolutely *not* about the particular, individual expressions. These zones of detail instead belonged to some narrow "specialized history" (*Spezialgeschichte*).

This dispensed with one flavor of contemporary *Kulturgeschichte*, the narrow-framed analysis. Droysen then turned to another: "Here we are not talking about cultural history in the sense referred to by Mr. Klemm," namely, "the fullest possible collection of all ethnographic particularities. What he reports on the wild and half-wild peoples has as little to do with the true meaning of cultural history as the history of the wars and peace of these tribes, in our opinion, belongs to general history." If humans were like animals, Klemm's definition would be perfect—but since they were not, *Kulturgeschichte* had to be restricted to the higher notion of culture. Ethnography provided "much more evidence of the absence of culture [*Nicht-kultur*]." Yes, he concluded, "it is of interest to know all peoples and their circumstances." This kind of curiosity would be sufficient if human beings were "just another category of creation." But they weren't. Hence Droysen's conclusion, directly opposing Klemm—and reaffirming, ultimately, the divide between politics and ethnology—that "we retain cultural history only for the cultured peoples."[72] If Klemm had to be rejected as incompatible with received opinion, we can imagine how Droysen would have reacted to Nietzsche's discovery of deep history.

The *Historische Zeitschrift*, edited by Heinrich von Sybel, published volume 1 in 1859. The editor's foreword proclaimed the desire to be neither antiquarian—which is to say, totally unconnected to the present—nor political—too connected to the present. It aimed to illustrate the "the form of states and culture produced [as if by] inner necessity." The journal was, therefore, about "the life of the present" (*Leben der Gegenwart*). Writing from a kind of inevitably Hegelian perspective—"if the highest task of history is to understand the Lawful-ness and Unity of all being and Lives . . . then the past is made present"—a focus on the past as past made no sense. This followed Hegel's sharp break with the world of the antiquarian, like that depicted on Keats's "Grecian Urn," as he presents it in his *Phenomenology of Spirit*.[73]

The lead article in that first number of volume 1, by Wilhelm von Giesebrecht, was dedicated to a historical overview of "modern German historical science." At its beginnings, he wrote, history was a *Hilfswissenschaft* for theology, jurisprudence, and humane letters and emerged out of collections of ecclesiastical history, antiquarian studies, and *Statistik*. As early yearnings he pointed to the handbooks published by Göttingen professors like Gatterer or Schönemann.[74] B. G. Niebuhr and Theodor Mommsen were the modern heroes, the monograph was the message, and the MGH the model for all great ventures. (Mommsen would himself, in the vainglorious years after 1871, present the Reich's *Grossindustrie* as the model for his *Grosswissenschaft*.)

In this constellation, "cultural history" was a problem—"such a many-sided and much-misused name." It was either an "Olla podrida of a thousand little curiosities or a dry enumeration of newer discoveries and fashions." How could this be taken seriously? "One who wishes to find out about the life of the nation must grasp the inner connectedness of its state- and church-lives, must comprehend its manners and law, its language and literature."[75]

This constituted a clear leave-taking from cultural history. But it was not clear enough for the editors of this new journal. For they devoted the second article to an explicit attack on the school of German *Kulturgeschichte* embodied by the Germanisches Nationalmuseum. "False Directions" was Georg Waitz's title, in case readers had any doubts. The enemies of good history lay at both ends of the spectrum: "learned special investigations" and "popular entertainment." Conveniently, they could also be found united in the same production: the *Zeitschrift für deutsche Kulturgeschichte*. The provincial historical associations had done important work, even if few of their number understood how to undertake "special historical research." The provincials ought to have left history for the professionals; their work, like the *Hilfswissenschaften*, was really "Vorarbeit" (preparatory studies) rather than history proper. Dilettantism and "dry as dust" were both dead ends.

The *Zeitschrift für deutsche Kulturgeschichte* ceased publication in 1859. The second volume of the *Historische Zeitschrift* appeared in 1860 containing a laudatory review of Burckhardt's *Culture of the Renaissance in Italy* (*Kultur der Renaissance in Italien*), just then published. (S. G. C. Middlemore's Victorian discomfort, reflected in his inadequate translation of Burckhardt's key term as "civilization" in 1878, has helped obscure Burckhardt's relationship to the story being told here.) Though Burckhardt would later be treated as an antiquarian by many German historians, if there was an acceptable kind of cultural history, it was his, devoted as it was to the higher things in life: art, philosophy, nature, and politics. In 1862 Aufseß resigned as museum director, worn out from the long years of struggling to establish the museum.

Together, these mark the end of an era—and the beginning of another.

The Burckhardt supernova has blinded almost everyone to the prior existence of a thriving practice of cultural history.[76] For students of history, and of cultural history in particular, 1860 is Year One. But for the story we have been telling, it is the end of days. What came after, at Nuremberg, in the later series of the *Zeitschrift für deutsche Kulturgeschichte*, and then at Bonn with Lamprecht, has a very different feel. How are we to assess the pre-1860 period of enormous effort? Most obviously, the closure of the journal represents a failure: a failure, in the first instance, to engage the community of academic historians. Cultural history simply did not catch on in the university except for some very marginal positions. But it also represents the failure of the idea of the museum as a research institution (even as a research institute inside a popular foundation, which was Aufseß's precise vision), a failure that has persisted into our own time. (How many Getty-like research institutes are there embedded within museums? They can be counted on one hand.)

When August von Essenwein took over as director of the Germanisches Nationalmuseum in 1866, he dropped Aufseß's "System," with its dependence on antiquarianism. He shifted to an emphasis on the aesthetics of the art museum. He organized items based on object type and material: viz. sculpture, painting, decorative arts, instruments, furniture. This was very close to the way applied art was then being displayed. Indeed, while the founding of the Germanisches Nationalmuseum is exactly contemporary with that of the South Kensington Museum (later the Victoria and Albert Museum), we would be very wrong to see them as related. It was only Essenwein's turn to the object and away from history that produced this superficial resemblance. His gesture pointed the Germanisches Nationalmuseum in the direction of the contemporary museum foundations dedicated to "Kunst und Industrie" or "Kunst und Gewerbe." The first of these was the Austrian Museum for Art and Industry in Vienna (1864). After the Austro-Prussian War, the German Applied Art Museum opened in Berlin in 1867, followed by similar institutions in Leipzig, Nuremberg, Hamburg, and Frankfurt over the next decade. A few years later, even Nuremberg got its own, "Bavarian Applied Art Museum," showing that despite Essenwein's efforts, the Germanisches Nationalmuseum was in its bones not seen as an applied art museum.[77]

The difference between the South Kensington and German National museums, to put a fine point on it, is that the applied art museum looked forward, not backward—to progress and celebrating achievement and not to salvaging fragments from time's eating teeth. The applied art museum reflected the marriage of industry and art, the historical or cultural museum the curious exploration of past life forms. The Germanisches Nationalmuseum also stood at the head of the whole late nineteenth-century efflorescence of ethnological and folklore museums. The same tension between aesthetic and "historical" valuation of objects runs through the relationships linking the different museums containing these objects. There is much that is instructive in that later nineteenth-century debate about the distinctions dividing history, art, and ethnology museums.[78]

A further comparison may be illuminating. In both the Germany of our story and the United States up until very recently, the study of material culture happened outside of the universities, and often ran up against the disdain of the professoriate. Local historians, amateurs, curators, connoisseurs—they were the ones who knew about the "small things," or about materials, or about practices that did not fall into the neat boxes constituted by academic disciplines. In both Germany and the United States, exhibiting was very important for the development of material culture studies, though perhaps more so in the United States where the Centennial Exposition (Philadelphia 1876) and the Columbian Exposition (Chicago 1893) play roles unlike anything in Germany. Even the founding of the American Wing at the Metropolitan Museum of Art did more to catalyze the study of American objects in the wider culture than did, for instance, the founding of the Germanisches Nationalmuseum. Finally, the study of things in both countries was directly inspired by national politics. In the case of Germany, however, because it was triggered by Napoleon's invasion and the collapse of national politics, cultural history and material culture was from the start an "oppositional" practice. Those who studied it, and this continued on through Burckhardt, who turned down the offer of a professorship in Berlin because of his distaste for the politics of chauvinism after the founding of the German *Reich* in 1871, did so in order *not* to study politics. In the United States, however, the turn to things was a way of celebrating the nation—indeed, of "doing" politics by other means. Those national "fairs" were self-celebratory events. The "Colonial Revival," which included the creation of that American Wing, was part of the mood of self-affirmation that accompanied the post–World War I ascendency. There was no need to justify remembering the small things because these fit the national mythology. In Germany the things pushed against it. In the United States, in short, "1848" was meaningless. (On the other hand, "1865" was not, and that triggered its own oppositional kinds of cultural history, both Southern and African-American, but that is another story, and one that has not run its course.)[79]

Culture and Economy

When the *Zeitschrift für deutsche Kulturgeschichte* came back to life in 1872 in Hanover under the sole editorship of Johannes von Müller, it focused a bit more narrowly on national economy, though without coming out and saying so.[80] The founding of the Reich the previous year had shifted the landscape of debate. No longer was the pre-1848 quest for unity of the *Volk* across the plurality of its "organism" the burning issue. There was greater willingness to identify with the new journal on the part of university-based historians. Even Wilhelm von Giesebrecht, who celebrated Ranke and attacked antiquarianism in the first number of the *Historische Zeitschrift*, contributed an article—on women's history, no less!—and Droysen finally associated his name with the journal's efforts. The affiliation of these few, but pre-eminent, professors shows that the crux of their resistance was to the type of subject matter studied and to the museum as publisher. A focus on economic life and a shift to a commercial publisher alleviated their fears of abetting a decline in professional standards.

Johannes Falke's lead article, "Cultural History and National Economic Theory," staked out the distance traveled from the first series. He began from the realm of the state, acknowledged its importance, and then argued that its sphere did not embrace the whole life of people. Historians needed to take into account those activities that supported material existence. For it was in the pursuit of fundamental needs such as food, clothing, and shelter, that is, in economic activity, that human beings distinguished themselves from animals. While these had only their senses and instincts to work with, humans had spiritual resources and aspirations with which they transformed nature into culture.

For Falke, there was no hard-and-fast line separating the economic from the spiritual life of man, no way to mark precisely the difference between, to use his example, commerce and the technical arts. At the margins, as with "Archäologie der Kunst," the material and the spiritual blurred together. "And so," Falke summed up, "what is economic life other than a history of what happens from day to day, from year to year, and from century to century, for individuals, for a people, for all humankind?" This is a vision of economic history–as–cultural history that would characterize the work of Lamprecht but that Falke in 1872 identified with the work of Lamprecht's teacher, Wilhelm Roscher.[81]

Roscher was already identified with the application of a historical method to the study of economic thought. As early as 1843 he was subsuming a whole series of cultural questions within his economic history (see chapters 2 and 7). It was precisely during the years of the second series of the *Zeitschrift für deutsche Kulturgeschichte* that Roscher published his last book, *History of National Economy in Germany* (1874). Roscher anchored the forerunners of "national economic" thought in the history of history in Germany. In the beginning, he wrote, there was Winckelmann but also Heyne and the Göttingen school. He noted that at the same time "very dry, but influential textbooks" from the era showed that political history was "bound up also with cultural history in the widest sense." He specifically enumerated bourgeois constitutionalism, commerce, and trade as well as the arts and sciences.[82] This broad reach was complemented outside of history, Roscher wrote, by developments in philology and geography. He identified Wolf's *Altertumswissenschaft* as a kind of *Statistik* for the ancient world and Boeckh and K. O. Müller in the next generation as following Wolf's commitment to the material context of ancient life. Geography, as practiced by travelers such as Alexander von Humboldt, was full of discussions of natural products. Geography, as the academic field practiced by scholars like Carl Ritter (1779–1859), led directly to questions of how people lived.[83]

Roscher's ambition was "to take men as they really are"—almost Marx's very words in *The German Ideology*. To do this, he argued, a historical perspective was absolutely necessary. Only history revealed the changing needs, capacities, and relationships of people. Without it, an assessment of any of these would be doomed to error. The two questions that political economy had to answer—and he thought them equally important—were "What is?" and "What should be?" They had to be answered not by theoretical modeling of states of nature but in terms of historical reality.[84] In essays such as "On the

Agriculture of the Most Ancient Germans" or "A Main National-Economic Principle of Forestry," questions of culture—how people lived and worked—were frequently addressed.[85]

When Falke asked the question, "What is economic life other than the day to day?" he was speaking Roscher's language. When Lamprecht, just a few years later, declared that he would "investigate the legal and economic aspects of the development of all of the countryside's material culture, an investigation based on the conviction that in the total development of culture, one may indeed supplement a specific, ideal circle of faith, of art, and of science with the sphere of specific, real or material culture, that is, of economy and of law, and that it must be possible to subject the development of each particular circle, as well as their reciprocal relationships, to distinct investigations" he too was speaking Roscher's language.[86]

In short, with Falke and the second series of the the *Zeitschrift für deutsche Kulturgeschichte* we have found the point of contact between the type of antiquarian-inspired cultural history done in Nuremberg and the economics-inspired cultural history that Lamprecht took away from his studies with Roscher. If we had proceeded entirely genealogically from the present back to Braudel and Bloch, and from Bloch to Lamprecht, and from Lamprecht to Roscher, we would never have found this point of contact with the Nuremberg circle. Instead, we would have continued backwards from Roscher to his teacher Ranke. And then we would have wound up with yet another variant of the received view in which Ranke stands as the father of modern scientific history. We never would have found this deeper-running history of cultural history and never would have been able to identify its points of contact with the still older antiquarian way of studying the past.

The *Zeitschrift für deutsche Kulturgeschichte* failed for a second time, ceasing publication in 1875 (it would have yet another, brief lease on life in the 1890s). And Lamprecht himself over the course of the next decade moved away from economic history-as-cultural history to a greater interest in art and then the laws of social psychology. Yet right here, in the middle of the 1870s, we have found what we set out to find: the narrow pass connecting the deeper history of studying the past through things to our wider present.[87]

❧ CONCLUSION

Toward a Future Theory of the Historical Document

My father had died in April. The week of mourning passed, and then the month. The days began to grow longer, and the feathery blossoms on the trees, which had wept themselves away as I walked to and from the hospital, had long since given way to the hardy green leaves of summer. But summer, in turn, had to yield to fall before I could begin to go through his things. His desk was covered with papers bearing his signature, the overlarge curving *S* whose dramatic stroke exhilarated me as a child when I watched him make it. Then there were the props on his desk, some relics of his long career in the printing business, like the T-square, the extra black pencils, and the sharp rectangular stone on which he scored and cut paper. Some of these I took for my own desk.

All of this was sad, of course, and full of memories. The shock of it all only came later, when I got around to emptying his closet. The shoes he had worn, the shirts, even the suits—all so familiar, and so ghostly, now that the fabrics and leather had lost their animating spirit. But it was only when I finally turned to the hats—and maybe part of me knew this, and that is why I had saved them for last—the hats he wore on all occasions when he went out of doors, the hats that crowned his head, framed his smile, sheltered his dancing eyes . . . that is when I dissolved.

That was also when the idea for this book was conceived, though I did not know it then. What I learned in that instant was that our histories are deeply connected to objects. Of course, I could have learned this from books, but in the end I learned about the power of things from the things themselves. Over the years that followed it was the study of things, rather than the experience of them, that became the focus of my work. But just as Hermanus Posthumus provided me with a picture of the antiquary's emotional world, forever wrestling *tempus edax rerum*, Nietzsche gave me the word for it: *Sehnsucht*. It was then only a matter of time before my interest in how we study things in the world converged with my interest in how we feel through the things that live in us. This book is the result.

Of course, there is much more about our "entanglement" with things, to use the word prominently featured in two provocative books by Nicholas Thomas and Ian Hodder, than the scholarly study of things as historical evidence.[1] I have tried to give some indication of this wider horizon as well, in the hope that historians of scholarship will pay more attention to the world of the imagination and that historians of the arts will avail themselves of the precision in the self-conscious discussions of scholars. If, once upon a time, the handbooks of the early modern *Ars Historica* proclaimed chronology and geography the two "eyes of history," we might rename them *precision* and *imagination*.

In 1907 the leading German journal of museum studies published a six-part article exploring the boundaries between the art museum and the history museum. We could see this as the culmination of the century-long discussion that was conducted under the heading "Archäologie der Kunst." For here as well, it was the unaesthetic but interesting object that was the flashpoint. Could it go into an art museum? It might, if art history was seen as cultural history, but not if art history was about refined, or refining, taste. But if it went into a history museum, was that to imply that aesthetics did not matter at all for history? If, then, history museums were entirely about the story that made an object "interesting," perhaps the objects themselves were but occasions for the spilling of words. Maybe copies could do this job just as well? We have not escaped the gravitational pull of these paradoxes.[2]

A hundred years ago, the author of that remarkable article proposed that the "history museum" distribute its materials according to Biondo's reworking of Varro's antiquarian categories. He spoke of *"Altertümer"* instead of "objects" or "things." And his history museum was organized according to family, household, political and social, legal, religious, artistic, learned, and military *Altertümer*. Otto Lauffer also offered an alternate taxonomy based on materials, such as portraits and seals, and function, such as dwelling or social life, which is more familiar, at least in post-Boas American museums.[3]

The museum's appropriation of the discussion about how to make meaning from objects marks an endpoint in the intense exploration of material evidence that we have been tracking. By 1900 Stark, Lamprecht, and even Dilthey had each independently of the other come to the brink of making the argument for a "material culture studies"—together they had assembled all the pieces needed to press the case—before pulling back. It was the combination of Stark's death and the fact that he presented his argument in terms of an archaic discourse, the controversy surrounding Lamprecht, and Dilthey's disciplinary location in philosophy that permitted later historians and art historians to ignore their arguments.

Similarly, Heinrich Rickert's presentation of the "historical cultural sciences" (historische Kulturwissenschaften) as a solution to the problem of accommodating the individuating nature of historical research and the need for some generalization in order to rise above the welter of detail—perhaps the most conceptually aware presentation of the tension between history and antiquarianism up to that time—seems to have had no obvious echo among practicing historians or historians of history.[4] Only Aby Warburg, who fully integrated objects into a study of imagery, seems to have followed Rickert by identifying his own approach with the field of "Cultural Science." In 1925, he explained to that same Otto Lauffer, no longer a very young museum director but Ordinarius Professor of Folklore at the University of Hamburg and Founding Director of Hamburg's History Museum, that the Kulturwissenschaftliche Bibliothek Warburg was an institution devoted to "comparative cultural science" (vergleichende Kulturwissenschaft). The field he was creating he repeatedly called an "art-historical cultural science" (kunstgeschichtliche Kulturwissenschaft).[5] But he died before he could systematize these thoughts. His followers tried but when forced into exile after 1933 found the effort linguistically unsustainable. One of them, Edgar Wind, explicitly rejected Rickert as a model for Warburg in the one place where he sought to contextualize Warburg's key term.[6]

So did another: Ernst Cassirer, whose Logic of the Cultural Sciences, written in one burst during the desperate summer of 1940 and published in an obscure Swedish journal in 1942 after Cassirer had already emigrated to the United States, was a final contribution to the post-Dilthey conversation. For him, as it had for Rickert, Kulturwissenschaft served as an explicitly synthetic vehicle. On the one hand, religion, art, language "are never tangible for us except in the monuments that they themselves have created." On the other, to focus only on the marble of Michelangelo's sculptures or the canvas and pigments used by Raphael would be to ignore that the material is a means to something else—first, a narration and second, a personal expression. These three layers, which he terms the physical, the historical and the psychological, are each insufficient in themselves to explain any "object of culture." Because the goal of studying the past—Cassirer works with Rickert's notion of "*historische* Kulturwissenschaften" without mentioning it—is understanding, then, as in Dilthey but also as in Nietzsche, when we study "specific historical monuments . . . in words and writing, in image and in bronze," we do this not only for the sake of those lost worlds: "we are able to restore them for ourselves."[7]

The *Logic of the Cultural Sciences* was Cassirer's last German-language publication. A contribution to a debate that now seemed from an entirely different planet, the volume had little resonance in the new geography and climate of postwar history and philosophy. It was seldom read in German and was not translated into English until 2000. The later twentieth century had to regrow its approaches to the object from seeds newly planted by Warburg and Pirenne in the second and third decades of the century.

This is where we began, eight chapters ago. But we can push that moment when the thread was lost even closer to the present. The one English writer who was familiar with this whole German tradition and was himself both a student of historical research and a practicing student of objects was R. G. Collingwood. Professor of both archaeology and philosophy at Oxford, Collingwood understood that history was the history of research practices. For all of these reasons we might have expected him to seize on the antiquarians in order to develop a deep history of the study of objects as evidence.[8]

Collingwood himself described the excavation site as his "laboratory of knowledge." "Experience soon taught me," he wrote, "that under these laboratory conditions one found out nothing at all except in answer to a question; and not a vague question either, but a definite one." Moreover, even in as concrete an inquiry as archaeology, "what one learnt depended not merely on what turned up in one's trenches but also on what questions one was asking." That meant that three different people looking at the same object in the ground but asking three different questions of it might describe what they saw in three different ways.[9] In his *Autobiography* Collingwood identified this question-driven practice with the empirical revolution of Bacon and Descartes. He then extended its implications from the material world to the textual. As a practicing archaeologist, he had all the tools and dispositions needed to reclaim the achievement of the antiquaries, and he was looking at exactly the right moment, 1600 to 1640—but he did not discuss their work at all.[10]

If Collingwood learned the "priority of the question," as Hans-Georg Gadamer was to call it, from digging, it also made him intensely aware of the differences between the laboratory and the library as sites of questioning. Collingwood recalls that Rosencrantz and Guildenstern think they can discover what Plato's *Parmenides* is about by reading it. "But if you took them to the south gate of Housesteads and said, 'Please distinguish the various periods of construction here, and explain what purpose the builders of each period had in mind,' they would protest 'Believe me, I cannot.'"[11]

That the world simply does not present itself to us in the same categories into which it is cut up and arranged in books and by authors was a truth repeatedly remarked upon in the early seventeenth century. As the Roman antiquary Lelio Pasqualini explained to Peiresc in 1608: "There is a very great difference between learning something from writers and seeing the thing itself." Or the French philologist Claude Saumaise, who in 1635 proclaimed that Peiresc was superior to all other students of antiquity because "the majority of our learned men, having worked in only one of these parts, are content with what they can learn from books, which is not at all worth what the things themselves teach us, once we look at them, handle them, and hold them in our hands."[12] In this, the fundamental curatorial encounter, knowledge of the thing can and must come from the thing. Letting it is far from easy work. As Collingwood concludes, "Do they think the *Parmenides* is easier to understand than a rotten little Roman fort?"[13]

This is why material culture studies are important. Where books—let's use the term *disciplines*—cut up knowledge in self-affirming and internally consistent ways, the world is indifferent to classroom categories. The gap between the two has been bridged by what we call "applied learning." The frontier where theory meets practice has always been stormy; think of the relationship between history and political science, between biology and medicine, or between mathematics and engineering. This is what Collingwood was pointing to by contrasting Plato's *Parmenides* with the Roman fort Housesteads. He never got around to connecting the dots from this epistemological truth to any curricular consequences but we well might: Our knowledge of the world will always remain incomplete, and maybe our sense of what constitutes knowledge itself will remain a little distorted, if we don't work from the world back to the books as often as we do from the books to the world. Teaching from objects, or landscapes, is a way of forcing an epistemological revolution. Think about the typical relationship of the library and museum on a college campus: the one central and the other peripheral. Collingwood helps us see why they belong next to each other, as they did at the beginning, in Hellenistic Alexandria's Musaeum, a library and object space rolled into one, and again later in early modern Europe's *Kunst- und Wunderkammer* (often reproduced of late, though nowhere as well as in the British Museum's Enlightenment Gallery).

Even if we were to grant Collingwood that the wordlessness of things is a corrective to the artificiality of the disciplines, we would still be faced with a problem: How do we extract knowledge from the muteness shrouding them? In other words, how do we proceed from the discovery of the question back toward an answer? Collingwood points to "imagination." Not as ornament, the way Macaulay offered that imagination was needed to make a narrative "affecting and picturesque"—a comment that itself looks back to Gatterer's essay on the role of evidence—but as structure. That there are any stories to tell about the past is a triumph of imagination. Surviving sources add up to history only after the historian's imagination weaves them into a fabric with a recognizable pattern.[14]

Imagination played a key role for Dilthey, whose work Collingwood knew well. In his 1867 inaugural lectures in Basel—Burckhardt was already teaching there; Nietzsche would arrive in two years—Dilthey had argued that understanding involved a re-creation that was an imaginative process based on intuition as well as erudition. Dilthey had specifically addressed its function in the poet and the historian.[15] Collingwood, in one of the pieces on method published with *The Idea of History* in 1946, yoked the historian to the novelist.[16] He embraced the way that Dilthey used imagination to allow a later interpreter to enter into the life of an earlier one. This historical afterlife Dilthey termed "re-experiencing" (*Nacherleben*). For Collingwood this concept was the basis of the historian's specific kind of knowledge. For what the historian possessed was "knowledge of the past in the present, the self-knowledge of the historian's own mind as the present revival and reliving of past experiences."[17]

What, in turn, gave imagination such authority was our common humanity. We can enter—more properly, re-enter—a past life because it was lived by another human being with whose range of experiences and feelings we can feel familiar because as humans we share them. Rocks and bones, by contrast, are not human, and thus a rock's long experience of being a rock is simply not accessible to us. What Collingwood calls the pseudo-historical disciplines, such as geology and paleontology, are not history because they are not about humans. But would this also be true for what we call "material culture"? If it were—if Stone Age objects, for instance, were like stones—then there could be no history from things. We would then have come, in all scholarly self-awareness, to discover an adamantine frontier between the post-Renaissance study of material culture and a renaissance of things in our own time.

But Collingwood does not say this. On the contrary, he tells us that when an archaeologist studies things, he views them "as artifacts serving human purposes and thus expressing a particular way in which men have thought about their own life."[18] Things made by people are, and even more importantly remain, proxies for those people and thus can be re-experienced and understood in the same way that we might an individual. Collingwood is no Kantian, and Kant was not interested in material culture, but his transcendental turn—his argument that our categories of perception precede and prepare us for our encounter with the external world—has the effect of similarly eliminating the barrier between humans and things. As he explained in the *Prolegomena to Any Future Metaphysics* (1783), "Nature is the existence of things, so far as it is determined according to universal laws. Should nature signify the existence of things in themselves, we could never know it either a priori or a posteriori." It is only because we can bring the external world under our categories of perception that we can talk about things scientifically—as *knowledge*. Without us, things might exist, but they could not have meaning.

Kant made understanding of the world contingent on the awareness of our prior positioning. For Rickert, this reflexivity made scientific cognition possible. For Dilthey, reflexivity described the hermeneutical turn; it also explains how he could conceive of his work as a way toward the "Critique of Historical Reason" that Kant never attempted. Thinking hermeneutically about Kant's statement on things, we might conclude that just as we need objects to help understand the past, objects need people to fully realize their own potential. This was what Rilke meant when he explained that "transient, they look to us for deliverance: us, the most transient of all."[19] Indeed, this is why we need his poetry and that of Francis Ponge or William Carlos Williams—or even Neil MacGregor: to help us see the world through the eyes of the object. Michael Shanks has coined a word that explains the convergence between poems and things: *pragmatology*, from the Greek word meaning both "things" and "things done." Shanks further notes that the verb at the root of *pragmata* is *prattein*, to act in the material world. This is cognate, he writes, with the verb that signifies making in the poetic sphere: *poiein*. As Williams put it in his account of the genesis of the epic poem *Paterson*, "That is why I started to write *Paterson*: a man is indeed a city, and for the poet there are no ideas but in things."[20]

Rilke's training in this kind of seeing came from sitting with Rodin in Paris and watching his hands. "Hands," he wrote, "have their own culture." From close observation in Paris, Rilke moved to Duino and metaphysics. Without the centuries of thinking and writing that fed that long monographic article on Rodin, Rilke's invocation of the rope maker in Rome or the potter on the Nile might seem casual, even adventitious. But without the seriousness—the deadly seriousness, we might insist—of Rilke, we might treat the study of things as just another academic subject among many. And then we would have fallen into the trap sprung by Nietzsche, who lamented those for whom the choice of subject for academic study was a technical matter and not something that came from or went to their souls: too broad, as he complained about Boeckh's blurring of history and philology, and at the same time far too narrow. This narrowness produced scholarship that was as much a form of alienated labor as what Marx complained about. We might instead see the antiquary's passion—Proust's identification of his curiosity for facts about the past with the endless curiosity of the lover for his beloved is as important a statement about studying the past as anything written by Ranke—as a necessary corrective.

This is not, however, the kind of antiquarianism that Arnaldo Momigliano wrote about, beginning in 1950 with his "Ancient History and the Antiquarian." If we are puzzled by Collingwood's silence about antiquaries, then what of Momigliano's, in turn, about Dilthey and Collingwood? Dilthey, in his Burckhardtian essay of 1901 on the historical world of the eighteenth century, highlights the seventeenth-century contribution of philology to the study of sources and method, often inspired by theological needs, as with seventeenth-century French Jansenist historians of the ancient world such as Sébastian le Nain de Tillemont, the role of documents as the basis for argument, and then in the eighteenth century the importance of Hume, Gibbon, Robertson, and Winckelmann for the writing of a new kind of history. Dilthey called Gibbon "the century's greatest historian" and his argument about the shift from barbarism to civilization the "real problem of eighteenth-century historiography." Collingwood insisted that this kind of "second-order history, or the history of history," was a necessary component of understanding the practice of historical research.[21]

How was it that Momigliano, who we know read Dilthey and Collingwood, neither cites nor incorporates their work on the early modern history of philology and archaeology, even as he makes exactly the same points in his path-breaking essays on antiquarianism?[22] Where Momigliano does give sustained attention to Dilthey and Collingwood in print, the choice of venue is telling: Dilthey in the context of thinking about historicism, not antiquarianism or classical philology; Collingwood in a review of 1945 on the state of ancient history in England. (All the other, scattered, references to Collingwood come in relation to his work on Croce.)[23] Momigliano is ambivalent about Collingwood, acknowledging the merit of his "insisting on history as research, and not narration or description," but viewing that very insistence as being carried on to the point of error. As for Collingwood's question-and-answer method, again Momigliano seems of two minds, describing the chapters Collingwood devotes to it as the best in the *Autobiography* but also siding with those who argued that it led Collingwood to crude errors.[24]

Only a few years later, though, in the summer of 1950, Collingwood was at the center of a very important turn in Momigliano's intellectual life. The connection was Croce. Writing an appreciation of the older man's work, Momigliano concluded that Croce's reception in England was complicated by the fact that he "found here the most intelligent of his pupils—but he was a queer pupil" who never understood the depth of his debt to Croce. This was Collingwood. Momigliano noted that there were now university lecture courses devoted to Collingwood's philosophy, but he implied that it was derivative.

At this point, Momigliano's assessment of the relationship between Croce and Collingwood, master and disciple, moves into a new domain. A comparison of the work of the two men, he concluded, will help us understand "what so far is the most comprehensive—and perhaps also the most difficult—attempt at a philosophy of history in our time: a philosophy of history accompanied by and leading to solid historical research."[25] From earlier in the essay we know that Momigliano admired Croce for the way he expressed much of his philosophical work through historical scholarship. Momigliano was implying that, by comparison, this was what Collingwood did not quite do. Yet, nevertheless, another long-unpublished essay from that same summer shows how much Momigliano learned from Collingwood, adopting for himself—silently, as he claimed Collingwood did with Croce—Collingwood's question-and-answer approach. "Philology and History" begins exactly as Collingwood might have written: "A problem is the starting point of any historical research. We mean by a historical problem a situation which can be explained only with the help of some evidence which at the moment is not available to the historian or if it is available is not fully clear. . . . Thus, the historian looks for evidence."[26]

Like the presence of Collingwood, it is the word *research* that connects these two essays and brings them together with a third, also written that summer: a short précis of "Ancient History and the Antiquarian," the article that would be published later that year and would eventually launch the renaissance of the history of antiquarianism. More unequivocally than in the published article, Momigliano puts the contemporary importance of the history of antiquarianism in terms of its rebuke to loose forms of argument. In the later seventeenth century hyperbolic skepticism was dubbed "Pyrrhonian," and the antiquarians had entered the lists to combat this challenge to the possibility of knowledge. Momigliano's act of historical recovery was motivated by a present fear: "Against conjecturalism and Pyrrhonism there is only the old remedy: the cautious and methodical examination of documents with all the skills that were developed in the collaboration of antiquaries and textual critics in the seventeenth and eighteenth centuries." This is the "solid historical research" of the Croce-Collingwood conclusion, and Momigliano is now deploying it as the foundation for a new kind of historical scholarship inspired by the antiquarians. He even ended the essay calling for a "future, modern *ars historica*." Between the wars there was much discussion of hermeneutics, he wrote, but it all focused on Schleiermacher, who derived its principles from theology and then imported them into philology. This was the line that extended from his student Boeckh all the way through the nineteenth century, as we have seen. But this hermeneutics, with its slide toward subjectivism and misology, had led to its own sort of "trahison des clercs." In its place, Momigliano now argued, "there exists a hermeneutic of the antiquaries, much more complex and more productive than that of the theologians, which merits attention in any future theory of the historical document."[27] Momigliano had, in fact, digested that whole nineteenth-century literature on hermeneutics and its application to the study of past artifacts. But by the summer of 1950 he had come to the conclusion that the study of historical scholarship as practiced offered a better understanding of how to understand the past, one that could not be tortured into advocating for whatever ideology the scholar himself supported.

Momigliano never explicitly returned to the "future theory of the historical document," never explicitly tried to paint a future historical practice inspired by the antiquarians. But if we follow the return of the other word from the parallel Croce essay, we might find a clue: research. The lecture he devoted to antiquarianism in his 1963 Sather Lectures at Berkeley was entitled "The Rise of Antiquarian *Research*." He argued that while premodern historians worked by rewriting ancient historians, antiquaries scoured literary and material remains for new information, turning these things, some of which actually were "things," into sources. For Momigliano, this would mark the path toward the deep engagement with the social and cultural sciences that colored his last decades' work as well as a re-engagement of history with the cultural sciences. The Greek title of Herodotus' great book was, after all, "Researches" and belonged to the broader Ionian exploration of the world (Herodotus was born in Halicarnassus, modern-day Bodrum). Only later, and because of him, did the word he used, *historia*, come to mean our "history" and acquire an emphasis on story. Thinking about Momigliano's wagering of antiquarianism against Pyrrhonism, we can understand how research is also an ethical stance. Acknowledging the endlessness of the task and the impossibility of perfection because of both the limitations of evidence and the limitations of our ability to interpret evidence—but always with a commitment to pursuing truth—makes historical research into a form of philosophical exercise. It is a way of living in the world.

Nietzsche thought more about pedagogy than research and much more about texts than things.[28] Reading through the *Untimely Meditations* today, it is astonishing how contemporary "We Historians" and "We Philologists" remain. But the kind of disengagement Nietzsche laments—philology ignoring the philologist, that is, imagining that we can separate knowledge acquisition in the humanities from the person who is acquiring and processing that knowledge—is actually a comment on the dissociation of research from the person doing the research. It is an ethical argument. If Herodotus represented a last moment in which research knit together human and natural concerns, then we can read *The Birth of Tragedy* as being as much about Herodotus as Socrates.

This is where objects come in. Because we can hold them in our hands or lay our hands on them, because we can sometimes actually feel the past, the connection between learning and person endures. Because objects do not themselves speak we are always forced into an empathic, imaginative relationship if we are to find a way to represent them, whether to ourselves or to others. Far from there being no hermeneutic of the object, as the nineteenth century came to conclude, we might turn things around. That we can make sense of objects at all is only because we experience them hermeneutically.

Returning in *The Gay Science* (1882) to many of the themes of the *Untimely Meditations* of the early 1870s but broadening their address, Nietzsche pointed to the antiquarian in everyone and connected it to the deepest feeling of loss-over-time: "Anyone who manages to experience the history of humanity as a whole as *his own history* will feel in an enormously generalized way all the grief of an invalid who thinks of health, of an old man who thinks of the dreams of his youth, of a lover deprived of his beloved, of the martyr whose ideal is perishing, of the hero on the evening after a battle that has decided nothing but brought him wounds and the loss of a friend." But if this is a longing drenched in melancholy, the Nietzsche of the 1880s found a way to turn *Sehnsucht* into affirmation—and antiquarianism into something like an old-new vision of history as the guide to life, or *magistra vitae*.

> If one could finally contain all this in one soul and crowd it into a single feeling—this would surely have to result in a happiness that humanity has not known so far: the happiness of a god full of power and love, full of tears and laughter, a happiness that, like the sun in the evening, continually bestows its inexhaustible riches, pouring them into the sea, feeling richest, as the sun does, only when even the poorest fisherman is still rowing with golden oars! This godlike feeling would then be called—humaneness [*Menschlichkeit*].[29]

🦋 ACKNOWLEDGMENTS

For a long time I described this book to friends as the series of lectures I never had the chance to deliver. It helped explain its style and structure—at least to me. Even if it didn't have its origin in a series of lectures I was invited to deliver, one source of the idea that became this book derived from lectures delivered in a series I organized at Bard Graduate Center in 2004–2005 on "The Auxiliary Sciences Today." I am grateful to the inspiration offered by the speakers that year: Anders Winroth, Jacob Soll, Marcello Simonetta, Matt Jones, Elisheva Carlebach, Jonathan Hay, and Michael McCormick. About a year earlier, though, I had been a guest of Lorraine Daston at the Max-Planck-Institut für Wissenschaftsgeschichte in Berlin for a project run by Nancy Siraisi and Gianna Pomata, and its patient librarians had collected for me the materials that made the skeleton of this book. I then ran a research seminar on the subject through several iterations, "Foundations of Material Culture." It was a wonderful opportunity for me to be able to assemble my arguments and sharpen them against the wits of my students. I am sure, however, that it did not always make for a thrilling in-class experience. But it is clear to me now that I could never have developed this book manuscript without that time in the classroom. I was grateful to my students then, and I am even more grateful now. I thank them all by name: Maude Bass-Krueger, Donna Bilak, Adam Brandow, Christine Brennan, Yenna Chan, Doug Clouse, Joyce Denney, Erin Eisenbarth, Rina Fuji, Sierra Gonzalez, Elise Hodson, Roisin Ingelsby, Rita Jules, Matt Keagle, Hannah Kinney, Evelyn Leong, Elizabeth MacMahon, Casey Mathern, Jessica Mizrahi, Kate Nyhan, Amy Osborne, Maria Perers, Rebecca Perten, Shax Riegler, Jorge Rivas-Perez, Amy Sande-Friedman, Frederun Scholz, Kate Tahk, Jon Tavares, and Tom Tredway.

My colleagues at the Bard Graduate Center over the past fifteen years have taught me an enormous amount. Our sustained conversation about material culture has been great—and great fun. I think it is a rare thing for an institution to function also as a symphony, with different voices carrying different parts and doing different work, but all towards the same end. I feel fortunate to have been part of this and I know how much it has shaped me.

I also want to thank the librarians who have kept me supplied with books and inter-library loans, including Heather Topcik, Janis Ekdahl, Rebecca Kranz Friedman, Cheryl Costello, Karyn Hinkle, and Anna Helgeson. During the semester in which I was on leave finishing this book, Jeffrey Collins and Elena Pinto Simon generously took on more responsibilities so that I could feel fewer. I am very grateful to them.

Though never delivered as a series, I am grateful to friends and colleagues for opportunities to air some of the themes and content. I thank Martin Mulsow, who gave me the gift of a day's seminar at his Forschungszentrum Gotha devoted to discussion of an early version of this book. Felipe Rojas invited me to give a lecture at Brown that sparked what appears here as the core of the introduction. Rilke, who inspired chapter 1, featured in many speeches and introductions I delivered in my capacity as dean of the Bard Graduate Center between 2006 and 2010. Other parts of that chapter, on Emmanuel Ringelblum and David Macaulay, were the subject of reviews published in *The New Republic*. I thank my friend Leon Wieseltier for giving me the opportunity to explore these topics. Part of chapter 3, on Peiresc and the *Hilfswissenschaften*, was presented at a joint BGC-Columbia Medieval/ Renaissance Seminar. The core of chapter 7, on Gustav Friedrich Klemm, was discussed at the kick-off meeting for the "Cultural Histories of the Material World" book series, and its conclusion, on *Kulturwissenschaft*, was presented at a conference at the Warburg Institute. The content of chapter 8, Aufseß and the Germanisches Nationalmuseum, were the subject of talks given at a joint BGC/INHA workshop and at the CIHA 2012 meeting at Nuremberg. For the last four years Michael Shanks and I have been running an informal, bi-coastal collaborative seminar on "Neo-Antiquarianism"; the writing of this book has been part of that conversation. Drafts of the complete manuscript were read at different times by Ken Ames, Anthony Grafton, Joan-Pau Rubiés, Marina Rustow, Michael Shanks, and Chris Wood. I am grateful to them for their time and thoughtfulness. There have been many moments, especially when I was trying to make sense of the connection between political economy and social theory in the middle of the nineteenth century, that I longed for just one more conversation with my dear friend and teacher Istvan Hont. I can see his face and I can hear his voice, but I no longer have his words. From one book to the next, Aleš Debeljak, a poet and a professor of *Kulturwissenschaft*, also slipped in among the shades. "Hugs"—that was how he always signed off. Now this word makes me think of thrice-foiled Odysseus in the Underworld.

John Ackerman, then the director of Cornell University Press, wanted to publish this book. I am grateful to him for his interest in, and support for, this project. Mahinder Kingra has my thanks for the way he then helped the book ripen with just a few astute observations about the manuscript's structure. Bethany Wasik, Karen Laun, and Martin Schneider helped me through the production phase. I am in debt to Nils Schott for his exceptional skills as a copyeditor. Antonia Behan, Elizabeth Neil, and Michelle Jackson helped me with very practical tasks at the end, and I thank them warmly. Above all, I thank everyone mentioned here for their patience!

For as long as I have lived I have thanked my parents, Samuel Miller and Naomi Churgin Miller, and for as long as they have lived I have thanked my children, Livia and Samuel. Rilke enjoined us to think about childhood in order to find a way back to the power of objects: "If, amongst your early experiences, you knew kindness, confidence and the sense of not being alone—do you not owe it to that thing?" So, in addition to everything else about them that I give thanks for, I have to thank my children for helping me find my way back to this world—their world—from which I have learned so much. I have sometimes wondered what the "Tempus Edax Rerum" of Posthumus might look like if painted today. I think it would be a child with a divining rod.

Notes

Introduction

1. Robert B. Pippin, *Interanimations: Receiving Modern German Philosophy* (Chicago: University of Chicago Press, 2015), 1–4.

2. Friedrich Nietzsche, "Encyclopädie der klassischen Philologie," in *Nietzsche Werke*, pt. 2, vol. 3, ed. Fritz Bornmann and Mario Carpitella (Berlin: Walter de Gruyter, 1993), 349. See James I. Porter, *Nietzsche and the Philology of the Future* (Stanford: Stanford University Press, 2000), ch. 4, though he does not discuss this passage.

3. See Nietzsche, *Anti-Education*, introduction and notes by Paul Reitter and Chad Wellmon, trans. Damion Searls (New York: New York Review Books, 2015). This course of lectures was delivered in 1872.

4. Nietzsche, "History in the Service and Disservice of Life," in *Unmodern Observations/Unzeitgemässe Betrachtungen*, ed. William Arrowsmith (New Haven and London: Yale University Press, 1990), 99–103. I have compared this translation with that of Peter Preuss, *On the Advantage and Disadvantage of History for Life* (Indianapolis: Hackett, 1980), 19–21, and preferred occasionally the one or the other. Raymond Geuss, "Nietzsche and Genealogy," *European Journal of Philosophy* 2 (1994): 274–92.

5. "Alles Erinnern ist Vergleichen d.h. Gleichsetzen. Jeder Begriff sagt uns das; es ist das 'historische' Urphäonomen . . . Diesen Trieb bezeichne ich als den Trieb nach dem Klassischen und Mustergültigen: die Vergangenheit dient der Gegenwart als Urbild. Entgegen steht der antiquarische Trieb, der sich bemüht das Vergangne als vergangen zu fassen und nicht zu entstellen, nicht zu idealisiren. Das Lebensbedürfniss nach dem Klassischen, das Wahrheitsbedürfniss nach dem Antiquarischen." "Nachgelassene Fragmente. Sommer 1872 bis Ende 1874," in *Nietzsche Werke: Kritische Gesamtausgabe*, series 3, vol. 4, ed. Giorgio Colli and Mazzino Montinar (Berlin and New York: De Gruyter, 1978), 244.

6. Nietzsche, "History in the Service and Disservice of Life," 103; 110–11.

7. Nietzsche, "History in the Service and Disservice of Life," 124.

8. Nietzsche, "We Philologists," *Unmodern Observations/Unzeitgemässe Betrachtungen*, 340. I have silently altered some of the translations.

9. Friedrich Hölderlin, *Selected Poems and Fragments*, trans. Michael Hamburger, ed. Jeremy Adler (London: Penguin, 1998), 258–59.

10. Nietzsche, "History in the Service and Disservice of Life," 100; Rainer Maria Rilke, *Ahead of All Parting: The Selected Poetry and Prose of Rainer Maria Rilke* [henceforth *Selected Poetry and Prose*], 384–85. This "antiquarian" link between Nietzsche and Rilke is obscured in Walter Kaufmann, "Nietzsche and Rilke," *The Kenyon Review*, 17 (1955), 7.

11. Nietzsche, "Encyclopädie der klassischen Philologie," 369.

12. Marc Bloch, *The Historian's Craft*, trans. Peter Putnam (Manchester: Manchester University Press, 1992), 36.

13. Henry David Thoreau, *The Journal, 1837–1861*, ed. Damion Searls (New York: New York Review Books, 2009), 557.

14. Thoreau, *Journal*, 557.

15. Plato, *Hippias Major*, 285d, *The Collected Dialogues of Plato*, ed. Edith Hamilton and Huntington Cairns, trans. Lane Cooper (Princeton: Princeton University Press, 1961), 1538. See F. Osann, "Der Sophist Hippias als Archaeolog," *Rheinisches Museum für Philologie*, new series 2 (1843): 495–521.

16. Plato, *Cratylus*, 439b, *Collected Dialogues of Plato*, 473. See Francesco Ademollo, *The* Cratylus *of Plato: A Commentary* (Cambridge, U.K.: Cambridge University Press, 2011), 446–47.

17. We can now make these kinds of comparisons because Alain Schnapp undertook the project that resulted in *World Antiquarianism*, ed. Alain Schnapp et al. (Los Angeles: Getty Publications, 2013).

18. For all of these, see my *Peiresc's Mediterranean World* (Cambridge, MA: Harvard University Press, 2015).

19. See Alain Schnapp, *La Conquête du passé* (Paris: Carré, 1994), translated as *The Discovery of the Past* (London: British Museum, 1996); idem, "Between Antiquarians and Archaeologists—Continuities and Ruptures," *Antiquity* 76 (2002): 134–40; Richard Bradley, *The Past in Prehistoric Societies* (London: Routledge, 2002).

20. Arnaldo Momigliano, *The Classical Foundations of Modern Historiography* (Berkeley, Los Angeles, and Oxford, U.K.: University of California Press, 1990), 54.

21. Arnaldo Momigliano, "Ancient History and the Antiquarian," *Journal of the Warburg and Courtauld Institutes* 13 (1950): 285–315; on which, see Ingo Herklotz, "Arnaldo Momigliano's 'Ancient History and the Antiquarian': A Critical Review," in *Momigliano and Antiquarianism: Foundations of the Modern Cultural Sciences*, ed. Peter N. Miller (Toronto: University of Toronto Press, 2007), 127–53.

22. Momigliano's decision not to study the history of cultural history emerges in a correspondence with Frances Yates in the Fall of 1950. See Anthony Grafton, "Momigliano's Method and the Warburg Institute: Studies in His Middle Period," *Momigliano and Antiquarianism*, 115. Hans Schleier, *Geschichte der deutschen Kulturgeschichtsschreibung* (Waltrop, Germany: Hartmut Spenner, 2008).

23. Eduard Fueter, *Geschichte der neueren Historiographie* (Munich: Oldenbourg, 1911). Fueter left out antiquarianism entirely. The new twenty-first-century history of history, *The Oxford History of Historical Writing*, ed. Daniel Woolf, 5 vols. (Oxford, U.K.: Oxford University Press, 2013) devotes a single chapter to early modern antiquarianism in volume three. On questions, see Paul Veyne, *Writing History: Essay on Epistemology*, tr. Mina Moore-Rinvolucri (Middletown, CT: Wesleyan University Press, 1984), 224.

24. On the complexity of the German-American nexus, see Emily J. Levine, "Baltimore Teaches, Göttingen Learns: Cooperation, Competition, and the Research University," *The American Historical Review* 121 (2016): 780–823.

25. For example, Astrid Swenson, *The Rise of Heritage: Preserving the Past in France, Germany, and England, 1789–1914* (Cambridge, U.K.: Cambridge University Press, 2013); Stephen Bann, *The Clothing of Clio: A Study of the Representation of History in Nineteenth-Century Britain and France* (Cambridge, U.K.: Cambridge University Press,

1984); Bonnie Effros, *Uncovering the Germanic Past: Merovingian Archaeology in France, 1830–1914* (Oxford, U.K.: Oxford University Press, 2012); Philippa Levine, *The Amateur and the Professional: Antiquarians, Historians, and Archaeologists in Victorian England, 1838–1886* (Cambridge, U.K.: Cambridge University Press, 1986).

26. Lionel Gossman, *Medievalism and the Ideologies of the Enlightenment: The World and Work of La Curne de Sainte-Palaye* (Baltimore: The Johns Hopkins University Press, 1968), 354.

27. This analogy was inspired by reading Yuval Noah Harrari, *Sapiens: A Brief History of Humankind* (New York: HarperCollins, 2015).

28. William Stenhouse, "Antiquarianism," in *The Classical Tradition*, ed. Anthony Grafton, Glenn Most, and Salvatore Settis (Cambridge, MA, and London: Harvard University Press, 2010), 51–53; idem, "The Renaissance Foundations of European Antiquarianism," in *World Antiquarianism*, ed. Alain Schnapp et al. (Los Angeles: Getty Publications, 2013), 295–316; Miller, "Major Trends in European Antiquarianism, Petrarch to Winckelmann," in *The Oxford History of Historical Writing*. Volume 3: 1400–1800, ed. Jose Rabasa, Masayuki Sato, Edoardo Tartarolo, and Daniel Woolf (Oxford, U.K.: Oxford University Press, 2012), 244–60; idem, "A Tentative Morphology of European Antiquarianism, 1500–2000," in *World Antiquarianism*, 67–88; Peter N. Miller and François Louis, eds., *Antiquarianism and Intellectual Life in Europe and China, 1500–1800* (Ann Arbor: University of Michigan Press, 2012).

29. Exploring Momigliano's suggestion is the premise of Miller, *Momigliano and Antiquarianism*.

30. Examples include Pamela Smith's "Making and Knowing" project at Columbia University and the Institute of Making at University College, London.

31. Françoise Choay, "Introduction" in Camillo Boito, *Conserver ou restaurer? (1893)* (Paris: Éditions de l'Encyclopédie des Nuisances, 2013), 9–10 and more generally *L'allegorie du patrimoine* (Paris: Éditions du seuil, 1992), ch. 2. Academic initiatives in this direction have been promoted by the Mellon and Kress Foundations in the United States.

32. "The Germanisches Nationalmuseum and the Museums Debate in Later 19th Century Germany," in *The Challenge of the Object: 33rd Congress of the International Committee of the History of Art, Nuremberg, 15th–20th July 2012*, ed. Georg Ulrich Großmann and Petra Krutisch, 4 vols. (Nuremberg: Verlag des Germanischen Nationalmuseums, 2013), 1, 370–73.

33. Warburg, "Italian Art and International Astrology in the Palazzo Schifanoia, Ferrara," in Warburg, *The Renewal of Pagan Antiquity* (Los Angeles: Getty Research Institute, 1999), 585.

34. "We Philologists" and "We Historians" were two of the "untimely" or "anti-modern" meditations written during the years immediately following. The former was left unfinished, while the latter was published with the title *Vom Nutzen und Nachteil der Historie für das Leben*. But in 1887, a prospective second edition was announced with the title "We Historians: Towards a History of the Sickness of the Modern Soul."

35. Momigliano, review of Lionel Gossman, *Orpheus Philologicus*, *Ottavo Contributo alla Storia degli Studi Classici e del Mondo Antico* (Rome: Edizioni di Storia e Letteratura, 1987), in *Journal of Modern History* 57 (1985): 328–30.

36. Nietzsche, *Human, All Too Human (I)*, trans. Gary Handwerk, *The Complete Works of Friedrich Nietzsche, Volume III* (Stanford: Stanford University Press, 1990),

no. 2, p. 16; no. 41, p. 49; no. 45, pp. 51–52. This last is one of a series of observations that are later developed into the first essay of his *Genealogy of Morality* (1887). I have seen this point noted only in Saul Tobias, "Nietzsche as Deep Historian," *The European Legacy* 20 (2015): 606–7. Christian Benne describes Nietzsche's interest in comparative ethnology as "astounding and astoundingly early" but does not specifically call attention to his attention to prehistory (*Nietzsche und die historisch-kritische Philologie* (Berlin and New York: Walter de Gruyter, 2005), 120).

37. Nietzsche, *Human, All Too Human*, no. 111, p. 91.

38. Alfred Weber, *Kulturgeschichte als Kultursoziologie* (Leiden: Sijthoff, 1935), 13–14. His response to Nietzsche is the subject of Franz zu Solms-Laubach, *Nietzsche and Early German and Austrian Sociology* (New York and Berlin: De Gruyter, 2007), ch. 8, but there is no discussion there of "prehistory."

39. I am thinking of the way Cyprian Broodbank approaches the history of the Mediterranean before writing in *The Making of the Middle Sea* (Oxford, U.K.: Oxford University Press, 2014).

Chapter One. History and Things in the Twentieth Century

1. Rainer Maria Rilke, *Rodin and Other Prose Pieces*, trans. C. Craig Houston, introduction by William Tucker (London: Quartet Books, 1986), 19.

2. Rilke, *Rodin*, 45.

3. Rilke, *Rodin*, 45–46.

4. Rilke, *Rodin*, 47.

5. Rilke, *Selected Poetry and Prose*, 370–71.

6. Rilke, *Selected Poetry and Prose*, 372–73.

7. "Solche Entberbte, / denen das Frühere nicht und noch nicht das Nächste gehört."

8. Rilke, *Selected Poetry and Prose*, 384–85.

9. Rilke, *Selected Poetry and Prose*, 384–85.

10. Horst Bredekamp, "Warburg, Berlin, the Middle Ages," paper presented at *Aby Warburg 150: Work. Legacy. Promise: A Conference in London June 13–15, 2016*.

11. Aby M. Warburg, *Schlangenritual: Ein Reisebericht*, afterword by Ulrich Raulff (Berlin: Wagenbach, 1988); *Schlangenritual: Der Transfer der Wissensformen vom Tsu'ti'kive der Hopi bis zu Aby Warburgs Kreuzlinger Vortrag*, ed. Cora Bender, Thomas Hensel, and Erhard Schüttpelz (Berlin: Akademie Verlag, 2007).

12. Quoted in Ernst Gombrich, "Warburg Centenary Lecture," in *Art History as Cultural History: Warburg's Projects*, ed. Richard Woodfield (Amsterdam: OPA, 2001), 41. On the Hamburg School, see Emily Levine, *Dreamland of Humanists: Warburg, Cassirer, Panofsky, and the Hamburg School* (Chicago: University of Chicago Press, 2013).

13. Bernd Roeck, *Florence 1900: The Quest for Arcadia* (Chicago: University of Chicago Press, 2009 [2004]), 71. I thank Horst Bredekamp for this fact. Warburg, *Werke in einem Band*, ed. Martin Treml, Sigrid Weigel, and Perdita Ladwig (Frankfurt a.M.: Suhrkamp Verlag, 2010), 222: "Die Antike war ihm . . . die wiedererwachte Vergangenheit des eigenen heimatlichen Bodens." I am grateful to Ulrich Raulff for this reference.

14. Edgar Wind, "Warburg's Concept of *Kulturwissenschaft*," in *The Eloquence of Symbols: Studies in Humanist Art*, ed. Jaynie Anderson (Oxford, U.K.: Clarendon Press, 1993), 24.

15. None of what is presented in chapter 7 is, for example, found in Claus Leggewie et al., eds., *Schlüsselwerke der Kulturwissenschaften* (Bielefeld: transcript, 2012).

16. Wilhelm Ostwald, *Energetische Grundlagen der Kulturwissenschaft* (Leipzig: Klinkhardt Verlag, 1909). That Ostwald in the end used the word *Kulturwissenschaft* in the title is less telling than his explanation that he initially planned to call it *Soziologie* because he thought it represented the "most general and highest synthesis of human affirmation" (v). I am grateful to Kurt Forster for referring me to this title.

17. The story of the death of "Kulturwissenschaft" is fascinating: Edgar Wind had devoted pages to explaining it in the German introduction to Hans Meier, Richard Newald, and Edgar Wind, eds., *Kulturwissenschaftliche Bibliographie zum Nachleben der Antike: Erster Band: Die Erscheinungen des Jahres 1931* (Leipzig and Berlin: B. G. Teubner, 1934), vii–xi, but omitted these pages in his English version of the introduction, after proclaiming the word *Kulturwissenschaft* as itself untranslatable.

18. Paolo Baldacci, *Giorgio De Chirico: The Metaphysical Period, 1888–1919*, trans. Jeffrey Jennings (New York: Bullfinch, 1997), 69–70. More specifically, see Baldacci, "The Function of Nietzsche's Thought in De Chirico's Art," in *Nietzsche and "An Architecture of Our Minds,"* ed. Alexandre Kostka and Irving Wohlfarth (Los Angeles: Getty Publications, 1999), 91–114, esp. 95–96. For more on the deep Greece of prehistory, see Ara H. Merjian, "'Il faut méditerraniser la peinture': Giorgio de Chirico's Metaphysical Painting, Nietzsche, and the Obscurity of Light," *California Italian Studies* 1 (2010): 11.

19. Ponge's prose poem on snails, dated 1936, compares directly with Peiresc's essay on copulating slugs. Carpentras, Bibliothèque Inguimbertine, MS 1821, fols. 82–83, quoted in Miller, "Description Terminable and Interminable: Looking at the Past, Nature, and Peoples in Peiresc's Archive," in *'Historia': Empricism and Erudition in Early Modern Europe*, ed. Gianna Pomata and Nancy Siraisi (Cambridge, MA: MIT, 2005), 369.

20. Quoted in Stuart Gillespie and Philip R. Hardie, eds., *The Cambridge Companion to Lucretius* (Cambridge, U.K.: Cambridge University Press, 2007), 317.

21. In "A Sort of Song," Williams writes, "of words, slow and quick, sharp/ to strike, quiet to wait,/ sleepless./ —through metaphor to reconcile/ the people and the stones./ Compose. (No ideas/ but in things) Invent!"

22. See my discussion of De Certeau in *Peiresc's Mediterranean World*, 150–51.

23. Bertolt Brecht, "Der Messingkauf," in *Brecht on Performance: Messingkauf and Modelbooks*, ed. Tom Kuhn, Steve Giles, and Marc Silberman (London: Bloomsbury, n.d.), 17. I thank Freddie Rokem for pointing me toward this literary encounter between Brecht and Benjamin. See Rokem, *Philosophers and Thespians: Thinking Performance* (Stanford: Stanford University Press, 2009), 121–22.

24. Despite a fame in France almost equal, at least among anthropologists, with that of Claude Lévi-Strauss, Leroi-Gourhan hardly exists for English readers. This will change with an edition of a selection of his works edited by Nathan Schlanger and published by the Bard Graduate Center in the series "Cultural Histories of the Material World."

25. Fernand Braudel, "Vie matérielle et comportements biologiques," and "Histoire de la vie matérielle," both in Braudel, *L'Histoire au quotidien* (Paris: Éditions de Fallois, 2001), 215–27.

26. Sigfried Giedion, *Mechanization Takes Command: A Contribution to Anonymous History* (Minneapolis: University of Minnesota Press, 2013 [1948]), 2.

27. James Deetz, *In Small Things Forgotten: The Archaeology of Early American Life* (New York: Doubleday, 1977), 7–8.

28. Thomas J. Schlereth, "Material Culture Studies in America, 1876–1976," in *Material Culture Studies in America*, ed. Thomas J. Schlereth (Nashville: American Association for State and Local History, 1982), 1. Schlereth also believed that up to that point "no one had attempted a synoptic historical overview that might try to answer these questions." Ames's assessment of Schlereth's contribution is found in his foreword to Schlereth, *Cultural History and Material Culture: Everyday Life, Landscapes, Museums* (Charlottesville and London: University Press of Virginia, 1992), xix.

29. Schlereth, "Material Culture Studies in America," 31–32. As late as 1981, when this essay was first published, Schelreth could write the following: "Unfortunately, the official history establishment, the American Historical Association and its membership residing in college and university departments of history, remains largely indifferent to this scholarly activity" (73).

30. Schlereth, *Cultural History and Material Culture*, 6.

31. This exhibition has recently itself become the object of scholarly study: Anke te Heesen and S. Padberg, eds., *Musée Sentimental 1979* (Ostfildern, Germany: Hatje Cantz Verlag, 2011).

32. Available at www.muenchner-stadtmuseum.de/en/sonderausstellungen/i-am-the-only-one-who-owns-these-things-thepassionofcollecting.html, accessed October 2, 2015.

33. Available at http://collectiegebouw.boijmans.nl/en/, accessed October 29, 2015.

34. Frederic Marès Deulorol, *El mundo fascinante del coleccionismo y de las antigüedades: Memorias de la vida de un coleccionista* (Barcelona, 1977).

35. Peter N. Miller, "Thinking with Thomas Browne: Sebald and the *Nachleben* of the Antiquarian," in *Sir Thomas Browne: The World Proposed*, edited by Reid Barbour and Claire Preston (Oxford, U.K.: Oxford University Press, 2008), 318–19; Kurt W. Forster, "Bilder geistern durch Sebalds Erzählungen, Geister bewohnen ihre Zeilen" in *Wandernde Schatten: W. G. Sebalds Unterwelt*, ed. Ulrich von Bülow, Heike Gfrereis, and Ellen Strittmatter (Marbach: Deutscher Schillergesellschaft, 2008), 87–99. The contrast is with the linguistic manipulation documented in Viktor Klemperer, *Lingua Tertii Imperii: Notizbuch eines Philologen* (Berlin: Aufbau-Verlag, 1947).

36. Petra Lange-Berndt, ed., *Materiality* (London and Cambridge, MA: Whitechapel Gallery and MIT Press;, 2015), especially the editor's "Introduction: How to Be Complicit with Materials," 12–23. The book is part of the "Documents of Contemporary Art" series.

37. "Is Marxism, a component of the era of modernity, our new ideological antiquity? Will we return, excavate, research, and rediscover the ideas of Marx? Will they become the eternal 'antiquity', that truth which will give rise to new renaissances as it is recalled?" Grisha Bruskin, "Shattered Truth: Has Marxism become the Antiquity of our Times? Notes for the *Archaeologist's Collection* Installation in the Former Church of Santa Caterina in Venice," in Grisha Bruskin, *An Archaeologist's Collection*, ed. Giuseppe Barbieri and Silvia Burini (Crocetta del Montello, Italy: Terra Ferma, 2015), 7. The notion that the Soviet experience is so strange as to need excavation is the theme of Karl Schlögel's latest work, announced in *Archäologie des*

Kommunismus oder Russland im 20. Jahrhundert: Ein Bild neu zusammensetzen (Munich: Carl Friedrich von Siemens Stiftung, 2014).

38. These include "Museum of Proletarian Culture. The Industrialization of Bohemia," and "The Archive of the Future Museum of History," both partially recreated at the Casa dei Tre Oci in Venice (May 9–August 23, 2015). For background, see Ilya Budraitskis and Arseniy Zhilyaev, eds., *Pedagogical Poem: The Archive of the Future Museum of History* (Vicenza, Italy: Marsilio Editori, 2014).

39. The pathway is in the sectioning of the exhibition galleries: "The studiolo. The production room. The dirty finish room. The varnishing and finishing room. The display space."

40. *Joseph Cornell: Wanderlust* (London: Royal Academy of Arts, 2015). The connection between Cornell and Dion is made on page 61.

41. Paul Feyerabend, *Against Method*, introduction by Ian Hacking (London and New York: Verso, 2010, 4th ed. [1st ed. 1975], 281). Veyne, *Writing History*, 215.

42. Mike Pearson and Michael Shanks, *Theatre/Archaeology* (London and New York: Routledge, 2001), esp. 159–77. A new edition is currently being planned.

43. Neil MacGregor, *History of the World in 100 Objects*; *The Real Jane Austen: A Life in Small Objects* (London: HarperPerennial, 2014); Deborah Lutz, *The Brönte Cabinet: Three Lives in Nine Objects* (New York: W. W. Norton, 2015); Sam Roberts, *A History of New York in 101 Objects* (New York: Simon and Schuster, 2014); Richard Kurin, *The Smithsonian's History of America in 101 Objects* (New York: Penguin, 2013); S. Brent Plate, *A History of Religion in 5½ Objects: Bringing the Spiritual to Its Senses* (Boston: Beacon Press, 2014).

44. Leanne Shapton, *Important Artifacts and Personal Property from the Collection of Lenore Doolan and Harold Morris, including Books, Street Fashion, and Jewelry* (New York: Farrar Straus and Giroux, 2009).

45. Peter Stallybrass, "Marx's Coat," in *Border Fetishisms: Material Objects in Unstable Spaces*, ed. P. Spyer (London: Routledge, 1998), 183–207.

46. The discussion of "commodity fetishism" appears in *Capital*, ch. 1, sec. 4.

47. Leo S. Klejn, *Soviet Archaeology: Trends, Schools, and History* (Oxford, U.K.: Oxford Univesity Press, 2013), 15–16. I am grateful to Nathan Schlanger for bringing this to my attention.

48. Nadezhda I. Platonova, "The Phenomenon of Pre-Soviet Archaeology: Archival Studies in the History of Russian Archaeology—Methods and Results," in *Archives, Ancestors, Practices: Archaeology in the Light of its History*, ed. Nathan Schlanger and Jarl Nordbladh (Oxford and New York: Berghahn Books, 2008), 48.

49. A selection might include: Ivan Gaskell and Sarah Carter, eds., *The Oxford Handbook of History and Material Culture* (Oxford, U.K.: Oxford University Press, forthcoming); Laurel Thatcher Ulrich et al., *Tangible Things: Making History through Objects* (Oxford, U.K.: Oxford University Press, 2015); Anne Gerritsen and Giorgio Riello, eds., *Writing Material Culture History* (London and New York: Bloomsbury, 2015); Dan Hicks and Mary C. Beaudry, eds., *The Oxford Handbook of Material Culture Studies* (Oxford, U.K., and New York: Oxford University Press, 2010); Victor Buchli, ed., *The Material Culture Reader* (Oxford, U.K.: Berg, 2002); Christopher Tilley et al., eds., *Handbook of Material Culture* (London: SAGE, 2006); Karen Harvey, *History and Material Culture: A Student's Guide to Approaching Alternative Sources* (London and New

York: Routledge, 2009); W. Kingery, ed., *Learning from Things: Method and Theory of Material Culture Studies* (Washington, DC: Smithsonian Institution Press, 1996); S. Lubar and W. Kingery, eds., *History from Things: Essays on Material Culture* (Washington, DC: Smithsonian Institution Press, 1995); Thomas J. Schlereth, ed., *Material Culture: A Research Guide* (Lawrence: University Press of Kansas, 1985).

Chapter Two. Karl Lamprecht and the "Material Turn" c. 1885

1. Ernst Cassirer, *The Problem of Knowledge: Philosophy, Science, and History since Hegel* (New Haven: Yale University Press, 1950), ch. 17; Karl J. Weintraub, *Visions of Culture: Voltaire, Guizot, Burckhardt, Lamprecht, Huizinga, Ortega y Gasset* (Chicago: University of Chicago Press, 1966); Bruce Lyon, "The Letters of Henri Pirenne to Karl Lamprecht (1894–1915)," *Bulletin de la Commission Royale d'Histoire* 132 (1966): 161–231; Roger Chickering, *Karl Lamprecht: A German Academic Life* (Leiden: E. J. Brill, 1993); Luise Schorn-Schütte, *Karl Lamprecht: Kulturgeschichtsschreibung zwischen Wissenschaft und Politik* (Göttingen: Vandenhoeck & Ruprecht, 1984). Note that even Hans Schleier, whose *Alternative zu Ranke* (Leipzig: Reclam, 1988) really opened up the question of Lamprecht's key role, and who then went on to build a whole genealogy of cultural history that led up to Lamprecht, did not emphasize his central role in the modern study of material culture—in fact, his 1022-page *summa* does not include even a section devoted to Lamprecht's study of *realia*. See Schleier, *Geschichte der deutschen Kulturgeschichtsschreibung* (Waltrop, Germany: Hartmut Spenner, 2008).

2. Schorn-Schütte, *Karl Lamprecht*, 31.

3. The comparison with Savigny was made in Roscher, *Grundriss zu Vorlesungen über die Staatswirtschaft. Nach Geschichtlicher Methode* (Göttingen, 1843), v. On Roscher, see Thanasis Giouras, "Wilhelm Roscher: The 'Historical Method' in the Social Sciences: Critical Observations for a Contemporary Evaluation," *Journal of Economic Studies* 22 (1995): 106–7; Karl Milford, "Roscher's Epistemological and Methodological Position: Its Importance for the *Methodenstreit*," *Journal of Economic Studies* 22, no. 3 (1995): 26–52; Erich W. Streissler, "Wilhelm Roscher als führender Wirtschaftshistoriker," in *Vademecum zu einem Klassiker der historischen Schule*, ed. Bertram Schefold (Düsseldorf, 1994), 37–121. Studies of the "Historical School" touch on him only glancingly; see, for example, Erik Grimmer-Solem, *The Rise of Historical Economics and Social Reform in Germany, 1864–1894* (Oxford, U.K.: Clarendon Press, 2003); Yuicihi Shionya, ed., *The German Historical School: The Historical and Ethical Approach to Economics* (London: Routledge, 2000).

4. Herbert Schönebaum, "Gustav Mevissen und Karl Lamprecht," *Rheinische Vierteljahresblätter* 17 (1952): 180–96. Mevissen helped found the newspaper *Rheinsichen Zeitung*, to which Karl Marx contributed articles.

5. Ursula Lewald, "Karl Lamprecht und die Rheinische Geschichtsforschung," *Rheinische Vierteljahresblätter* 21 (1956): 282. This text is quoted, but without attribution to either Lewald or Lamprecht, in Schorn-Schütte, *Karl Lamprecht*, 114.

6. Mevissen had the idea of founding a "Verein für rheinisch-westfälische Geschichte" as early as 1868. His motivations, like those of Aufseß and the generation of the 1820s, were both to document the past of his region and to provide a connection and context for those now living in it. Schorn-Schütte, *Karl Lamprecht*, 42, quoting a letter of Mevissen from 1890.

7. Luise Schorn-Schötte, "Karl Lamprecht: Wegbereiter einer Historischen Sozialwissenschaft," in *Deutsche Geschichtswissenschaft um 1900*, ed. Notker Hammerstein (Stuttgart: Steiner Verlag, 1988), 157.

8. Schorn-Schütte, *Karl Lamprecht*, 46.

9. Quoted in Schorn-Schötte, "Karl Lamprecht: Wegbereiter einer Historischen Sozialwissenschaft," 173.

10. Schorn-Schütte, *Karl Lamprecht*, 44.

11. "What is at stake here is to ground *any historical provincial research* on a foundation of solid historical methodology." Lamprecht to E. Bernheim (late 1881), quoted in Luise Schorn-Schütte, "Territorialgeschichte Provinzialgeschichte—Landesgeschichte—Regionalgeschichte. Ein Beitrag zur Wissenschaftsgeschichte der Landesgeschichtsschreibung," in *Civitatum Communitas: Studien zum Europäischen Städtewesen: Festschrift Heinz Stoob zum 65. Geburtstag*, ed. Helmut Jäger, Franz Petri, and Heinz Quirin, 2 vols. (Cologne and Vienna: Böhlau Verlag, 1984), 394.

12. Lamprecht, *Deutsches Wirtschaftsleben im Mittelalter: Untersuchungen über die Entwicklung der Materiellen Kultur des platten Landes auf Grund der Quellen zunächst des Mosellandes*, 3 vols. (Leipzig, 1885–1886, rpt. Darmstadt: Scientia Verlag Aalen, 1969). For the reception of the book, see Schorn-Schütte, *Karl Lamprecht*, 50–52.

13. ". . . so wird für ihn der Begriff der materiellen Kultur als einer einheitlichen Gesamterscheinung massgebend. . . . Das ist die Auffassung, welche dieser Arbeit zu Grunde liegt." Lamprecht, *Deutsches Wirtschaftsleben*, vol. 2, 4.

14. Lamprecht, *Deutsches Wirtschaftsleben*, vol. 2, 4: "sie will die Entwicklung der materiellen Kultur des platten Landes in ihrer Gesamtheit, nach rechtlicher wie wirtschaftlicher Seite hin, untersuchen von der Überzeugung aus, dass man in der Gesamtentwicklung der Kultur sehr wohl der Sphäre der specifisch realen oder materiellen Kultur der Wirtschaft und des Rechtes einen specifisch idealen Kreis des Glaubens, der Kunst und der Wissenschaft gegenübersetzen könne, und dass es möglich sein müsse, die Entwicklung eines jeden dieser Kreise sowie die ihrer gegenseitigen Beziehungen gesonderten Untersuchungen zu unterwerfen."

15. Lamprecht to Friedrich Althoff, 1884, quoted in Schorn-Schütte, "Territorialgeschichte—Provinzialgeschichte—Landesgeschichte—Regionalgeschichte," 395.

16. Lamprecht, "Berichte über die Verhandlungen der Königlich Sächsischen Gesellschaft der Wissenschaften zu Leipzig, Phil.-hist. Klasse, bd. 52 (Leipzig, 1900)," quoted in Lamprecht, *Alternative zu Ranke*, 359.

17. Heinrich Schmidt, *Heimat und Geschichte: Zum Verhältnis von Heimatbewußtsein und Geschichtsforschung* (Hildesheim, 1967).

18. Quoted in Schorn-Schütte, "Territorialgeschichte—Provinzialgeschichte—Landesgeschichte—Regionalgeschichte," 411.

19. Schorn-Schütte, "Territorialgeschichte—Provinzialgeschichte—Landesgeschichte—Regionalgeschichte," 409–12. For important background on "space" studies, see Karl Schlögel, *In Space We Read Time* (New York: Bard Graduate Center, 2016 [2003]), ch. 1.

20. Lamprecht, *Deutsches Wirtschaftsleben*, vol. I.1, v.

21. "Praktisch, weil bei der langsamen aber ununterbrochenen Entwicklung gerade der ländlichen Kultur eine große Anzahl von Fragen der Gegenwart nicht zu lösen ist ohne wahrhafte und allseitige Kenntnis einer weit zurückreichenden Vergangenheit; wissenschaftlich, weil die neuere Entwicklung der geschichtlichen

Studien eine allseitige und wohlbegründete Ansicht über die Geschichte gerade der ländlichen Kultur noch nicht erreicht hat." Lamprecht, *Deutsches Wirtschaftsleben*, vol. I.1, vi.

22. Lamprecht, *Deutsches Wirtschaftsleben*, vol. I.2, 1485.

23. Lamprecht, *Deutsches Wirtschaftsleben*, vol. I.2, 1485–86.

24. Lamprecht, *Deutsches Wirtschaftsleben*, vol. I.2, 1485–86.

25. Schorn-Schütte, *Karl Lamprecht*, 116.

26. "Inzwischen war mir aber klar geworden, daß alle diese Studien in der Luft stehen würden, wenn ich nicht ihr Komplement, die Entwicklung der materiellen Kultur, wie ich mich damals und noch lange nachher nach Roschers Vorgang ausdrückte, mit heranzöge. Ich begann also auf diesem Gebiete zu arbeiten. So entstand, nach einer Vorarbeit auf dem Gebiete der französischen Geschichte, mein deutsches Wirtschaftsleben im Mittelalter (1886)." Lamprecht, "Was ist Kulturgeschichte?" quoted in Lamprecht, *Alternative zu Ranke*, 253–54.

27. Lamprecht, "Was ist Kulturgeschichte?" quoted in Lamprecht, *Alternative zu Ranke*, 255.

28. Lamprecht, "Was ist Kulturgeschichte?" quoted in Lamprecht, *Alternative zu Ranke*, 267n.

29. Lamprecht, "Was ist Kulturgeschichte?" quoted in Lamprecht, *Alternative zu Ranke*, 254.

30. Schorn-Schütte, *Karl Lamprecht*, 114.

31. Schorn-Schütte, *Karl Lamprecht*, 115.

32. Karl Lamprecht, *Initial-Ornamentik des VIII. bis XIII. Jahrhunderts* (Leipzig: Alphons Dürr, 1882), 1.

33. Lamprecht, "Was ist Kulturgeschichte?" quoted in Lamprecht, *Alternative zu Ranke*, 254.

34. Quoted in Ursula Lewald, "Karl Lamprecht und die Rheinische Geschichtsforschung," *Rheinische Vierteljahresblätter*, 21 (1956): 290.

35. Aby Warburg attended lectures of *Grundzüge der deutschen Kulturentwickelung im Mittelalter* in the 1887–1888 winter semester, and his notes are preserved in Warburg Institute Archive, 32.1.2. I thank Claudia Wedepohl for her assistance in deciphering Warburg's handwriting. See Kathryn Brush, "The Cultural Historian Karl Lamprecht: Practitioner and Progenitor of Art History," *Central European History* 26 (1993): 155.

36. Lamprecht, *Einführung in das historische Denken*, 2nd ed. (Leipzig, 1913), 15.

37. ". . . einer toten Masse in sich wohl zubereiteten antiquarischen Stoffes." Lamprecht, "Was ist Kulturgeschichte?" in Lamprecht, *Alternative zu Ranke*, 214.

38. Quoted in Herbert Schönebaum, ed., *Karl Lamprecht, Ausgewählte Schriften zur Wirtschafts- und Kulturgeschichte und zur Theorie der Geschichtswissenschaft* (Aalen, Germany: Scientia, 1974), 250.

39. Lamprecht, "Was ist Kulturgeschichte?" in Lamprecht, *Alternative zu Ranke*, 271. See also Jeannine Guichardet, *Balzac "Archéologue" de Paris* (Paris: Sedes, 1986).

40. "The historical artisan generally possesses good knowledge, at least on individual matters. . . . But he remains confined to the simple collection of material. To copy out a mouldy and unreadable document, and have it printed on beautiful paper, that is his joy. Mind and heart have little involvement in this, and there is little profit from it. In collecting material he is thorough, as hard-working as an ant. . . .

He is always a pedant, that is to say he mistakes great things for small ones and small things for great." Roscher, *Leben, Werk und Zeitalter des Thukydides* (Göttingen, 1842), 11–12, quoted in Neville Morley, "Thucydides, History, and Historicism in Wilhelm Roscher," in *Thucydides and the Modern World: Reception, Reinterpretation and Influence from the Renaissance to the Present,* ed. Katherine Harloe and Neville Morley (Cambridge, U.K.: Cambridge University Press, 2012), 125.

41. Morley, "Thucydides, History, and Historicism in Wilhelm Roscher," 131.

42. Review of Karl Theodor v. Inama-Sternegg, *Deutsche Wirtschaftsgeschichte des 10. bis 12. Jahrhunderts (1891)* [1895], in Lamprecht, *Alternative zu Ranke,* 138.

43. Goethe, *Scientific Studies. Collected Works,* vol. 12, ed. and trans. Douglas Miller (Princeton University Press, 1995), 55, 56; Goethe, "Vorarbeiten zu einer Physiologie der Pflanzen," *Schriften zur Morphologie* [=Johann Wolfgang Goethe, *Sämtliche Werke, Briefe, Tagebücher und Gespräche,* part I, vol. 24], ed. Dorothea Kuhn (Frankfurt a.M: Deutscher Klassiker Verlag, 1987), 357.

44. Lamprecht, *What is History?* (New York: Macmillan, 1905), lecture 1, 3.

45. Lamprecht, *What is History?* lecture 1, 28.

46. Lamprecht, *What is History?* lecture 1, 32.

47. Rickert, *Kulturwissenschaft und Naturwissenschaft,* 9–10n2, 69, 90–91. In point of fact, I have found not found Lamprecht using the term *Kulturwissenschaft,* at least in his theoretical writing. His consistent preference is for *Geschichtswissenschaft.*

48. Lamprecht, "Denkschrift über Entwicklung, gegenwärtigen Stand und Zukunft des Königlich Sächsischen Instituts für Kultur- und Universal-Geschichte bei der Universität Leipzig," in Lamprecht, *Alternative zu Ranke,* 426.

49. Quoted in Schorn-Schütte, *Karl Lamprecht,* 117.

50. Weintraub, *Visions of Culture,* 164; Stefan Haas, *Historische Kulturforschung in Deutschland, 1880–1930: Geschichtswissenschaft zwischen Synthese und Pluralität,* (Cologne, Weimar, and Vienna: Böhlau Verlag, 1994), 113–16.

51. Quoted in Schorn-Schütte, *Karl Lamprecht,* 129.

52. Lamprecht, *What is History?* lecture 6, 190.

53. Lamprecht, *What is History?* lecture 6, 191.

54. For this, see Chickering, *Karl Lamprecht,* 175.

55. "Dem geistigen Kulturbesitz liegt der matierelle zu Grunde. Geistige Schöpfungen kommen als Luxus nach der Befriedigung der körperlichen Bedürfnisse. Jede Frage nach der Entstehung der Kultur löst sich daher auf in die Frage: Was begünstigt die Entwicklung der materiellen Grundlagen der Kultur?" Lamprecht, "Was ist Kulturgeschichte?" in Lamprecht, *Alternative zu Ranke,* 271n.

56. On the debate, see Haas, *Historische Kulturforschung,* 116–26, 149–58. Schäfer and Gothein are quoted in Kelley, *Fortunes of History: Historical Inquiry from Herder to Huizinga* (New Haven and London: Yale University Press, 2003), 305. Chickering's discussion of Treitschke's debut essay as editor of the *Historische Zeitschrift* is representative of this view; see *Karl Lamprecht,* 180. On Doren, see Gerald Diesener and Jaroslav Kudrna, "Alfred Doren (1869–1934)—ein Historiker am Institut für Kultur- und Universalgeschichte" in *Karl Lamprecht weiterdenken: Universal- und Kulturgeschichte heute,* ed. Gerald Diesener (Leipzig: Leipziger Universitätsverlag, 1993), 65.

57. On the reaction to Lamprecht, see Dietrich Fischer, *Die deutsche Geschichtswissenschaft von J. G. Droysen bis O. Hintze in ihrem Verhältnis zur Soziologie: Grundzüge eines*

Methodenproblems (Cologne, 1966), esp. 78–80, 130–31; on Weber, see Sam Whimster, "Karl Lamprecht and Max Weber: Historical Sociology within the Confines of a Historians' Controversy," in *Max Weber and his Contemporaries*, ed. Wolfgang J. Mommsen and Jürgen Osterhammel (London: German Historical Institute/Unwin Hyman, 1987), 278–80; on Meinecke, see Chickering, *Karl Lamprecht*, 260.

58. Lamprecht, "Die kultur- und universalgeschichtlichen Bestrebungen an der Universität Leipzig" (1908), in Lamprecht, *Alternative zu Ranke*, 370.

59. On Huizinga and Lamprecht, see Weintraub, *Visions of Culture*, 232; Gerhard Oestreich, "Huizinga, Lamprecht und die deutsche Geschichtsphilosophie: Huizingas Groninger Antrittsvorlesung von 1905," *Bijdragen en Mededelingen betreffende de Geschiedenis der Nederlanden* 88 (1973): 143–70; on Bloch and Lamprecht, see Catherine Devulder, "Karl Lamprecht, Kulturgeschichte et histoire totale," *Revue d'Allemagne* 17 (1985): 516; on Pirenne and Lamprecht, see Schorn-Schütte, *Karl Lamprecht*, 320–28; on Berr and Lamprecht, see Schorn-Schütte, *Karl Lamprecht*, 309–17.

60. Weintraub, *Visions of Culture*, 166.

61. Chickering, *Karl Lamprecht*, 359. On the institute more generally, see Haas, *Historische Kulturforschung*, section 4.3.1.

62. Kathryn Brush, "Aby Warburg and the Cultural Historian Karl Lamprecht," in *Art History as Cultural History: Warburg's Projects*, ed. Richard Woodfield (Amsterdam: OPA, 2001), 78.

Chapter Three. Things as Historical Evidence in the Late Renaissance and Early Enlightenment

1. See Marina Belozerskaya, *To Wake the Dead: A Renaissance Merchant and the Birth of Archaeology* (New York: W. W. Norton, 2009); Angelo Mazzocco and Marc Laureys, eds., *A New Sense of the Past: The Scholarship of Biondo Flavio (1392–1463)* (Louvain: Leuven University Press, 2016); Anthony Grafton, *Leon Battista Alberti: Master Builder of the Italian Renaissance* (New York: Hill and Wang, 2000). For a survey of the more fragmentary treatment of Poggio, see Craig Kallendorf's Oxford Bibliography available at www.oxford bibliographies.com/view/document/obo-9780195399301/obo-9780195399301-0095. xml, accessed March 5, 2016. Choay also singles out the 1430s (*Alegoría del patrimonio*), as does Henning Wrede, "Die Entstehung der Archäologie und das Einsetzen der neuzeitlichen Geschichtsbetrachtungen," in *Geschichtsdiskurs vol. 2 Anfänge modernen historischen Denkens*, ed. Wolfgang Küttler, Jörn Rüsen, Ernst Schulin (F.a.M: Fischer Verlag, 1993), 95. 35. Emphasizing this "material moment" is not meant to challenge Ronald Witt's masterful argument about the sense of a classical past emerging in Petrarch's time See *In the Footsteps of the Ancients: The Origins of Humanism from Lovato to Bruni* (Leiden: E. J. Brill, 2000) and *The Two Latin Cultures and the Foundation of Renaissance Humanism in Medieval Italy* (Cambridge, U.K.: Cambridge University Press, 2012).

2. Ingrid Rowland, "Raphael, Angelo Colocci, and the Genesis of the Architectural Orders," *Art Bulletin* 76 (1994): 81–104; Nicole Dacos, *"Roma Quanta Fuit": Tre pittori fiamminghi nel Domus Aurea* (Rome: Donzelli Editore, 1995).

3. William Stenhouse, "Antiquarianism," in *The Classical Tradition*, ed. Anthony Grafton, Glenn Most, and Salvatore Settis (Cambridge, MA, and London: Harvard University Press, 2010), 51–53; idem, "The Renaissance Foundations of European

Antiquarianism," in *World Antiquarianism*, ed. Alain Schnapp et al. (Los Angeles: Getty Publications, 2013), 295–316; and idem, *Reading Inscriptions and Writing Ancient History: Historical Scholarship in the Late Renaissance* (London: Institute of Classical Studies, 2005). His work is replacing what was for long the flawed standard: Roberto Weiss, *The Renaissance Discovery of Classical Antiquity* (Oxford, U.K.: Oxford University Press, 1969, 2nd ed.). Art historians have been the most attentive to the antiquarian legacy. Several years ago Joseph Connors put together an online bibliography of antiquarianism for art historians that came to over seven hundred titles.

4. Cropper, Perini, and Solinas, eds., *Documentary Culture*; Francesco Solinas, ed., *Cassiano dal Pozzo: Atti del Seminario Internazionale di Studi* (Rome, 1989); and Herklotz, *Cassiano dal Pozzo und die Archäologie des 17. Jahrhunderts*; idem, *Die Academia Basiliana: Griechische Philologie, Kirchengeschichte und Unionsbemühungen im Rom der Barberini* (Rome-Freiburg-Vienna: Herder, 2008); idem, *La Roma degli antiquari: cultura e erudizione tra cinquecento e settecento* (Rome: De Luca Editori d'Arte, 2012); idem, "Arnaldo Momigliano's 'Ancient History and the Antiquarian': A Critical Review," in *Momigliano and Antiquarianism: Foundations of the Modern Cultural Sciences*, ed. Peter N. Miller (Toronto: University of Toronto Press, 2007), 127–53.

5. Arnaldo Momigliano, *The Classical Foundations of Modern Historiography* (Los Angeles and Berkeley: University of California Press, 1990), 57. On how Peiresc was viewed by posterity, see *Peiresc's Mediterranean World*, Appendix A.

6. Carpentras, Bibliothèque Inguimbertine [henceforth CBI], MS. 1861, fols. 166r–v.

7. "Dans la premiere caisse du coin De la liasse Aurasicae. Trois grandes chartres l'une bulle de plomb les aultres sans seau./ De la liasse Arles {deux grands parchemins, deux petits parchemins, une feuille de papier. Le registre des causes de Porcellet./ De la liasse Avignon {deux petits parchemins, l'un tout rongé l'autre du Vicomte de Nimes. Deux grand, l'un à 4 seaux de cire et l'autre à un./ Du fonds du coffre. un parchemin sans seau. cotté 0." CBI, MS. 1863, fol. 333r.

8. Peiresc to Grotius, November 20, 1629, in *Grotius Briefwisseling*, ed. P. C. Molhuysen and B. L. Meulenbroek (The Hague, 1964), vol. 4, no. 1447, 127.

9. On seals, see Brigitte Bedos-Rezak, *When Ego Was Imago* (Leiden: E. J. Brill, 2010).

10. Such as: "Le seau est de cire verte, pendu en soye verte fort grand, et y a la figure du prince à cheval armé de toutes pieces portant son espee à la droitte et son escu à la gauche sur lequel ne paroissent que deux chasteaux. La valdrappe de son cheval est semee de fleurs de lis par le devant, et de chasteaux par le derriere. L'inscription au tour est S. ALFONSUS.FILI.REG. FRANC.COMES.PICT.&.THOLOSE. Au contreseel qui est fort petit, n'y a rien qu'un escusson avec la croix pour mettre de Thousoulse." CBI, MS. 1791, fol. 474r.

11. See Peter N. Miller, "Description Terminable and Interminable: Looking at the Past, Nature, and Peoples in Peiresc's Archive," in *"Historia": Empricism and Erudition in Early Modern Europe*, ed. Gianna Pomata and Nancy Siraisi (Cambridge, MA: MIT, 2005), 355–97. Gianna Pomata suggests "epistemic genre." See "Epistemic Genres or Styles of Thinking? Tools for the Cultural History of Knowledge," Available at www.unige.ch/rectorat/maison-histoire/mediatheque/professeursinvites/pomata/, accessed August 1, 2016.

12. There are examples of this from the Church of St François in Hyères (CBI, MS. 1771, fol.195r), from St. Victor in Marseille (CBI, MS. 1771, fol. 202r.), and from smaller towns in northern Provence such as Moustiers and Digne (CBI, MS. 1771, fol. 196r).

13. Michel Pastoureau, *Une histoire symbolique du Moyen Âge occidental* (Paris: Le Seuil, 2004), among many others.

14. CBI, MS. 1805, fol. 150v.; see also fol. 156r.

15. Peter N. Miller, *Peiresc's "History of Provence" and the Discovery of a Medieval Mediterranean* (Philadelphia: American Philosophical Society, 2012).

16. Peiresc's study of the genealogy of the Regno Italico, for example, was based on a study of the kings of Italy (in tabular form) drawn up by Théodore Godefroy (CBI, MS. 1792, fol.45r). His discussion of the genealogy of the House of Baux includes an exchange of letters with André Duchesne in correspondence during July and August 1626 (Duchesne to Peiresc, July 31, 1626, CBI, MS. 1811, fol. 120; Peiresc to Duchesne, August 25, 1626, fols. 123–24). A "Memoire pour Mompelier [*sic*]" was sent to Peiresc's teacher, Giulio Pace, seeking birth and death dates of various thirteenth-century Langedocians. This episode is especially interesting from the point of view of terminology. For, apparently, the volume containing testaments in the archives at Montpelier was called the "Talmud," and there was a "Grand" as well as a "petit" (CBI, MS. 1811, fol. 163r).

17. Peter N. Miller, "The Antiquary's Art of Comparison: Peiresc and *Abraxas*," in *Philologie und Erkenntnis: Beiträge zu Begriff und Problem frühneuzeitlicher "Philologie,"* ed. Ralph Häfner (Tübingen: Max Niemeyer Verlag, 2001), 57–94.

18. Peiresc to Alvares, 28 Nov 1633, Carpentras, Bibliothèque Inguimbertine, MS. 1871, fol. 335v, also printed in *Lettres de Peiresc*, ed. Philippe Tamizey de Larroque, 7 vols. (Paris: Imprimerie Nationale, 1888–98), vol. 1, 33; Alois Riegl, "The Modern Cult of Monuments: Its Character and Its Origin," *Oppositions* 25 (1982): 20–51. On Peiresc in the history of conservation, see the very brief notice in Françoise Choay, *Alegoría del patrimonio* (Barcelona: Editorial Gustavo Gili, 2007 [1992]), 63–64.

19. CBI, MS. 1791, fol. 446r. Peiresc's paleographic skills remain formidable; Bruce Eastwood makes them a centerpiece of his analysis of the Roman Calendar of 354. "Origins and Contents of the Leiden Planetary Configuration (MS Voss. Q.79, Fol. 93v), An Artistic Astronomical Schema of the Early Middle Ages," *Viator* 14 (1983): 36–40. I thank Ittai Weinryb for bringing this article to my attention.

20. CBI, MS. 1791, fol. 33r.

21. CBI, MS. 1791, fols. 69r–70r.

22. CBI, MS. 1791, fol. 500r.

23. For an overview, see Roland Étienne and Jean-Claude Mossière, eds., *Jacob Spon: Un humaniste lyonnais du XVIIᵉ siècle* (Lyon: Publications de la bibliothèque Salomon-Reinach, 1993).

24. Jacob Spon, *Voyage d'Italie, de Dalmatie, de Grèce et du Levant. Fait es Années 1675 & 1676* (Amsterdam: Henry & Theodore Boom, 1679).

25. "Archaeographia est declaratio sive notitia antiquorum monumentorum, quibus veteres sui temporis religionem historiam politicam aliasque tum artes tum scientias propagare posterisque tradere studerunt," from his *Miscellanea eruditae antiquitatis*, quoted in Karl Bernhard Stark, *Handbuch der Archäologie der Kunst* (Stuttgart: A. Heitz, 1880), 46.

26. "Il luy [Guillet] plait d'apeller les Livres imprimez *l'histoire mesme*: mais pour les Inscriptions & les medailles, il leur fait seulement l'honneur de les traiter *de monumens qui servent à l'histoire.*" Jacob Spon, *Réponse a la critique publiée par M. Guillet, sur le Voyage de Grece de Iacob Spon* (Lyon, 1679), 59.

27. Francis Bacon, *The Advancement of Learning*, book 2.

28. "Pour moy qui ne cherche pas ces distinctions rafinées, je dis que les livres ne sont pas plus l'histoire que les medailles, ou les inscriptions, & qu'il ne sont les uns & les autres que les pieces d'où elle est tirée. Il ne doit pas mesme s'imaginer que les livres ont un grand avantage parce qu'ils sont plus diffus, & qu'il y a plus de matiere pour en compiler l'histoire," Spon, *Réponse*, 59.

29. Spon, *Réponse*, 70.

30. Interestingly, however, he only mentioned Peiresc in the last category of angeiography, or material culture, which is somewhat surprising given that Spon, like Montfaucon and Caylus, is one of the few figures we know to have looked at the Peiresc papers and thus was aware of his activity across the range of these fields.

31. Spon, *Réponse*, 72.

32. Spon, *Réponse*, 74–77.

33. Peter N. Miller, "Peiresc and the Benedictines of Saint-Maur: Further Thoughts on the 'Ethics of the Historian,'" in *Europäische Geschichtskulturen um 1700 zwischen Gelehrsamkeit, Politik und Konfession*, ed. Thomas Wallnig, Ines Peper, Thomas Stockinger, and Patrick Fiska (Berlin: De Gruyter, 2012), 361–78, and bibliography there.

34. Mabillon, *De re Diplomatica libri VI. In quibus quidquid ad veterum instrumentorum antiquitatem, materiam, scripturam, & stilum; quidquid ad sigilla, monogrammata, subscriptiones, ac notas chronologicas; quidquid inde ad antiquariam, historicam, forensemque discplinam pertinet, explicatur & illustratur* (Paris: Louis Billaine, 1681).

35. Mabillon, *De re Diplomatica*, 1.

36. "Quam ob rem magnopere interest ad antiquariam historicam forensemque disciplinam haec tractatio." Mabillon, *Librorum de re Diplomatica Supplementum* (Paris, 1704), 8.

37. Mabillon, *De re Diplomatica*, 135, citing Pierre Gassendi, *Viri Illustris Nicolai Claudii Fabricii de Peiresc, Senatoris Aquisextiensis Vita* (Paris: Sebastian Cramoisy, 1641), book 2.

38. A long page in Peiresc's volume on French antiquities discusses a sculptural bust of Charlemagne in the Louvre. He identified it, carefully, as "The head of Charlemagne, or of some other Prince of his family, held to be Attila." He then offered a detailed description of the hairstyle and facial hair before moving on to describe the crown. "Une teste de marbre d'ouvrage de 800 ans environ, ayant le barbe quasi du tout rase, les ieux fort grands, le nez rompu (mais dont la racine convient aulcunement a celuy de CHARLEMAGNE) le devant du menton sans poil quelconque, un peu d'apparance de moustache. Les cheveulx semblent estre fondus fort bas sur le teste, et toutefoys assez longnets sur le front et tout à l'entour de la chevelleure, faisants d'assez gros bouillons de cheveux. La Couronne qui les serre est en forme de diademe chargé de pierreries, comme ceulx de Constantin, sans aulcunes infules pendantes, mais plus large que ceulx des empereurs, et plus convenable au siecle de Charlemagne. Au droict du front, il n'y a pas de medaille comme aux couronnes des empereurs d'occident, mais il y avoit en quelque fleuron montant plus hault que le reste du diademe, qui a

esté cassé par succcession de temps car il en reste des vestiges et de la peirre, qui servoit à le supporter par derriere. Or dans les seaux de Pepin roy d'Aquitaine filz de Louys le debonnaire on void sa couronne enrichie d'un semblable fleuron, sur le devant. & dans le mosaique du Vatican & de S.te Susanne, Charlesmagne à un pareil fleur sur le front. & la barbe rasee ne paroissent que par la couleur chenüe au reste du visage, et des ieulx fort gros" (CBI, MS. 1791, fol.132r). But all this detail was in turn then mobilized to compare one medium's depiction with another: the image of Charlemagne on a seal at St Denis and on a bull of Rome. The former, from the beginning of his reign, showed less of a beard, but corresponded to the portrayal of nose and crown, while the latter corresponded in all ways except that the moustache was more pronounced and the crown swapped for a laurel wreath, reflecting his status as emperor (CBI, MS. 1791, fol.132r). Peiresc was fascinated by the iconography of Charlemagne. We know of his work with the Roman antiquarian Lelio Pasqualini on the ancient depiction at the Lateran. Peiresc also sent his brother, Vallavez, to Aachen in 1609 with instructions to copy and identify depictions in the Palatine Chapel. The detailed, and sometimes colored, drawings survive (CBI, MS. 1791, 479–491r).

39. Mabillon, *De re Diplomatica*, 143.

40. See Jan Marco Sawilla, *Antiquarianismus, Hagiographie und Historie im 17. Jahrhundert : Zum Werk der Bollandisten; ein wissenschaftshistorischer Versuch* (Tübingen: Niemeyer Verlag, 2009).

41. See Francis Haskell, *History and Its Images: Art and the Interpretation of the Past* (New Haven: Yale University Press, 1993), ch. 5.

42. Francis W. Gravit, *The Peiresc Papers* (Ann Arbor, 1950).

43. Günter Scheel, "Leibniz und die deutsche Geschichtswissenschaft um 1700," in *Historische Forschung im 18. Jahrhundert. Organisation. Zielsetzung. Ergebnisse*, ed. Karl Hammer and Jürgen Voss (Bonn, 1976), 86.

44. Gottfried Wilhelm Leibniz, *Schriften und Briefe zur Geschichte*, ed. Malte-Ludolf Babin and Gerd van den Heuvel (Hanover: Verlag Hahnsche Buchhandlung, 2004), 24.

45. Quoted in Louis Davillé, *Leibniz Historien: Essai sur l'activité et la méthode historique de Leibniz* (Darmstadt: Scientia Verlag Allen, 1996 [1909]), 386, note 2: "Rerum monumenta sunt reliquiae humanorum corporum, ossa silicet . . . artis humanae vestigia ut in suppellectile, in sepulchris, substructionibusque."

46. Quoted in Davillé, *Leibniz Historien*, 384.

47. The idea "Historie zu Materialien," that is, of turning history into source materials, is also found, for example, in more purely academic contexts, such as Johann Georg Sulzer, *Kurzer Begriff aller Wissenschaften und anderen Theile der Gelehrsamkeit*, 2nd ed. (Frankfurt and Leipzig, 1759), 34.

48. Leibniz, "Zu Gegenstand, Geschichte und Methoden der Geschichtswissenschaft," *Schriften und Briefe zur Geschichte*, 70.

49. "Je ne meprise point qu'on epluche les antiquités jusqu'aux moindres bagatelles, car quelquefois la connoissance que les critiques en tirent, peut servir aux choses plus importantes." Leibniz, *Nouveaux Essais sur l'entendement humain* (1703), quoted in *Schriften und Briefe zur Geschichte*, 111.

50. Leibniz, "Scriptores rerum Brunsvicensium illustrationi inservientes," *Schriften und Briefe zur Geschichte*, 240.

51. Momigliano, *Classical Foundations of Modern Historiography* (Berkeley and London, 1990), ch. 6; see also Anthony Grafton, *Past Belief: Visions of Early Christian-*

ity in Renaissance and Reformation Europe. The Sixty-Third A. W. Mellon Lectures in the Fine Arts (2014).

52. Leibniz, *Schriften und Briefe zur Geschichte*, 839, 855. "Je veux que [souvent] l'Histoire tienne quelques fois un peu du Roman," cited in Louis Couturat, *Opuscules et fragments inédits de Leibniz* (Paris: Alcan, 1903), 225–26.

53. Leibniz, *Schriften und Briefe zur Geschichte*, 840–41.

54. Gottfried Wilhelm Leibniz, Protogaea: De l'aspect primitif de la terre et des traces d'une histoire très ancienne que renferment les monuments mêmes de la nature. Sive de prima facie telluris et antiquissimae historiae vestigiis in ipsis naturae monumentis dissertatio, ex schedis manuscriptis viri illustris in lucem edita. Trans. Bertrand de Saint-Germain, edited by with an introduction and notes by Jean-Marie Barrande (Toulouse: Presses Universitaires du Mirail, 1993), ch. 39, 139. For more on the contemporary sense of the world's history, see Ivano dal Prete, " 'Being the World Eternal': The Age of the Earth in Renaissance Italy," *Isis* 105 (2014): 292–317; Rienk Vermij, "Subterranean Fire: Changing Theories of the Earth during the Renaissance," *Early Science and Medicine* 3 (1998): 323–47.

55. Horst Bredekamp, *Die Fenster der Monade: Gottfried Wilhelm Leibniz' Theater der Natur und Kunst* (Berlin: Akademie Verlag, 2004), 157.

56. Bredekamp, *Fenster der Monade*, 27.

57. Bredekamp, *Fenster der Monade*, 178.

58. Henri Berr and Lucien Febvre, "History and Historiography," *Encyclopaedia of the Social Sciences*, editor-in-chief Edwin R. A. Seligman, associate editor Alvin Johnson (New York: Macmillan, 1937), 363–64.

59. Leibniz, *Schriften und Briefe zur Geschichte*, 272–73.

60. Leibniz to Vinzenz Placius, 2 / March 21 February 1696: "qui me non nisi editis novit, non novit."

61. Benjamin Hederich, *Anleitung zu den fürnehmsten Historischen Wissenschaften* (Berlin 1742, 6th edn [1711]), sig.)(2r. Hederich's *Anleitung zu den fürnehmsten Philologischen Wissenschaften, nach der Grammatica, Rhetorica und Poetica* (Wittenberg & Zerbst, 1746) loosely curricularizes the bibliographical treatments of Morhof and Fabricius.

62. The full title was *Auxilia historica oder Behülff zu den Historischen und dazu erforderlichen Wissenschaften* (Regensburg, 1741–1747).

63. Histories of academies and books at no. 130 "Critica" (Critique), and no. 131 "diplomatica." On Mabillon's *Diplomatica* he commented "Opus in hoc genere sine pari." The other tools for history of learning follow immediately: no. 132 "Bücher von Altherthümern oder Antiquarii," no. 133 Numismatics, no. 134 Art History, no. 137 Oriental languages, no. 153 Geography, no. 154 Heraldry, no. 155 Genealogy. These would become, a generation later, in Göttingen, the canonical auxiliary sciences. Desing also suggests interrelationships between the fields; his marking of genealogy, for instance, also includes geography, history and public law.

64. Johann David Köhler, *Kurze Anweisung zu den nöthigen Subsidia bey Erlernung der Teutschen Reichs-Historie* comprises the first twenty pages of his *Teutsche Reichs-Historie von dem Anfang des Teutschen Reichs . . .* (Riegel, 1736). See Notker Hammerstein, *Jus und Historie: ein Beitrag zur Geschichte des historischen Denkens an deutschen Universitäten im späten 17. und im 18. Jahrhundert* (Göttingen: Vandenhoeck & Ruprecht, 1972), 354.

65. Köhler's very detailed account of the documents includes also a list of "approved" published sources. *Kurze Anweisung*, 6–12.

66. Eckart Henning adds to these the unspecified mention of various "Hülffs-Mittel" for history made in Friedrich Christophe Schmicke, foreword to *Monumenta Hassica* 1 (1747), ("Die Historischen Hilfswissenschaften—historisch gesehen!" in *Vom Nutz und Frommen der Historischen Hilfswissenschaften* [=*Herold Studien*, 5 (2000)], (Neustadt a. d. Aisch: Degener & Co., 2000), 13).

67. [Charles-François Toustain, René-Prosper Tassin], *Nouveau Traité de Diplomatique, ou l'on examine les fondemens de cet art: on etablist des regles sur le discernement des titres, et l'on expose historiquement les caracteres des bulles Pontificales et des diplomes donné en chaque siècle: avec des éclaircissemens sur un nombre considerable de points d'Histoire, de Chronologie, de Critique & de Discipline; & la Réfutation de diverses accusations intentées contre beaucoup d'Archives célèbres, & sur tout contre celles des anciennes Eglises*, 5 vols. (Paris, 1750–1765).

68. *Nouveau Traité*, vol. 1, ii.

69. *Nouveau Traité*, vol. 1, 75.

70. *Nouveau Traité*, vol. 1, 593. They do not, however, acknowledge the work of Peiresc, who was responsible for first publishing the Samaritan Pentateuch and whose Samaritana, when entering the collection of the Royal Library, supplied six of the first ten items catalogued. If Peiresc remained known to Mabillon, he had disappeared to Mabillon's heirs.

71. *Nouveau Traité*, vol. 2, 146.

72. *Nouveau Traité*, vol. 2, 303.

73. Comte de Caylus, *Recueil d'Antiquités Egyptiennes, Etrusques, Grecques et Romanes*, 7 vols. (Paris, 1752), vol. 2, ii.

Chapter Four. Material Evidence in the History Curriculum in Eighteenth-Century Göttingen

1. Notker Hammerstein's argument that Gatterer's originality here is overstated and that he drew much from the theologians and philologists can be sustained without diminishing the importance of the systematization of the *Hilfswissenschaften*, which gave them an independent identity and new primacy in of historical training. See Hammerstein, *Jus und Historie*, 357; Herman Wesendonck, *Die Begründung der neueren deutschen Geschichtsschreibung durch Gatterer und Schlözer* (Leipzig: Krüger, 1876), 227.

2. Some handbooks contain some introductory approaches. For example, R. C. van Caenegem et al., *Introduction aux sources de l'histoire médiévale* (Turnholt: Brepols, 1997), pt. 3, ch. 1. I thank Michael McCormick for this reference. For the ancient world, the limited range of sources simply do not allow for as many *Hilfswissenschaften*. Curt Wachsmuth's *Einleitung in das Studium der alten Geschichte* (Leipzig, 1895), for example, covers only literary sources, inscriptions, coins, art objects, chronology, and metrology.

3. The point was made forcefully long ago in Herbert Butterfield, *Man on his Past: The Study of the History of Historical Scholarship* (Cambridge, U.K.: Cambridge University Press, 1955), 15. See also Luigi Marino, *I Maestri della Germania: Göttingen, 1770–1820* (Turin: Einaudi, 1975). More recently, on biblical studies see Jonathan Sheehan, *The Enlightenment Bible: Translation, Scholarship, Culture* (Princeton: Princeton

University Press, 2005), esp. ch. 7 on comparative religion; Michael C. Carhart, *The Science of Culture in Enlightenment Germany* (Cambridge, MA: Harvard University Press, 2007), esp. ch. 3; and Han F. Vermeulen, "Early History of Ethnography and Ethnology in the German Enlightenment: Anthropological Discourse in Europe and Asia, 1710–1808," PhD dissertation, Leiden University, 2008.

4. Ludwig Wachler, *Geschichte der Künste und Wissenschaften seit der Wiederherstellung derselben bis an das Ende des achtzehnten Jahrhunderts. Fünfte Abtheilung. Geschichte der historischen Wissenschaften* (Gottingen: Johann Friedrich Rower, 1812), vol. 2, 274.

5. Wachler, *Geschichte der Künste und Wissenschaften*, vol. 2, 865–66.

6. We know remarkably little about the institute, whose founding seems, remarkably, not to have been thought worthy of scholarly study.

7. Details can be found in *Geseze des Königl. Instituts des historischen Wissenschaften*, 23.12.1766, UAG Kur 7540, Göttingen University Archive, but not in the published manifesto "Vom historischen Plan, und der darauf sich gründenden Zusammenfügung der Erzählungen," which is really a vision of hoped for publication outputs. See Johann Christoph Gatterer, "Vom historischen Plan, und der darauf sich gründenden Zusammenfügung der Erzählungen," *Allgemeine historische Bibliothek* 1 (1767), 15–89.

8. Martin Gierl, *Geschichte als präzisierte Wissenschaft: Johann Christoph Gatterer und die Historiographie des 18. Jahrhunderts im ganzen Umfang* (Stuttgart–Bad Cannstatt: frommann-holzboog, 2012), 19.

9. *Historische Encyclopädie, d.h. die vornehmsten Kapitel der Heraldik, Geographie, Chronologie, Numismatik, Genealogie, Diplomatik und allgemeine Geschichte.* There is some bibliographical information on Gatterer and Göttingen but little on the *Hilfswissenschaften* there. See Rudolf Vierhaus, "Göttingen und die Anfänge der modernen Geschichtswissenschaft im 18.Jahrhundert," in *Geschichtswissenschaft in Göttingen*, ed. Harmut Bookman and Hermann Wellenreuther (Göttingen: Vandenhoeck & Ruprecht, 1987), 14–15; Georg Iggers, "The University of Göttingen, 1760–1800, and the Transformation of Historical Scholarship," *Storia della Storiografia* 2 (1982): 11–37; Hans Erich Bödeker, Philippe Büttgen, and Michel Espagne, eds., *Göttingen vers 1800: L'Europe des sciences de l'homme* (Paris: Éditions du Cerf / Bibliothèque franco-allemande, 2010); Georg G. Iggers, "Die Göttinger Historiker und die Geschichtswissenschaft des 18. Jahrhunderts," *Mentalitäten und Lebensverhältnisse: Beispiele aus der Sozialgeschichte der Neuzeit. Rudolf Vierhaus zum 60. Geburtstag* (Göttingen: Vandenhoeck & Ruprecht, 1982), 385–98; Hammerstein, *Jus und Historie*, 357–74; Peter Reill, "History and Hermeneutics in the Aufklarung: The Thought of Johann Christoph Gatterer," *Journal of Modern History* 45 (1973); and A. H. L. Heeren, "Johann Christoph Gatterer," in *Biographische und litterarische Denkschriften* (Göttingen, 1823), 450–68.

10. Johann Christoph Gatterer, "Räsonnement über die jezige Verfassung der Geschichtskunde in Teutschland," *Historisches Journal* 1 (1772), in Horst Walter Blanke and Dirk Fischer, ed., *Theoretiker der deutschen Aufklärungshistorie* (Stuttgart-Bad Canstatt: frommann-holzboog, 1990), vol. 2, 719–20. For orientation to the contemporary German context—not mine, it needs be added—for the project of recovering "Aufklärungshistorie," see D. A. Jeremy Telman, review of *Theoretiker der deutschen Aufklärungshistorie*, in *History and Theory* 33 (1994): 249–65; and Alexandre Escudier, "De Chladenius à Droysen. Théorie et méthodologie de l'histoire de langue allemande (1750–1860)," *Annales HSS* (2003): 743–77.

11. *Abriss der Universalhistorie* (1765), *Einleitung in die synchronistische Universal-historie* (1771), *Kurzer Begriff der Weltgeschichte* (1785), *Weltgeschichte in ihrem ganzen Umfange* (1785), *Versuch einer allgemeinen Weltgeschichte* (1792).

12. Johann Christoph Gatterer, *Handbuch der Universalhistorie nach ihrem gesam-ten Umfange von Erschaffung der Welt bis zum Ursprunge der meisten heutigen Reiche und Staaten*, 2nd ed. (Göttingen: Vandenhoeck, 1765), pt. 1, ch. 3.

13. For example, Marino, *I Maestri della Germania*, 288.

14. He suggests that one combine genealogy, heraldry, numismatics, and so on to create a sort of game. The coats of arms and coins could be painted, the coins could be catalogued or copied with plaster, tin, lead, or glass, family trees could be painted, and so on. Gatterer, "Von der historischen Erziehung [1771]," in *Theoretiker der deutschen Aufklärungshistorie*, vol. 2, 713.

15. Gatterer, *Praktsiche Heraldik* (Nuremberg, 1791), 5.

16. See Gierl, *Geschichte als präzisierte Wissenschaft*, 95–96.

17. Gatterer, "Die kluge Auswal der Begebenheiten ist der eigentliche Probier-stein eines historischen Genies," *Handbuch der Universalhistorie*, 2. This emphasis on events is maintained in Heeren, *Andenken an Deutsche Historiker aus den letzten funfzig Jahren*, quoted in Daniel Fulda, *Wissenschaft aus Kunst: Die Entstehung der modernen deutschen Geschichtsschreibung 1760–1860* (Berlin and New York: Walter de Gruyter, 1996), 86.

18. Gatterer, "Von der Evidenz in der Geschichtskunde" (1767), in *Die Allge-meine Welthistorie die in England durch eine Gesellschaft von Gelehrten ausgefertiget wor-den: In einem vollständigen und pragmatischen Auszuge*, ed. Friedrich Eberhard Boysen, *Alte Historie*, vol. 1 (Halle: Gebauer, 1767), 1–38. See also Fulda, *Wissenschaft aus Kunst*, 157–66.

19. Gatterer, "Von der Evidenz," 10.

20. Gatterer, "Von der Evidenz," 11.

21. Gatterer, "Von der Evidenz," 13.

22. Gatterer, "Von der Evidenz," 17, emphasis in original.

23. Gatterer, *Handbuch der Univeralhistorie*, 1.

24. A. H. L. Heeren, "Etwas über die Seltenheit klassischer Geschichtschreiber, besonders in Deutschland," *Biographische und litterarische Denkschriften* (Göttingen, 1823), 434. Typically, Heeren devotes nearly all of his discussion to the qualities of the *Geschichtsschreiber*, with the researcher identified only in terms of shared prac-tices such as "Kritik" and the pursuit of truth.

25. The Italian theorist Agostino Mascardi, for example, distinguished between antiquaries, who studied the things that remained, and historians, who "teach how properly to weave a tale of the most memorable human events." *Dell'arte historica* (1636), quoted in William Stenhouse, "The Renaissance Foundations of European Antiquarianism," in *World Antiquarianism*, ed. Alain Schnapp et al. (Los Angeles: Getty Publications, 2013), 303.

26. Mark Phillips, *Society and Sentiment: Genres of Historical Writing in Britain, 1740–1820* (Princeton: Princeton University Press, 2000). Gatterer's contemporary Johann Georg Sulzer similarly likened the history-writer to the portrait painter in his ability to characterize deftly and through all manner of signs. Johann Georg Sulzer, *Kurzer Begriff aller Wissenschaften und anderen Theile der Gelehrsamkeit*, 2nd ed. (Frank-furt and Leipzig: University of Leipzig, 1759), 27.

27. Johan Huizinga, "On the Task of Cultural History," *Men and Ideas* (London: Eyre & Spottieswoode, 1960), 45–49.

28. Gatterer, "Von der Evidenz," 17, emphasis in original.

29. Gatterer, "Von der Evidenz," 18.

30. Gatterer, "Von der Evidenz," 19. This point was emphasized a generation later in Heeren, "Etwas über die Seltenheit klassischer Geschichtschreiber," 436–37.

31. Gatterer, "Von der Evidenz," 20–21.

32. Gatterer, "Von der Evidenz," 24.

33. Gatterer, "Von der Evidenz," 27.

34. Gatterer, "Von der Evidenz," 36–37.

35. Johann Huizinga, "The Task of Cultural History," *Men and Ideas*, trans. James S. Holmes and Hans van Marle (New York: Meridian Books, 1959), 55.

36. Gatterer, *Handbuch der Universalhistorie*, 63.

37. On Biondo and the history of antiquarianism, see Angelo Mazzocco, "Biondo Flavio and the Antiquarian Tradition," PhD dissertation, University of California, Berkeley, 1973; and Miller, "Major Trends in European Antiquarianism, Petrarch to Peiresc," in *Oxford History of Historical Writing*, vol. 3, ed. Jose Rabasa et al. (Oxford, U.K.: Oxford University Press, 2012), 250–53.

38. Johann Christoph Gatterer, *Ideal einer allgemeinen Weltstatistik: in der öffentlichen Versammlung des Köngl. histor. Instituts den 2 Oct 1773 vorgelesen* (Gottingen: Vandenhoeck) 41, emphasis in original.

39. Hammerstein, *Jus und Historie*, 360.

40. Gatterer, *Ideal einer allgemeinen Weltstatistik*.

41. Gatterer, *Ideal einer allgemeinen Weltstatistik*, 24.

42. Gatterer, *Ideal einer allgemeinen Weltstatistik*, 36.

43. Giovanni Botero, *Le relationi universali* (Venice, 1597); Samuel von Pufendorf, *Einleitung zu der Historie der vornehmsten Reiche und Staaten, so itziger Zeit in Europa sich befinden* (Frankfurt a.M., 1684).

44. See Carhart, *Science of Culture in Enlightenment Germany*.

45. Gérard Laudin, "L'histoire comme science de l'homme chez Gatterer et Schlözer," in *Göttingen vers 1800: L'Europe des sciences de l'homme*, ed. Hans Erich Bödeker, Philippe Büttgen, and Michel Espagne (Paris: Cerf, 2011), 483–514; Peter Hans Reill, "History and Hermeneutics in the Aufklärung: The Thought of Johann Christoph Gatterer," *Journal of Modern History* 45 (1973): 40.

46. For a perceptive discussion, see Justin Stagl, "Chapter 6: August Ludwig Schlözer and the Study of Mankind According to Peoples" *A History of Curiosity: The Theory of Travel, 1550–1800* (Chur, Switzerland: Harwood Academic Publications, 1995), 233–68.

47. August Ludwig Schlözer, "Vorstellung seiner Universal-Historie" (1772), *Theoretiker deutscher Aufklärungshistorie*, 683. The Parisian *Société de Statistique* in 1803 is reported to have divided up into six commissions with different areas of study: (1) physical and medical topography; (2) statistical meteorology and natural history; (3) population and its institutions; (4) farming and agriculture (5) industry, commerce, and trades (6) public education and the fine arts. Schlözer, *Theorie der Statistik*, 21.

48. Schlözer, "Vorstellung seiner Universal-Historie," 678–79.

49. Schlözer, *Theorie der Statistik*, 31–32.

50. Schlözer, *Theorie der Statistik*, 34.

51. Schlözer, *Theorie der Statistik*, 34–38.

52. Schlözer, *Theorie der Statistik*, 45.

53. Miller, *Peiresc's Mediterranean World* (Cambridge, MA: Harvard University Press, 2015), §8. See Pascale Hummel, *Moeurs Érudites. Étude sur la micrologie littéraire* (Allemagne, XVIe-XVIIIe siècles) (Droz: Geneva, 2002).

54. Stagl, *History of Curiosity*, 261.

55. Schlözer, *Theorie der Statistik*, 63.

56. See Martin Peters, *Altes Reich und Europa: Der Historiker, Statistiker und Publizist August Ludwig (v.) Schlözer (1735–1809)* (Münster, 2005) and the essays collected in Heinz Duchhardt and Marin Espenhorst, eds., *August Ludwig (von) Schlözer in Europa* (Göttingen: Vandenhoeck & Ruprecht, 2012), especially Ulrich Muhlack, "Der Vermittler der Welt: Ein Zugang zum Verständnis des 'ganzen' Schlözer," 7–20.

57. Schlözer, *Theorie der Statistik*, 34–38.

58. "Warum nicht auch Statistiken der Vergangenheit? Geschichte ist eine fortlaufende Statistik; und Statistik ist eine stillstehende Geschichte." Schlözer, *Theorie der Statistik*, 86.

59. Schlözer, *Theorie der Statistik*, 87.

60. Schlözer, *Theorie der Statistik*, 92.

61. Schlözer, *Theorie der Statistik*, 93.

62. Schlözer, *Theorie der Statistik*, 93.

63. Schlözer, *Weltgeschichte*, quoted in Hans Schleier, *Geschichte der deutschen Kulturgeschichtsschreibung* (Waltrop, Germany: Hartmut Spenner, 2008), 110.

64. "Oder mit andern Worten: Geschichte ist das Ganze, Statistik ein Teil derselben." Schlözer, *Theorie der Statistik*, 93.

65. Will, "Einleitung in die historische Gelahrtheit und die Methode, die Geschichte zu lehren und zu lernen," printed in *Theoretiker der deutschen Aufklärungshistorie*, vol. 1, 329. The manuscript was first printed in Horst Walter Blanke, "Georg Andreas Wills 'Einleitung in die historische Gelartheit' (1766) und die Anfange der modernen Historik-Vorlesungen in Deutschland," *Dilthey-Jahrbuch* 2 (1984): 193–265.

66. Friedrich Maier, "Versuch einer Encyclopädie der Geschichte, nach allen ihren Theilen, in einem natürlichen Zusammenhang (1796)," in *Theoretiker der deutschen Aufklärungshistorie*, vol. 2, 370.

67. W. T. Krug, *Versuch einer systematischen Encyclopädie der Wissenschaften* (Wittenberg and Leipzig, 1796), part 1, 54–96; Christian Jacob Kraus, "Encyclopädische Ansichten der historischen Gelehrsamkeit," in *Theoretiker der deutschen Aufklärungshistorie*, vol. 2, 385; idem, *Vermischte Schriften über staatswirthschaftliche, philosophische und andere wissenschaftliche Gegenstände*, ed. Hans von Auserwald (Königsberg: Friedrich Ricolovius, 1809), vol. 3, 17. These textbooks typically reflect lecture courses delivered over some period of time, making the initial formulation of the ideas contained within somewhat difficult to determine.

68. For description as a paradigmatic signifer of antiquarian practice, see Peter N. Miller, "Description Terminable and Interminable: Looking at the Past, Nature and Peoples in Peiresc's Archive," in *"Historia": Empiricism and Erudition in Early Modern Europe*, ed. Gianna Pomata and Nancy Siraisi (Cambridge, MA: MIT Press, 2005), 355–97.

69. Maier, "Versuch einer Encyclopädie der Geschichte," 371.

70. Maier, "Versuch einer Encyclopädie der Geschichte," 372.

71. Maier, "Versuch einer Encyclopädie der Geschichte," 373.

72. Maier, "Versuch einer Encycklopädie der Geschichte," 373–74.

73. See Stephanie-Gerrit Bruer, "Jacob Burckhardt. Systematische Kunstbetrachtung ein Jahrhundert nach Winckelmann," in *Jacob Burckhardt und die Antike*, ed. Peter Betthausen and Max Kunze (Mainz: Verlag Phillip von Zabern, 1998), 105.

74. Maier, "Versuch einer Encycklopädie der Geschichte," 375.

75. D. C. T. G. Schönemann, *Grundriß einer Encyclopädie der historischen Wissenschaften zum Gebrauch seiner Vorlesungen entwerfen* (Göttingen, 1799), 5: "der Geschichte *in specie*; Geschichtskunde in engerer Bedeutung" focused on "der successiven Betrachtung und Erzählung von Ereignissen." The other kind study, which also traveled under the name of *history*, was based on "der stillsehenden Betrachtung eines Landes, Volkes, Staats, der Statistik."

76. Schönemann, *Grundriss*, 5.

77. Schönemann, *Grundriss*, 17–18.

78. Johann Georg Fessmaier, *Grundriss der historischen Hilfswissenschaften vorzüglich nach Gatterers Schriften zum akademischen Gebrauche bearbeitet* (Landshut: Anton Weber 1802), iii.

79. Fessmaier, *Grundriss*, 2.

80. One form of *Geschlechts-* or *Stammtafeln* gives all the known persons in a family in their lines, with the oldest at the top. A second follows one person only, with his relations. A third focused on the figure of a ruler and studied him only. A fourth mapped inheritance from closer relations to those further away. A fifth kind of table, called "synchronistische," presented the trees of several families together, showing their interrelationship. The sixth kind was the "historical," which differed from the ordinary family tree "in that it includes biographies of the main members of the family tree as well as their descendants." Finally, the seventh chart was the "national and detailed chart that included tribal families and population fluctuation as well as a family's wealth." Fessmaier, *Grundriss*, 47, descriptions of the different kinds of tables are found at 47–49.

81. Fessmaier, *Grundriss*, 232–36; Johann Christoph Gatterer, *Praktische Heraldik* (Nuremberg: Bauer und Mann, 1791), 5.

82. Fessmaier, *Grundriss*, 79.

83. Fessmaier, *Grundriss*, 73.

84. "Es ist also ein Archiv nichts weniger als eine Antiquitätenkammer, sondern ein Institut von dem reichhaltigsten Gebrauche." Fessmaier, *Grundriss*, 184.

85. Fessmaier, *Grundriss*, 297.

86. Fessmaier, *Grundriss*, 298.

87. Fessmaier, *Grundriss*, 297–98.

88. Fabri, *Encyclopädie der Historischen Hauptwissenschaften und deren Hülfs-Doctrinen: Archäologie, Alterthumskunde, Chronologie, Diplomatik, Epigraphik, Genealogie, Heraldik, Hieroglyphik, Mythologie, Mythographie, Numismatik, Sphragistik, Toponomie, politischen Arithmetik* (Erlangen: Johann Jakob Palm, 1808), 2r.

89. Fabri, *Encyclopädie*, 116–17.

90. Gerhard Lutz, "Johann Ernst Fabri und die Anfänge der Volksforschung im ausgehenden 18. Jahrhundert," *Zeitschrift für Volkskunde* 69 (1973): 36.

91. Fabri, *Encyclopädie*, 124.

92. Fabri, *Encyclopädie*, 125.

93. Fabri, *Encyclopädie*, 353.

94. Fabri, *Encyclopädie*, 380, emphasis in original.

95. Fabri, *Encyclopädie*, 407.

96. Fabri, *Encyclopädie*, 420.

97. Fabri, Encyclopädie, 436.

98. *L'École nationale des chartes: histoire de l'École depuis 1821* (Thionville, France: Gérard Klopp, 1997); Jean-François Delmas, "La Figure du Chartiste dans la littérature: Entre mythe et réalité," *Mémoires de l'académie de Nîmes*, 9th series, 88 (2014): 49–72.

Chapter Five. Archaeology as a Way of Talking about Things, 1750–1850

1. This is Spon quoted by Millin, cited in François Lissarrague and Alain Schnapp, "Klassische Archäologie in Frankreich," in *Klassische Archäologie: Eine Einführung*, ed. Adolf H. Borbein, Tonio Hölscher, and Paul Zanker (Berlin: Reimer Verlag, 2000), 370.

2. Christian Jürgenson Thomsen, *Ledetraad til Nordisk Oldkyndighed* (Copenhagen, 1836) was translated into English as *Guide to Northern Archaeology* (London, 1848).

3. Thomsen, *Guide to Northern Archaeology* (London, 1848).

4. On English antiquarianism, see Stuart Piggott, *Ruins in a Landscape: Essays in Antiquarianism* (Edinburgh: University Press, 1976); idem, *William Stukeley, An Eighteenth-Century Antiquary* (New York: Thames and Hudson, 1985); Stan A. E. Mendyk, *"Speculum Britanniae": Regional Study, Antiquarianism, and Science in Britain to 1700* (Toronto: University of Toronto Press, 1989); Graham Parry, *The Trophies of Time: English Antiquarians of the Seventeenth Century* (Oxford, U.K.: Oxford University Press, 1995); Rosemary Sweet, *Antiquaries: The Discovery of the Past in Eighteenth-Century Britain* (London and New York: Hambledon and London, 2004); David Starkey and David Gaimster, *Making History: Antiquaries in Britain, 1707–2007* (London: Royal Academy Books, 2007). On Aubery, Michael Hunter's *John Aubrey and the World of Learning* (London: Duckworth, 1975) is not surpassed by Ruth Scurr, *John Aubrey: My Life* (London: Chatto & Windus, 2015).

5. *The Archaeologist and Journal of Antiquarian Science*, opening address of vol. 1 (1841): 2, quoted in David Westherall, "The Growth of Archaeological Societies," in *The Study of the Past in the Victorian Age*, ed. Vanessa Brand (Oxford, 1998), 21.

6. On Millin, see G. Adkins, "The Renaissance of Peiresc: Aubin-Louis Millin and the Postrevolutionary Republic of Letters," *Isis* 99 (2008): 675–700.

7. Guy Verron, "Arcisse de Caumont et la naissance de l'archéologie moderne," in *Arcisse de Caumont (1801–1873) Érudit Normand et Fondateur de l'Archéologie française*, ed. Vincent Juhel (Caen: Société des antiquaires de Normandie, 2004), 127.

8. Ève Gran-Aymerich, *Naissance de l'archéologie moderne 1798–1945* (Paris: CNRS Éditions 1998), 24, 136.

9. Corinne Saminadayar-Perrin, "Pages de pierre: Les apories du roman archéologique" in *Rêver l'archéololgie au XIXe siècle: de la science à l'imaginaire*, ed. Éric Perrin-Saminadayar (Saint-Étienne, France: Publications de l'Université de Saint-Étienne, 2001), 123–46.

10. 1763: "Veterum monumentorum et arteficiorum notitiam deinceps traditus." 1764: "rem gemmarium et numismaticam veterum." 1767: "Archaeologiam,

seu notitiam monumentorum antiquorum eorumque comparationem cum praecep-
tis artium elegantiorum nunc primum docebit." 1772: "Die Archäologie oder die
Kenntniss der Kunst und der Kunstwerke des Alterthums." Martin Vöhler, "Chris-
tian Gottlob Heyne und das Studium des Altertums in Deutschland," in *Disciplining
Classics: Altertumswissenschaft als Beruf*, ed. Glenn W. Most (Göttingen: Vandenhoek &
Ruprecht, 2002), 44–49.

11. Io. Augusti Ernesti, *Archaeologia Literaria* (Leipzig, 1768), iv.

12. Ernesti, *Archaeologia Literaria*, v. Wilhelm Dilthey identifies Ernesti as employ-
ing a thoroughly literary approach and places him in the line leading to Gottfried Hermann, *Hermeneutics and the Study of History: Selected Works*, ed. Rudolf A. Makkreel
and Frithjof Rodi (Princeton: Princeton University Press, 1996), vol. 4, 79–82.

13. Daniel Grapeler, "Einleitung: Christian Gottlob Heyne und die Archäologie,"
in *Das Studium des schönen Altertums: Christian Gottlob Heyne und die Entstehung der
Klassischen Archäologie*, ed. Daniel Grapeler and Joachim Migl (Göttingen: Niedersächsische Staats- und Universitätsbibliothek Göttingen, 2007), 13.

14. Heyne, *Einleitung in das Studium der Antike* (Göttingen, 1772), no. 6, p. 7.

15. Heyne, *Sammlung antiquarischer Aufsätze. Erstes Stück* (Leipzig, 1778), iii–viii.

16. Thus, his posthumously published lectures on archaeology contain an appendix entitled "Das Antiquarische der Kunst" devoted to the beards and hairstyles
depicted in ancient reliefs. Heyne, *Akademische Vorlesungen über die Archäologie der
Kunst des Alterthums, besonders der Griechen und Römer* (Braunschweig, 1822), 496.

17. For the question of impact, see Grapeler, "Ausblick: Heynes Wirkung auf die
Archäologie," in *Das Studium des schönen Altertums*, 121–22.

18. Heyne, *Akademische Vorlesungen über die Archäologie der Kunst des Alterthums*,
35–36. On Heyne and Winckelmann, see Grapeler, "Heyne und Winckelmann," *Das
Studium des schönen Altertums*, 17–28.

19. René Sternke, *Böttiger und der archäologische Diskurs* (Berlin: Akademie Verlag,
2008).

20. Christian Jacob Kraus, *Encyclopädische Ansichten einiger Zweige der Gelehrsamkeit*, in *Vermischte Schriften über staatswirthschaftliche, philosophische und andere wissenschaftliche Gegenstände*, ed. Hans von Auserwald, 4 vols. (Königsberg: Friedrich Ricolovius, 1809), 3, 95–100.

21. Kraus explicitly declares that *Altertumskunde* is not a *Hilfswissenschaft* but a
constitutive part of history. "Encyclopädische Ansichten einiger Zweige der Gelehrsamkeit" in *Vermischte Schriften* 3, 275–76.

22. Christian Daniel Beck, *Grundriss der Archäologie oder Anleitung zur Kenntniß
der Geschichte der alten Kunst und der Kunst-Denkmäler und Kunstwerke des classischen
Alterthums* (Leipzig, 1816), 1. Despite this insistence, Beck nevertheless does have a
detailed, if brief, section focusing in detail on some non-visual ancient materials, such
as coins or inscriptions (119).

23. Johann Philipp Siebenkees, *Handbuch der Archäologie oder Anleitung zur Kenntniss der Kunstwerke des Alterthums und zur Geschichte der Kunst der Alten Völker* (Nuremberg, 1799), 2–3.

24. Siebenkees, *Handbuch der Archäologie*, 4.

25. Siebenkees, *Handbuch der Archäologie*, 6.

26. On Wolf in this context, see Anthony Grafton, "Prolegomena to Friedrich
August Wolf," *Journal of the Warburg and Courtauld Institutes* 44 (1981): 101–29; idem,

"Polyhistor into *Philolog*: Notes on the Transformation of German Classical Scholarship, 1780–1850," *History of Universities* 3 (1983): 159–92.

27. Friedrich August Wolf, *Darstellung der Altertumswissenschaft nach Begriff, Umfang, Zweck und Wert*, afterword by Johannes Irmscher (Weinheim: Acta humaniora, VCH, 1986), 30. The *Darstellung* was printed in Friedrich August Wolf and Philipp Buttman, eds., *Museum der Alterthums-Wissenschaft* (Berlin: Realschulbuchhandlung, 1807). For a comparison of this version of the lectures with those published in 1831, see Christiane Hackel, *Die Bedeutung August Boeckhs für den Geschichtstheoretiker Johann Gustav Droysen* (Würzburg: Königshausen & Neumann, 2006).

28. Wolf, *Museum*, 55.

29. Friedrich August Wolf, *Vorlesungen über die Alterthumswissenschaft*, ed. J. D. Gürtler (Leipzig: August Lehnhold, 1831), 17–18.

30. Wolf, *Vorlesungen*, 26.

31. Wolf, *Museum*, 91.

32. Wolf, *Vorlesungen*, 29.

33. Wolf, *Museum*, 125.

34. Wolf, *Vorlesungen*, 16.

35. "Nichtig ist daher die Philologie, wenn sie entweder bloss als historische und antiquarische Gelehrsamkeit, oder als gelehrtes Sprachstudium betrachtet wird. Die Alterthumskunde hat keine Bedeutung und Wahrheit, wenn sei das Einzelne bloss faktisch und empirisch auffasst, ohne sein höheres und eigentliches Wesen in der Idee des Ganzen zu erkennen: eben so gehaltlos und todt ist das bloss gelehrte Sprachstudium, das die Sprache nicht als Organ des Geistes erkennt und deutet, sondern sie in ihrer atomistischen Einzelnheit als ein nicht höher beziehbares, also zufälliges und blindes Wesen behandelt." Friedrich Ast, *Grundriss der Philologie* (Landshut: Philipp Krüll, 1808), 2.

36. This publication may have heavily been influenced by Boeckh's final version of the lecture course, which was delivered twice in his final four years of teaching, both times with his editor—and former student—Ernst Bratuscheck in attendance. Bratuscheck also incorporated materials found in Boeckh's nachlass. He began to undertake a revision but died before it was completed; this second, incomplete edition was published in 1886. A critical edition, accounting for layers of composition and posthumous editorial re-working, is currently being planned.

37. August Boeckh, "De studia antiquitatis," *Gesammelte Kleine Schriften* (Leipzig: G. B. Teubner, 1858), vol. 1, 105.

38. Boeckh, *Encyklopädie und Methodologie der philologischen Wissenschaften*, ed. Ernst Bratuscheck, with Rudolf Klussman (Leipzig: Teubner, 1886), 53. All references are to this edition unless otherwise specified.

39. "Historischen Construction des ganzen Erkennens und seiner Teile" (14); "Nachconstruction der Constructionen des menschlichen Geistes in ihrer Gesammtheit" (16); "Wiedererkenntnis und Darstellung des ganzen vorhandenen menschlichen Wissens" (16); "die richtige Reproduction des Ueberlieferten" (17); "Reconstruction der Gesammtheit des Erkennens" (19). All references are to Boeckh, *Encyklopädie*.

40. Axel Horstmann, *Antike Theoria und moderne Wissenschaft: August Boeckhs Konzeption der Philologie* (Frankfurt a.M., Berlin, and Bern: Peter Lang, 1992), 171.

41. Boeckh, *Encyklopädie*, 25.

42. "Der Begriff Bökhs ist zu weit: Unterschied zwischen Philologie und Ge-schichte verschwindet: und zu eng (vergl. Z.B. die homerische Frage. Der Sprach-vergleich.)" Quoted in Benn, *Nietzsche und die historisch-kritische Philologie*, 79n129.

43. Stark, "Ueber Kunst und Kunstwissenschaft auf deutschen Universitäten," *Vorträge und Aufsätze aus dem Gebiete der Archäologie und Kunstgeschichte*, ed. Gottfried Kinkel (Leipzig: G. B. Teubner, 1880), 6–7. We find exactly the same point being made in 1851 in an essay "On the Study of Archaeology" written by Charles New-ton, first Yates Professor of Classical Archaeology at University College London: "He who would master the manifold subject-matter of Archaeology, and appreci-ate its whole range and compass, must possess a mind in which the reflective and perceptive faculties are duly balanced; he must combine with the aesthetic culture of the Artist, and the trained judgment of the Historian, not a little of the learning of the Philologer; the plodding drudgery which gathers together his materials must not blunt the critical acuteness required for their classification and interpretation." Quoted in Levine, *Amateur and the Professional*, 87.

44. Quoted in Levine, *Amateur and the Professional*, 90.

45. Boeckh, *Encyklopädie*, 16.

46. Boeckh, *Encyklopädie*, 7, 27.

47. Boeckh, *Encyklopädie*, 258.

48. Ernst Gombrich, *In Search of Cultural History* (London: Oxford University Press, 1969), 31. The relationship between Boeckh and Hegel is discussed in Bene-detto Bravo, *Philologie, histoire, philosophie de l'histoire: étude sur J. G. Droysen, historien de l'antiquité* (Wrocław, Poland: Zakład Narodowy Imienia Ossolińskich, Wydawn, 1968), 90–96. What might this coincidence of simile say about the relationship between Boeckh and Gombrich, or indeed between philology and art history? I can only raise this question here.

49. Boeckh, *Encyklopädie*, 375.

50. Boeckh, *Gesammelte Kleine Schriften* (1859), 2, 189.

51. Wilfried Nippel, "Boeckhs Beitrag zur Alten Geschichte," in *August Boeckh: Philologie, Hermeneutik und Wissenschaftspolitik*, ed. Christiane Hackel and Sabine Seifert (Berlin: Berliner Wissenschafts Verlag, 2013) 52.

52. Jacob Burckhardt, *The Greeks and Greek Civilization*, trans. Sheila Stern, ed. Oswyn Murray (New York: St. Martin's Griffin, 1998), 3–4.

53. Eduard Platner, *Ueber wissenschaftliche Begründung und Behandlung der Anti-quitäten insbesondere der römischen* (Marburg, 1818), vi.

54. Platner, *Ueber wissenschaftliche Begründung*, 5.

55. Platner, *Ueber wissenschaftliche Begründung*, 10.

56. Platner, *Ueber wissenschaftliche Begründung*, 15.

57. Platner, *Ueber wissenschaftliche Begründung*, 18.

58. "Der antiquarische Forscher, um auf diesen zurück zu kommen, muss alle Eigenheiten des darzustellenden Volkes allerdings kennen, weil das, was auf den ersten Anblick ganz ausserwesentlich scheint, doch zuweilen durch Combination mit dem Ganzen in Verbindung gebracht werden kann, und oft über Dunkelheiten wesentlicher Gegenstände Licht verbreitet." Platner, *Ueber wissenschaftliche Begründung*, 20.

59. Thomas Poiss, "Die Unendliche Aufgabe: August Boeckh als Begründer des Philologischen Seminars," in *Die modernen Väter der Antike: Die Entwicklung der*

Altertumswissenschaften an Akademie und Universität im Berlin des 19. Jahrhunderts, ed. A. M. Baertschi and C. G. King (Berlin: Walter de Gruyter, 2009), vol. 3, 65.

60. Boeckh, *Encyklopädie*, 375.

61. Boeckh, *Encyklopädie*, 492.

62. Boeckh, *Encyklopädie*, 493. A whole section devoted to a review of the literature followed.

63. On this tension, see Serena Fornaro, "Das 'Studium der Antike' von Heyne bis Boeckh," in *August Boeckh*, ed. Hackel and Seifert, 197–209.

64. "Critical" answered the questions "Is it all here?" "What is its material?" "Who is its maker and when was it made?" "Historical" asked about what the object tells us about the myths it was based on. "Aesethetic" was about the choices made by the artist and how well he or she achieved the stated goal. "Technical" referred to the way the materials or the tools shaped and motivated the work. F. Christian Petersen, *Allgemeine Einleitung in das Studium der Archäologie*, trans. P. Friedrichsen (Leipzig: Hahn'schen verlag, 1829 [Denmark 1825]), 285–89.

65. René Sternke, *Böttiger und der archäologische Diskurs* (Berlin: Akademie Verlag, 2008); Eve Gran-Aymerich and Jürgen von Ungern-Sternberg, eds., *L'Antiquité partagée: Correspondances franco-allemandes (1823–1861)* (Paris: Memoires de l'Academie des Inscriptions et Belles-Lettres, 2012).

66. Only by the late nineteenth century was this remedied. *The Nouveau Larousse Illustré* (1898) divided it into *archéologie de l'art* (architecture, sculpture, painting) and *archéologie des utensiles* (small and domestic objects), while the *Grand Dictionnaire Universel du XIXᵉ siècle* (1867–1890), added a third category, *archéologie littéraire*. I am grateful to my former student, Maude Bass-Krueger, for sharing this with me.

67. Pierre Judet de la Combe, "'Le savant antiquaire de Goettingue': Karl Otfried Müller en France," in *Zwischen Rationalismus und Romantik: Karl Otfried Müller und die antike Kultur*, ed. William M. Calder III and Renate Schleiser with Susanne Gödde (Hildesheim, Germany: Weidmann, 1998), 285–88.

68. Gran-Aymerich, *Naissance de l'archéologie moderne 1798–1945*, 153; idem, "Archéologie et préhistoire: les effets d'une révolution," in *Rêver l'archéologie au XIXe siècle: de la science à l'imaginaire*, ed. Éric Perrin-Saminadayar (Saint-Étienne, France: Publications de l'Université de Saint-Étienne, 2001), 20.

69. Boeckh, *Encyklopädie*, 5.

70. Boeckh, *Encyklopädie*, 27. This fear was already real in the generation of Boeckh's teachers. Heeren, Gatterer's heir at Göttingen, worried in 1797 that "these studies led only too often to a simplistic micrology" that risked turning philology into a *Hilfswissenschaft*. A. H. L. Heeren, *Geschichte der Künste und Wissenschaften seit der Wiederherstellung derselben bis an das Ende des achtzehnten Jahrhunderts* (Göttingen: Georg Rosenbusch, 1797), vol. 1, 6.

71. Boeckh, *Encyklopädie*, 307.

72. The Romans called those who knew things "philologists" and those who thought abstractly "philosophers." Boeckh, *Encyklopädie*, 23.

73. "Man kann sich im Einzelnen so vertiefen, dass man in ihm, wie in einem Mikrokosmos das Ganze, den Makrokosmos erfasst. In jeder einzelnen Idee wird das Ganze erreicht." Boeckh adds, quite honestly, that no one can actually grasp all the ideas and thus the entirety of the whole. Boeckh, *Encyklopädie*, 15.

74. Boeckh, *Encyklopädie*, 27.

75. Boeckh, *Encyklopädie*, 307.

76. Boeckh, *Die Staatshaushaltung der Athener*, 2nd ed. (Berlin: G. Reimer, 1851), xiii.

77. Boeckh, *Encyklopädie*, 376–79, 390–427.

78. Boeckh, *The Public Economy of Athens in Four Books* (London: John Murray, 1828), 7–8.

79. August Boeckh, *Corpus Inscriptionum Graecarum* (Berlin, 1828), vii.

80. Roscher, *Leben, Werk und Zeitalter des Thukydides*, vii. Only a few decades later this had changed: Friedrich Jodl described the flourishing expansion of the subjects of historical research in terms of the revolution produced by the microscope for the study of nature. *Die Culturgeschichtsschreibung, ihre Entwickelung und ihr Problem* (Halle: CEM Pfeffer, 1878), 2.

81. Roscher, *Leben, Werk und Zeitalter des Thukydides*, 11–12. On Mommsen and antiquarianism, see Wilfried Nippel, "Der 'antiquarische Bauplatz': Theodor Mommsen's *Römisches Staatsrecht*," in *Theodor Mommsen: Gelehrter, Politiker und Literat*, ed. Josef Wiesehöfer (Stuttgart: Franz Steiner Verlag, 2005), 165–84.

82. Boeckh, *Encyklopädie*, 83.

83. Boeckh, *Encyklopädie*, 81.

84. Boeckh, *Encyklopädie*, 256.

85. Konrad Levezow, *Über archäologische Kritik und Hermeneutik: Eine Abhandlung gelesen in der Königlichen Akademie der Wissenschaften zu Berlin am 21. November 1833* (Berlin: Königliche Akademie der Wissenschaften, 1834), 18. On him and his work, see Werner Fuchs, "Fragen der archäologischen Hermeneutik in der ersten Hälfte des 19. Jahrhunderts," in *Philologie und Hermeneutik im 19. Jahrhundert: Zur Geschichte und Methodologie der Geisteswissenschaften*, ed. Hellmut Flashar, Karlfried Gründer, and Axel Horstmann (Göttingen: Vandenhoeck & Ruprecht, 1979), 201–24.

86. Levezow, *Über archäologische Kritik und Hermeneutik*, 3.

87. Levezow, *Über archäologische Kritik und Hermeneutik*, 20.

88. Levezow, *Über archäologische Kritik und Hermeneutik*, 5, 7.

89. Levezow, *Über archäologische Kritik und Hermeneutik*, 11.

90. Levezow, *Über archäologische Kritik und Hermeneutik*, 15.

91. Carl Robert in *Archäologische Hermeneutik: Anleitung zur Deutung klassischer Bildwerke* (Berlin: Weidmannsche Buchhandlung, 1919) acknowledged that any systematic questions would have to be left for those with "philosophical heads" to decipher ("Vorwort"). By this point, however, a different kind of answer was being developed in French-speaking Europe. See W. Deonna, *L'Archéologie. Son domaine, son but* (Paris: Flammarion, 1922): pt. 1, "Origine et Constitutions de l'Archéologie. Son Champ d'étude."

92. Ludwig Preller, "Ueber die wissenschaftliche Behandlung der Archäologie [1845]," in *Ausgewählte Aufsätze aus dem Gebiete der classischen Alterthumswissenschaft*, ed. Reinhold Köhler (Berlin: Weidmannsche Buchhandlung, 1864), 385–90.

93. Preller, "Ueber die wissenschaftliche Behandlung der Archäologie," 414, 392, 396, 414.

94. On the clash between them, see Ernst Vogt, "Der Methodenstreit zwischen Hermann und Böckh und seine Bedeutung für die Geschichte der Philologie," in *Philologie und Hermeneutik im 19. Jahrhundert*, 103–21; Brita Rupp-Eisenreich, "La Leçon des mots et des choses: philologie, linguistique et ethnologie (de August Boeckh à

Heymann Steinthal)," in *Philologiques I: Contribution à l'histoire des disciplines littéraires en France et en Allemagne au XIXe siècle*, ed. Michel Espagne and Michel Werner (Paris: Éditions de la Maison des Sciences de l'Homme, 1990), 367. Constanze Güthenke, "'Enthusiasm Dwells Only in Specialization." Classical Philology and Disciplinarity in Nineteenth-Century Germany," *World Philology*, ed. Sheldon Pollack, Benjamin Elman, Ku-ming Kevin Chang (Cambridge, MA: Harvard University Press, 2015), 281–83; Wilfried Nippel, "Philologenstreit und Schulpolitik: Zur Kontroverse zwischen Gottfried Hermann und August Boeckh," in *Geschichtsdiskurs* vol. 3, 244–53.

95. Axel Horstmann, *Antike Theoria und moderne Wissenschaft*, 109–10. This differs from Lehmann's interpretation, which rather clumsily tries to paint Hermann as rejecting the relationship between philology and history. Cornelia Lehmann, *Die Auseinandersetzung zwischen Wort- und Sachphilologie in der deutschen klassischen Altertumswissenschaft des 19. Jahrhunderts*, PhD dissertation, Humboldt University, Berlin, 1964, 51–53.

96. Axel Horstmann, "'Erkenntnis des Erkannten': Philologie und Philosophie bei August Boeckh (1785–1867)," *Zeitschrift für Germanistik* 20 (2010): 68; Josine H. Blok, "'Romantische Poesie, Naturphilosophie, Construktion der Geschichte': K. O. Müller's Understanding of History and Myth," in *Zwischen Rationalismus und Romantik: Karl Otfried Müller und die antike Kultur*, ed. William M. Calder III and Renate Schleiser (Hildesheim, Germany: Weidmann, 1998), 67–69; both seem preceded by Vogt, "Der Methodenstreit zwischen Hermann und Böckh," 116–17.

97. Vogt, "Der Methodenstreit zwischen Hermann und Böckh," 107.

98. On Nietzsche (and Ritschl's) relationship to Hermann and the Hermann-Boeckh debate, see Christian Benne, *Nietzsche und die historisch-kritische Philologie* (Berlin and New York: Walter de Gruyter, 2005), 26, 52, 56. In his lecture course on Latin grammar from the winter semester 1869–70, Nietzsche wrote: "Die tiefsten philosoph. Erkenntnisse liegen schon vorbereitet in der Sprache. Kant sagt: 'ein grosser Theil, viell der grösste Theil von dem Geschäfte der Vernunft besteht in Zergliederungen der Begriffe, die er schon in sich vorfindet (72).'"

99. Salomon Reinach, *Manuel de philologie classique*, 2nd ed. (Paris: Hachette, 1883–1884), vol. 2, 267.

100. For the insistence that such a view, otherwise associated with Herder and Hamann, could only be linked to the late Kant, see Michael N. Forster, "Kant's Philosophy of Language," *Tijdschrift voor Filosofie* 74 (2012): 485–511. I am grateful to Robert N. Pippin for directing me to this article and to Michael N. Forster for personal communication. See more generally, Frederick Beiser, *The Fate of Reason: German Philosophy from Kant to Fichte* (Cambridge, MA: Harvard University Press, 1987).

101. Conrad Bursian, *Geschichte der klassichen Philologie in Deutschland* (Munich and Leipzig: R. Oldenbourg, 1883), book 4, chs. 3 and 5.

102. The classic, if very old, treatment is K. Hillebrand, *Étude sur Otfried Müller et sur l'École historique de la philologie allemande* (Paris: Auguste Durand, 1866); see also Bravo, *Philologie, histoire, philosophie de l'histoire*, 105–27, and Calder and Schleiser, eds., *Zwischen Rationalismus und Romantik*.

103. Stephanie-Gerrit Bruer, "Jacob Burckhardt: Systematische Kunstbetrachtung ein Jahrhundert nach Winckelmann," in *Jacob Burckhardt und die Antike*, ed. Peter Betthausen and Max Kunze (Mainz, Germany: Verlag Phillip von Zabern, 1998), 106.

104. Fittschen, "Karl Otfried Müller und die Archäologie," *Zwischen Rationalismus und Romantik*, 197.

105. K. O. Müller, *Ancient Art and its Remains: Or a Manual of the Archaeology of Art*, ed. F. G. Welcher, trans. John Leitch (London: A. Fullarton, 1850), vi. Müller's disproportionate reliance on coins and inscriptions reflected the existing state of material evidence of antiquity. Fittschen, "Karl Otfried Müller und die Archäologie," 188.

106. Müller, *Handbuch der Archäologie der Kunst*, 2nd ed. (Göttingen, 1835), 4.

107. Müller, *Handbuch der Archaeologie der Kunst*, ed. Fr. G. Welcker, 3rd ed., 2nd printing (Stuttgart: Albert Heitz, 1878), 12. On the specific nature of Goethe's historical work in that book, see Peter N. Miller, "Goethe and the End of Antiquarianism," in *For the Sake of Learning. Essays in Honor of Anthony Grafton*, ed. Ann Blair and Anja-Silvia Goeing, 2 vols. (Leiden: E. J. Brill, 2016), vol. 2, 904–5.

108. Müller, *Handbuch*, 18–24.

109. Müller, *Ancient Art and its Remains*, 18. The translation is of the formulation in the second edition (22); it does not appear in the first edition.

110. Müller, *Handbuch*, 22.

111. Eduard Gerhard, *Grundriss der Archäologie: Für Vorlesungen nach Müllers Handbuch* (Berlin, 1853), 23.

112. Gerhard, *Grundriss*, 23, see also 37–38n18.

113. Gerhard, *Grundriss*, 3–4. For his relationship to Boeckh, see Lehmann, *Die Auseinandersetzung zwischen Wort- und Sachphilologie*, 19.

114. Eduard Gerhard and Karl Otfried Müller, "Ueber das Verhältniss der Archäologie zur Philologie und zur Kunst," Supplement, *Grundriss*, 39–41.

115. Karl Bernhard Stark, review of Müller, *Handbuch der Archäologie der Kunst*, in *Zeitschrift für die Alterthumswissenschaft* 10 (1852): 43–45.

116. Stark, review of Müller, *Handbuch der Archäologie der Kunst*, 47.

117. Momigliano, "Ancient History and the Antiquarian," *Journal of the Warburg and Courtauld Institutes* 13 (1950): 285–315; Schnapp, *Discovery of the Past*.

118. Stark, *Handbuch der Archäologie der Kunst*, (Stuttgart: A. Heitz, 1880), 1.

119. Boeckh, *Encyklopädie*, iii. The idea was first mooted at the 1867 gathering of German philologists.

120. Stark, *Handbuch*, 4–6.

121. Stark, *Handbuch*, 58. For Stark's history of antiquarianism, see Miller, "Writing Antiquarianisms: Prolegomenon to a History," *Antiquarianism and Intellectual Life in Europe and China, 1500–1800*, esp. 28–39.

122. For an example of Dilthey's attack on Ranke and contempt for Nietzsche, see Dilthey, *The Formation of the Historical World in the Human Sciences. Selected Works. Volume III*, ed. Rudolf A. Makkreel and Frithjof Rodi (Princeton: Princeton University Press, 2002), 269. There is surprisingly little on Nietzsche and Dilthey and nothing focusing on their historical thinking. See, for example, Rudolf A. Makkreel, *Dilthey: Philosopher of the Human Studies* (Princeton: Princeton University Press, 1992 [1975]), 159; Gerard Visser, "Dilthey und Nietzsche: Unterschiedliche Lesarten des Satzes der Phänomenalität," *Dilthey-Jahrbuch* 10 (1996): 224–45; Werner Stegmaier, *Philosophie der Fluktuanz—Dilthey und Nietzsche* (Göttingen: Vandenhoek & Ruprecht, 1992). See Porter, Nietzsche, 180.

123. Dilthey, "On Understanding and Hermeneutics," in *Hermeneutics and the Study of History: Selected Works: Volume IV*, ed. Rudolf A. Makkreel and Frithjof Rodi (Princeton: Princeton University Press, 1996), 233.

124. Dilthey, "The Rise of Hermeneutics," in *Hermeneutics and the Study of History*, ed. Makkreel and Rodi, 237.

125. Dilthey, *The Formation of the Historical World in the Human Sciences*, 168–69.

126. Dilthey, "Rise of Hermeneutics," 237.

127. Dilthey, *Formation of the Historical World in the Human Sciences*, 118.

128. Dilthey, "The Rise of Hermeneutics," *Hermeneutics and the Study of History*, 237. Momigliano, by calling attention to Usener's influence on Dilthey, helps explain this: Usener followed Hermann and rejected Boeckh's vision of philology as a guide to everything—and thus Dilthey could remain insensitive to the possibilities of material evidence. Momigliano, "Hermann Usener," *History and Theory* 21 (1982), Beiheft 21: "New Paths of Classicism in the Nineteenth Century," 47).

129. Hubert Cancik and Hildegard Cancik-Lindemaier, *Philolog und Kultfigur: Friedrich Nietzsche und seine Antike in Deutschland* (Stuttgart and Weimar: J. B. Metzlar, 1999), ch. 1.

Chapter Six. Material Culture in the Amateur Historical Associations of Early Nineteenth-Century Germany

1. For an older statement of the question, see Hartmut Boockmann and Hermann Wellenreuther, eds., *Geschichtswissenschaft in Göttingen: eine Vorlesungsreihe* (Göttingen: Vandenhoeck & Ruprecht, 1987); for a newer one, see Hans Erich Bödeker, Philippe Büttgen, and Michel Espagne, eds., *Die Wissenschaft vom Menschen in Göttingen um 1800: Wissenschaftliche Praktiken, institutionelle Geographie, europäische Netzwerke* (Göttingen: Vandenhoek & Ruprecht, 2008).

2. Franz Eisel, "Geschichts- und Altertumsvereine als Keimzellen und Wegbereiter der Heimatmuseen," *Neue Museumskunde* 27 (1984): 173–82. This early nineteenth-century story does not figure in Felix Gilbert's otherwise sensitive treatment of "Burckhardt and the Cultural History of His Time," *History: Politics or Culture?* (Princeton: Princeton University Press, 1986), ch. 5; see also Susan Crane, *Collecting and Historical Consciousness in Early Nineteenth-Century Germany* (Ithaca, NY: Cornell University Press, 2000).

3. Stephen Bann, *The Clothing of Clio: A Study of the Representation of History in Nineteenth-Century Britain and France* (Cambridge, U.K.: Cambridge University Press, 1984); Mark Phillips, *Society and Sentiment in Eighteenth-Century Britain* (Princeton: Princeton University Press, 2000); François Lissarrague and Alain Schnapp, "Tradition und Erneuerungin der Klassischen Archäologie in Frankreich," in *Klassische Archäologie: Eine Einführung*, ed. A. Borbein, T. Hölscher, and P. Zanker (Berlin: Reimer, 2000), 368.

4. Bonnie Efros, *Uncovering the Germanic Past: Merovingian Archaeology in France, 1830–1914* (Oxford, U.K.: Oxford University Press, 2012), ch. 3.

5. See Jean-Pierre Chaline, *Sociabilité et érudition: Les Sociétés savantes en France* (Paris: Éditions du Comité des travaux historiques et scientifiques, 1995); Charles-Olivier Carbonell, *Histoire et historiens: Une mutation idéologique des historiens français 1865–1885* (Toulouse: Privat, 1976), esp. 71–90, 117–26, 134–43.

6. Efros, *Uncovering the Germanic Past*, 38, 51, 60; Philippa Levine, *The Amateur and the Professional: Antiquarians, Historians, and Archaeologists in Victorian England, 1838–1886* (Cambridge, U.K.: Cambridge University Press, 1986), ch. 3.

7. Y. S. S. Chung, "John Britton (1771–1857): A Source for the Exploration of the Foundations of County Archaeological Society Museums," *Journal of the History of Collections* 15 (2003): 113–25.

8. Stark, *Handbuch der Archäologie der Kunst*, 266–67; 294–314.

9. Tim Murray, "Colonial and Postcolonial Contexts of Antiquarian Practice," in *World Antiquarianism*, ed. Schnapp et al. (Los Angeles: Getty Publications, 2013), 27.

10. Friedrich Rühs, *Entwurf einer Propädeutik des historischen Studiums (Berlin 1811)*, edited and introduction by Hans Schleier and Dirk Fleischer (Waltrop, Germany: Hartmut Spenner, 1997), xxiii; for Boeckh's numbers, see August Boeckh, *On Interpretation and Criticism*, ed. and trans. John Paul Pritchard (Norman: University of Oklahoma Press, 1968), ix.

11. See Georg Winter, "Zur Vorgeschichte der Monumenta Germaniae Historica," *Neues Archiv der Gesellschaft für ältere deutsche Geschichtskunde* 47 (1928): 1–30.

12. Hans Schleier and Dirk Fleischer, introduction, "Über die methodische Kompetenz eines Historikers. Friedrich Rühs' Konzept für historische Forschung und Darstellung," in Rühs, *Entwurf*, xlii (note 85).

13. Hans Schleier suggests that some footnotes in Rühs's proposals show that he had in mind foreign antiquarian societies and publications, as in England, France, or Sweden. Schleier and Fleischer, "Introduction," Rühs, *Entwurf*, xlii (note 85).

14. Rühs, *Entwurf*, 22.

15. Rühs, *Entwurf*, 184.

16. Rühs, *Entwurf*, 184.

17. Rühs, *Entwurf*, 185.

18. Rühs, *Entwurf*, 213–14.

19. Rühs, *Entwurf*, 215.

20. He thought Meiners's *Beschreibung alter Denkmäler, deren Errichtung unbekannt oder ungewiss* (Nuremberg, 1786) and J. J. Oberlin's *Orbis antiqui monumentis suis illustrati primae lineae* (Strasbourg, 1790) were a start but were mostly bibliographical in orientation. Rühs, *Entwurf*, 215.

21. Rühs, *Entwurf*, 248.

22. ". . . dagegen theilen die Franzosen mit den Deutschen den Ruhm, vortreffliche Kritiker hervorgebracht zu haben, die, wenn sie auch oft sich bis zu Micrologien verirren, doch gründliche Aufschlüsse geben, wie *Ducange, Duchesne, Mabillon*, u.s.w." Rühs, *Entwurf*, 272.

23. On the history of the MGH, see Winter, "Zur Vorgeschichte der Monumenta Germaniae Historica," 6–9; Robert Hering, "Freiherr vom Stein, Goethe und die Anfänge der MGH," *Jahrbuch des freien deutschen Hochstifts* (1907): 278–323.

24. On the associations movement, see Jürgen Voss, "Akademien, gelehrte Gesellschaften und wissenschaftliche Vereine in Deutschland, 1750–1850," in *Sociabilité et Société*, ed. Etienne Francois (Paris, 1986), 149–67. Still rich with information and thought is K. A. Klüpfel, "Die historischen Vereine und Zeitschriften Deutschlands," *Zeitschrift für Geschichtswissenschaft* 1 (1844): 518–59.

25. Schleier, *Geschichte der deutschen Kulturgeschichtsschreibung*, 300–302. A history of association foundations would include, for example, 1819: Stein's *Monumenta*, Naumburg; 1824: Königlich-sächsischer Verein zur Erforschung und Erhaltung vaterländischer Geschichts- und Kunstdenkmale; 1826: Halle, Thüringisch-sächsischer Verein für Erforschung des vaterländischen Alterthums und seiner Denkmale; 1833: Gesellschaft

für Schleswig-Holsteinische Geschichte; 1835: Königlich Hannöverscher Historischer Verein für Niedersachsen; 1835: Grossherzoglich Mecklenburg-Schwerinscher Geschichts- und Altertums-Verein; 1838: Sachsen-Altenburgische Geschichts- und Altertumsforschende Gesellschaft des Oberlandes; 1843: Königlich Württembergischer Altertumsverein; 1846: Königlich Preussischer Verein für Geschichte Schlesiens; 1850: Steiermark; 1852: Sonderhausen und Thüringen, Rottenburg am Neckar; 1853: Wien; 1854: Niederrhein. See also Ulrike Sommer, "Choosing Ancestors: The Mechanisms of Ethnic Ascription in the Age of Patriotic Antiquarianism (1815–1850)," in *Archives Ancestors Practices. Archaeology in the Light of its History*, ed. Nathan Schlanger and Jarl Nordbladh (Oxford, U.K.: Berghahn, 2008), 236–38.

26.   Philipp A. F. Walther, *Systematisches Repertorium über die Schriften sämmtlicher historischer Gesellschaften Deutschlands* (Darmstadt, 1845).

27.   Walther, *Systematisches Repertorium*, xii.

28.   Friedrich David Gräter, "Uebersicht der Alterthümer der ehmaligen Reichsstadt Hall: Als eine Probe wie ungefähr die Alterthümer der teutschen Städte aufzunehmen wären," *Idunna und Hermode* 2, no. 14 (1813): 65–72.

29.   Anonymous, "Plan und Ankündigung dieser Zeitschrift," *Curiositäten der physisch-literarisch-artistisch-historischen Vor- und Mitwelt* 1 (1811): 5–6.

30.   Wigand's plan is discussed in Wilhelm Steffens, "Paul Wigand und die Anfänge planmäßiger landesgeschichtlicher Forschung in Westfalen," *Westfälische Zeitschrift* 94 (1938): 143–237, reprinted in Harald Seiler, *Die Anfänge der Kunstpflege in Westfalen (Beitrag zur Wesensforschung des Biedermeier)* (Münster: Univ. Buchhandlung Coppenrath, 1937).

31.   Wigand, in Seiler, *Die Anfänge*, quoted in Bernward Deneke, "Konzeption einer Altertumskunde des deutschsprachigen Gebietes in der ersten Hälfte des 19. Jahrhunderts," in *Volkskunde im Museum*, ed. Wolfgang Brückner und Bernward Deneke (Würzburg: Bayerische Blätter für Volkskunde, 1976), 86n26.

32.   Eduard Mühle, *Für Volk und deutschen Osten: Der Historiker Hermann Aubin und die deutsche Ostforschung* (Düsseldorf: Droste Verlag, 2005).

33.   Johann Gustav G. Büsching, *Abriß der Deutschen Alterthumskunde: Zur Grundlage von Vorlesungen bestimmt* (Weimar, 1824), 5–6. On Busching, see Marek Halub, *Johann Gustav Gottlieb Bushing* (Wrocław, Poland, 1997). Cf. C. J. Thomsen, from 1822: "No less important is that the antiquarian should observe which objects are found together—we have been neglectful in this respect. I hope the careful inventory we keep on everything that comes into our museum will be of some help." Quoted in Kristian Kristiansen, "A Short History of Danish Archaeology," in *Archaeological Formation Processes: The Representativity of Archaeological Remains from Danish Prehistory*, ed. Kristian Kristiansen (Copenhagen: National Museum Copenhagen, 1985), 21.

34.   Büsching, *Abriß der Deutschen Alterthumskunde*, esp. 21–36.

35.   Johann Büsching, "Blick auf die Forschungen über deutsche Vorzeit" in *Morgenblatt für gebildete Stände* 19 (May 1825). Quoted in Deneke, *Konzeption*, 80n2.

36.   Ernst Hermann Jospeh Münch, *Grundriß einer teutschen Alterthumskunde zum Gebrauche für Vorlesungen und zum Selbststudium* (Freiburg im Breisgau: Friedrich Wagner, 1827), 1.

37.   Münch, *Grundriß*, 2.

38.   Münch, *Grundriß*, 24–28, 34–35.

39. *Deutsche Alterthümer oder Archiv für alte und mittlere Geschichte, Geographie und Alterthümer in Sonderheit der germanischen Völkerstämme* 2 (Halle, 1827), 94.

40. *Deutsche Alterthümer*, 94.

41. "Because of the tremendous deficiencies of the source texts concerning the specific description of the upper north, one cannot hope to gain a clear picture of our early people from ancient sources alone.—The relics of our ancient ancestors must speak where the tongues of yore fall silent, and the Thuringian-Saxon Association, just like all similar antiquarian associations in Germany and Scandinavia, have made it their great aim to one day provide answers to those questions through the careful study and collection of the vestiges of ancient times. This is why the earlier task shifted from the specific to the general, and we would be very pleased if we could soon report on the happy resolution of these questions." *Deutsche Alterthümer*, 95.

42. "The following main objectives should be formulated in this survey of mountain peoples: 1. Identify peoples in their largest and smallest divisions and segmentations, grouped by historians, by language classes, dialects, civic bodies, native customs and how often outsiders interact with the people. 2. Define current living areas using natural landmarks and political boundaries and describe the current state of each grouping. 3. Describe each people's historical development from its origin or immigration, settlement, commingling, expansion into a larger area, or concentration in a smaller territory, including references to the ancestors of the present-day people in history and monuments. This will be especially important for the diffusion of Slavic tribes in the West. 4. The language as people speak it, dialects, poetry, music, language remnants from older times, and the appellative meanings of the names of places, rivers, mountains, forests, etc. and the entire range of geographically extant appellatives from this language family. When comparing languages, do not merely consider words that are the same; pay special attention to the grammatical structure of the languages in order to draw conclusions. 5. Works of art, architecture, gravesites, bulwarks of defense and their historical monuments, and the context in which they were created. 6. Physical appearance, structure, morals, number of individuals, lifestyle, special knowledge and skills, characteristics with regard to agriculture, animal husbandry, warfare, and civic institutions. 7. Characteristics of and relations of each specific sub-group to the whole within the specifications given." *Deutsche Alterthümer*, 99–100.

43. On Preusker, see Schleier, *Geschichte der deutschen Geschichtsschreibung*, 297–99; Regina Smolnik, ed., *Karl Benjamin Preusker: Archäologe—Reformer—Netzwerker* (Beucha, Germany: Markkleeberg, 2011). The title page of his *Ober-Lausitzische Alterthümer* (Görlitz, Germany: Johann Gottlieb Dressler, 1828) identifes him as Royal Saxon "Rentamtmann" in Grossenhayn, Lieutenant in the Army, member of the Ober-Lausitzische Society of Sciences in Görlitz, of the Royal Saxon Association for the Research and Preservation of Patriotic Antiquities in Dresden, the German, Nature Researching, and Economic Socities of Leipzig, and the Thurinigian-Saxon Association for Antiquities at Halle.

44. Karl Benjamin Preusker, *Beschreibung einiger bei Radeberg im Königreiche Sachsen aufgefundenen Urnen mit unbekannten Charakteren* (Halle, 1828), 1.

45. See *Uebersicht der mit der Königlichen Antiken-Sammlung in Dresden vereinigten Preusker'schen Sammlung vaterländischer Alterthümer* (Leipzig: Hermann Fritzsche / Grossenhain: Carl Bornemann, 1856).

46. Karl Benjamin Preusker, *Blicke in die vaterländische Vorzeit: Sitten, Sagen, Bau-werke und Geräthe* . . . (Leipzig, n.d. [1841]), 3–4, 6.

47. Karl Benjamin Preusker, *Ueber Mittel und Zweck der vaterländischen Alterthums-forschung. Eine Andeutung: Der Oberlausitzischen Gesellschaft der Wissenschaften zu Gör-litz bei deren funfzigjährigen Stiftungsfeier am 29. Julius 1829* (Leipzig: Nauck, 1829), 3. Preusker uses "antiquarian" and "Altertumskunde" interchangeably, viz. "Die Ver-breitung historischer und antiquarischer Kenntnisse mittelst eingeleiteter Lesever-eine unter den Mitgliedern." Preusker, *Ueber Mittel und Zweck*, 51; see also uses of "historisch-antiquarisch," 16.

48. "Often, the term 'study of antiquities' (*Altertumswissenschaft, Altertumskunde*) is used to mean all knowledge of ancient times—of all peoples or individuals that have changed their mores since then to create a new order of things at least one or two ages ago. Sometimes it is intended to mean the knowledge about these peoples with respect to their political, civic, and moral life and being, supported by the spiritual and material remains of that people. Sometimes it means knowledge about the monuments that remain available to us, particularly with respect to the visual arts, without even consider-ing numerous other assumptions in a general or specific sense; elucidating the various definitions of this science is outside the scope of this work; we will merely touch upon the means and purposes of same here." Preusker, *Ueber Mittel und Zweck*, 4.

49. Preusker, *Ueber Mittel und Zweck*, 4.

50. Preusker, *Ueber Mittel und Zweck*, 4. He restates this as a twofold distinction between antiquities in the narrow sense (remains) and the larger one (cultural prac-tices seen from a material point of view) in Preusker, *Ober-Lausitzische Alterthümer*, 8.

51. "Therefore, it is understandable that the terms are often used interchange-ably. Many things are labeled as historical description that can really only properly apply to the study of antiquities, and many antiquarian treatises include the history of individual objects or periods of time. However, this cannot reduce the value of these two disciplines, as the labels and external forms are not what matter—only the presented results can be considered the main subject of scientific study. Nonetheless, to avoid misunderstandings, this difference should be taken into consideration as often as possible in the future." Preusker, *Ueber Mittel und Zweck*, 5n1.

52. Preusker, *Ueber Mittel und Zweck*, 5.

53. Preusker, *Ueber Mittel und Zweck*, 5–6.

54. Preusker, *Ueber Mittel und Zweck*, 6.

55. Preusker, *Ueber Mittel und Zweck*, 23–24.

56. Preusker, *Ueber Mittel und Zweck*, 24.

57. Preusker, *Ueber Mittel und Zweck*, 22.

58. Preusker, *Ueber Mittel und Zweck*, 26.

59. Preusker, *Ueber Mittel und Zweck*, 37.

60. Preusker, *Ueber Mittel und Zweck*, 38.

61. Karl Preusker, "Ueber die deutsche Alterthumsforschung der neuesten Zeit," *Neue Zeitschrift für die Geschichte der germanischen Völker* 1, no. 3 (1832): 93.

62. Preusker, *Blicke in die vaterländische Vorzeit, Sitten, Sagen, Bauwerke und Geräthe, zur Erläuterung des öffentlichen aund häuslichen Volkslebens im heidnischen Alterthume und im christlichen Mittelalter* (Leipzig, 1841), 24.

63. Glyn Daniel, *A Hundred and Fifty Years of Archaeology* (Cambridge, MA: Har-vard University Press, 1975 [1950]), 45.

64. [Thomsen], *Leitfaden zur Nordischen Altertumskunde* (Copenhagen, 1837), 3.

65. [Thomsen], *Leitfaden zur Nordischen Altertumskunde*, 25.

66. [Thomsen], *Leitfaden zur Nordischen Altertumskunde*, 26.

67. [Thomsen], *Leitfaden zur Nordischen Altertumskunde*, 80, 84.

68. Quoted in Daniel, *A Hundred and Fifty Years of Archaeology*, 52.

69. Gran-Aymerich, *Naissance de l'archéologie moderne*, 153.

70. Chr. v. Rommel, "Ueber Quellen und Hülfsmittel der hessischen Geschichte" in *Zeitschrift des Vereins für hessische Geschichte und Landeskunde* 1 (1837), 77.

71. Rommel, "Ueber Quellen und Hülfsmittel der hessischen Geschichte," 77.

72. Rommel, "Ueber Quellen und Hülfsmittel der hessischen Geschichte," 78.

73. Rommel, "Ueber Quellen und Hülfsmittel der hessischen Geschichte," 79.

74. Rommel, "Ueber Quellen und Hülfsmittel der hessischen Geschichte," 104.

75. Karl Wilhelmi, *Ueber die Entstehung, den Zweck und die Einrichtung der gegenwärtigen Geschichts- und Alterthumsvereine Deutscher Zunge. Eine Rede, bei der ersten General-Versammlung des Alterthums Vereins für das Grossherzogthum Baden in Baden gehalten den 5. November 1844* (Heidelberg: Mohr Verlag, 1844), 8.

76. Wilhelmi, *Ueber die Entstehung*, 9.

77. Wilhelmi, *Ueber die Entstehung*, 15–16.

78. Wilhelmi, *Ueber die Entstehung*, 17–18.

79. Wilhelmi, *Ueber die Entstehung*, 19.

80. Matti Bunzl, "Franz Boas and the Humboldtian Tradition," in *Volksgeist as Method and Ethic: Essays on Boasian Ethnography and the German Anthropological Tradition*, ed. George W. Stocking (Madison: University of Wisconsin Press, 1986), 17–78.

81. J. F. Knapp, "Ueber das Wirken der historischen und antiquarischen Vereine in Bezug auf die Wissenschaft," *Archiv für hessische Geschichte und Alterthumskunde* 5 (1846): 3.

82. Knapp, "Ueber das Wirken der historischen und antiquarischen Vereine," 4.

83. "Scherben, Ringe und Waffen, aus Gräbern hervorgeholt, mögen allerdings für den Forscher im Fache der politischen Geschichte keinen oder einen nur sehr secundären Werthe haben; wer sich aber mit Erforschung der Gebräuche, der Kunstfertigkeit, der Geschmacksbildung und den Kenntnissen in der Metalurchie der Vorzeit beschäftigt, dürfte wohl auch solchen Gegenständen gern seine volle Aufmerksamkeit widmen." Knapp, "Ueber das Wirken der historischen und antiquarischen Vereine," 4–5.

84. Effros, *Uncovering the Germanic Past: Merovingian Archaeology in France, 1830–1914* (Oxford, U.K.: Oxford University Press, 2012).

85. Knapp, "Ueber das Wirken der historischen und antiquarischen Vereine," 6.

86. Knapp, "Ueber das Wirken der historischen und antiquarischen Vereine," 6.

87. Knapp, "Ueber das Wirken der historischen und antiquarischen Vereine," 6–7.

88. "Die Aufsuchung germanischer und celtischer Alterthümer, die Ermittelung der Wohnsitze der religiösen Culten der germanischen Völkerstämme, die Verfolgung römischer Straßen, Befestigungswerke und Niederlassungen, die Erforschung der alten Gau-, Diöcesan-, Herrschafts- und Gerichtsgränzen, der Rechtsgewohnheiten, der Sagen; die Sammlungen von Urkunden über Länder und Gebietstheile, die jetzt getrennt sind, sowie über Geschlechter, die in verscheidenen Gebieten angesessen waren, und viele andere Gegenstände, womit sich die Vereine befassen, greifen in den Wirkungskreis mehrerer derselben über, und können von einzelnen Vereinen

nur in mangelhaften Bruchstücken erörtert werden." Knapp, "Ueber das Wirken der historischen und antiquarischen Vereine," 8.

89. Knapp, "Ueber das Wirken der historischen und antiquarischen Vereine," 10.

90. J. F. Lange, "Entwurf zu einer historisch-artistischen Darstellung der hessischen Kunstdenkmale," *Zeitschrift des Vereins für hessische Geschichte und Landeskunde* 4 (1847): xxviii.

91. Lange, "Entwurf," xxix.

92. Lange, "Entwurf," xxxii–xxxiii.

93. Lange, "Entwurf," xxxv.

Chapter Seven. Gustav Klemm, Cultural History and *Kulturwissenschaft*

1. A note on spelling: We find a variable use of *Kulturgeschichte* and *Culturgeschichte* in the 1830s, 1840s, and 1850s, with *Culturgeschichte* predominating. By the 1880s a clear preference had arisen for *Kulturgeschichte* (and *Kulturwissenschaft*) and this has remained. Thus, wherever I am quoting I preserve the original orthography. But when I use the terms I follow the contemporary convention.

2. Augustin Thierry, *The Historical Essays, published under the title of "Dix ans D'Études Historiques", and Narratives of the Merovingian era; or, scenes of the sixth century with Autobiographical Preface* (Philadelphia: Carey and Hart, 1845), xii.

3. Michael Shanks, *The Archaeological Imagination* (Walnut Creek, CA: Left Coast Press, 2012), 43–94.

4. Jacques-Joseph Champollion-Figeac, "Archéologie," in *Dictionnaire de la conversation et de la lecture*, ed. M. W. Duckett, vol. 2 (Paris: Belin-Mandar, 1833), 483–85.

5. Charles Lenormant, "Archéologie," *Revue archéologique* 1 (1844): 3.

6. See Jeannine Guichardet, *Balzac, "archéologue" de Paris* (Paris: Sedes, 1986), 15.

7. Walter Benjamin, "Eduard Fuchs: Collector and Historian," *Selected Writings: 1935–1938*, ed. Howard Eiland and Michael W. Jennings (Cambridge, MA: Harvard University Press, 2002), 260–302.

8. Eckhardt Fuchs, "Contemporary Alternatives to German Historicism in the Nineteenth Century," in *Oxford History of Historical Writing: Volume 4: 1800–1945*, ed. Stuart Macintyre, Juan Maiguashca, and Attila Pok (Oxford, U.K.: Oxford University Press, 2011), 57–77.

9. Jörn Garber, "Von der Menschheitsgeschichte zur Kulturgeschichte. Zum geschichtstheoretischen Kulturbegriff der deutschen Spätaufklärung," in *Kultur zwischen Bürgertum und Volk*, ed. Jutta Held (Berlin, 1983), 76–97. More narrowly, Volker Hartmann finds *Kulturgeschichte* (or *Culturgeschichte*) in 48 titles published between 1782 and 1815 and another 52 between 1815 and 1865. Hartmann, *Die deutsche Kulturgeschichtsschreibung von ihren Anfängen bis Wilhelm Heinrich Riehl*, PhD dissertation, University of Marburg, 1971.

10. Donald R. Kelley, "The Old Cultural History," *History of the Human Sciences* 9 (1996): 101–26; Hans Schleier, *Geschichte der deutschen Culturgeschichtsschreibung* (Waltrop, Germany: Harmut Spenner, 2002); Michael C. Carhart, *The Science of Culture in Enlightenment Germany* (Cambridge, MA: Harvard University Press, 2007); Hans Erich Bödeker, Philippe Büttgen, and Michel Espagne, eds., *Die Wissenschaft vom Menschen in Göttingen um 1800. Wissenschaftliche Praktiken, institutionelle Geographie, europäische Netzwerke* (Göttingen: Vandenhoek & Ruprecht, 2008).

11. See Gombrich, *In Search of Cultural History*; Felix Gilbert, "Cultural History and Its Problems," *Comité International des Sciences Historiques: Rapports* 1 (1960): 40–58; Peter Burke, *What Is Cultural History?* (Cambridge, U.K., and Malden, MA: Polity Press, 2004) documents, but no longer tries to define, its subject.

12. Istvan Hont, "Natural Jurisprudence, Political Economy, and the Concept of Civilisation: Samuel Pufendorf's Theory of *Cultura*," paper presented at "The Identity of Political Economy: Between Utopia and the Critique of Civilisation," King's College Research Centre, July 1–3, 1984, István Hont Papers, Special Collections, University of St. Andrews, Scotland. I am grateful to Richard Whatmore and Béla Kapossy for alerting me to the existence of this paper and for making it available to me. Hont, *Jealousy of Trade: International Competition and the Nation-State in Historical Perspective* (Cambridge, MA, and London: Harvard University Press, 2005), 46.

13. Wilhelm Wachsmuth, *Entwurf einer Theorie der Geschichte* (Halle, 1820), 80.

14. Hans Schleier, "Wachsmuths *Entwurf einer Theorie der Geschichte* aus dem Jahre 1820," *Jahrbuch für Geschichte* 37 (1988): 103–35.

15. Wilhelm Wachsmuth, *Europäische Sittengeschichte* (Leipzig, 1831), vol. 1, 19.

16. Stefan Hass, *Historische Kulturforschung in Deutschland 1880–1930: Kulturgeschichte zwischen Synthese und Pluralität* (Cologne, Weimar, and Vienna: Böhlau Verlag, 1994), 33.

17. For Marx, see *Marx-Engels Gesamtausgabe*, series 4, vol. 1 (Berlin, 1981) and, more generally, Jans-Peter Jaeck, *Die französische bürgerliche Revolution von 1789 im Frühwerk von Karl Marx (1843–1846): Geschichtsmethodologische Studien* (Berlin, 1979). In his *Londoner Heften* we find many references to two other works by Wachsmuth, the *Europäische Sittengeschichte vom Ursprunge volksthümlicher Gestaltungen bis auf unsere Zeit*, 5 vols. (Leipzig, 1831–1839) and *Allgemeine Kulturgeschichte*, 3 vols. (Leipzig, 1850–1852). Burckhardt read Wachsmuth's *Grundriss der Allgemeinen Geschichte der Volker und Staaten* (Leipzig, 1826) and also C. F. Hermann and Wachsmuth, *Hellenische Altertumskunde*, 2 vols. (n.p., 1846).

18. Wachsmuth, *Allgemeine Culturgeschichte* (Leipzig, 1850–1852), vol. 1, ix–x.

19. Wachsmuth, *Allgemeine Culturgeschichte*, vol. 1, x, footnote 1, xii.

20. Wachsmuth, *Allgemeine Culturgeschichte*, vol. 1, xiv–xv; Wachsmuth's categories are property, aristocracy, clerisy, constitution, national economy, law, and trade, xvii–xviii.

21. Wachsmuth, *Allgemeine Culturgeschichte*, vol. 1, xxi.

22. Compare the tables of contents of volume 1 with that of volume 2 (on the Middle Ages, published in 1851) and volume 3 (on "modern times," published 1852).

23. "Die kulturgeschichtliche Monographienliteratur der letzten fünf Jahre," *Zeitschrift für deutsche Kulturgeschichte* 1 (1856): 564.

24. Heinrich Dilly and James Ryding, "Kulturgeschichtsschreibung vor und nach der bürgerlichen Revolution von 1848," *Asthetik und Kommunikation* 21 (1975): 15–32.

25. Wachsmuth, *Allgemeine Culturgeschichte*, iii.

26. Falke, "Bucherschau," *Zeitschrift für deutsche Kulturgeschichte* 1 (1856): 402.

27. Thomas Nipperdey, "Kulturgeschichte, Sozialgeschichte, historische Anthropologie," *Vierteljahrschrift für Sozial- und Wirtschaftsgeschichte* 55 (1968): 145.

28. Compare J. J. Honegger, *Katechismus der Culturgeschichte* (Leipzig: Verlagsbuchhandlung von J.J. Weber, 1879), 7, 51; and Friedrich Jodl, *Die Culturgeschichtsschreibung, ihre Entwickelung und ihr Problem* (Halle: CEM Pfeffer, 1878), 22–24.

29. "It would be useful to see how far Jacob Burckhardt fits into the movement of German Kulturgeschichte, projected as early as Herder (1784–91) and popularized by the publication of Gustav Klemm's book (1843–52)." Fernand Braudel, *On History* (Chicago: University of Chicago Press, 1980), 186.

30. M. Heydrich, "Gustav Klemm und seine kulturhistorische Sammlung," in *Kultur und Rasse: Otto Reche zum 60. Geburtstag*, ed. Michael Hesch and Günther Spannaus (Munich and Berlin: J. F. Lehamnns Verlag, 1939), 305–17. More recently, see Ernst Germer, "Die Vorgeschichte der Gründung des Museums für Völkerkunde zu Leipzig, 1868–1869," *Jahrbuch des Museums für Völkerkunde zu Leipzig* 26 (1969): 5–40; Dietrich Drost, "Gustav Klemms kulturhistorisches Museum," *Jahrbuch des Museums für Völkerkunde zu Leipzig* 26 (1969): 41–83; Schleier, *Geschicthe der deutschen Geschichtsschreibung*, ch. III.3; I. Rödiger, "Gustav Friedrich Klemm: Allgemeine Cultur-Geschichte der Menschheit," in *Hauptwerke der Ethnologie*, ed. Christian F. Feest and Karl-Heinz Kohl (Stuttgart: Alfred Kröner Verlag, 2001), 188–92; Chris Manias, "The Growth of Race and Culture in Nineteenth-Century Germany: Gustav Klemm and the Universal History of Humanity," *Modern Intellectual History* 9 (2012): 1–31. However, his name appears only once, in a footnote, in a list of names, in Horst Walter Blanke's 809-page *Historiographiegeschichte als Historik* (Stuttgart–Bad Cannstatt: froommann-holzboog, 1991), 448; he does not rate a proper discussion in Han F. Vermeulen, *Before Boas: The Genesis of Ethnography and Ethnology in the German Enlightenment* (Omaha: University of Nebraska Press, 2015).

31. Gustav Klemm, *Allgemeine Culturwissenschaft*, 2 vols. (Leipzig: J. M. Romberg, 1855), vol. 1, 31–32.

32. Klemm, *Allgemeine Culturwissenschaft*, vol. 1, 34.

33. Grayna Orlinska, "Klemm as Archaeologist," *Catalogue of the "Germanic" Antiquities from the Klemm Collection in The British Museum* (London, 2001), 20–29.

34. Klemm, *Allgemeine Culturwissenschaft*, vol. 1, 35.

35. Gustav Klemm, *Die Königlich Sächsische Porzellan-Sammlung* (Dresden: Walther'schen Hofbuchhandlung, 1834).

36. Klemm, *Porzellan-Sammlung*, 3–7.

37. Klemm, *Porzellan-Sammlung*, 31–52.

38. Grayna Orlinska, *Catalogue of the "Germanic" Antiquities from the Klemm Collection in The British Museum* (London, 2001); "Klemm as Archaeologist," 20–29.

39. Klemm listed his titles as: Secretary of the Königlich Sächsischer Verein für Erforschung und Erhaltung Vaterländischer Alterthümer and member of the Deutsche Gesellschaft zu Erforschung vaterländischer Sprache und Alterthümer zu Leipzig, the Gesellschaft für Natur und Heilkunde zu Dresden, the Oberlausitzer Gesellschaft der Wissenschaften zu Görlitz, the Kurländische Gesellschaft für Literatur und Kunst und the Hennebergischer Historischer Verein zu Meinigen.

40. The letters are in the collection of the Sächsische Landesbibliothek.

41. Twenty-five letters are preserved in the Sächsische Landesbibliothek—Staats- und Universitätsbibliothek Dresden, available at http://kalliope-verbund.info/de/query?q=ead.creator.gnd%3D%3D%2210030396X%22, accessed February 26, 2016.

42. For more on him, see René Sternke, *C. A. Böttiger und die archaeologische Diskurs*. Thirteen letters from Klemm to Boöttiger are preserved in Böttiger's papers, Sächsische Landesbibliothek—Staats- und Universitätsbibliothek Dresden; Nachlass

Böttiger, Carl August (1760–1835), available at http://kalliope-verbund.info/de/query?q=ead.creator.gnd%3D%3D%2210030396X%22, accessed February 26, 2016.

43. Winfried Nerdinger, "Der Architekt Gottfried Semper: 'Der notwendige Zusammenhang der Gegenwart mit allen Jahrhunderten der Vergangenheit,'" *Gottfried Semper 1803–1879: Architektur und Wissenschaft* (Zurich: Prestel, 2003), 13, 28. See also Harry Francis Mallgrave, *Gottfried Semper: Architect of the Nineteenth Century* (New Haven and London: Yale University Press, 1996), 161, 163; Sonja Hildebrand, "'Nach einem Systeme zu ordnen, welches die inneren Verbindsfäden dieser bunten Welt am besten zusammenhält': Kulturgeschichtliche Modelle bei Gottfried Semper und Gustav Klemm," in *Gottfried Semper, Dresden und Europa: Die moderne Renaissance der Künste*, ed. Henrik Karge (Munich and Berlin: Deutscher Kunstverlag, 2006), 237–50; and Mari Hvattum, *Gottfried Semper and the Problem of Historicism* (Cambridge, U.K.: Cambridge University Press, 2004), 42–46, 66–67.

44. Hildebrand, "'Nach einem Systeme zu ordnen,'" 238–39.

45. Gustav Klemm, *Handbuch der Germanischen Alterthumskunde* (Dresden: Walther'schen Hofbuchhandlung, 1836), v.

46. These materials eventually found their way to the British Museum. See Orlinska, *Catalogue of the 'Germanic' Antiquities from the Klemm Collection*, 19–29.

47. Ole Worm, *Museum Wormianum* (Leiden, 1655); Jakob Benediktsson, ed., *Ole Worm's Correspondence with Icelanders* (Copenhagen: Munksgaard, 1948).

48. See Allison Meier, "Ole Worm Returns: An Iconic 17th Century Curiosity Cabinet is Obsessively Recreated," available at www.atlasobscura.com/articles/ole-worm-cabinet, accessed December 3, 2015.

49. Gustav Klemm, *Zur Geschichte der Sammlungen für Wissenschaft und Kunst in Deutschland* (Zerbst, Germany: G. A. Kummer, 1838), 165.

50. Klemm, *Zur Geschichte der Sammlungen*, 167–82, 184–88.

51. Klemm, *Zur Geschichte der Sammlungen*, 196–201, 214–19.

52. Klemm, *Zur Geschichte der Sammlungen*, 228, 239–40, 243, 268–73.

53. Klemm, *Zur Geschichte der Sammlungen*, 300.

54. Klemm, *Zur Geschichte der Sammlungen*, 304, 312–25.

55. Klemm, *Allgemeine Culturwissenschaft: Die materiellen Grundlagen menschlicher Cultur*, 2 vols. (Leipzig, 1854–1855), vol. 1, 35.

56. Klemm described his collecting as a salvage project saving indigenous materials from corruption and eventually destruction by Europeans. Klemm, *Allgemeine Cultur-Geschichte der Menschheit* (Leipzig: B. G. Teubner, 1843–1854), vol. 1, 27.

57. The figures are given in Heydrich, "Gustav Klemm und seine kulturhistorische Sammlung," 312; Klemm, *Allgemeine Culturwissenschaft*, 35.

58. "Nicht geringen Werth haben jene bildlosen, oft formlosen Sachen, Geräthe, Gefäße, Kleider, Waffen, Modelle von Fahrzeugen, Gebäuden u.s.w., welche aus fernen Zeiten oder Gegenden zu uns gelangen. . . . Wie in der Mineralogie, Zoologie, Botanik, Archäologie, Numismatik und Paläographie ist eigene Anschauung der Gegenstände auch in der Geschichte das beßte Hülfsmittel zur rechten Erkenntniß." Klemm, *Allgemeine Cultur-Geschichte*, vol. 1, 27

59. Klemm, *Allgemeine Cultur-Geschichte*, vol. 1, 21.

60. Klemm, *Allgemeine Cultur-Geschichte*, vol. 1, 26–27.

61. Klemm, *Allgemine Cultur-Geschichte*, vol. 2, table of contents.

62. Fabri, *Encyclopädie*, 353.

63. Klemm, *Allgemine Cultur-Geschichte*, vol. 5, table of contents.

64. Klemm, *Allgemeine Cultur-Geschichte*, vol. 9, table of contents.

65. Klemm, *Allgemeine Cultur-Geschichte*, vol. 1, 352–62.

66. Klemm, *Allgemeine Cultur-Geschichte* vol. 1, 355.

67. Jodl, *Die Culturgeschichtsschreibung*, 23.

68. Klemm, *Allgemeine Cultur-Geschichte*, vol. 1, 356.

69. Klemm, *Allgemeine Cultur-Geschichte*, vol. 1, 359.

70. Klemm, *Allgemeine Cultur-Geschichte*, vol. 1, 360.

71. Klemm, *Allgemeine Cultur-Geschichte*, vol. 1, 361.

72. Klemm, *Allgemeine Cultur-Geschichte*, vol. 1, 362.

73. Hildebrand, " 'Nach einem Systeme zu ordnen,' " 245–50.

74. Gottfried Semper, *The Ideal Museum: Practical Art in Metals and Hard Materials* (Vienna: Schlebrügge, 2007), 55.

75. Gustav Klemm, "Grundideen zu einer allgemeinen Cultur-Wissenschaft," *Sitzungsberichte der Kaiserlichen Akademie zu Wien. Historisch-philologische Klasse* 7 (1851): 175.

76. "Die Culturwissenchaft beginnt mit den materiellen Grundlagen des menschlichen Lebens, mit der Darstellung der körperlichen Bedürfnisse, den Mitteln zu deren Befriedigung und den daraus entspringenden Erzeugnissen. Sie stellt sodann die menschlichen Verhältnisse in der Familie und in ihrer Erweiterung zum Staate dar. Der letzte Abschnitt derselben aber hat die Betrachtung der Ergebnisse menschlicher Erforschung und Erfahrung, so wie die geistigen Schöpfungen des Menschen in der Wissenschaft und Kunst zu entwickeln." Klemm, "Grundideen zu einer allgemeinen Cultur-Wissenschaft," 184.

77. Klemm, *Allgemeine Culturwissenshaft*, vol. 2, 2.

78. Klemm, *Allgemeine Culturwissenschaft*, vol. 2, 18–25.

79. One has to marvel at Klemm's intuition here: The scholarly literature on encyclopedism is of very recent vintage and has oriented itself on precisely these two axes See for instance work of Ann Blair and Ann Moss on finding aids and commonplace books, on the one hand, and Helmut Zedelmaier's work on taxonomy, on the other.

80. Klemm, *Allgemeine Culturwissenschaft*, vol. 2, 28.

81. Klemm, *Allgemeine Culturwissenschaft*, vol. 2, 29.

82. Klemm, *Allgemeine Culturwissenschaft*, vol. 2, 37.

83. Klemm, *Allgemeine Cultur-Geschichte*, vol. 10, lii.

84. "Die Culturwissenschaft hat den Zweck nachzuweisen, wie die verschiedenen leiblichen und geistigen Triebe, Anlagen und Kräfte mit Hilfe der von der Vorsehung dargebotenen Naturerzeugnisse und Naturerscheinungen an dem einzelnen wie in den zur Familie und zum Stamm, Volk und Staat vereinigten Menschen eine neue Folge von Erzeugnissen und Erscheinungen allgemach hervorbringen und die Gesetze zu ermitteln, nach denen dieß in den verschiedenen Theilen der Erdoberfläche geschieht. Die Cultur ist das Resultat der Wechselwirkung zwischen Menschen und Natur und fortan des Verkehrs der Menschen unter einander." Klemm, *Allgemeine Culturwissenschaft*, vol. 2, 36–37.

85. ". . . mit einem Wort: die Culturwissenschaft hat die Aufgabe, die gesammte Menschenthätigkeit und deren Denkmale in allen Zonen und Zeiten zur Anschauung zu bringen." Klemm, *Allgemeine Culturwissenschaft*, vol. 2, 37–38. We have found

the view of history as a "science of experience" articulated already by Roscher in his *Leben, Werk und Zeitalter des Thukydides* (107) and by Fabri in his *Encyclopädie* (51).

86. "Nahrung, Kleidung und Schmuck, Werkzeuge, Wohnstätten, Fahrzeuge und Gefäße, diese sind die materiellen Grundlagen der menschlichen Cultur. . . ." Klemm, *Allgemeine Culturwissenschaft*, vol. 2, 42.

87. Klemm, *Allgemeine Culturwissenschaft*, vol. 2, 52.

88. Gustav Klemm, *Die Werkzeuge und Waffen, ihre Entstehung und Ausbildung* (Hondershausen, Germany: G. Neuse, 1858), 3–4. Originally published as *Allgemeine Culturwissenschaft*, volume 1, 1854.

89. Klemm, *Die Werkzeuge und Waffen*, 392–93; *Karl Marx Friedrich Engels Gesamtausgabe (MEGA)*, Abt. 4, vol. 32 (Berlin: Akademie Verlag, 1999), 374. Marx read the volume on tools much more carefully than the one devoted to food, drink, narcotics, and so on: After annotating only 8 pages from this volume, he covered the other with marginalia. Karl Arnd, again between Klemm and Marx, offers an anthropologically geared taxonomy of tools in *Die naturgemässe Volkswirthschaft, gegenüber dem Monopoliengeiste und dem Communismus, mit einem Rückblicke auf die einschlagende Literatur* (Hanau: Friedrich König, 1843), 26.

90. Gustav Klemm, *Die menschliche Kleidung: Culturgeschichtliche Skizze*. Lecture given on the twentieth anniversary of the Gewerbevereins of Dresden, January 31, 1854 (Dresden, 1856).

91. Klemm, *Die menschliche Kleidung*, 4.

92. Klemm, *Die menschliche Kleidung*, 5.

93. Klemm, *Die menschliche Kleidung*, 24.

94. Klemm, *Die menschliche Kleidung*, 26–27.

95. Gustav Klemm, "Der Hut," in *Gellertbuch*, ed. Ferdinand Naumann (Dresden, 1854), 129, 131.

96. Klemm, *Die Frauen: Culturgeschichtliche Schilderungen des Zustandes und Einflusses der Fauen in den verschiedenen Zonen und Zeitaltern*, 6 vols. (Dresden, 1854–1858). A comparison with Christoph Meiners's *Geschichte des weiblichen Geschlechts*, 4 vols. (1788–1800) and translated almost immediately into English in four volumes in 1808 would also underline the differences in their approach to cultural history.

97 In 1855 Klemm published with Heinrich Wilhelm Schulz a room-by-room guide to the Museum of the Society for the Research and Preservation of Patriotic Antiquities. *Führer durch das Museum des königlich Sächsischen Vereins zu Erforschung und Erhaltung vaterländischer Alterthümer im Königl. Palais des grossen Gartens*, ed. Franz Louis Bösigk, 2nd ed. (Dresden: Meinhold, 1868).

98. Klemm, *Vor fünfzig Jahren: Culturgeschichtliche Briefe* (Stuttgart: E. Schweizerbart, 1865), 72.

99. Klemm, *Vor fünfzig Jahren*, 101.

100. Klemm, *Vor fünfzig Jahren*, 126.

101. Klemm, *Vor fünfzig Jahren*, 72.

102. Klemm, *Vor fünfzig Jahren*, 137.

103. "In der geologischen Chronologie ist ein Jahrtausend etwa so viel wie eine Woche in der culturgeschichtlichen, ja, sogar vielleicht nur wie ein Tag oder eine Telegraphensecunde." Klemm, *Vor fünfzig Jahren*, 189–90.

104. Aby Warburg, *Images from the Region of the Pueblo Indians of North America*, ed. Michael P. Steinberg (Ithaca, NY, and London: Cornell University Press, 1995), 53.

105. "Die Kulturwissenschaft hat es daher nicht mit pädagogischen Untersuchungen zu thun, oder mit den Mitteln zur Bildung von Künstlern und Gelehrten, sie setzt vielmehr die dahin führenden Wege als bekannt voraus, wie denn überhaupt nicht das Individuum, sondern die Bevöllkerungsmasse Gegenstand ihrer Forschung ist." Moritz von Lavergne-Peguilhen, *Grundzüge der Gesellschaftswissenschaft*, 2 vols. in 1 (Leipzig, 1838), vol. 2, 3–4. Even Angela Stender, who surveys not only Lavernge-Peguilhen's reception history but also that of its constituent parts, treats "Kulturwissenschaft," by contrast, as utterly nonproblematic: With no history and needing no further elucidation. Stender, *Durch Gesellschaftswissenschaft zum idealen Staat: Moritz von Lavergne-Peguilhen (1801–1870)* (Berlin: Duncker & Humblot, 2005).

106. Lavergne-Peguilhen, *Grundzüge*, 3.

107. By defining the place of *Kulturwissenschaft* between philosophical and practical learning, Lavergne-Peguilhen indicates his triangulation between the positions of Kant and Herder; it is the linking of the term to social process and "Productionswissenschaft" that seems to mark off the start of a new trajectory. *Grundzüge*, 6.

108. Karl Arnd, *Die materiellen Grundlagen und sittlichen Forderungen der europäischen Cultur* (Stuttgart and Tübingen: J. G. Cotta'schen Buchhandlung, 1835).

109. Arnd, *Die materiellen Grundlagen*, 9, 24–25.

110. Arnd, *Die materiellen Grundlagen*, 30.

111. Arnd, *Die materiellen Grundlagen*, 34.

112. See Béla Kapossy, *Iselin contra Rousseau: Sociable Patriotism and the History of Mankind* (Basel, Switzerland: Schwabe, 2006).

113. Arnd, *Die materiellen Grundlagen*, 42.

114. Karl Arnd, *Die naturgemässe Volkswirthschaft*, 1–20, 38. Marx was dismissive of this work, calling it "naïve" and its author "the philosopher of the dog tax" because of his advocacy of something like it. Marx, *Das Capital*, vol. 3, part 5, ch. 22, note 7, available at www.marxists.org/archive/marx/works/1894-c3/ch22.htm, accessed on July 7, 2016.

115. Arnd, *Die naturgemässe Volkswirthschaft*, 116.

116. Wilhelm Roscher, *Grundriss zu Vorlesungen über die Staatswirtschaft: Nach geschichtlicher Methode* (Göttingen, 1842), iv.

117. Roscher, *Grundriss*, 3.

118. Roscher, *Grundriss*, 3–4.

119. Roscher, *Grundriss*, 27–31.

120. Roscher, *Grundriss*, 35.

121. Roscher, *Grundriss*, 54–57.

122. Roscher, *Grundriss*, ch. 2. On Weber, see Neville Morley, "Thucydides, History, and Historicism in Wilhelm Roscher," *Thucydides and the Modern World: Reception, Reinterpretation and Influence from the Renaissance to the Present*, ed. Katherine Harloe and Neville Morley (Cambridge, U.K.: Cambridge University Press, 2012), 136–38.

123. Roscher, *Grundriss*, 86.

124. Roscher, *Grundriss*, 93.

125. Lorenz von Stein, *Sozialismus und Kommunismus des heutigen Frankreich: Ein Beitrag zur Zeitgeschichte* (Leipzig: O. Wiegand, 1842); idem, *Die Geschichte der sozialen Bewegung in Frankreich von 1789 bis auf unsere Tage*, 3 vols. (Leipzig: O. Wiegand, 1850).

126. Von Stein, *Die Geschichte der sozialen Bewegung*, I, CXXVI.

127. Karl Marx, "The German Ideology," in *The Marx-Engels Reader*, ed. Robert Tucker (New York: W. W. Norton, 1978), 149. The latest biography of Marx devotes three pages to Stein and does not mention Lavergne-Peguilhen, Arnd, or Klemm (Gareth Stedman Jones, *Karl Marx: Greatness and Illusion* [Cambridge, MA: Harvard University Press, 2016]).

128. Keith Tribe, "Karl Marx's 'Critique of Political Economy," *The Economy of the Word: Language, History, and Economics* (Oxford, U.K.: Oxford University Press, 2015), 174; K. H. Hennings, "A Note on Marx's Reading List in His *Economic and Philosophical Manuscripts of 1844*," *Economy and Society* 14 (1985): 132, 133–36.

129. Marx, "German Ideology," 150.

130. Jodl, *Die Culturgeschichtsschreibung*, 31.

131. Kolb, quoted in Jodl, *Die Culturgeschichtsschreibung*, 32–33.

132. Marx, "German Ideology," 154.

133. Marx, "German Ideology," 154.

134. On Marx's dependence on Stein, see Kaethe Mengelberg, "Lorenz von Stein and His Contribution to Historical Sociology," *Journal of the History of Ideas* 22 (1961): 267n2–3.

135. Lorenz von Stein, *Die Gesellschaftslehre: Erste Abtheilung: Der Begriff der Gesellschaft* (Stuttgart and Augsburg: J. W. Cotta'scher Verlag, 1856), 37–38, 145.

136. "Die Dinge, welche im Innern der Gesellschaft vor sich gehen, treten durch die Beziehung zum Besitz an die Wirklichkeit, und so ensteht, das, was wir die Gestalt der Gesellschaft nennen." Stein, *Die Gesellschaftslehre*, 38.

137. See, for example, Stein, *Die Gesellschaftslehre*, 154–55, 158. For the Hegelian angle, see the perceptive review by the young Felix Gilbert in *Social Research* 4 (1937): 258–60; more recently, see Joachim Singelmann and Peter Singelmann, "Lorenz von Stein and the Paradigmatic Bifurcation of Social Theory in the Nineteenth Century," *British Journal of Sociology* 37 (1986): 431–52. Also, Christian Simon, "Gesellschaftsgeschichte in der ersten Hälfte des 19. Jahrhunderts—Frankreich und Deutschland," in *Geschichtsdiskurs vol. 3. die Epochen der Historisierung*, ed W. Küttler, J. Rüsen, E. Schulin (Frankfurt am Main: Fischer Verlag, 1993), 369–71.

138. Istvan Hont, "Alternative Political Economies? One Political Economy and Many Political Positions, (Outlines for the 'Introduction' of *After Adam Smith: Essays on the Development of Political Economy in the Early 19th Century*)," 4–6. István Hont Papers, University of St. Andrews Special Collections. I am grateful to Richard Whatmore for making this available to me.

139. Leopold von Ranke, quoted in Annelore Rieke-Müller and Siegfried Müller, "Konzeptionen der Kulturgeschichte um die Mitte des 19. Jahrhunderts: Das Germanische Nationalmuseum in Nürnberg und die Zeitschrift für deutsche Kulturgeschichte," *Archiv für Kulturgeschichte* 82 (2000): 347, 349; Karl Lamprecht, "Was ist Kulturgeschichte? Beitrag zu einer empirischen Historik," in Lamprecht, *Alternative zu Ranke*, 214; Henri Pirenne, "La specialisation en histoire," quoted in Warland, "Henri Pirenne and Karl Lamprecht's *Kulturgeschichte*," 423; Otto Brunner, "Abendländisches Geschichtsdenken," in *Neue Wege der Verfassungs- und Sozialgeschichte* (Göttingen: Vandenhoek & Ruprecht, 1968), 43. In general, see Anthony Nuttall, *Dead from the*

Waist Down: Scholars and Scholarship in Literature and the Popular Imagination (New Haven and London: Yale University Press, 2003).

140. Thesis IX: "The highest point attained by contemplative materialism, that is, materialism which does not comprehend sensuousness as practical activity, is the contemplation of single individuals in civil society." Thesis X: "The standpoint of the old materialism is 'civil' society; the standpoint of the new is *human* society, or socialised humanity." *Marx-Engels Reader*, 145.

141. Lawrence Krader, "Introduction," *The Ethnological Notebooks of Karl Marx* (Assen: Van Gorcum & Co., 1972), 81.

142. E. Germer, "Die Vorgeschichte der Gründung des Museums für Völkerkunde zu Leipzig 1868–1869," *Jahrbuch des Museums für Völkerkunde zu Leipzig* 26 (1969): 35n115.

143. Tylor, *Researches into the Early History of Mankind and the Development of Civilization* (1865), ed. Paul Bohannan (Chicago: University of Chicago Press, 1964), 1. For more on Tylor's notion of culture and its relation to Klemm and others, see Joan Leopold, *Culture in Comparative and Evolutionary Perspective: E. B. Tylor and the Making of Primitive Culture* (Berlin: D. Reimer, 1980); George W. Stocking Jr., "Matthew Arnold, E. B. Tylor, and the Uses of Invention," *American Anthropologist* 65 (1963): 785–86.

144. A. Lane Fox, "Primitive Warfare: Illustrated by Specimens from the Museum of the Institution," delivered June 28, 1867.

145. Schlereth, *Cultural History and Material Culture*, 19.

146. A description of the collection just prior to Klemm's death is found in "Die culturwissenschaftliche Sammlung des Hofrath Dr. Gustav Klemm in Dresden," *Das Ausland* 37 (1864): 12–17, and *Das Ausland* 38 (1865): 345–49. Additional information can be found in Germer, "Die Vorgeschichte der Gründung."

147. *Catalogue of the German Antiquities from the Klemm Collection in the British Museum.*

148. On this history, see Penny, *Objects of Culture*, 175–79, 199–202; Alfred Lehmann, "85 Jahre Museum für Völkerkunde zu Leipzig," *Jahrbuch des Museums für Völkerkunde zu Leipzig* 12 (1951): 11–51; and Fritz Krause, "Chronik des Museums 1926–1945," *Jahrbuch des Museums für Völkerkunde zu Leipzig* 10 (1926/1951): 1–46.

149. Robert Rydell, *All the World's a Fair: Visions of Empire at American Expositions, 1876–1916* (Chicago and London: University of Chicago Press, 1984), 23; Kathleen Curran, *The Invention of the American Art Museum. From Craft to "Kulturgeschichte"* (Los Angeles: Getty Research Institute, 2016), 1.

150. For recent Bastian bibliography, see Klaus-Peter Koepping, *Adolf Bastian and the Psychic Unity of Mankind: Foundations of Anthropology in Nineteenth Century Germany* (London and New York: LIT Verlag, 1983); H. Glenn Penny, "Bastian's Museum: On the Limits of Empiricism and the Transformation of German Ethnology," in *Worldly Provincialism: German Anthropology in the Age of Empire*, ed. Matti Bunzl and H. Glenn Penny (Ann Arbor: University of Michigan Press, 2003), 86–126.

151. Adolf Bastian, *Die Vorgeschichte der Ethnologie* (Berlin, 1881), 2.

152. Bastian, *Die Vorgeschichte*, 45–46n.

153. Bastian, *Die Vorgeschichte*, 60–61.

154. Bastian, *Die Vorgeschichte*, 62.

155. Bastian, *Die Vorgeschichte*, 63–64.

156. Bastian, *Die Vorgeschichte*, 74.

157. Bastian, *Die Vorgeschichte*, 114n.

158. Ernst Gombrich, *Aby Warburg: An Intellectual Biography* (Chicago: University of Chicago Press, 1986[1970]), 265.

Chapter Eight. The Germanisches Nationalmuseum

1. See Vincent Juhel, ed., *Arcisse de Caumont (1801–1873): Érudit Normand et Fondateur de l'Archéologie française* (Caen, France: Société des antiquaires de Normandie, 2004); Annette Frey, ed., *Ludwig Lindenschmit d. Ä.: Begleitbuch zur Ausstellung aus Anlass seines 200. Geburtstages* (Mainz, Germany: Verlag des Römisch-Germanischen Zentralmuseums, 2009).

2. See Theodore Hampe, ed., *Das Germanische Nationalmuseum von 1852 bis 1902: Festschrift zum Feier seines fünfzigjährigen Bestehens im Auftrage des Direktoriums* (Leipzig, 1902), 6.

3. Crane, *Collecting and Historical Consciousness in Early Nineteenth-Century Germany*; Bernward Deneke, "Das System der Deutschen Geschichts- und Altertumskunde des Hans von und zu Aufseß und die Historiographie im 19. Jahrhundert," in *Anzeiger des Germanischen Nationalmuseums 1974* (Nuremberg: Verlagseigentum des Germanischen Museums, 1974).

4. Of course Aufseß was, precisely, *not* interested in wonders or treasures. Hampe, *Das Germansiche Nationalmuseum*, 12.

5. Quoted in Hampe, *Das Germanische Nationalmuseum*, 13.

6. Quoted in Hampe, *Das Germanische Nationalmuseum*, 16.

7. Walter Hochreiter, *Vom Musentempel zum Lernort: Zur Sozialgeschichte deutscher Museen 1800–1914* (Darmstadt, Germany: Wissenschaftliche Buchgesellschaft, 1994), 61.

8. Jakob Grimm to Ritter von Lang in the 1830s, quoted in *Das Germanische Nationalmuseum*, 17.

9. *Das Germanische Nationalmuseum*, 18.

10. Heinrich Dilly and James Ryding, "Kulturgeschichtsschreibung vor und nach der bürgerlichen Revolution von 1848," *Ästhetik und Kommunikation* 21 (1975): 22.

11. *Das Germanische Nationalmuseum*, 20–21.

12. Hans v. u. zu Aufseß, *Sendschreiben an die erste allgemeine Versammlung deutscher Rechtsgelehrten, Geschichts- und Sprachforscher zu Frankfurt am Main* (Nuremberg: Riegel und Wiessner, 1846), 5–6.

13. Aufseß, *Sendschreiben*, 7–8.

14. Aufseß, *Sendschreiben*, 20–21. On the foundation of museums, see Barbara Mundt, *Die deutschen Kunstgewerbemuseen im 19. Jahrhundert* (Munich: Prestel, 1974).

15. Aufseß, *Sendschreiben*, 22.

16. Aufseß, *Sendschreiben*, 23.

17. For example, Baur, Geh. Staats- und Kabinettsarchivar, Darmstadt; Prof. Dr. Jacob Heinrich Ritter von Hefner, Munich; Prof Dr. Constantin Höfler, Prague; Prof. K. Klein, Mainz; Heinrich Künssberg, lawyer, Ansbach; Dr. v. Lanngen, König. Sachs. Wirl. Geheimen Rat und Präsident des Oberappellationsgerichts, Dresden; J. M. Lappenberg, archivist, Hamburg; Dr. Friddrich Lisch, archivist, Schwerin; Ferdinand von Quast, König. Preuss. Baurat and Konservator der Kunstdemkäler, Berlin.

18. The story is presented in *Mittheilungen des Königl. Sächs. Vereins für Erforschung und Erhaltung vaterländischer Alterthümer* (Dresden, 1852), "Versammlung deutscher Geschichts- u. Alterthumsforscher," 114–27 at 113. On this episode and its consequences, see Peter Burian, "Das Germanische Nationalmuseum und die deutsche Nation," in *Das Germanische National-museum Nürnberg 1852–1977*, ed. Bernward Deneke and Rainer Kahsnitz (Munich and Berlin: Deutschen Kunstverlag, 1978), 127–59.

19. *Mittheilungen des Königl. Sächs. Vereins*, 152.

20. Deneke, *Anzeiger des Germanischen Nationalmuseums*, 153, 154.

21. Aufseß, *System der deutschen Geschichts- und Alterthumskunde entworfen zum Zwecke der Anordnung der Sammlungen des germanischen Museums* (Nuremberg: Artistisch-literar. Anstalt des germ. Museums, 1853).

22. Aufseß, *System*, 3.

23. Aufseß, *System*, 3–4.

24. "Die historischen Zustände gründlich zu erforschen ist daher eben so wichtig als die Geschichtsforschung selbst, und in so fern gebührt ihnen mit Recht der Platz neben der Geschichte, nicht, wie bisher, unter ihr als blosse Gehülfen und Diener der Geschichte, als Hülfswissenschaften." Aufseß, *System*, 4.

25. W. Harless, *Erster Jahresbericht des Germanischen Nationalmuseums zu Nürnberg vom September 1853 bis Ende August 1854 mit Rückblick auf das Jahr 1852* (Nuremberg: Artistisch-literar. Anstalt des germ. Museums, 1854), 1.

26. Harless, *Erster Jahresbericht*, 4.

27. "Die Schematisierung des Stoffes, wie sie Herr von Aufseß aufstellt, mag ihren Wert haben für allerhand Merkwürdigkeiten und Curiosa: für lebendiges Wissen ist sie tödtlich," quoted in Annelore Rieke-Müller and Siegfried Müller, "Konzeptionen der Kulturgeschichte um die Mitte des 19. Jahrhunderts: Das Germansiche National-museum in Nürnberg und die Zeitschrift für deutsche Kulturgeschichte," *Archiv für Kulturgeschichte* 82 (2000): 347, 349.

28. *Dritter Jahresbericht des Germanischen Nationalmuseums zu Nürnberg: von Anfang September 1855 bis 1. October 1856* (Nurnberg and Leipzig: literarish-artist. Anstalt des germanischen Museums and Friedrich Fleischer, 1856), 1.

29. *Denkschriften des Germanischen Nationalmuseums. Erster Band. Das Germanische National-museum. Organismus und Sammlungen. Zweite Abtheilung. Kunst- und Alterthums-Sammlungen* (Nurnberg and Leipzig: literarisch-artist. Anstalt des germanischen Museums und Fried-rich Fleischer, 1856), 1.

30. *Denkschriften*, vol. 1, 4.

31. The production of these *Denkschriften* was in part driven by a desire to emu-late the *Monumenta* produced in Frankfurt by the "Archiv der Gesellschaft für ältere deutsche Geschichtskunde," but also in order to live up to the self-proclaimed aspira-tions of a national institutution.

32. *Denkschriften*, vol. 1, 9.

33. *Denkschriften*, vol. 1, 10.

34. *Denkschriften*, vol. 1, 48.

35. Quoted in Hochreiter, *Vom Musentempel zum Lernort*, 68.

36. Hochreiter, *Vom Musentempel zum Lernort*, 70–71.

37. Quoted in Hochreiter, *Vom Musentempel zum Lernort*, 76.

38. For an overview, see Schleier, *Geschichte der deutschen Geschichtsschreibung*, 516–31.

39. Johannes Falke, "Prospektus," *Zeitschrift für deutsche Kulturgeschichte* 1 (1856): 7.

40. I am grateful to Anthony Grafton for pointing me toward Freytag.

41. Johannes Falke, "Die deutsche Kulturgeschichte," *Zeitschrift für deutsche Kul-turgeschichte* 1 (1856): 7.

42. Falke, "Die deutsche Kulturgeschichte," 8–9.

43. Falke, "Die deutsche Kulturgeschichte," 24.

44. Falke, "Die deutsche Kulturgeschichte," 24.

45. Falke, "Die deutsche Kulturgeschichte," 28.

46. This last in particular is in *Zeitschrift für deutsche Kulturgeschichte* 2 (1857): 116–26.

47. R. Hoder, "Zu den Judenverfolgungen im Mittelalter," *Zeitschrift für deutsche Kulturgeschichte* 2 (1857): 399.

48. Karl Seifart, "Streitbare Juden im Mittelalter," *Zeitschrift für deutsche Kulturgeschichte* 2 (1857): 521–27.

49. Anon., "Der Dilettantismus in der Kulturgeschichte," *Zeitschrift für deutsche Kulturgeschichte* 1 (1856): 281–82. As if responding to this call, in the following year the *Journal* published a review of "Die kulturgeschichtliche Literatur der Zeitschriften," *Zeitschrift für deutsche Kulturgeschichte* 2 (1857): 347–50.

50. J. F. [Johannes Falke], "Zwischenrede," *Zeitschrift für deutsche Kulturgeschichte* 2 (1857): 425–26.

51. On Biedermann, see Schleier, *Geschichte der deutschen Kulturgeschichts-schreibung*, ch. 11; Richard J. Bazillion, *Modernizing Germany: Karl Biedermann's Career in the Kingdom of Saxony, 1835–1901* (New York: Peter Lang, 1990).

52. Biedermann, "Ein Beitrag zur kulturgeschichtlichen Betrachtung der Leibnitzischen Philosophie," *Zeitschrift für deutsche Kulturgeschichte* 1 (1856): 240. This is exactly the point of Pippin's *Interanimations*, discussed in the introduction.

53. Biedermann, "Die Leibnitzische Philosophie in kulturgeschichtlicher Auffassung," *Zeitschrift für deutsche Kulturgeschichte* 2 (1857): 295.

54. Biedermann, "Leibnitz und seine Zeit," *Zeitschrift für deutsche Kulturgeschichte* 2 (1857): 487–520.

55. Karl Biedermann, "Die Stellung der Kulturgeschichte in der Gegewart mit besonderer Hinsicht auf die Idee eines kulturgeschichtliches Vereins," *Zeitschrift für deutsche Kulturgeschichte* 2 (1857): 67–73.

56. Biedermann, "Die Stellung der Kulturgeschichte," 73.

57. "Die sog. materiellen Interessen—Ackerbau, Gewerbe, Handel und Verkehr, sammt den daraus resultirenden volkswirthschaftlichen und socialen Zuständen der verschiedenen Gesellschaftsklassen—diese Interessen, die trotz der nasenrümpfenden Verachtung, womit ein Theil unserer Gelehrtenwelt sie lange Zeit behandelt hat, dennoch nicht blos zu einer, sondern zu der socialen macht unsers Jahrhunderts erwachsen sind, bilden fortan auch für die Geschichtsforschung und Gehichtschreibung die nicht mehr zu entbehrende, breite und solide Basis, auf der allein mit Sicherheit der Bau eines wahrhaften Geschichtswerkes sich erheben kann." Biedermann, "Die Stellung der Kulturgeschichte," *Zeitschrift für deutsche Kulturgeschichte* 2 (1857): 69.

58. Biedermann, "Die Stellung der Kulturgeschichte," *Zeitschrift für deutsche Kulturgeschichte* 2 (1857): 71.

59. Biedermann, "In Sachen des 'Vereins für deutsche Kulturgeschichte,'" *Zeitschrift für deutsche Kulturgeschichte* 2 (1857): 547–48.

60. Dr. Peez [sic], "Berührungspunkte zwischen Kulturgeschichte und Nationalökonomie," *Zeitschrift für deutsche Kulturgeschichte* 3 (1858): 413–26.

61. A. von Eye, "Ueber die Bedeutung des Studiums der Kulturgeschichte für unsere Zeit," *Zeitschrift für deutsche Kulturgeschichte* 1 (1856): 419, 425. Strangely, aside from the initial mise-en-scène there is no further discussion of National Economy in the entire article.

62. Rieke-Müller and Müller, "Konzeptionen der Kulturgeschichte um die Mitte des 19. Jahrhunderts," 354.

63. Quoted in Rieke-Müller and Müller, "Konzeptionen der Kulturgeschichte um die Mitte des 19. Jahrhunderts," 356.

64. Quoted in Peter Burian, "Das Germanisches Nationalmuseum und die deutsche Nation," in Das Germanische National-museum Nürnberg, 1852–1977, ed. Bernward Deneke and Rainer Kahsnitz (Munich: Deutscher Kunst Verlag, 1978), 139.

65. Rieke-Müller and Müller, "Konzeptionen der Kulturgeschichte um die Mitte des 19. Jahrhunderts," 371–72.

66. Johann Gustav Droysen, Outline of the Principles of History (Grundriss der Historik), trans. E. Benjamin Andrews (New York: H. Fertig, 1967), 111, 118.

67. Droysen, Outline of the Principles of History, 117.

68. Droysen, Outline of the Principles of History, 118.

69. Droysen to von Sybel, September 26, 1857, cited in Rieke-Müller and Müller, "Konzeptionen der Kulturgeschichte," 373. Momigliano long ago made the point that Droysen invented the concept of "Hellenism" and was thus was the one German historian who could have recognized the importance of cultural history. See Momigliano, "J. G. Droysen between Greeks and Jews," History and Theory 9 (1970): 139–53.

70. Johann Gustav Droysen, Texte zur Geschichtstheorie. Mit ungedruckten Materialien zur "Historik," ed. Günter Birsch and Jörn Rüsen (Göttingen: Vandenhoeck & Ruprecht, 1972), 28.

71. Droysen, Texte zur Geschichtstheorie, 18. See ch. 5 above.

72. Droysen, Texte zur Geschichtstheorie, 28–30.

73. G. W. F. Hegel, Phenomenology of Spirit, trans. A. V. Miller (Oxford, U.K.: Oxford University Press, 1977), par. 755, 455–56.

74. Wilhelm Giesebrecht, "Die Entwicklung der modernen deutschen Geschichtswissenschaft," Historische Zeitschrift 1 (1859): 3.

75. Giesebrecht, "Die Entwicklung," 9.

76. Even the bibliography of works on cultural history assembled by Peter Burke begins with Burckhardt. See What Is Cultural History? (Cambridge, U.K., and Malden, MA: Polity Press, 2004). It was Donald R. Kelley who first pointed me toward this literature. Kelley, "The Old Cultural History," History of the Human Sciences 9 (1996): 101–26.

77. Barbara Mundt, "Über einige Gemeinsamkeiten und Unterschiede von kunstgewerblichen und kulturgeschichtlichen Museen," in Die deutschen Kunstgewerbemuseen im 19. Jahrhundert (Munich: Prestel, 1974), 143. The English influence on Germany remains the received view, as does the preeminence of the South Kensington and then Victoria and Albert Museum on the history of decorative arts. That there could be an entirely German path to design history is often ignored. See most recently Anthony Burton, "Art and Science Applied to Industry: Prince Albert's Plans for South Kensington," in Künstlerische Beziehungen zwischen England und Deutschland in der viktoriansichen Epoche, ed. Franz Bosbach and Frank Büttner (Munich: Saur, 1998), 169–86.

78. Peter N. Miller, "The Germanisches Nationalmuseum and the Museums Debate in Later 19th Century Germany," in The Challenge of the Object: 33rd Congress of the International Committee of the History of Art, Nuremberg, 15th–20th July 2012, ed. Georg Ulrich Großmann and Petra Krutisch (Nuremberg: Verlag des Germanischen Nationalmuseums, 2013), vol. 1, 370–73.

79. The American terms of the comparison I derive from Thomas J. Schlereth, "Material Culture Studies in America, 1876–1976," in Material Culture Studies in

America, ed. Thomas J. Schlereth (Nashville: American Association for State and Local History, 1982), 1–75.

80. The "Prospektus," written by Müller and introducing the first volume, repeats all of the generalities rolled out fourteen years earlier. *Zeitschrift für deutsche Kulturgeschichte*, 2nd series, vol. 1 (1872): [v]–[vii].

81. Johannes Falke, "Die Kulturgeschichte und die Volkswirtschaftslehre," *Zeitschrift für deutsche Kulturgeschichte*, 2nd series, vol. 1 (1872): 10, 28.

82. Roscher, *Geschichte der National-Oekonomik in Deutschland* (Munich: R. Oldenbourg, 1874), 913.

83. Roscher, *Geschichte der National-Oekonomik*, 913–15.

84. Roscher, *Geschichte der National-Oekonomik*, 1032–33.

85. Roscher, *Ansichten der Volkswirthschaft aus dem geschichtlichen Standpunkte* (Leipzig and Heidelberg, 1861), chs. 2 and 3.

86. Lamprecht, *Deutsches Wirtschaftsleben im Mittelalter*, vol. 2, 4.

87. For a summary discussion of this second series of the journal, see Schleier, *Geschichte der deutschen Kulturgeschichtsschreibung*, 531–37; titles of articles available at http://legacy.fordham.edu/mvst/magazinestacks/zsdtkg_nf.html, accessed December 6, 2015.

Conclusion

1. Nicholas Thomas, *Entangled Objects: Exchange, Material Culture, and Colonialism in the Pacific* (Cambridge, MA: Harvard University Press, 2009); Ian Hodder, *Entangled: An Archaeology of the Relationships between Humans and Things* (Oxford and Malden, MA: Wiley-Blackwell, 2012).

2. Otto Lauffer, "Das Historische Museum: Sein Wesen und Wirken und sein Unterschied von den Kunst- und Kunstgewerbe-Museen," *Museumskunde* 3 (1907): 1–14, 78–99, 179–85, 222–45.

3. Lauffer, "Das Historische Museum," 231.

4. Heinrich Rickert, *Kulturwissenschaft und Naturwissenschaft* (Tübingen, Germany: J. C. B. Mohr (Paul Siebeck), 1926), 80, 83.

5. Warburg to Otto Lauffer, November 11, 1925, quoted in Claudia Naber, "'Heuernte bei Gewitter': Aby Warburg, 1925–1929," in Aby M. Warburg, "Ekstatische Nymphe . . . trauernder Flußgott," in *Portrait eines Gelehrten*, ed. Robert Galitz and Brita Reimers (Hamburg, 1995), 112, 115.

6. Edgar Wind saw Dilthey and Rickert as the thinkers Warburg sought to break with in "Kritik der Geistesgeschichte," his introduction to *Kulturwissenschaftliche Bibliographie zum Nachleben der Antike: Erster Band: Die Erscheinungen des Jahres 1931*, ed. Hans Meier, Richard Newald, and Edgar Wind (Leipzig-Berlin: B. G. Teubner, 1934), vii–ix. This whole section was omitted from the extensive English translation: *A Bibliography on the Survival of the Classics: First Volume: The Publications of 1931: The Text of the German edition with an English Introduction* (London: Cassel & Company, 1934), v.

7. Ernst Cassirer, *The Logic of the Cultural Sciences* (New Haven and London: Yale University Press, 2000), 41, 57, 77.

8. The importance of his work as a student of things for his work as a theorist of the past remains underappreciated. Ian Hodder and Quentin Skinner both see them-

selves as Collingwood's heirs and yet neither—from opposite starting points—makes the connection between Collingwood the philosopher of historical method and Collingwood the archaeologist. See Hodder, ed., *Archaeology as Long-Term History* (Cambridge, U.K.: Cambridge University Press, 1987), 2; Hodder, "Digging for Symbols in Science and History: A Reply," *Proceedings of the Prehistoric Society* 52 (1987): 353; Hodder and Scott Hutson, *Reading the Past: Current Approaches to Interpretation in Archaeology*, 3rd ed. (Cambridge, U.K.: Cambridge University Press, 2003), 145–53; Skinner, "The Rise of, Challenge to and Prospects for a Collingwoodian Approach to the History of Political Thought," in *The History of Political Thought in National Context*, ed. Dario Castiglione and Iain Hampsher-Monk (Cambridge, U.K.: Cambridge University Press, 2001), 175–88; Fred Inglis, *History Man: The Life of R. G. Collingwood* (Princeton: Princeton University Press, 2009), 334. For a welcome alternative, see Charles G. Salas, "Collingwood's Historical Principles at Work," *History and Theory* 26 (1987): 53–71.

9. R. G. Collingwood, *An Autobiography*, ed. Stephen Toulmin (Oxford, U.K.: Clarendon Press, 2002 [1938]), 23, 25.

10. Collingwood, *Autobiography*, 31.

11. Collingwood, *Autobiography*, 40.

12. Lelio Pasqualini to Peiresc, June 3, 1608, Carpentras, Bibliothèque Inguimbertine, MS. 1831, fol. 60v; Claude Saumaise to Peiresc, June 1, 1635, *Les Correspondants de Peiresc*, ed. Philippe Tamizey de Larroque, 2 vols. (Geneva: Slatkine Reprints), vol. 1, 232.

13. Collingwood, *Autobiography*, 40. For Gadamer's engagement with Collingwood, see *Truth and Method* (New York: Crossroads, 1985 [1975]), 332.

14. R. G. Collingwood, *The Idea of History* (Oxford, U.K.: Oxford University Press, 1946), 241–45.

15. Dilthey, "On Understanding and Hermeneutics," *Selected Writings*, vol. 4, 233.

16. Collingwood, *Idea of History*, 245.

17. Collingwood, *Idea of History*, 174–45.

18. Collingwood, *Idea of History*, 212.

19. Rilke, *Selected Poetry and Prose*, 387.

20. Michael Shanks and Mike Pearson, *Theatre | Archaeology 1993–2013*, 93, accessed June 11, 2016; William Carlos Williams, reprinted in *Paterson* (Harmondsworth, U.K.: Penguin Books, 1983), [iii].

21. Dilthey, "The Eighteenth Century and the Historical World," *Selected Writings*, vol. 4, 335, 345–47, 375; Collingwood, *Autobiography*, 132–33.

22. In the archive there is a page of bibliography with the heading "Burckhardt & Dilthey: Kulturgeschichte," N-b 1 and a reference to Collingwood's "Human Nature and Human History," *Proceedings of the British Academy* 22 (1936) at n-b 1 "Storicismo." I am grateful to Riccardo di Donato for access to this material.

23. See, for example, Momigliano, "Historicism in Contemporary Thought," *Studies in Historiography* (London: Weidenfeld & Nicolson, 1968), 221–38; idem, "New Paths of Classicism in the Nineteenth Century," *History and Theory* 21 (1982): 460–67; Peter N. Miller, "Momigliano, Benjamin and Antiquarianism after the Crisis of Historicism," in *Momigliano and Antiquarianism: Foundations of the Modern Cultural Sciences*, ed. Peter N. Miller (Toronto: University of Toronto Press, 2007), 336–40.

24. Momigliano, "La Storia Antica in Inghilterra," *Sesto contributo alla storia degli studi classici e del mondo antico* (Rome: Edizioni di Storia e Letteratura, 1980), 764–65.

25. Momigliano, "Benedetto Croce (1950)," *Decimo contributo*, 541.

26. Momigliano, "Philology and History," *Decimo contributo*, 291.

27. Momigliano, "Antiquari e storici dell'antichità," in *Decimo Contributo alla storia degli studi classici e del mondo antico*, ed. Riccardo Di Donato (Rome: Edizioni di Storia e Letteratura, 2012), 285–90; also in Di Donato, "Arnaldo Momigliano from Antiquarianism to Cultural History: Some Reasons for a Quest," in *Momigliano and Antiquarianism*, 86–91. For a discussion of Momigliano's Pyrrhonism, see Miller, "Introduction: Momigliano, Antiquarianism, and the Cultural Sciences," and "Momigliano, Benjamin, and Antiquarianism after the Crisis of Historicism," in *Momigliano and Antiquarianism*, ed. Miller, 26–28, 338–44, 364.

28. Proof: Even one of the few opportunities Nietzsche makes for material culture, the section of his lecture course on Greek religion (winter semester 1875–1876) on ritual implements, speaks only generally, not by reference to specific finds or even material typologies. Nietzsche, *Le service divin des Grecs*, translation and introduction by Emmanuel Cattin (Paris: Édition de l'Herne, 1992), 119–26.

29. Friedrich Nietzsche, *The Gay Science*, trans. Walter Kaufmann (New York: Vintage Books, 1974), 268–69.

✒ BIBLIOGRAPHY

Ademollo, Francesco. *The Cratylus of Plato: A Commentary.* Cambridge, U.K.: Cambridge University Press, 2011.

Adkins, G. "The Renaissance of Peiresc: Aubin-Louis Millin and the Postrevolutionary Republic of Letters." *Isis* 99 (2008): 675–700.

Angela, Stender. *Durch Gesellschaftswissenschaft zum idealen Staat: Moritz von Lavergne-Peguilhen (1801–1870).* Berlin: Duncker & Humblot, 2005.

Anonymous. "Die culturwissenschaftliche Sammlung des Hofrath Dr. Gustav Klemm in Dresden." *Das Ausland* 37 (1864): 12–17.

Anonymous. "Die culturwissenschaftliche Sammlung des Hofrath Dr. Gustav Klemm in Dresden." *Das Ausland* 38 (1865): 345–49.

Anonymous. "Der Dilettantismus in der Kulturgeschichte." *Zeitschrift für deutsche Kulturgeschichte* 1 (1856): 281–82.

Arnd, Karl. *Die materiellen Grundlagen und sittlichen Forderungen der europäischen Cultur.* Stuttgart and Tübingen: J. G. Cotta'schen Buchhandlung, 1835.

Arnd, Karl. *Die naturgemässe Volkswirthschaft, gegenüber dem Monopoliengeiste und dem Communismus, mit einem Rückblicke auf die einschlagende Literatur.* Hanau: Friedrich König, 1843.

Ast, Friedrich. *Grundriss der Philologie.* Landshut: Philipp Krüll, 1808.

Aufseß, Hans von und zu. *Sendschreiben an die erste allgemeine Versammlung deutscher Rechtsgelehrten, Geschichts- und Sprachforscher zu Frankfurt am Main.* Nuremberg: Riegel und Wiessner, 1846.

Aufseß, Hans v. u. zu. *System der deutschen Geschichts- und Alterthumskunde entworfen zum Zwecke der Anordnung der Sammlungen des germanischen Museums.* Nuremberg: Artistisch-literar. Anstalt des germ. Museums, 1853.

Bacon, Francis, and Gilbert Watts. *Of the Advancement and Proficience of Learning; or, The Partitions of Sciences. Nine Books. Written in Latin by the Most Eminent, Illustrious, and Famous Lord Francis Bacon Baron of Verulam, Vicount St. Alban, Councellor of Estate, and Lord Chancellor of England.* Interpreted by Gilbert Watts. Oxford, U.K.: Printed by Leon Lichfield printer to the University, for Robert Young and Edward Forrest, 1640.

Bahnson, Kristian. "Ueber ethnographische Museen." *Mitteilungen der Anthropologischen Gesellschaft in Wien* 18 (1888): 109–64.

Baldacci, Paolo. "The Function of Nietzsche's Thought in De Chirico's Art." In *Nietzsche and "An Architecture of Our Minds,"* edited by Alexandre Kostka and Irving Wohlfarth, 91–114. Los Angeles: Getty Publications, 1999.

Baldacci, Paolo. *Giorgio De Chirico: The Metaphysical Period, 1888–1919.* Translated by Jeffrey Jennings. New York: Bullfinch, 1997.

Bann, Stephen. *The Clothing of Clio: A Study of the Representation of History in Nineteenth-Century Britain and France.* Cambridge, U.K.: Cambridge University Press, 1984.

Barthélemy, Jean-Jacques. *Voyage du jeune Anacharsis en Grèce, dans le Milieu du Quatrième Siècle avant l'ère Vulgaire.* Paris: Chez de Bure, 1789.

Bastian, Adolf. *Die Vorgeschichte der Ethnologie.* Berlin: Harrwitz und Gossmann, 1881.

Bazillion, Richard J. *Modernizing Germany: Karl Biedermann's Career in the Kingdom of Saxony, 1835–1901.* New York: Peter Lang, 1990.

Beck, Christian Daniel. *Grundriss der Archäologie oder Anleitung zur Kenntniß der Geschichte der alten Kunst und der Kunst-Denkmäler und Kunstwerke des classischen Alterthums.* Leipzig: J. C. Hinrichs, 1816.

Bedos-Rezak, Brigitte. *When Ego Was Imago.* Leiden: E. J. Brill, 2010.

Beiser, Frederick. *The Fate of Reason: German Philosophy from Kant to Fichte.* Cambridge, MA: Harvard University Press, 1987.

Benne, Christian. *Nietzsche und die historisch-kritische Philologie.* Berlin and New York: Walter de Gruyter, 2005.

Berr, Henri, and Lucien Febvre. "History and Historiography." In *Encyclopaedia of the Social Sciences,* edited by Edwin R. A. Seligman and Alvin Johnson. New York: The Macmillan Company, 1937.

Biedermann, Karl. "Die Leibnitzische Philosophie in kulturgeschichtlicher Auffassung." *Zeitschrift für deutsche Kulturgeschichte* 2 (1857): 295–323.

Biedermann, Karl. "Die Stellung der Kulturgeschichte in der Gegewart mit besonderer Hinsicht auf die Idee eines kulturgeschichtliches Vereins." *Zeitschrift für deutsche Kulturgeschichte* 2 (1857): 67–73.

Biedermann, Karl. "Ein Beitrag zur kulturgeschichtlichen Betrachtung der Leibnitzischen Philosophie." *Zeitschrift für deutsche Kulturgeschichte* 1 (1856): 237–52.

Biedermann, Karl. "In Sachen des 'Vereins für deutsche Kulturgeschichte.'" *Zeitschrift für deutsche Kulturgeschichte* 2 (1857): 547–50.

Biedermann, Karl. "Leibnitz und seine Zeit." *Zeitschrift für deutsche Kulturgeschichte* 2 (1857): 487–520.

Blanke, Horst Walter. *Historiographiegeschichte als Historik.* Stuttgart–Bad Cannstatt: froommann-holzboog, 1991.

Blanke, Horst Walter, and Dirk Fleischer. *Theoretiker der deutschen Aufklärungshistorie.* Stuttgart–Bad Cannstatt: frommann-holzboog, 1990.

Bloch, Marc. *The Historian's Craft.* Translated by Peter Putnam. Manchester: Manchester University Press, 1992.

Blok, Josine H. "'Romantische Poesie, Naturphilosophie, Construktion der Geschichte': K. O. Müller's Understanding of History and Myth." In *Zwischen Rationalismus und Romantik: Karl Otfried Müller und die antike Kultur,* edited by William M. Calder III and Renate Schleiser with Susanne Gödde, 55–97. Hildesheim, Germany: Weidmann, 1998.

Bödeker, Hans Erich, Philippe Büttgen, and Michel Espagne, eds. *Göttingen vers 1800: L'Europe des sciences de l'homme.* Paris: Éditions du Cerf (Bibliothèque franco-allemande), 2010.

Bödeker, Hans Erich, Philippe Büttgen, and Michel Espagne, eds. *Die Wissenschaft vom Menschen in Göttingen um 1800: Wissenschaftliche Praktiken, institutionelle Geographie, europäische Netzwerke.* Göttingen, Germany: Vandenhoek & Ruprecht, 2008.

Boeckh, August. "De antiquitatis studio." In *Gesammelte Kleine Schriften*, vol. 1, 103–9. Leipzig: G. B. Teubner, 1858.

Boeckh, August. *Die Staatshaushaltung der Athener.* 2nd ed. Berlin: G. Reimer, 1851.

Boeckh, August. *Encyklopädie und Methodologie der philologischen Wissenschaften.* Edited by Ernst Brautscheck, with Rudolf Klussman. Leipzig: Teubner, 1886.

Boeckh, August. *On Interpretation and Criticism.* Edited and translated by John Paul Pritchard. Norman: University of Oklahoma Press, 1968.

Boeckh, August. *The Public Economy of Athens in Four Books.* London: John Murray, 1828.

Boeckh, August. "Von der Philologie, besonders der klassischen in Beziehung zur morgenländischen, zum Unterricht und zur Gegenwart." In *Gesammelte Kleine Schriften*, vol. 2, 183–99. Leipzig: G. B. Teubner, 1859.

Boeckh, August, Johannes Franz, Ernst Curtius, A. Kirchhoff, and Hermann Roehl. *Corpus inscriptionum graecarum.* Berlin: ex Officina Academica, vendit G. Reimeri libraria, 1828.

Boockmann, Hartmut, and Hermann Wellenreuther, eds. *Geschichtswissenschaft in Göttingen: eine Vorlesungsreihe.* Göttingen: Vandenhoeck & Ruprecht, 1987.

Bradley, Richard. *The Past in Prehistoric Societies.* London: Routledge, 2002.

Braudel, Fernand. *L'Histoire au quotidien.* Paris: Éditions de Fallois, 2001.

Braudel, Fernand. *On History.* Chicago: University of Chicago Press, 1980.

Bravo, Benedetto. *Philologie, histoire, philosophie de l'histoire: étude sur J. G. Droysen, historien de l'antiquité.* Wrocław, Poland: Zakład Narodowy Imienia Ossolińskich, Wydawn, 1968.

Brecht, Bertolt. "Der Messingkauf." In *Brecht on Performance: Messingkauf and Modelbooks*, edited by Tom Kuhn, Marc Silberman, and Steve Giles. London: Bloomsbury, n.d.

Bredekamp, Horst. *Die Fenster der Monade: Gottfried Wilhelm Leibniz' Theater der Natur und Kunst.* Berlin: Akademie Verlag, 2004.

Broodbank, Cyprian. *The Making of the Middle Sea.* Oxford, U.K.: Oxford University Press, 2014.

Bruer, Stephanie-Gerrit. "Jacob Burckhardt: Systematische Kunstbetrachtung ein Jahrhundert nach Winckelmann." In *Jacob Burckhardt und die Antike*, edited by Peter Betthausen and Max Kunze, 103–16. Mainz, Germany: Verlag Phillip von Zabern, 1998.

Brush, Kathryn. "Aby Warburg and the Cultural Historian Karl Lamprecht." In *Art History as Cultural History: Warburg's Projects*, edited by Richard Woodfield. Amsterdam: OPA, 2001.

Brush, Kathryn. "The Cultural Historian Karl Lamprecht: Practitioner and Progenitor of Art History." *Central European History* 26, no. 2 (1993): 139–64.

Bruskin, Grisha. "Shattered Truth: Has Marxism become the Antiquity of Our Times? Notes for the Archaeologist's Collection Installation in the Former Church of Santa Caterina in Venice." In *Grisha Bruskin: An Archaeologist's Collection*, edited by Giuseppe Barbieri and Silvia Burini, 7–9. Crocetta del Montello, Italy: Terra Ferma, 2015.

Budraitskis, Ilya, and Arseniy Zhilyaev, eds. *Pedagogical Poem: The Archive of the Future Museum of History.* Vicenza, Italy: Marsilio Editore, 2014.

Büsching, Johann. "Blick auf die Forschungen über deutsche Vorzeit." In *Morgenblatt für gebildete Stände* 19 (May 1825).

Büsching, Johann Gustav Gottlieb. *Abriß der deutschen Alterthums-Kunde mit einer Charte des alten Germaniens.* Weimar: Landes-Industrie-Comptoir, 1824.

Bunzl, Matti. "Franz Boas and the Humboldtian Tradition." In *Volksgeist as Method and Ethic: Essays on Boasian Ethnography and the German Anthropological Tradition,* edited by George W. Stocking, 17–78. Madison: University of Wisconsin Press, 1986.

Burckhardt, Jacob. *The Greeks and Greek Civilization.* Translated by Sheila Stern. Edited by Oswyn Murray. New York: St. Martin's Griffin, 1998.

Burian, Peter. "Das Germanische Nationalmuseum und die deutsche Nation." In *Das Germanische Nationalmuseum Nürnberg 1852–1977,* edited by Bernward Deneke and Rainer Kahsnitz, 127–59. Munich and Berlin: Deutschen Kunstverlag, 1978.

Burke, Peter. *What Is Cultural History?* Cambridge, U.K., and Malden, MA: Polity Press, 2004.

Bursian, Conrad. *Geschichte der klassischen Philologie in Deutschland,* IV. Munich and Leipzig, 1883.

Burton, Anthony. "Art and Science Applied to Industry: Prince Albert's Plans for South Kensington." In *Künstlerische Beziehungen zwischen England und Deutschland in der viktoriansichen Epoche,* edited by Franz Bosbach and Frank Büttner, 169–86. Munich: Saur, 1998.

Butterfield, Herbert. *Man on His Past: The Study of the History of Historical Scholarship.* Cambridge, U.K.: Cambridge University Press, 1955.

Byrne, Paula. *The Real Jane Austen: A Life in Small Things.* New York: Harper, 2013.

Caenegem, R. C. van, F. L. Ganshof, Lucas Jocqué, and Baudouin van den Abeele. *Introduction aux sources de l'histoire médiévale.* Turnhout, Belgium: Brepols, 1997.

Cancik, Hubert, and Hildegard Cancik-Lindemaier. *Philolog und Kultfigur: Friedrich Nietzsche und seine Antike in Deutschland.* Stuttgart: J. B. Metzlar, 1999.

Carbonell, Charles-Olivier. *Histoire et historiens: Une mutation idéologique des historiens français 1865–1885.* Toulouse: Privat, 1976.

Carhart, Michael C. *The Science of Culture in Enlightenment Germany.* Cambridge, MA: Harvard University Press, 2007.

Cassirer, Ernst. *The Problem of Knowledge: Philosophy, Science, and History since Hegel.* New Haven: Yale University Press, 1950.

Chaline, Jean-Pierre. *Sociabilité et érudition : Les Sociétés savantes en France.* Paris: Éditions du Comité des travaux historiques et scientifiques, 1995.

Champollion-Figeac, Jacques-Joseph. "Archéologie." In *Dictionnaire de la conversation et de la lecture,* edited by M. W. Duckett, vol. 2, 483–85. Paris: Belin-Mandar, 1833.

Chickering, Roger. *Karl Lamprecht: A German Academic Life.* Leiden: E. J. Brill, 1993.

Choay, Françoise. *Alegoría del patrimonio.* Barcelona: Editorial Gustavo Gili, 2007 [1992].

Choay, Françoise. "Introduction" in Camillo Boito, *Conserver ou restaurer?* Paris: Éditions de l'Encyclopédie des Nuisances, 2013 [1893].

Chung, Y. S. S. "John Britton (1771–1857): A Source for the Exploration of the Foundations of County Archaeological Society Museums." *Journal of the History of Collections* 15 (2003): 113–25.

Cornell, Joseph. *Wanderlust.* London: Royal Academy of Arts, 2015.

Couturat, Louis. *Opuscules et fragments inédits de Leibniz.* Paris: Alcan, 1903.

Crane, Susan. *Collecting and Historical Consciousness in Early Nineteenth-Century Germany.* Ithaca, NY: Cornell University Press, 2000.

Cropper, Elizabeth, G. Perini, and Francesco Solinas, eds. *Documentary Culture: Florence and Rome from Grand-Duke Ferdinand I to Pope Alexander.* Bologna: Nuova Alfa Editoriale, 1992.

Curran, Kathleen. *The Invention of the American Art Museum. From Craft to "Kulturgeschichte."* Los Angeles: Getty Research Institute, 2016.

Dacos, Nicole. *Roma quanta fuit: Tre pittori fiamminghi nel Domus Aurea.* Rome: Donzelli Editore, 1995.

Daniel, Glyn. *A Hundred and Fifty Years of Archaeology.* Cambridge, MA: Harvard University Press, 1975 [1950].

Davillé, Louis. *Leibniz Historien: Essai sur l'activité et la méthode historique de Leibniz.* Darmstadt: Scientia Verlag Allen, 1996 [1909].

de la Combe, Pierre Judet. "'Le savant antiquaire de Goettingue': Karl Otfried Müller en France." In *Zwischen Rationalismus und Romantik: Karl Otfried Müller und die antike Kultur,* edited by William M. Calder III and Renate Schleiser with Susanne Gödde, 283–311. Hildesheim, Germany: Weidmann, 1998.

Deetz, James. *In Small Things Forgotten: The Archaeology of Early American Life.* New York: Doubleday, 1977.

Delmas, Jean-François. "La Figure du Chartiste dans la littérature: Entre mythe et réalité." *Mémoires de l'académie de Nîmes,* 9th series, 88 (2014): 49–72.

Deneke, Bernward. "Das System der Deutschen Geschichts- und Altertumskunde des Hans von und zu Aufseß und die Historiographie im 19. Jahrhundert." In *Anzeiger des Germanischen Nationalmuseums 1974,* 144–58. Nuremberg: Verlagseigentum des Germanischen Museums, 1974.

Deneke, Bernward. "Zur Sammlungsgeschichte Volkskundlicher Museumsbestände." In *Volkskunde im Museum,* edited by Wolfgang Brückner and Bernward Deneke, 261–76. Würzburg, 1976.

Deneke, Petra. *Konzeption zur Einführung der Kostenstellenrechnung in die Kassenärztliche Vereinigung Brandenburg.* Wildau, Germany: TH Diplomarbeit, 2009.

Deonna, W. "Origine et Constitutions de l'Archéologie. Son Champ d'étude." In *L'Archéologie, son domaine, son but,* 1. Paris: Flammarion, 1922.

Desing, Anselm. *Auxilia historica, oder Behülff zu den historischen und dazu erforderlichen Wissenschaften.* Stadt am Hof, nächst Regenspurg, Germany: Gastl, 1741.

Devulder, Catherine. "Karl Lamprecht, Kulturgeschichte et histoire totale." *Revue d'Allemagne* 17 (1985): 1–16.

"Die kulturgeschichtliche Literatur der Zeitschriften." *Zeitschrift für deutsche Kulturgeschichte* 2 (1857): 347–50.

Diesener, Gerald, and Jaroslav Kudrna. "Alfred Doren (1869–1934)—ein Historiker am Institut für Kultur- und Universalgeschichte." In *Karl Lamprecht weiterdenken: Universal- und Kulturgeschichte heute,* edited by Gerald Diesener, 60–85. Leipzig: Leipziger Universitätsverlag, 1993.

Dilly, Heinrich, and James Ryding. "Kulturgeschichtsschreibung vor und nach der bürgerlichen Revolution von 1848." *Ästhetik und Kommunikation* 21 (1975): 15–32.

Drost, Dietrich. "Gustav Klemms kulturhistorisches Museum." *Jahrbuch des Museums für Völkerkunde zu Leipzig* 26 (1969): 41–83.

Droysen, Johann Gustav. *Outline of the Principles of History (Grundriss der Historik).* Translated by E. Benjamin Andrews. New York: H. Fertig, 1967.

Droysen, Johann Gustav. *Texte zur Geschichtstheorie: Mit ungedruckten Materialien zur "Historik."* Edited by Günter Birsch and Jörn Rüsen. Göttingen: Vandenhoeck & Ruprecht, 1972.

Duchhardt, Heinz, and Martin Espenhorst. *August Ludwig (von) Schlözer in Europa.* Göttingen: Vandenhoek & Ruprecht, 2012.

Eastwood, Bruce. "Origins and Contents of the Leiden Planetary Configuration (MS Voss. Q.79, Fol. 93v), An Artistic Astronomical Schema of the Early Middle Ages," *Viator* 14 (1983): 36–40.

Effros, Bonnie. *Uncovering the Germanic Past: Merovingian Archaeology in France, 1830–1914.* Oxford, U.K.: Oxford University Press, 2012.

Eisel, Franz. "Geschichts- und Altertumsvereine als Keimzellen und Wegbereiter der Heimatmuseen." *Neue Museumskunde* 27 (1984): 173–82.

Ellesmere. Francis Egerton. *Guide to Northern Archeology.* London: Bain, 1848.

Engels, Friedrich, Karl Marx, and Robert Cinnamond Tucker. *The Marx-Engels Reader.* New York: Norton, 1978.

Ernesti, Johann August. *Io. Augusti Ernesti Archaeologia literaria.* Leipzig: Impensis Caspari Fritsch, 1768.

Escudier, Alexandre. "De Chladenius à Droysen: Théorie et méthodologie de l'histoire de langue allemande (1750–1860)." *Annales HSS* 58 (2003): 743–77.

Eye, A. von. "Ueber die Bedeutung des Studiums der Kulturgeschichte für unsere Zeit." *Zeitschrift für deutsche Kulturgeschichte* 1 (1856): 419–31.

Fabri, Johann Ernst. *Encyclopädie der Historischen Hauptwissenschaften und deren Hülfs-Doctrinen. Archäologie, Alterthumskunde, Chronologie, Diplomatik, Epigraphik, Genealogie, heraldik, Hieroglyphik, Mythologie, Mythographie, Numismatik, Sphragistik, Toponomie, politischen Arithmetik.* Erlangen, Germany: Johann Jakob Palm, 1808.

Falke, Johannes. "Bücherschau." *Zeitschrift für deutsche Kulturgeschichte* 1 (1856): 401–11.

Falke, Johannes. "Die deutsche Kulturgeschichte." *Zeitschrift für deutsche Kulturgeschichte* 1 (1856): 5–30.

Falke, Johannes. "Prospektus." *Zeitschrift für deutsche Kulturgeschichte* 1 (1856): 1–3.

Falke, Johannes. "Zwischenrede." *Zeitschrift für deutsche Kulturgeschichte* 2 (1857): 423–30.

Fessmaier, Johann Georg. *Grundriss der historischen Hilfswissenschaften vorzüglich nach Gatterers Schriften zum akadmeischen Gebrauche bearbeitet.* Landeshut: Anton Weber, 1802.

Fiorillo, J. D. *Geschichte der zeichnenden Künste in Deutschland und die Niederlanden,* 5 vols. Göttingen, 1708–1808.

Fischer, Dietrich. *Die deutsche Geschichtswissenschaft von J. G. Droysen bis O. Hintze in ihrem Verhältnis zur Soziologie: Grundzüge eines Methodenproblems,* Ph.D thesis, Cologne, 1966.

Fittschen, Klaus. "Karl Otfried Müller und die Archäologie." In *Zwischen Rationalismus und Romantik: Karl Otfried Müller und die antike Kultur,* edited by William M. Calder III and Renate Schlesier, 187–216. Hildesheim, Germany: Weidmann, 1988.

Flashar, Hellmut, Karlfried Gründer, and Axel Horstmann, eds. *Zur Geschichte und Methodologie der Geisteswissenschaften*. Göttingen: Vandenhoeck & Ruprecht, 1979.

Fornaro, Serena. "Das 'Studium der Antike' von Heyne bis Boeckh." In *August Boeckh: Philologie, Hermeneutik und Wissenschaftspolitik*, edited by Christiane Hackel and Sabine Seifert, 197–209. Berlin: Berliner Wissenschafts Verlag, 2013.

Forster, Kurt W. "Bilder geistern durch Sebalds Erzählungen, Geister bewohnen ihre Zeilen." In *Wandernde Schatten: W. G. Sebalds Unterwelt*, edited by Ulrich von Bülow, Heike Gfrereis, and Ellen Strittmatter, 87–99. Marbach, Germany: Deutscher Schillergesellschaft, 2008.

Forster, Michael N. "Kant's Philosophy of Language." *Tijdschrift voor Filosofie* 74 (2012): 485–511.

Freedberg, David. *The Eye of the Lynx: Galileo, His Friends, and the Beginnings of Modern Natural History*. Chicago: University of Chicago Press, 2002.

Frey, Anette, ed. *Ludwig Lindenschmit d. Ä: Begleitbuch zur Ausstellung aus Anlass seines 200. Geburtstages*. Edited by Annette Frey. Mainz: Verlag des Römisch-Germanischen Zentralmuseum, 2009.

Fuchs, Werner. "Fragen der archäologischen Hermeneutik in der ersten Hälfte des 19. Jahrhunderts." In *Philologie und Hermeneutik im 19. Jahrhundert: zur Geschichte und Methodologie der Geisteswissenschaften*, edited by Hellmut Flashar, Karlfried Gründer, and Axel E.-A. Horstmann, 201–24. Göttingen: Vandenhoeck und Ruprecht, 1979.

Fueter, Eduard. *Geschichte der neueren Historiographie*. Munich: Oldenbourg, 1911.

Fulda, Daniel. *Wissenschaft aus Kunst: Die Entstehung der modernen deutschen Geschichtsschreibung 1760–1860*. Berlin and New York: Walter de Gruyter, 1996.

Garber, Jörn. "Von der Menschheitsgeschichte zur Kulturgeschichte. Zum geschichtstheoretischen Kulturbegriff der deutschen Spätaufklärung." In *Kultur zwischen Bürgertum und Volk*, edited by Jutta Held, 76–97. Berlin: Argument-Verlag, 1983.

Gassendi, Pierre. *Viri Illustris Nicolai Claudii Fabricii de Peiresc, Senatoris Aquisextiensis Vita*. Paris: Sebastian Cramoisy, 1641.

Gatterer, Johann Christoph. *Abriß der Universalhistorie nach ihrem gesamten Umfange von Erschaffung der Welt bis auf unsere Zeiten Hälfte 1*. Göttingen: Vandenhöck, 1765.

Gatterer, Johann Christoph. *Einleitung in die synchronistische Universalhistorie*. Göttingen: Vandenhoek, 1771.

Gatterer, Johann Christoph. *Geseze des Königl. Instituts des historischen Wissenschaften*, 23.12.1766, Göttingen University Archive, Kur 7540.

Gatterer, Johann Christoph. *Handbuch der Universalhistorie nach ihrem gesamten Umfange von Erschaffung der Welt bis zum Ursprunge der meisten heutigen Reiche und Staaten*. 2nd ed. Göttingen: Vandenhoeck, 1765.

Gatterer, Johann Cristoph. *Ideal einer allgemeinen Weltstatistik. in der öffentlichen Versammlung des Köngl. histor. Instituts den 2 Oct 1773 vorgelesen*. Göttingen: Vandenhokischen, 1773.

Gatterer, Johann Christoph. *Kurzer Begriff der Weltgeschichte*. 1785.

Gatterer, Johann Christoph. *Praktische Heraldik*. Nuremberg: Bauer und Mann, 1791.

Gatterer, Johann Christoph. *Versuch einer allgemeinen Weltgeschichte bis zur Entdeckung Amerikens*. Göttingen: Vandenhoeck and Ruprecht, 1792.

Gatterer, Johann Christoph. "Vom historischen Plan, und der darauf sich gründenden Zusammenfügung der Erzählungen." *Allgemeine historische Bibliothek* 1 (1767): 15–89.

Gatterer, Johann Christoph. *Weltgeschichte in ihrem ganzen Umfange*. Göttingen, 1785–1787.

Gerhard, Eduard. "Ueber das Verhältniss der Archäologie zur Philologie und zur Kunst." In *Grundriss der Archäologie: für Vorlesungen nach Müllers Handbuch*, edited by Eduard Gerhard, 39–41. Berlin: G. Reimer, 1853.

Germanisches Nationalmuseum Nürnberg. *Das Germanische Nationalmuseum: Organismus und Sammlungen*. Nuremberg: Im Verlag der lit.-artist. Anstalt des German. Museums, 1856.

Germer, Ernst. "Die Vorgeschichte der Gründung des Museums für Völkerkunde zu Leipzig, 1868–1869." *Jahrbuch des Museums für Völkerkunde zu Leipzig* 26 (1969): 5–40.

Geuss, Raymond. "Nietzsche and Genealogy." *European Journal of Philosophy* 2 (1994): 274–92.

Giedion, Sigfried. *Mechanization Takes Command: A Contribution to Anonymous History*. Minneapolis: University of Minnesota Press, 2013 [1948].

Gierl, Martin. *Geschichte als präzisierte Wissenschaft. Johann Christoph Gatterer und die Historiographie des 18. Jahrhunderts im ganzen Umfang*. Stuttgart–Bad Cannstatt: frommann-holzboog, 2012.

Giesebrecht, Wilhelm. "Die Entwicklung der modernen deutschen Geschichtswissenschaft." *Historische Zeitschrift* 1 (1859): 1–17.

Gilbert, Felix. *History: Politics or Culture? Reflections on Ranke and Burckhardt*. Princeton: Princeton University Press, 1986.

Gillespie, Stuart, and Philip R. Hardie, eds. *The Cambridge Companion to Lucretius*. Cambridge, U.K.: Cambridge University Press, 2007.

Giouras, Thanasis. "Wilhelm Roscher: The 'Historical Method' in the Social Sciences: Critical Observations for a Contemporary Evaluation." *Journal of Economic Studies* 22 (1995).

Goethe, Johann Wolfgang von. *Scientific Studies: Collected Works*. Vol. 12. Edited and translated by Douglas Miller. Princeton: Princeton University Press, 1995.

Goethe, Johann Wolfgang von. "Vorarbeiten zu einer Physiologie der Pflanzen." In *Schriften zur Morphologie*, edited by Dorothea Kuhn. Frankfurt a.M.: Deutscher Klassiker Verlag, 1987.

Gombrich, Ernst. *Aby Warburg: An Intellectual Biography*. Chicago: University of Chicago Press, 1986 [1970].

Gombrich, Ernst. *In Search of Cultural History*. London: Oxford University Press, 1969.

Gombrich, Ernst. "Warburg Centenary Lecture." In *Art History as Cultural History: Warburg's Projects*, edited by Richard Woodfield, 33–54. Amsterdam: OPA, 2001.

Gossman, Lionel. *Medievalism and the Ideologies of the Enlightenment: The World and Work of La Curne de Sainte-Palaye*. Baltimore: Johns Hopkins University Press, 1968.

Gräter, Friedrich David. "Uebersicht der Alterthümer der ehmaligen Reichsstadt Hall. Als eine Probe wie ungefähr die Alterthümer der teutschen Städte aufzunehmen wären." *Idunna und Hermode* 2, no. 14 (1813): 65–72.

Grafton, Anthony. "Past Belief: Visions of Early Christianity in Renaissance and Reformation Europe." Paper presented at the Sixty-Third A. W. Mellon Lectures in the Fine Arts, 2014.

Grafton, Anthony. "Polyhistory into Philolog: Notes on the Transformation of German Classical Scholarship, 1780–1850." *History of Universities* 3 (1983): 159–92.

Grafton, Anthony. "Prolegomena to Friedrich August Wolf." *Journal of the Warburg and Courtauld Institutes* 44 (1981): 101–29.

Gran-Aymerich, Ève. "Archéologie et préhistoire: les effets d'une revolution." In *Rêver l'archéologie au XIXe siècle: de la science à l'imaginaire*, ed. Éric Perrin-Saminadayar, 17–46. Saint-Étienne, France: Publications de l'Université de Saint-Étienne, 2001.

Gran-Aymerich, Ève. *Naissance de l'archéologie moderne 1798–1945.* Paris: CNRS Éditions 1998.

Gran-Aymerich, Ève, and Jürgen von Ungern-Sternberg. *L'Antiquité partagée: Correspondances franco-alleamndes (1823–1861).* Paris: Memoires de l'Academie des Inscriptions et Belles-Lettres, 2012.

Grapeler, Daniel. "Ausblick: Heynes Wirkung auf die Archäologie." In *Das Studium des schönen Altertums: Christian Gottlob Heyne und die Entstehung der Klassischen Archäologie*, edited by Daniel Grapeler and Joachim Migl, 121–28. Göttingen: Niedersächsische Staats- und Universitätsbibliothek Göttingen, 2007.

Grapeler, Daniel. "Einleitung: Christian Gottlob Heyne und die Archäologie." In *Das Studium des schönen Altertums: Christian Gottlob Heyne und die Entstehung der Klassischen Archäologie*, edited by Daniel Grapeler and Joachim Migl, 11–15. Göttingen: Niedersächsische Staats- und Universitätsbibliothek Göttingen, 2007.

Grapeler, Daniel. "Heyne und Winckelmann." In *Das Studium des schönen Altertums: Christian Gottlob Heyne und die Entstehung der Klassischen Archäologie*, edited by Daniel Grapeler and Joachim Migl, 17–28. Göttingen: Niedersächsische Staats- und Universitätsbibliothek Göttingen, 2007.

Gravit, Francis W. *The Peiresc Papers.* Ann Arbor: University of Michigan Press, 1950.

Grimmer-Solem, Erik. *The Rise of Historical Economics and Social Reform in Germany, 1864–1894.* Oxford, U.K.: Clarendon Press, 2003.

Guichardet, Jeannine. *Balzac, 'archéologue' de Paris.* Paris: Sedes, 1986.

Güthenke, Constanze. "'Enthusiasm Dwells Only in Specialization.' Classical Philology and Disciplinarity in Nineteenth-Century Germany." In *World Philology*, ed. Sheldon Pollack, Benjamin Elman, Ku-ming Kevin Chang. Cambridge, MA: Harvard University Press, 2015.

Haas, Stefan. *Historische Kulturforschung in Deutschland 1880–1930: Geschichtswissenschaft zwischen Synthese und Pluralität.* Cologne, Weimar, and Vienna: Böhlau Verlag, 1994.

Hackel, Christiane. *Die Bedeutung August Boeckhs für den Geschichtstheoretiker Johann Gustav Droysen.* Würzburg: Königshausen & Neumann, 2006.

Hałub, Marek. *Johann Gustav Gottlieb Büsching, 1783–1829: ein Beitrag zur Begründung der schlesischen Kulturgeschichte.* Wrocław, Poland: Wydawnictwo Uniwersytetu Wriclawskiego, 1997.

Hamilton, Edith, and Huntington Cairns, eds. *The Collected Dialogues of Plato.* Translated by Lane Cooper. Princeton: Princeton University Press, 1961.

Hammerstein, Notker. *Jus und Historie: ein Beitrag zur Geschichte des historischen Denkens an deutschen Universitäten im späten 17. und im 18. Jahrhundert.* Göttingen: Vandenhoeck & Ruprecht, 1972.

Hampe, Theodore, ed. *Das Germanische Nationalmuseum von 1852 bis 1902. Festschrift zum Feier seines fünfzigjährigen Bestehens im Auftrage des Direktoriums.* Leipzig, 1902.

Harless, W. *Erster Jahresbericht des Germanischen Nationalmuseums zu Nürnberg vom September 1853 bis Ende August 1854 mit Rückblick auf das Jahr 1852.* Nuremberg: Artistisch-literar. Anstalt des germ. Museums, 1854.

Harrari, Yuval Noah. *Sapiens: A Brief History of Humankind.* New York: HarperCollins, 2015.

Hartmann, Volker. *Die deutsche Kulturgeschichtsschreibung von ihren Anfängen bis Wilhelm Heinrich Riehl.* PhD dissertation, University of Marburg, 1971.

Haskell, Francis. *History and Its Images: Art and the Interpretation of the Past.* New Haven: Yale University Press, 1993.

Hass, Stefan. *Historische Kulturforschung in Deutschland 1880–1930. Kulturgeschichte zwischen Synthese und Pluralität.* Cologne, Weimar, and Vienna: Böhlau Verlag, 1994.

Hederich, Benjamin. *Anleitung zu den fürnehmsten Philologischen Wissenschaften, nach der Grammatica, Rhetorica und Poetica.* Wittenberg & Zerbst, 1746.

Heeren, A. H. L. "Etwas über die Seltenheit klassischer Geschichtschreiber, besonders in Deutschland." In *Biographische und litterarische Denkschriften*, 433–49. Göttingen: Roewer, 1823.

Heeren, A. H. L. "Johann Christoph Gatterer." In *Biographische und litterarische Denkschriften*, 450–68. Göttingen: Roewer, 1823.

Heeren, A. H. L. *Geschichte der Künste und Wissenschaften seit der Wiederherstellung derselben bis an das Ende des achtzehnten Jahrhunderts.* 2 vols. Göttingen: Georg Rosenbusch, 1797.

Heesen, Anke te, and S. Padberg, eds. *Musée Sentimental 1979.* Ostfildern, Germany: Hatje Cantz Verlag, 2011.

Hegel, G. W. F. *Phenomenology of Spirit.* Translated by A. V. Miller. Oxford, U.K.: Oxford University Press, 1977.

Henning, Eckart. "Die Historischen Hilfswissenschaften—historisch gesehen!" In *Vom Nutz und Frommen der historischen Hilfswissenschaften*, edited by Friedrich Beck and Eckart Henning, 11–22. Neustadt an der Aisch, Germany: Degener, 2000.

Hennings, K. H. "A Note on Marx's Reading List in His *Economic and Philosophical Manuscripts* of 1844." *Economy and Society* 14 (1985), 128–37.

Hering, Robert. "Freiherr vom Stein, Goethe und die Anfänge der MGH." *Jahrbuch des freien deutschen Hochstifts* (1907): 278–323.

Herklotz, Ingo. "Arnaldo Momigliano's 'Ancient History and the Antiquarian': A Critical Review." In *Momigliano and Antiquarianism: Foundations of the Modern Cultural Sciences*, edited by Peter N. Miller, 127–53. Toronto: University of Toronto Press, 2007.

Herklotz, Ingo. *Cassiano dal Pozzo und die Archäologie des 17. Jahrhunderts.* Munich: Hirmer Verlag, 1999.

Herklotz, Ingo. *Die Academia Basiliana: Griechische Philologie, Kirchengeschichte und Unionsbemühungen im Rom der Barberini.* Rome, Freiburg, and Vienna: Herder, 2008.

Herklotz, Ingo. *La Roma degli antiquari: cultura e erudizione tra cinquecento e settecento.* Rome: De Luca Editori d'Arte, 2012.

Heydrich, M. "Gustav Klemm und seine kulturhistorische Sammlung." In *Kultur und Rasse. Otto Reche zum 60. Geburtstag,* edited by Michael Hesch and Günther Spannaus, 305–17. Munich and Berlin: J. F. Lehamnns Verlag, 1939.

Heyne, Christian Gottlob. *Akademische Vorlesungen über die Archäologie der Kunst des Alterthums, besonders der Griechen und Römer.* Braunschweig, 1822.

Heyne, Christian Gottlob. *Einleitung in das Studium der Antike.* Göttingen, 1772.

Heyne, Christian Gottlob. *Sammlung antiquarischer Aufsätze.* Vol. 1. Leipzig, 1778.

Hildebrand, Sonja. " 'Nach einem Systeme zu ordnen, welches die inneren Verbindsfäden dieser bunten Welt am besten zusammenhält': Kulturgeschichtliche Modelle bei Gottfried Semper und Gustav Klemm." In *Gottfried Semper, Dresden und Europa: Die moderne Renaissance der Künste,* edited by Henrik Karge, 237–49. Munich and Berlin: Deutscher Kunstverlag, 2006.

Hillebrand, K. *Étude sur Otfried Müller et sur l'École historique de la philologie allemande.* Paris: Auguste Durand, 1866.

Hochreiter, Walter. *Vom Musentempel zum Lernort: Zur Sozialgeschichte deutscher Museen 1800–1914.* Darmstadt: Wissenschaftliche Buchgesellschaft, 1994.

Hoder, R. "Zu den Judenverfolgungen im Mittelalter." *Zeitschrift für deutsche Kulturgeschichte* 2 (1857): 399–406.

Hölderlin, Friedrich. *Selected Poems and Fragments.* Translated by Michael Hamburger. Edited by Jeremy Adler. London: Penguin, 1998.

Honegger, J. J. *Katechismus der Culturgeschichte.* Leipzig: Verlagsbuchhandlung von J.J. Weber, 1879.

Hont, Istvan. *Jealousy of Trade: International Competition and the Nation-State.* Cambridge, MA, and London: Harvard University Press, 2005.

Hont, Istvan. "Natural Jurisprudence, Political Economy and the Concept of Civilization: Samuel Pufendorf's Theory of *Cultura*." Istvan Hont Papers, Special Collections, University of St Andrews, Scotland.

Horstmann, Axel. *Antike Theoria und moderne Wissenschaft: August Boeckhs Konzeption der Philologie.* Frankfurt a.M., Berlin, and Bern: Peter Lang, 1992.

Horstmann, Axel. " 'Erkenntnis des Erkannten': Philologie und Philosophie bei August Boeckh (1785–1867)." *Zeitschrift für Germanistik* 20, no. 1 (2010): 64–78.

Huizinga, Johan. "The Task of Cultural History." In *Men and Ideas: History, the Middle Ages, the Renaissance: Essays,* 17–76. London: Eyre & Spottieswoode, 1960.

Hummel, Pascale. *Moeurs Érudites. Étude sur la micrologie littéraire* (Allemagne, XVIe–XVIIIe siècles). Droz: Geneva, 2002.

Hunter, Michael. *John Aubrey and the World of Learning.* London: Duckworth, 1975.

Hvattum, Mari, *Gottfried Semper and the Problem of Historicism.* Cambridge, U.K.: Cambridge University Press, 2004.

Iggers, Georg G. "Die Göttinger Historiker und die Geschichtswissenschaft des 18. Jahrhunderts." In *Mentalitäten und Lebensverhältnisse: Beispiele aus der Sozialgeschichte der Neuzeit: Rudolf Vierhaus zum 60. Geburtstag,* edited by Siegfried Bahne, 385–98. Göttingen: Vandenhoeck & Ruprecht, 1982.

Jaeck, Jans-Peter. *Die französische bürgerliche Revolution von 1789 im Frühwerk von Karl Marx (1843–1846): Geschichtsmethodologische Studien.* Berlin: Akademie-Verlag, 1979.

Jahresbericht des Germanischen Nationalmuseums zu Nürnberg von Anfang September 1855 bis 1 October 1856. Vol. 3. Nuremberg and Leipzig: literarisch-artist. Anstalt des germanischen Museums und Friedrich Fleischer, 1856.

Jodl, Friedrich. *Die Culturgeschichtsschreibung, ihre Entwickelung und ihr Problem.* Halle, Germany: CEM Pfeffer, 1878.

Juhel, Vincent, ed. *Arcisse de Caumont (1801–1873): Érudit Normand et Fondateur de l'Archéologie française.* Caen, France: Société des antiquaires de Normandie, 2004.

Kapossy, Béla. *Iselin contra Rousseau: Sociable Patriotism and the History of Mankind.* Basel, Switzerland: Schwabe. 2006.

Kaufmann, Walter. "Nietzsche and Rilke." *Kenyon Review* 17 (1955): 1–22.

Kelley, Donald R. *Fortunes of History: Historical Inquiry from Herder to Huizinga.* New Haven and London: Yale University Press, 2003.

Kelley, Donald R. "The Old Cultural History." *History of the Human Sciences* 9 (1996): 101–26.

Klejn, Leo S. *Soviet Archaeology: Trends, Schools, and History.* Oxford, U.K.: Oxford University Press, 2013.

Klemm, Gustav Friedrich. *Allgemeine Cultur-Geschichte der Menschheit.* 10 vols. Leipzig: B. G. Teubner, 1843–1854.

Klemm, Gustav Friedrich. *Allgemeine Culturwissenschaft: Die materiellen Grundlagen menschlicher Cultur.* 2 vols. Leipzig, 1854–1855.

Klemm, Gustav Friedrich. "Der Hut." In *Gellertbuch*, edited by Christian Fürchtegott and Ferdinand Naumann, 129–35. Dresden: E. E. Meinhold, 1854.

Klemm, Gustav Friedrich. *Die Frauen: culturgeschichtliche Schilderungen des Zustandes und Einflusses der Frauen in den verschiedenen Zonen und Zeitaltern.* 6 vols. Dresden: Arnoldi, 1859.

Klemm, Gustav Friedrich. *Die Königlich Sächsische Porzellan-Sammlung: Eine Uebersicht ihrer vorzüglichsten Schätze, nebst Nachweisungen über die Geschichte der Gefässbildnerei in Thon und Porzellan.* Dresden: Walther'schen Hofbuchhandlung, 1834.

Klemm, Gustav Friedrich. "Die menschliche Kleidung: Culturgeschichtliche Skizze." Dresden, 1856.

Klemm, Gustav Friedrich. "Grundideen zu einer allgemeinen Cultur-Wissenschaft." *Sitzungsberichte der Kaiserlichen Akademie zu Wien. Historisch-philologische Klasse* 7 (1851): 167–90.

Klemm, Gustav Friedrich. *Handbuch der Germanischen Alterthumskunde.* Dresden: Walther'schen Hofbuchhandlung, 1836.

Klemm, Gustav Friedrich. *Vor fünfzig Jahren: Culturgeschichtliche Briefe.* Stuttgart, 1865.

Klemm, Gustav Friedrich. *Zur Geschichte der Sammlungen für Wissenschaft und Kunst in Deutschland.* Zerbst, Germany: G. A. Kummer, 1838.

Klemm, Gustav, and Heinrich Wilhelm Schulz. *Führer durch das Museum des königlich Sächsischen Vereins zu Erforschung und Erhaltung vaterländischer Alterthümer im Königl. Palais des grossen Gartens*, exp. Franz Louis Bösigk. 2nd ed. Dresden: Meinhold, 1868.

Klemm, Heinrich. *Die menschliche Kleidung vom Standpunkte der Gesundheitspflege und Aesthetik.* Dresden: Klemm, 1860.

Klemperer, Viktor. *Lingua Tertii Imperii: Notizbuch eines Philologen*. Berlin: Aufbau-Verlag, 1947.

Klüpfel, K. A. "Die historischen Vereine und Zeitschriften Deutschlands." *Zeitschrift für Geschichtswissenschaft* 1 (1844): 518–59.

Knapp, J. F. "Ueber das Wirken der historischen und antiquarischen Vereine in Bezug auf die Wissenschaft." *Archiv für hessische Geschichte und Alterthumskunde* 5, no. 1 (1846).

Koepping, Klaus-Peter. *Adolf Bastian and the Psychic Unity of Mankind: Foundations of Anthropology in Nineteenth Century Germany*. London and New York: LIT Verlag, 1983.

Koetschau, Karl. "Randbermerkungen zu Denkschrift Wilhelm Bodes über die Berliner Museen." *Museumskunde* 3 (1907): 57–61.

Köhler, Johann David. *Johann David Köhlers P. P. Teutsche Reichs-Historie von Dem Anfang des Teutschen Reichs mit König Ludwigen dem Teutschen biß auf den Badenschen Frieden: Wobey Eines jeglichen Teutschen Königes und Kaysers Handzeichen oder Monogramma in Kupfer accurat vorgestellet wird*. Nuremberg: Riegel, 1736.

Königlich Sächsische Gesellschaft der Wissenschaften zu Leipzig. *Berichte über die Verhandlungen der Königlich Sächsischen Gesellschaft der Wissenschaften zu Leipzig*. Leipzig: Weidmann, 1847.

Königlich Sächsischer Verein für Erforschung und Erhaltung Vaterländischer Alterthümer. *Mittheilungen des Königlich-Sächsischen Vereins für Erforschung und Erhaltung Vaterländischer Alterthümer*. Dresden, 1852.

Krader, Lawrence. "Introduction." In *The Ethnological Notebooks of Karl Marx*, edited by Lawrence Krader. Assen, the Netherlands: Van Gorcum & Co., 1972.

Kraus, Christian Jacob. *Vermischte Schriften über staatswirthschaftliche, philosophische und andere wissenschaftliche Gegenstände*. Edited by Hans von Auserwald. 4 vols. Königsberg: Friedrich Ricolovius, 1809.

Krause, Fritz. "Chronik des Museums 1926–1945." *Jahrbuch des Museums für Völkerkunde zu Leipzig* 10 (1926/1951): 1–46.

Kristiansen, Kristian. "A Short History of Danish Archaeology." In *Archaeological Formation Processes: The Representativity of Archaeological Remains from Danish Prehistory*, edited by Kristian Kristiansen. Copenhagen: National Museum Copenhagen, 1985.

Krug, W. T. *Versuch einer systematischen Encyclopädie der Wissenschaften*. Leipzig, 1796; Jena, 1797.

Kruse, Friedrich. "Preisaufgaben in Betreff der Germanischen und Nordischen Alterthümer überhaupt." *Deutsche Alterthümer oder Archiv für alte und mittlere Geschichte, Geographie und Alterthümer in Sonderheit der germanischen Völkerstämme* 2, no. 7 (1827): 94–101.

Kurin, Richard. *The Smithsonian's History of America in 101 Objects*. New York: Penguin, 2013.

Küttler, Wolfgang, Jörn Rüsen, and Ernst Schulin. *Geschictsdiskurs vol. 2 Anfänge modernen historischen Denkens*. Frankfurt am Main: Fischer Verlag, 1993.

L'École nationale des chartes: histoire de l'École depuis 1821. Thionville, France: Gérard Klopp, 1997.

Lamprecht, Karl. *Alternative zu Ranke: Schriften zur Geschichtstheorie*, ed. Hans Schleier. Leipzig: P. Reclam, 1988.

Lamprecht, Karl. *Deutsches Wirtschaftsleben im Mittelalter: Untersuchungen über die Entwicklung der Materiellen Kultur des platten Landes auf Grund der Quellen zunächst des Mosellandes*, 3 vols. in 4. Leipzig, 1885–1886. Reprinted Aalen: Scientia Verlag, 1969.

Lamprecht, Karl. *Einführung in das historische Denken*. 2nd ed. Leipzig, 1913.

Lamprecht, Karl. *Initial-Ornamentik des VIII. Bis XIII. Jahrhunderts*. Leipzig: Alphons Dürr, 1882.

Lamprecht, Karl. *What is History?* New York: Macmillan, 1905.

Lange, J. F. "Entwurf zu einer historisch-artistischen Darstellung der hessischen Kunstdenkmale." *Zeitschrift des Vereins für hessische Geschichte und Landeskunde* 4 (1847).

Lange-Berndt, Petra. *Materiality*. Documents of Contemporary Art. London and Cambridge, MA: Whitechapel Gallery and MIT Press, 2015.

Larousse, Pierre, and Claude Augé. *Nouveau Larousse Illustré : Dictionnaire Universel Encyclopédique*. Paris: Librairie Larousse, 1904.

Larousse, Pierre. *Grand dictionnaire universel du XIXe siècle, français, historique, géographique, mythologique, bibliographique, littéraire, artistique, scientifique, etc. etc.* Paris: Administration du Grand dictionnaire universel, 1866.

Larroque, Philippe Tamizey de. *Lettres de Peiresc*. 7 vols. Paris: Imprimerie Nationale, 1888–98.

Laudin, Gérard. "L'histoire comme science de l'homme chez Gatterer et Schlözer." In *Göttingen vers 1800: L'Europe des sciences de l'homme*, edited by Hans Erich Bödeker, Philippe Büttgen, and Michel Espagne. Paris: Cerf, 2011.

Lauffer, Otto. "Das Historische Museum: Sein Wesen und Wirken und sein Unterschied von den Kunst- und Kunstgewerbe-Museen." *Museumskunde* 3 (1907): 1–14, 78–99, 179–85, 222–45.

Lauffer, Otto. "Moriz Heyne und die archäologischen Grundlagen der historischen Museen." *Museumskunde* 2 (1906): 153–62.

Lavergne-Peguilhen, Moritz von. *Grundzüge der Gesellschaftswissenschaft*. 2 vols. in 1. Leipzig, 1838.

Lehmann, Alfred. "85 Jahre Museum für Völkerkunde zu Leipzig." *Jahrbuch des Museums für Völkerkunde zu Leipzig* 12 (1951): 11–51.

Lehmann, Cornelia. *Die Auseinandersetzung zwischen Wort- und Sachphilologie in der deutschen klassischen Altertumswissenschaft des 19. Jahrhunderts*. PhD dissertation, Humboldt University Berlin, 1964.

Leibniz, Gottfried Wilhelm. *Protogaea: De l'aspect primitif de la terre et des traces d'une histoire très ancienne que renferment les monuments mêmes de la nature. Sive de prima facie telluris et antiquissimae historiae vestigiis in ipsis naturae monumentis dissertatio, ex schedis manuscriptis viri illustris in lucem edita*. Translated by Bertrand de Saint-Germain. Edited with introduction and notes by Jean-Marie Barrande. Toulouse: Presses Universitaires du Mirail, 1993.

Leibniz, Gottfried Wilhelm. *Schriften und Briefe zur Geschichte*. Edited by Malte-Ludolf Babin and Gerd van den Heuvel. Hanover: Verlag Hahnsche Buchhandlung 2004.

Lenormant, Charles. "Archéologie." *Revue archéologique* 1 (1844): 1–17.

Leopold, Joan. *Culture in Comparative and Evolutionary Perspective: E. B. Tylor and the Making of Primitive Culture.* Berlin: D. Reimer, 1980.

Levezow, Konrad. *Über archäologische Kritik und Hermeneutik: Eine Abhandlung gelesen in der Königlichen Akademie der Wissenschaften zu Berlin am 21. November 1833.* Berlin: Königlich Akademie der Wissenschaften, 1834.

Levine, Emily. *Dreamland of Humanists: Warburg, Cassirer, Panofsky, and the Hamburg School.* Chicago: University of Chicago Press, 2013.

Levine, Philippa. *The Amateur and the Professional. Antiquarians, Historians, and Archaeologists in Victorian England, 1838–1886.* Cambridge, U.K.: Cambridge University Press, 1986.

Lewald, Ursula. "Karl Lamprecht und die Rheinische Geschichtsforschung." *Rheinische Vierteljahresblätter* 21, nos. 1/4 (1956): 279–304.

Lissarrague, François, and Alain Schnapp. "Tradition und Erneurung in der Klassischen Archäologie in Frankreich." In *Klassische Archäologie. Eine Einführung,* edited by A. Borbein, T. Hölscher, and P. Zanker. Berlin, Reimer, 2000.

Lutz, Deborah. *The Brönte Cabinet: Three Lives in Nine Objects.* New York: W. W. Norton, 2015.

Lutz, Gerhard. "Johann Ernst Fabri und die Anfänge der Volksforschung im ausgehenden 18. Jahrhundert." *Zeitschrift für Volkskunde* 69 (1973): 19–42.

Mabillon, Jean. *De re Diplomatica libri VI. In quibus quidquid ad veterum instrumentorum antiquitatem, materiam, scripturam, & stilum; quidquid ad sigilla, monogrammata, subscriptiones, ac notas chronologicas; quidquid inde ad antiquariam, historicam, forensemque discplinam pertinet, explicatur & illustratur.* Paris: Louis Billaine, 1681.

Mabillon, Jean, Charles Robustel, and Alan de Bovard de Laforest. *Librorum de re diplomatica supplementum.: In quo archetypa in his libris pro regulis proposita, ipsaeque regulae denuo confirmantur, novisque speciminibus & argumentis asseruntur & illustrantur.* Paris, 1704.

MacGregor, Neil. *A History of the World in 100 Objects.* New York: Viking, 2011.

Mallgrave, Harry Francis. *Gottfried Semper: Architect of the Nineteenth Century.* New Haven and London: Yale University Press, 1996.

Manias, Chris. "The Growth of Race and Culture in Nineteenth-Century Germany: Gustav Klemm and the Universal History of Humanity." *Modern Intellectual History* 9 (2012): 1–31.

Marès Deulorol, Frederic. *El mundo fascinante del coleccionismo y de las antigüedades: Memorias de la vida de un coleccionista.* Barcelona, 1977.

Marino, Luigi. *I Maestri della Germania. Göttingen 1770–1820.* Turin: Einaudi, 1975.

Marx, Karl. *Karl Marx, Friedrich Engels Gesamtausgabe.* Vol. 4. Berlin: Dietz, 1981.

Mazzocco, Angelo. "Biondo Flavio and the Antiquarian Tradition." PhD dissertation, University of California, Berkeley, 1973.

Meier, Allison. "Ole Worm Returns: An Iconic 17th Century Curiosity Cabinet Is Obsessively Recreated." Available at www.atlasobscura.com/articles/ole-worm-cabinet, accessed December 3, 2015.

Meiners, Christoph. *Geschichte des weiblichen Geschlechts.* 4 vols. Hanover: Helwingsche Hofbuchhandlung, 1788–1800.

Mendyk, Stan A. E. *"Speculum Britanniae": Regional Study, Antiquarianism, and Science in Britain to 1700.* Toronto: University of Toronto Press, 1989.

Merjian, Ara H. " 'Il faut méditerraniser la peinture': Giorgio de Chirico's Metaphysical Painting, Nietzsche, and the Obscurity of Light." *California Italian Studies* 1 (2010).

Milford, Karl. "Roscher's Epistemological and Methodological Position: Its Importance for the *Methodenstreit*." *Journal of Economic Studies* 22, 3 (1995): 26–52.

Miller, Peter N. "The Antiquary's Art of Comparison: Peiresc and Abraxas." In *Philologie und Erkenntnis. Beiträge zu Begriff und Problem frühneuzeitlicher "Philologie,"* edited by Ralph Häfner, 57–94. Tübingen: Max Niemeyer Verlag, 2001.

Miller, Peter N. "Description Terminable and Interminable: Looking at the Past, Nature, and Peoples in Peiresc's Archive." In *"Historia": Empricism and Erudition in Early Modern Europe*, edited by Gianna Pomata and Nancy Siraisi, 355–97. Cambridge, MA: MIT, 2005.

Miller, Peter N. "The Germanisches Nationalmuseum and the Museums Debate in Later 19th Century Germany." In *The Challenge of the Object: 33rd Congress of the International Committee of the History of Art, Nuremberg, 15th–20th July 2012*, edited by Georg Ulrich Großmann and Petra Krutisch. 4 vols. Nuremberg: Verlag des Germanischen Nationalmuseums, 2013.

Miller, Peter N. "Major Trends in European Antiquarianism, Petrarch to Winckelmann." In *The Oxford History of Historical Writing*, edited by Daniel Woolf, vol 3, 244–60. Oxford, U.K.: Oxford University Press, 2012.

Miller, Peter N. "Peiresc and the Benedictines of Saint-Maur: Further Thoughts on the 'Ethics of the Historian.' " In *Europäische Geschichtskulturen um 1700 zwischen Gelehrsamkeit, Politik und Konfession*, edited by Thomas Wallnig, Ines Peper, Thomas Stockinger, and Patrick Fiska, 361–78. Berlin: De Gruyter, 2012.

Miller, Peter N. *Peiresc's "History of Provence": Antiquarianism and the Discovery of a Medieval Mediterrranean*. Philadelphia: American Philosophical Society, 2011.

Miller, Peter N. *Peiresc's Mediterranean World*. Cambridge, MA: Harvard University Press, 2015.

Miller, Peter N. "Thinking with Thomas Browne: Sebald and the Nachleben of the Antiquarian." In *Sir Thomas Browne: The World Proposed*, edited by Reid Barbour and Claire Preston, 311–28. Oxford, U.K.: Oxford University Press, 2008.

Miller, Peter N., and Peter Burke. *Momigliano and Antiquarianism: Foundations of the Modern Cultural Sciences*. Toronto: University of Toronto Press, 2015.

Miller, Peter N., and François Louis, eds. *Antiquarianism and Intellectual Life in Europe and China, 1500–1800*. Ann Arbor: University of Michigan Press, 2012.

Molhuysen, P. C., and B. L. Meulenbroek, eds. *Briefwisseling van Hugo Grotius*. Vol. 4. The Hague, 1964.

Momigliano, Arnaldo. "Ancient History and the Antiquarian." *Journal of the Warburg and Courtauld Institutes* 13 (1950): 285–315.

Momigliano, Arnaldo. *Classical Foundations of Modern Historiography*. Berkeley and London, 1990.

Momigliano, Arnaldo. "J. G. Droysen between Greeks and Jews." *History and Theory* 9 (1970): 139–53.

Momigliano, Arnaldo. "La Storia Antica in Inghilterra." In *Sesto contributo alla storia degli studi classici e del mondo antico*, 761–68. Rome: Edizioni di Storia e Letteratura, 1980.

Momigliano, Arnaldo. Review of Lionel Gossman, *Orpheus Philologus*. In *Ottavo Contributo alla Storia degli Studi Classici e del Mondo Antico*, 409–13. Rome: Edizioni di Storia e Letteratura, 1987

Momgliano, Arnaldo. "Antiquari e storici dell'antichità." In *Decimo Contributo alla storia degli studi classici e del mondo antico*, edited by Riccardo Di Donato, 285–90. Rome: Edizioni di Storia e Letteratura, 2012.

Momigliano, Arnaldo. "Benedetto Croce (1950)." In *Decimo Contributo alla storia degli studi classici e del mondo antico*, edited by Riccardo Di Donato, 531–41. Rome: Edizioni di Storia e Letteratura, 2012.

Momigliano, Arnaldo. "Philology and History." In *Decimo Contributo alla storia degli studi classici e del mondo antico*, edited by Riccardo Di Donato, 291–95. Rome: Edizioni di Storia e Letteratura, 2012.

Morley, Neville. "Thucydides, History, and Historicism in Wilhelm Roscher." In *Thucydides and the Modern World: Reception, Reinterpretation, and Influence from the Renaissance to the Present*, edited by Katherine Harloe and Neville Morley, 115–39. Cambridge, U.K.: Cambridge University Press, 2012.

Mühle, Eduard. *Für Volk und deutschen Osten: Der Historiker Hermann Aubin und die deutsche Ostforschung*. Düsseldorf: Droste Verlag, 2005.

Müller, K. O. *Ancient Art and its Remains: Or a Manual of the Archaeology of Art*. Edited by F. G. Welcher. Translated by John Leitch. London A. Fullarton, 1850.

Müller, K. O. *Handbuch der Archäologie der Kunst*. 2nd ed. Göttingen, 1835.

Müller, K. O. *Handbuch der Archaeologie der Kunst*. Edited by Fr. G. Welcker. 3rd ed. Stuttgart: Albert Heitz, 1878.

Münch, Ernst Hermann Joseph. *Grundriß einer teutschen Alterthumskunde zum Gebrauche für Vorlesungen und zum Selbststudium*. Freiburg im Breisgau: Friedrich Wagner, 1827.

Münchner Stadtmuseum. "'I am the only one who owns these things.' The Passions of Collecting." Available at www.muenchner-stadtmuseum.de/en/sonderausstellungen/archive/2015/i-am-the-only-one-who-owns-these-things-thepassionofcollecting.html, accessed October 2, 2015.

Mundt, Barbara. *Die deutschen Kunstgewerbemuseen im 19. Jahrhundert*. Munich: Prestel, 1974.

Mundt, Barbara. "Über einige Gemeinsamkeiten und Unterschiede von kunstgewerblichen und kulturgeschichtlichen Museen." In *Das Kunst- und kulturgeschichtliche Museum im 19. Jahrhundert: Vorträge des Symposions im Germanischen Nationalmuseum, Nürnberg*, edited by Bernward Deneke and Rainer Kahsnitz, 143–49. Munich: Prestel, 1977.

Museum Boijmans Van Beuningen. "Collection Building—Rotterdam's Treasure House." Available at http://collectiegebouw.boijmans.nl/en/, accessed October 29, 2015.

Nerdinger, Winfried. "Der Architekt Gottfried Semper: 'Der notwendige Zusammenhang der Gegenwart mit allen Jahrhunderten der Vergangenheit.'" In *Gottfried Semper, 1803–1879: Architektur und Wissenschaft*, 9–50. Zurich: Prestel, 2003.

Nietzsche, Friedrich. *Anti-Education.* Introduction and notes by Paul Reitter and Chad Wellmon. Translated by Damion Searls. New York: New York Review Books, 2015.

Nietzsche, Friedrich. *The Complete Works of Friedrich Nietzsche.* Vol. 3. Translated by Gary Handwerk. Stanford: Stanford University Press, 1990.

Nietzsche, Friedrich. "Encyclopädie der klassischen Philologie." In *Nietzsche Werke,* edited by Fritz Bornmann and Mario Carpitella. Pt. 2, vol. 3. Berlin: Walter de Gruyter, 1993.

Nietzsche, Friedrich. "History in the Service and Disservice of Life." In *Unmodern Obsevations/Unzeitgemässe Betrachtungen,* edited by William Arrowsmith, 99–103. New Haven and London: Yale University Press, 1990.

Nietzsche, Friedrich. *Werke: Kritische Gesamtausgabe,* Vol. 3, no. 4. Berlin: W. de Gruyter, 1978.

Nippel, Wilfried. "Boeckhs Beitrag zur Alten Geschichte." In *August Boeckh: Philologie, Hermeneutik und Wissenschaftspolitik,* edited by Christiane Hackel and Sabine Seifert, 45–58. Berlin: Berliner Wissenschafts Verlag, 2013.

Nippel, Wilfried. "Der 'antiquarische Bauplatz': Theodor Mommsen's Römisches Staatsrecht." In *Theodor Mommsen: Gelehrter, Politiker und Literat,* edited by Josef Wiesehöfer, 165–84. Stuttgart: Franz Steiner Verlag, 2005.

Nippel, Wilfried. "Philologenstreit und Schulpolitik: Zur Kontroverse zwischen Gottfried Hermann und August Boeckh." In *Geschichtsdiskurs,* vol. 3, ed. W. Küttler, J. Rüsen, E. Schulin, 244–53. Frankfurt am Main: Fischer Verlag, 1993.

Nipperdey, Thomas. "Kulturgeschichte, Sozialgeschichte, historische Anthropologie." *Vierteljahrschrift für Sozial- und Wirtschaftsgeschichte* 55 (1968): 145–64.

Oestreich, Gerhard. "Huizinga, Lamprecht und die deutsche Geschichtsphilosophie: Huizingas Groninger Antrittsvorlesung von 1905." *Bijdragen en Mededelingen betreffende de Geschiedenis der Nederlanden* 88 (1973): 143–70.

Orlinska, Grayna. *Catalogue of the "Germanic" Antiquities from the Klemm Collection in The British Museum.* London: British Museum, 2001.

Osann, F. "Der Sophist Hippias als Archaeolog." *Rheinisches Museum für Philologie,* new series 2 (1843): 495–521.

Parry, Graham. *The Trophies of Time: English Antiquarians of the Seventeenth Century.* Oxford, U.K.: Oxford University Press, 1995.

Pastoureau, Michel. *Une histoire symbolique du Moyen Âge occidental.* Paris: Le Seuil, 2004.

Peez, Dr. "Berührungspunkte zwischen Kulturgeschichte und Nationalökonomie." *Zeitschrift für deutsche Kulturgeschichte* 3 (1858): 415–26.

Penny, H. Glenn. "Bastian's Museum: On the Limits of Empiricism and the Transformation of German Ethnology." In *Worldly Provincialism: German Anthropology in the Age of Empire,* edited by Matti Bunzl and H. Glenn Penny, 86–126. Ann Arbor: University of Michigan Press, 2003.

Penny, H. Glenn. *Objects of Culture Ethnology and Ethnographic Museums in Imperial Germany.* Chapel Hill: University of North Carolina Press, 2002.

Peters, Martin. *Altes Reich und Europa: Der Historiker, Statistiker und Publizist August Ludwig (v.) Schlözer (1735–1809).* Münster: Lit, 2003.

Petersen, F. Christian. *Allgemeine Einleitung in das Studium der Archäologie.* Translated by P. Friedrichsen. Leipzig: Hahn'schen verlag, 1829 [1825].

Phillips, Mark. *Society and Sentiment: Genres of Historical Writing in Britain, 1740–1820.* Princeton: Princeton University Press, 2000.

Piggott, Stuart. *Ruins in a Landscape: Essays in Antiquarianism.* Edinburgh: Edinburgh University Press, 1976.

Pigott, Stuart. *William Stukeley, An Eighteenth-Century Antiquary.* New York: Thames and Hudson, 1985.

Pippin, Robert B. *Interanimations: Receiving Modern German Philosophy.* Chicago: University of Chicago Press, 2015.

Plate, S. Brent. *A History of Religion in 5½ Objects: Bringing the Spiritual to Its Senses.* Boston: Beacon Press, 2014.

Platner, Eduard. *Ueber wissenschaftliche Begründung und Behandlung der Antiquitäten insbesondere der römischen.* Marburg, 1818.

Platonova, Nadezhda I. "The Phenomenon of Pre-Soviet Archaeology: Archival Studies in the History of Russian Archaeology—Methods and Results." In *Archives, Ancestors, Practices: Archaeology in the Light of its History,* edited by Nathan Schlanger and Jarl Nordbladh, 47–58. Oxford and New York: Berghahn Books, 2008.

Poiss, Thomas. "Die Unendliche Aufgabe: August Boeckh als Begründer des Philologischen Seminars." In *Die modernen Väter der Antike: Die Entwicklung der Altertumswissenschaften an Akademie und Universität im Berlin des 19. Jahrhunderts,* edited by A. M. Baertschi and C. G. King, vol. 3, 45–72. Berlin: Walter de Gruyter, 2009.

Pomata, Gianna. "Epistemic Genres or Styles of Thinking? Tools for the Cultural History of Knowledge." Available at www.unige.ch/rectorat/maison-histoire/mediatheque/professeursinvites/pomata/, accessed August 1, 2016.

Porter, James I. *Nietzsche and the Philology of the Future.* Stanford: Stanford University Press, 2000).

Preller, Ludwig. "Ueber die wissenschaftliche Behandlung der Archäologie [1845]." In *Ausgewählte Aufsätze aus dem Gebiete der classischen Alterthumswissenschaft,* edited by Reinhold Köhler, 385–90. Berlin: Weidmannsche Buchhandlung, 1864.

Prete, Ivano dal. "'Being the World Eternal': The Age of the Earth in Renaissance Italy." *Isis* 105 (2014): 292–317.

Preusker, Karl Benjamin. *Beschreibung einiger bei Radeberg im Königreiche Sachsen aufgefundenen Urnen mit unbekannten Charakteren: nebst Nachrichten von einigen andern alterthümlichen Gegenständen dasiger Gegend.* Halle, Germany: Ruff, 1828.

Preusker, Karl Benjamin. *Blicke in die vaterländische Vorzeit, Sitten, Sagen, Bauwerke und Geräthe, zur Erläuterung des öffentlichen aund häuslichen Volkslebens im heidnischen Alterthume und im christlichen Mittelalter.* Leipzig: Hinrichs, 1841.

Preusker, Karl Benjamin. *Ober-Lausitzische Alterthümer: erster Beitrag.* Görlitz, Germany: Dressler, 1828.

Preusker, Karl Benjamin. "Ueber die deutsche Alterthumsforschung der neuesten Zeit." *Neue Zeitschrift für die Geschichte der germanischen Völker* 1, no. 3 (1832): 86–94.

Preusker, Karl Benjamin. *Ueber Mittel und Zweck der vaterländischen Alterthumsforschung: eine Andeutung; der Oberlausitzischen Gesellschaft der Wissenschaften zu Görlitz bei deren funfzigjährigen Stiftungsfeier am 29. Julius 1829 ehrerbietigst dargebracht.* Leipzig: Nauck, 1829.

Reill, Peter Hans. "History and Hermeneutics in the Aufklärung: The Thought of Johann Christoph Gatterer." *Journal of Modern History* 45, no. 1 (1973): 24–51.

Reinach, Salomon. *Manuel de philologie classique.* 2nd ed. Paris: Hachette, 1883–1884.

Rieke-Müller, Annelore and Siegfried Müller. "Konzeptionen der Kulturgeschichte um die Mitte des 19. Jahrhunderts: Das Germanische Nationalmuseum in Nürnberg und die Zeitschrift für deutsche Kulturgeschichte." *Archiv für Kulturgeschichte* 82 (2000): 345–76.

Rilke, Rainer Maria. *Ahead of All Parting: The Selected Poetry and Prose of Rainer Maria Rilke.* Translated by Stephen Mitchell. New York: Modern Library Edition, 1995.

Rilke, Rainer Maria. *Rodin and Other Prose Pieces.* Translated by C. Craig Houston with an introduction by William Tucker. London: Quartet Books, 1986.

Rilke, Rainer Maria, and Auguste Rodin. *Auguste Rodin.* Leipzig: Insel-Verlag, 1919.

Robert, Carl. *Archäologische Hermeneutik: Anleitung zur Deutung klassischer Bildwerke.* Berlin: Weidmannsche Buchhandlung, 1919.

Roberts, Sam. *A History of New York in 101 Objects.* New York: Simon and Schuster, 2014.

Rödiger, I. "Gustav Friedrich Klemm: Allgemeine Cultur-Geschichte der Menschheit." In *Hauptwerke der Ethnologie,* edited by Christian F. Feest and Karl-Heinz Kohl, 188–92. Stuttgart: Alfred Kröner Verlag, 2001.

Rokem. Freddie. *Philosophers and Thespians: Thinking Performance.* Stanford: Stanford University Press, 2009.

Rommel, Chr. v. "Ueber Quellen und Hülfsmittel der hessischen Geschichte." *Zeitschrift des Vereins für hessische Geschichte und Landeskunde* 1 (1837): 77–119.

Roscher, Wilhelm. *Ansichten der Volkswirthschaft aus dem geschichtlichen Standpunkte.* Leipzig and Heidelberg, 1861.

Roscher, Wilhelm. *Geschichte der National-Oekonomik in Deutschland.* Munich: R. Oldenbourg, 1874.

Roscher, Wilhelm. *Grundriss zu Vorlesungen über die Staatswirtschaft nach geschichtlicher Methode.* Göttingen: Vandenhoeck und Ruprecht, 1842.

Roscher, Wilhelm. *Leben, Werk und Zeitalter des Thukydides.* Göttingen, 1842.

Rowland, Ingrid. "Raphael, Angelo Colocci, and the Genesis of the Architectural Orders." *Art Bulletin* 76 (1994): 81–104.

Rühs, Friedrich. *Entwurf einer Propädeutik des historischen Studiums (Berlin 1811).* Edited with an introduction by Hans Schleier and Dirk Fleischer. Waltrop, Germany: Hartmut Spenner, 1997.

Rupp-Eisenreich, Brita. "La Leçon des mots et des choses: philologie, linguistique et ethnologie (de August Boeckh à Heymann Steinthal)." In *Philologiques I: Contribution à l'histoire des disciplines littéraires en France et en Allemagne au XIXe siècle,* edited by Michel Espagne and Michel Werner, 365–91. Paris: Éditions de la Maison des Sciences de l'Homme, 1990.

Rydell, Robert. *All the World's a Fair: Visions of Empire at American Expositions, 1876–1916.* Chicago and London: University of Chicago Press, 1984.

Saminadayar-Perrin, Corinne. "Pages de pierre. Les apories du roman archéologique." In *Rêver l'archéololgie au XIXe siècle: de la science à l'imaginaire,* edited by Éric Perrin-Saminadayar, 123–46. Saint-Étienne, France: Publications de l'Université de Saint-Étienne, 2001.

Sawilla, Jan Marco. *Antiquarianismus, Hagiographie und Historie im 17. Jahrhundert: Zum Werk der Bollandisten; ein wissenschaftshistorischer Versuch.* Tübingen: Niemeyer Verlag, 2009.

Scheel, Günter. "Leibniz und die deutsche Geschichtswissenschaft um 1700." In *Historische Forschung im 18. Jahrhundert: Organisation. Zielsetzung. Ergebnisse,* edited by Karl Hammer and Jürgen Voss, 82–101. Bonn, 1976.

Schleier, Hans. *Alternative zu Ranke.* Leipzig: Reclam, 1988.

Schleier, Hans. *Geschichte der deutschen Kulturgeschichtsschreibung. Band 1 Vom Ende des 18. Bis Ende des 19. Jahrhunderts.* Waltrop, Germany: Hartmut Spenner, 2008.

Schleier, Hans. "Wachsmuths Entwurf einer Theorie der Geschichte aus dem Jahre 1820." *Jahrbuch für Geschichte* 37 (1988): 103–35.

Schlereth, Thomas J. "Material Culture Studies in America, 1876–1976." In *Material Culture Studies in America,* edited by Thomas J. Schlereth, 1–75. Nashville: American Association for State and Local History, 1982.

Schlereth, Thomas J. *Cultural History and Material Culture: Everyday Life, Landscapes, Museums.* Charlottesville and London: University Press of Virginia, 1992.

Schlözer, August Ludwig von. *Theorie der Statistik: nebst Ideen über das Studium der Politik.* Göttingen: Vandenhoek und Ruprecht, 1804.

Schlözer, August Ludwig. "Vorstellung seiner Universal-Historie." In *Theoretiker Deutscher Aufklärungshistorie,* edited by Horst Walter Blanke and Dirk Fleisher, 663–88. Stuttgart–Bad Cannstatt, 1990.

Schmidt, Heinrich. "Heimat und Geschichte: Zum Verhältnis von Heimatbewußtsein und Geschichtsforschung." *Niedersächsiches Jahrbuch für Ladesgeschichte* 39 (1967): 1–44.

Schönebaum, Herbert, ed. *Karl Lamprecht, Ausgewählte Schriften zur Wirtschafts- und Kulturgeschichte und zur Theorie der Geschichtswissenschaft.* Aalen, Germany: Scientia, 1974.

Schnapp, Alain. "Between Antiquarians and Archaeologists—Continuities and Ruptures." *Antiquity* 76 (2002): 134–40.

Schnapp, Alain. *La Conquête du Passé.* Paris: Carré, 1994. Translated as *The Discovery of the Past.* London: British Museum, 1996.

Schnapp, Alain, Lothar von Falkenhausen, Peter N. Miller, and Tim Murray, eds. *World Antiquarianism: Comparative Perspectives.* Los Angeles: Getty Research Institute, 2013.

Schönebaum, Herbert. "Gustav Mevissen und Karl Lamprecht." *Rheinische Vierteljahresblätter* 17 (1952): 180–96.

Schönemann, D. C. T. G. *Grundriß einer Encyclopädie der historischen Wissenschaften zum Gebrauch seiner Vorlesungen entworfen.* Göttingen: Dieterich, 1799.

Schorn-Schütte, Luise. *Karl Lamprecht: Kulturgeschichtsschreibung zwischen Wissenschaft und Politik.* Schriftenreihe der historischen Kommission bei der Bayerischen Akademie der Wissenschaften, Bd. 22. Göttingen: Vandenhoeck & Ruprecht, 1984.

Schorn-Schötte, Luise. "Karl Lamprecht: Wegbereiter einer Historischen Sozialwissenschaft." In *Deutsche Geschichtswissenschaft um 1900,* edited by Notker Hammerstein, 144–90. Stuttgart: Steiner Verlag, 1988.

Schorn-Schütte, Luise. "Territorialgeschichte—Provinzialgeschichte—Landesgeschichte—Regionalgeschichte. Ein Beitrag zur Wissenschaftsgeschichte der

Landesgeschichtsschreibung." In *Civitatum Communitas: Studien zum Europäischen Städtewesen. Festschrift Heinz Stoob zum 65. Geburtstag*, edited by Helmut Jäger, Franz Petri, and Heinz Quirin, vol. 2, 390–416. Cologne and Vienna: Böhlau Verlag, 1984.

Scurr, Ruth. *John Aubrey: My Life*. London: Chatto & Windus, 2015.

Seifart, Karl. "Streitbare Juden im Mittelalter." *Zeitschrift für deutsche Kulturgeschichte* 2 (1857): 521–27.

Seiler, Harald. *Die Anfänge der Kunstpflege in Westfalen (Beitrag zur Wesensforschung des Biedermeier)*. Münster in Westfalen: F. Coppenrath, 1937.

Semper, Gottfried. *The Ideal Museum: Practical Art in Metals and Hard Materials*. Vienna: Schlebrügge, 2007.

Shapton, Leanne. *Important Artifacts and Personal Property from the Collection of Lenore Doolan and Harold Morris, including Books, Street Fashion, and Jewelry*. New York: Farrar Straus and Giroux, 2009.

Sheehan, Jonathan. *The Enlightenment Bible: Translation, Scholarship, Culture*. Princeton: Princeton University Press, 2005.

Shionya, Yuicihi, ed. *The German Historical School: The Historical and Ethical Approach to Economics*. London: Routledge, 2000.

Siebenkees, Johann Philipp. *Handbuch der Archäologie oder Anleitung zur Kenntniss der Kunstwerke des Alterthums und zur Geschichte der Kunst der Alten Völker*. Nuremberg: Stein, 1799.

Simon, Christian. "Gesellschaftsgeschichte in der ersten Hälfte des 19. Jahrhunderts—Frankreich und Deutschland." In *Geschichtsdiskurs vol. 3. die Epochen der Historisierung*, ed W. Küttler, J. Rüsen, E. Schulin, 355–76. Frankfurt am Main: Fischer Verlag, 1993.

Smail, Daniel Lord, and Andrew Shryock. *Deep History: The Architecture of Past and Present*. Ann Arbor: University of Michigan Press, 2011.

Solinas, Francesco, ed. *Cassiano dal Pozzo: atti del seminario internazionale di studi*. Rome: De Luca, 1989.

Sommer, Ulrike. "Choosing Ancestors: The Mechanisms of Ethnic Ascription in the Age of Patriotic Antiquarianism (1815–1850)." In *Archives Ancestors Practices: Archaeology in the Light of its History*, edited by Nathan Schlanger and Jarl Nordbladh, 236–38. Oxford, U.K.: Berghahn, 2008.

Spies, Gerd. "Die kunst- und kulturgeschichtlichen Lokal- und Regionalmuseen." In *Das Germanische National-museum Nürnberg 1852–1977*, edited by Bernward Deneke and Rainer Kahsnitz, 77–81. Munich and Berlin: Deutschen Kunstverlag, 1978.

Spon, Jacob. *Réponse a la critique publiée par M. Guillet, sur le Voyage de Grece de Iacob Spon*. Lyon, 1679.

Spon, Jacob. *Un humaniste lyonnais du xviie siècle*. Edited by Roland Étienne and Jean-Claude Mossière. Lyon: Publications de la bibliothèque Salomon-Reinach, 1993.

Spon, Jacob. *Voyage d'Italie, de Dalmatie, de Grèce et du Levant. Fait es Années 1675 & 1676*. Amsterdam: Henry & Theodore Boom, 1679.

Stagl, Justin. "Chapter 6: August Ludwig Schlözer and the Study of Mankind According to Peoples." In *A History of Curiosity: The Theory of Travel 1550–1800*, edited by Justin Stagl, 233–68. Chur, Switzerland: Harwood Academic Publications, 1995.

Stallybrass, Peter. "Marx's Coat." In *Border Fetishisms: Material Objects in Unstable Spaces*, edited by P. Spyer, 183–207. London: Routledge, 1998.

Stark, Karl Bernhard. *Handbuch der Archäologie der Kunst*. Stuttgart: A. Heitz, 1880.

Stark, Karl Bernhard. Review of Müller, *Handbuch der Archäologie der Kunst*. In *Zeitschrift für die Alterthumswissenschaft* 10 (1852): 43–45.

Stark, Karl Bernhard. "Ueber Kunst und Kunstwissenschaft auf deutschen Universitäten." In *Vorträge und Aufsätze aus dem Gebiete der Archäologie und Kunstgeschichte*, edited by Gottfried Kinkel, 6–7. Leipzig: G. B. Teubner, 1880.

Starkey, David, and David Gaimster. *Making History: Antiquaries in Britain, 1707–2007*. London: Royal Academy Books, 2007.

Stedman Jones, Gareth. *Karl Marx: Greatness and Illusion*. Cambridge, MA and London: Harvard University Press, 2016.

Steffens, Wilhelm. "Paul Wigand und die Anfänge planmäßiger landesgeschichtlicher Forschung in Westfalen." *Westfälische Zeitschrift* 94 (1938): 143–237.

Stenhouse, William. "Antiquarianism." In *The Classical Tradition*, edited by Anthony Grafton, Glenn Most, and Salvatore Settis, 51–53. Cambridge, MA, and London: Harvard University Press, 2010.

Stenhouse, William. *Reading Inscriptions and Writing Ancient History: Historical Scholarship in the Late Renaissance*. London: Institute of Classical Studies, University of London School of Advanced Study, 2005.

Stenhouse, William. "The Renaissance Foundations of European Antiquarianism." In *World Antiquarianism*, edited by Alain Schnapp, et al., 295–316. Los Angeles: Getty Publications, 2015.

Sternke, René. *Böttiger und der archäologische Diskurs*. Berlin: Akademie Verlag, 2008.

Stocking, Jr., George W. "Matthew Arnold, E. B. Tylor, and the Uses of Invention." *American Anthropologist* 65 (1963): 783–99.

Streissler, Erich W. "Wilhelm Roscher als führender Wirtschaftshistoriker." In *Vademecum zu einem Klassiker der historischen Schule*, edited by Bertram Schefold, 37–121. Düsseldorf, 1994.

Sulzer, Johann Georg. *Kurzer Begriff aller Wissenschaften und anderen Theile der Gelehrsamkeit*. 2nd ed. Frankfurt: University of Leipzig, 1759.

Sweet, Rosemary. *Antiquaries: The Discovery of the Past in Eighteenth-Century Britain*. London and New York: Hambledon and London, 2004.

Swenson, Astrid. *The Rise of Heritage: Preserving the Past in France, Germany, and England, 1789–1914*. Cambridge, U.K.: Cambridge University Press, 2013.

Telman, Jeremy D. A. Review of *Theoretiker der deutschen Aufklärungshistorie*. In *History and Theory* 33 (1994): 249–65.

Thierry, Augustin. *"Dix ans D'Études Historiques," and Narratives of the Merovingian Era; or, Scenes of the Sixth Century with Autobiographical Preface*. Philadelphia: Carey and Hart, 1845.

Thomsen, Christian Jürgenson, Paul Detlev Christian Paulson, and N. M. Petersen. *Leitfaden zur Nordischen Altertumskunde*. Copenhagen: Die Gesellschaft, 1837.

Thoreau, Henry David. *The Journal, 1837–1861*. Edited by Damion Searls. New York: New York Review Books, 2009.

Thurnwald, R. "Über Völkerkundemuseen, ihre wissenschaftlichen Bedingungen und Ziele." *Museumskunde* 8, no. 4 (1912).

Toustain, Charles-François, and René-Prosper Tassin. *Nouveau Traité de Diplomatique, ou l'on examine les fondemens de cet art: on etablist des regles sur le discernement des titres, et l'on expose historiquement les caracteres des bulles Pontificales et des diplomes donné en chaque siècle: avec des éclaircissemens sur un nombre considerable de points d'Histoire, de Chronologie, de Critique & de Discipline; & la Réfutation de diverses accusations intentées contre beaucoup d'Archives célèbres, & sur tout contre celles des anciennes Eglises.* 5 vols. Paris, 1750–1765.

Tribe, Keith. *The Economy of the Word: Language, History, and Economics.* Oxford: Oxford University Press, 2015.

Tylor, Edward B., and Paul Bohannan. *Researches into the Early History of Mankind and the Development of Civilization.* Chicago: University of Chicago Press, 1964.

Übersicht der mit der Königlichen Antiken-Sammlung in Dresden vereinigten Preusker'schen Sammlung vaterländischer Alterthümer. Leipzig: Fritzsche, 1856.

Vermeulen, Han F. *Before Boas: The Genesis of Ethnography and Ethnology in the German Enlightenment.* Omaha: University of Nebraska Press, 2015.

Vermeulen, Han F. *Early History of Ethnography and Ethnology in the German Enlightenment: Anthropological Discourse in Europe and Asia, 1710–1808.* PhD dissertation, Leiden University, 2008.

Vermij, Rienk. "Subterranean Fire: Changing Theories of the Earth during the Renaissance." *Early Science and Medicine* 3 (1998), 323–47.

Veyne, Paul. *Writing History: Essay on Epistemology,* tr. Mina Moore-Rinvolucri. Middletown, CT: Wesleyan University Press, 1984.

Vierhaus, Rudolf. "Göttingen und die Anfänge der modernen Geschichtswissenschaft im 18. Jahrhundert." In *Geschichtswissenschaft in Göttingen,* edited by Harmut Bookman and Hermann Wellenreuther, 1–29. Göttingen: Vandenhoeck and Ruprecht, 1987.

Vöhler, Martin. "Christian Gottlob Heyne und das Studium des Altertums in Deutschland." In *Disciplining Classics: Altertumswissenschaft als Beruf,* edited by Glenn W. Most, 44–49. Göttingen: Vandenhoek & Ruprecht, 2002.

Vogt, Ernst. "Der Methodenstreit zwischen Hermann und Böckh und seine Bedeutung für die Geschichte der Philologie." In *Philologie und Hermeneutik im 19. Jahrhundert: zur Geschichte und Methodologie der Geisteswissenschaften,* edited by Hellmut Flashar, Karlfried Gründer, and Axel E.-A. Horstmann, 103–21. Göttingen: Vandenhoeck und Ruprecht, 1979.

Voss, Jurgen. "Akademien, gelehrte Gesellschaften und wissenschaftliche Vereine in Deutschland, 1750–1850." In *Sociétés et sociabilité au XIXe siècle: colloque à l'Université de Lausanne, 13–14 juin 1986,* edited by Etienne Francois, 149–67. Lausanne: Université de Lausanne, 1986.

Vulpius, Christian August. "Plan und Ankündigung dieser Zeitschrift." *Curiositäten der physisch-literarisch-artistisch-historischen Vor- und Mitwelt* 1 (1811): 3–7.

Wachler, Ludwig. *Geschichte der Künste und Wissenschaften seit der Wiederherstellung derselben bis an das Ende des achtzehnten Jahrhunderts. Fünfte Abtheilung. Geschichte der historischen Wissenschaften.* Gottingen: Johann Friedrich Rower, 1812.

Wachsmuth, Kurt. *Einleitung in das Studium der alten Geschichte.* Leipzig: S. Hirzel, 1895.

Wachsmuth, Wilhelm. *Allgemeine Culturgeschichte*. Leipzig: Bogel, 1850.

Wachsmuth, Wilhelm. *Entwurf einer Theorie der Geschichte*. Halle: Bei Hemmerde und Schwetschke, 1820.

Wachsmuth, Wilhelm. *Europäische Sittengeschichte vom Ursprunge volksthümlicher Gestaltungen bis auf unsere Zeit*. 5 vols. Leipzig: C. W. Vogel, 1831.

Walther, Philipp Alexander Ferdinand. *Systematisches Repertorium über die Schriften sämmtlicher historischer Gesellschaften Deutschlands*. Darmstadt: G. Jonghaus, 1845.

Warburg, Aby. *Images from the Region of the Pueblo Indians of North America*. Edited by Michael P. Steinberg. Ithaca, NY, and London: Cornell University Press, 1995.

Warburg, Aby. "Italian Art and International Astrology in the Palazzo Schifanoia, Ferrara." In *The Renewal of Pagan Antiquity: Contributions to the Cultural History of the European Renaissance*, edited by Aby Warburg, 563–91. Los Angeles: Getty Research Institute, 1999.

Warland, Geneviève. "Henri Pirenne and Karl Lamprecht's *Kulturgeschichte*. Intellectual transfer or *théorie fumeuse?*" *Revue belge d'histoire contemporaine* 41 (2011): 427–55.

Weber, Alfred. *Kulturgeschichte als Kultursoziologie*. Leiden: Sijthoff, 1935.

Weintraub, Karl J. *Visions of Culture: Voltaire, Guizot, Burckhardt, Lamprecht, Huizinga, Ortega y Gasset*. Chicago: University of Chicago Press, 1966.

Weiss, Roberto. *The Renaissance Discovery of Classical Antiquity*. 2nd ed. Oxford, U.K.: Oxford University Press, 1969.

Wesendonck, Herman. *Die Begründung der neueren deutschen Geschichtsschreibung durch Gatterer und Schlözer*. Leipzig: Krüger, 1876.

Westherall, David. "The Growth of Archaeological Societies." In *The Study of the Past in the Victorian Age*, edited by Vanessa Brand, 21–34. Oxford, U.K.: Oxbow Books, 1998.

Whimster, Sam. "Karl Lamprecht and Max Weber: Historical Sociology within the Confines of a Historians' Controversy." In *Max Weber and his Contemporaries*, ed. Wolfgang J. Mommsen and Jürgen Osterhammel, 268–83. London: The German Historical Institute/Unwin Hyman, 1987.

Wilhelmi, Karl. *Ueber die Entstehung, den Zweck und die Einrichtung der gegenwärtigen Geschichts- und Alterthumsvereine deutscher Zunge: Eine Rede, bei der ersten General-Versammlung des Alterthums-Vereins für das Grossherzogthum Baden in Baden gehalten den 5. November 1844*. Heidelberg: Mohr Verlag, 1844.

Winter, Georg. "Zur Vorgeschichte der Monumenta Germaniae Historica." *Neues Archiv der Gesellschaft für ältere deutsche Geschichtskunde* 47 (1928): 1–30.

Witt, Ronald. *In the Footsteps of the Ancients: The Origins of Humanism from Lovato to Bruni*. Leiden: E.J. Brill, 2000.

Witt, Ronald. *The Two Latin Cultures and the Foundation of Renaissance Humanism in Medieval Italy*. Cambridge: Cambridge University Press, 2012.

Wolf, Friedrich August. *Darstellung der Altertumswissenschaft nach Begriff, Umfang, Zweck und Wert*. Afterword by Johannes Irmscher. Weinheim: Acta humaniora, VCH, 1986. Reprint of Friedrich August Wolf and Philipp Buttman, eds., *Museum der Alterthums-Wissenschaft*. Berlin: Realschulbuchhandlung, 1807.

Wolf, Friedrich August. *Vorlesungen über die Alterthumswissenschaft*. Edited by J. D. Gürtler. Leipzig: August Lehnhold, 1831.

Woolf, Daniel, ed. *The Oxford History of Historical Writing.* 5 vols. Oxford, U.K.: Oxford University Press, 2013.

Worm, Ole. *Museum Wormianum: seu historia rerum rariorum, tam naturalium, quam artificialium, tam domesticarum, quam exoticarum, quæ Hafniæ Danorum in œdibus authoris fervantur.* Leipzig: Apud Iohannem Elsevirium, 1655.

Worm, Ole. *Ole Worm's Correspondence with Icelanders.* Edited by Jakob Benediktsson. Copenhagen: Munksgaard, 1948.

✺ INDEX

Abraxas gem, 62
aesthetics, 62–63, 109, 132
age value *vs.* historical value, 63
Alberti, Leon Battista, 12, 56
Altertumskunde (antiquities)
    Aufseß on, 175
    concept of, 250n48
    cultural history and, 140
    Fabri on, 95
    Gatterer on, 100
    Krauss on, 239n21
    Preusker on, 131–132, 250n47
    Rühs on, 126
amateur historical associations, 43–44,
    128–140, 142
anthropology, 95, 148
antiquarianism
    archaeology and, 95–99, 123–124, 141
    continued popularity of, 16–17
    decline of, 14–15
    definition, 56, 95
    Germanisches Nationalmuseum and,
    175, 180, 182, 195
    historical associations and, 134–139
    history of concept, 7–14, 55–56, 101, 128
antiquarians / antiquaries
    Droysen on, 193
    in eighteenth century Göttingen, 76–96;
    Gatterer, 80–86; Gatterer's followers,
    89–96; *Statistik*, 85–89, 94–95
    historians *vs.*, 7, 9–10, 14–15, 128, 132,
    234n25
    Lamprecht on, 48
    in Late Renaissance / early Enlighten-
    ment, 55–75; Leibniz, 68–72; Mabil-
    lon, 65–68; Peiresc, 57–63
    Nietzsche on, 4–5
    Platner on, 108
    Warburg on, 26–27
antiquitates, 126, 130
applied learning, 204

archaeographia, 64
archaeology
    antiquarianism and, 95–99, 123–124, 141
    Archäologie der Kunst, 62, 99–105, 109,
    116–124, 162, 201
    Collingwood on, 203–204, 205–206
    concept / use of term, 95, 96–103, 118
    Dilthey on, 121
    Greeks / Romans on, 8–9
    historians *vs.*, 99
    language of, use of, 36
    Newton on, 241n43
    Preusker on, 132
    rise of as discipline, 10, 15, 81, 97
archives, 74, 93–94, 175. *See also* collections;
    museums
Arnd, Karl, 161–162
art history, 47–48
    Archäologie der Kunst, 62, 99–105, 109,
    116–124, 162, 201
    art objects as sources, 138, 151, 172
    material culture *vs.*, 62–63
art museums, 195–196
artists, as historians, 15, 37
Aufseß, Hans von und zu, 173–184
aura. *See* spiritual aspect of objects
auxilia historica, 73, 77, 80

Bachofen, Johann Jakob, 18
Bacon, Francis, 9, 64, 69, 104
Balzac, Honoré de, 141
Bann, Stephen, 125
Bastian, Adolf, 170–172
Beck, Christian Daniel, 103
Benjamin, Walter, 30
Berlin, University of, 112
Berr, Henri, 71–72
Bertrand, Alexandre, 134
Biedermann, Karl, 144, 184, 187–189
Biondo, Flavio, 12, 56, 85, 105, 138, 201
Bloch, Marc, 7, 12, 14, 31, 41, 52

books and texts as, 60, 63, 64
categorizations of, 69, 74, 127, 129,
    132–133, 138, 178–183
historians and, 10, 33, 46, 77, 81–83
philology and, 102, 123
science and, 151, 170–171
texts, as parallel to, 113–114
university scholars and, 37, 39–40, 196
See also Hilfswissenschaften; spiritual aspect
    of objects
Ovid, 134–135

paleography, 63, 68, 103–104
Pamuk, Orhan, 35–36
Pasqualini, Lelio, 204
patriotism. *See* politics and nationalism
Peiresc, Nicolas-Claude Fabri de, 10, 16,
    57–63, 230n38
    Mabillon and, 65, 67–68
Petersen, Frederik Christian, 109
Phillips, Mark, 125
philological archaeology, 103
philology
    archaeology *vs.*, 119–120
    Boeckh and, 105–107, 111–112
    development of, 11–12
    Nietzsche on, 3, 5–6
    objects, acceptance of, 102, 123
    'real philology,' 72–73, 107
    Wolf and, 104
philosophy, 106, 107, 108
philosophy of history, 208
Pippin, Robert, 1
Pirenne, Henri, 7, 14, 31, 52, 54, 127, 203
Pitt Rivers, Augustus Henry Lane-Fox, 167
Platner, Eduard, 108
Plato, 8
political economy, 162–167
political history, 130, 137, 138, 145, 198
politics and nationalism
    1840/1850s, 144–145
    French Revolution/Napoleon, impact of,
        131, 134, 136, 140, 142, 151, 196–197
    Germanisches Nationalmuseum (GNM)
        and, 175–176, 183–184
    Jews, attitudes to, 186–187
    regional history and, 124
Ponge, Francis, 28, 30
Posthumus, Hermanus (Herman Postma),
    3–4, 55, 56
pragmatic archaeology, 103
pragmatology, 206
prehistory, 18–19, 98, 134, 152–153, 166–167

Preller, Ludwig, 114
Preusker, Karl, 131–133, 148, 250n47
prize competitions, 130–131
Protogaea (Leibniz), 71
Proust, Marcel, 7
psychology, 171
Pufendorf, Samuel, 142–143

Ranke, Leopold von, 53, 112, 143, 155, 180,
    185, 199
Ravdonikas, V.I., 39
real Cultur. See material culture
reconstruction, 9, 16–17, 106, 119
regional history, 43–44, 45, 124, 128–131
Reinach, Salomon, 115
research
    antiquarianism as, 7, 10, 128, 132, 166,
        208–209
    the arts and, 37
    Gatterer and, 82, 83
    imagination as complement to, 5, 37–38,
        82, 106–107, 141
    museums and, 17, 21–22, 195
    writing and, 69–70, 82–83, 84–85, 128
    See also Hilfswissenschaften
Rhenish Historical Society, 43–44
Rickert, Heinrich, 27, 49, 202, 206
Rilke, Rainer Maria, 6, 22–25, 38, 46,
    206–207, 212, 213
Ringelblum, Emanuel, 30–31
Robertson, William, 83
Rodin, Auguste, 22
Rome, 56–57
Rommel, Christoph von, 134–135
Roscher, Wilhelm, 42–43, 48, 53, 112, 127,
    162–163, 198–199, 225n40
Rousseau, Jean-Jacques, 18
Rühs, Friedrich, 125–128, 143

Sachphilologie, 72–73, 116, 244
Saumaise, Claude, 204
Schäfer, Dietrich, 51
Schelling, Friedrich Wilhelm Joseph, 106
Schleier, Hans, 11, 222n1
Schlereth, Thomas, 32–33
Schlözer, Ludwig von, 86–89, 124
Schnapp, Alain, 119, 125
Schönemann, K.T.G., 92
science and objects, 151, 170–171
seals, 60, 61fig, 62, 67–68
Sebald, W.G., 35
Sehnsucht, 6–7, 8, 201, 210
Semper, Gottfried, 148

CPSIA information can be obtained
at www.ICGtesting.com
Printed in the USA
LVOW11*1936250717

542596LV00005B/99/P